Literature and the
English Civil War

Literature and the English Civil War

Edited by
THOMAS HEALY AND JONATHAN SAWDAY

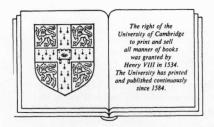

The right of the
University of Cambridge
to print and sell
all manner of books
was granted by
Henry VIII in 1534.
The University has printed
and published continuously
since 1584.

CAMBRIDGE UNIVERSITY PRESS

CAMBRIDGE

NEW YORK   PORT CHESTER   MELBOURNE   SYDNEY

CAMBRIDGE UNIVERSITY PRESS
Cambridge, New York, Melbourne, Madrid, Cape Town, Singapore,
São Paulo, Delhi, Dubai, Tokyo

Cambridge University Press
The Edinburgh Building, Cambridge CB2 8RU, UK

Published in the United States of America by Cambridge University Press, New York

www.cambridge.org
Information on this title: www.cambridge.org/9780521128551

First published 1990
This digitally printed version 2009

A catalogue record for this publication is available from the British Library

Library of Congress Cataloguing in Publication data
Literature and the English Civil War / edited by Thomas Healy and
Jonathan Sawday
    p.   cm.
Includes index.
ISBN 0-521-37082-5
1. English literature – Early modern, 1500–1700 – History and
criticism. 2. Great Britain – History – Civil War, 1642–1649 –
Literature and the war. 3. Politics and literature – Great Britain –
History – 17th century. 4. Literature and society – Great Britain –
History – 17th century. I. Healy, Thomas F. II. Sawday, Jonathan.
PR435.L58 1990
820.9′358 – dc20 89-7062 CIP

ISBN 978-0-521-37082-0 Hardback
ISBN 978-0-521-12855-1 Paperback

Contents

Notes on contributors

FRANCIS BARKER is a Senior Lecturer in Literature at the University of Essex where he teaches Renaissance literature and contemporary theory. Among his principal publications are: *The Tremulous Private Body: Essays on Subjection* (1984) and *Literature, Politics and Theory* (1986) of which he is co-editor.

MARTIN BUTLER is a Lecturer in the School of English at the University of Leeds. He is the author of *Theatre and Crisis 1632–1642* (1984) and co-editor of *The Selected Plays of Ben Jonson* (1988).

THOMAS N. CORNS is a Senior Lecturer in the Department of English, University College of North Wales, Bangor. His publications include: *The Development of Milton's Prose Style* (1982) and (with B. H. Rudall) *Computers and Literature: A Practical Guide* (1987). He edited *The Literature of Controversy Polemical Strategy from Milton to Junius* (1987), original essays by several hands, and he contributed the chapter on Milton's prose to the forthcoming *Cambridge Companion to Milton*. He is reviews editor of *Prose Studies* and honorary secretary of the Association for Literary and Linguistic Computing.

PATRICIA COUGHLAN lectures in the English Department, University College, Cork. Her doctoral research was on Marvell, and she is the editor of a collection of essays, *Spenser and Ireland: An Interdisciplinary Perspective* (1989). She has published articles on Anglo-Irish literature in various periods, especially on Anglo-Irish Gothic fiction.

THOMAS HEALY is a Lecturer in English at Birkbeck College, University of London. He is the author of *Richard Crashaw* (1986) and is presently completing a study of Renaissance literature and literary theory. He is a co-editor of this volume.

N. H. KEEBLE is a Reader in English at the University of Stirling. He has edited *The Autobiography of Richard Baxter* (1974), *The Pilgrim's Progress* (1985), and a collection of essays: *John Bunyan: Conventicle and Parnassus*

(1988). He is the author of *Richard Baxter: Puritan Man of Letters* (1982) and *The Literary Culture of Nonconformity in later Seventeenth-century England* (1987).

DAVID NORBROOK is a Fellow of Magdalen College, Oxford and Lecturer in English at the University of Oxford. He is the author of *Poetry and Politics in the English Renaissance* (1984).

GRAHAM PARRY is a Senior Lecturer in English at the University of York. He is the author of *Hollar's England* (1980), *The Golden Age Restor'd* (1981), *Seventeenth-Century Poetry: The Social Context* (1985), and *The Intellectual and Cultural Context of Seventeenth-Century Literature* (1989).

ANNABEL PATTERSON is Professor of Literature and English at Duke University. She is the author of *Hermogenes and the Renaissance* (1970), *Marvell and the Civic Crown* (1978), *Censorship and Interpretation* (1984), *Pastoral and Ideology* (1987) and *Shakespeare and the Renaissance* (1989). She has edited *Roman Images* for the English Institute, co-edits *The Journal of Medieval and Renaissance Studies* at Duke with Marcel Tutel, and will be editing the volume on Milton for the Longman Critical Reader Series.

JONATHAN SAWDAY is a Lecturer in English at the University of Southampton where he teaches Renaissance Literature and Critical Theory. He is presently completing a book *Bodies by art Fashioned* – a study of the Renaissance culture of dissection. He is a co-editor of this volume.

NIGEL SMITH is Fellow and Tutor in English at Keble College, Oxford. He has edited the Ranter pamphlets and is the author of *Perfection Proclaimed. Language and Literature in English Radical Religion 1640–1660* (1988). He is currently writing a history of literature in the English Civil War and Interregnum.

HELEN WILCOX lectures in English at Liverpool University, researching devotional and autobiographical writing of the seventeenth century. She is the co-editor of *Her own Life: Autobiographical Writings of Seventeenth-Century Englishwomen* (1989) and *Teaching Women: Feminism and English Studies* (1989). She is currently editing the poetical works of George Herbert.

SUSAN J. WISEMAN is a Lecturer in the Department of English, University of Kent at Canterbury. She is completing a study of drama in the period 1640–60.

THOMAS HEALY AND JONATHAN SAWDAY

Introduction: 'Warre is all the world about'

The anniversary of the execution of King Charles I was celebrated as normal on 30 January by the Society of King Charles the Martyr, an esoteric group on the rainbow fringes of high church/right-wing/monarchist/anglo-catholic frontiers who hope and pray for the king's canonization. An altar was set up in the Banqueting House in Whitehall – the scene of his execution supposedly consecrated by his spilled blood. Much gin was drunk. All in all a funny sort of gathering for Mr John (Selwyn) Gummer to be found addressing, expressing his hope that the spirit of King Charles would enter the heart of the Bishop of Durham.

The Guardian, 2 February 1985

This day the Parliament voted that the bodies of Oliver, Ireton, Bradshaw, &c, should be taken up out of their graves in the Abbey, and drawn to the gallows, and there hanged and buried under it: which (methinks) do trouble me that a man of so great courage as he was, should have that dishonour, though otherwise he might deserve it enough. Samuel Pepys, *Diary* 4 December 1660

I

THIS BOOK is concerned with remembering the events of the mid-seventeenth century which we have come to term the English Civil War, and with reading the literature which emerged from that conflict. The two quotations with which we begin this introduction reflect some of the problems which have faced interpreters of that period. They record attempts not just to recollect what *happened* in the 1640s and 1650s in England, but to (literally) *re-present* those events. They are, in fact, reproductions of history reflecting both the participants' and the observers' sectarian and historical perspectives.

At the same time, these two accounts point to the problematic relationship with the Civil War which British writers, historians, scholars, literary critics and, indeed, politicians enjoy. In Pepys's 1660 account, parliament's action is designed not merely to signal a restoration but to recast events into a different mould. The dead and buried (but not forgotten) resurface in order to meet a different end. In the 1985 account, we hear of an altar – a key symbol and point of confrontation in the mid-seventeenth century – rather than a scaffold being erected in Whitehall. It seems that seventeenth-century

1

divisions cannot be repressed. A minister in a parliament 325 years after the Restoration registers the fact that the social, political and religious oppositions which were inescapable in 1649 still lurk within the imagination, if not the actuality, of the present.

These quotations further identify problems interpreters face in establishing their own perspective. Pepys reveals the unease many (though not all) contemporary recorders felt in judging recent events.[1] He is troubled by the significance of what is performed. He is also uncovering a commonly found confusion in assessing what was actually done in the Civil War and how it should be remembered. Cromwell might, in Pepys's view, have deserved hanging for what he did, but his reputation ('a man of so great courage') does not. Or does it? The record of the latter-day commemoration of the execution of Charles I isolates a somewhat different problem. Superficially, the event recounted seems to exist on the fringes of mainstream British social and political debate. Stylistically, the author of the piece is hoping to confirm that marginalisation. Here, in popular British political parlance, is the 'Loony Right' at play. Yet, the account also reveals how a participant at the centre of modern British political life (a government minister) uses an adopted seventeenth-century platform and mode of discourse to address another recognised player in the political debate – the 'progressive' Bishop of Durham. The apparent irony of reversals – a member of parliament speaking for monarchy and established religion against a Bishop who is perceived of as representing radical opinion – is revealed only when we replace this act of remembrance into the historical context which it sets out to celebrate.

The essays in this volume are all concerned with this process of remembering and replacing. Their focus is on the literature which has come down to us from what is regarded as a key moment in British history, but where a bewildering variety of conflicting opinion, analysis and interpretation is invested. The contributors to this volume reflect that diversity in their own adoption of a variety of perspectives and methodologies to explore the ways literary texts anticipated and participated in events of this period.

But for all their differences in approach, the essays share a number of common concerns. All recognise that literature does not act as a passive register of historical events but exists in a dynamic engagement with its context. The poems, plays, masques, diaries, pamphlets and records which are the subjects of these essays are understood as texts which are involved in the actual production of history. The 'literary' shapes and provides a framework, a narration, not only for the events which are witnessed, but also for intellectual and imaginative participation in the social and political world. Literary texts may adopt any number of rhetorical, generic, and imaginative patterns through which to investigate the present. So, it might be added, does historiography. But literature reads and interprets history intertextually. It recalls other texts in other historical moments which have attempted to frame the present – just as we, as readers, are aware of other texts pressing upon our interpretations. In this sense, literature is continually engaged in a process of revising its own moment of production. This revisionary process is the textual equivalent of that desire to re-enact the past which Samuel Pepys recorded in December 1660.

In terms of the literature which was produced in the revolutionary period, a desire to recapture and, if necessary, re-shape the past is an overwhelming concern, and one that is investigated in a number of essays in this collection. That urge to call on the resources of the past is manifested in those early attempts, after the Restoration, to shape what 'happened' into a narrative which can serve to order the present. Clarendon's *History of the Rebellion* begins, for example, by invoking both present and future, in the belief that it is all too easy for those 'few' who, in Clarendon's words, 'opposed and resisted that torrent', to 'lose the recompense due to their virtue in the present'. Here, Clarendon is investigating what he terms the 'general combination, and universal apostasy in the whole nation from their religion and allegiance'. The 'castigation of heaven', Clarendon is willing to believe, may await this majority in the future. But the intervention of providence might be assisted a little by the historian. In the present it is Clarendon's task, in framing a 'full and clear narration', to indicate where virtue should be rewarded.[2]

Clarendon's desire to record those 'few', who, in his opinion, stood out against the 'madness' of the times might alert us to a similar model of heroic resistance to the tyranny of the majority:

> So spake the seraph Abdiel faithful found,
> Among the faithless, faithful only he;
> Among inummerable false, unmoved,
> Unshaken, unseduced, unterrified
> His loyalty he kept, his love, his zeal;
> Nor number, nor example with him wrought
> To swerve from truth, or change his constant mind
> Though single.[3]

Milton's Abdiel stands as a witness to match Clarendon's 'few' who were moved by 'duty and conscience' to resist the force of rebellion. For Milton and for Clarendon, both of them recorders of revolutions and participants, though on opposite sides, in the English Revolution, the post-revolutionary task is to authorise the present.

How, in concrete terms, does this fusion of the past and the present display itself? In 1630, Sir Richard Fanshawe, later to become Charles II's ambassador to Portugal and Spain, wrote his celebratory 'Ode Upon Occasion of His Majesties Proclamation in the Yeare 1630'. The proclamation to which Fanshawe would appear to be referring is that of 9 September 1630, which urged all country gentlemen with no particular business at court to return to their estates. This proclamation was itself only the latest in a long line of such royal suggestions that the gentry were best employed in the provinces rather than in London – the earliest being that of James I in May 1603. James had himself written an elegy, in 1622, whose title was very similar to that of Fanshawe's piece: 'An Elegie written by the king concerning his counsell for Ladies and gentlemen to depart the city of London according to his Majesties proclamation'.[4] Fanshawe's poem, though, opens as follows:

> Now warre is all the world about,
> And everywhere *Erynnis* raignes,
> Or else the Torch so late put out
>   The stench remaines.[5]

Ostensibly the poem then proceeds to celebrate Britain's preservation from the Thirty Years War raging on the continent. Only Britain, the poem argues, is preserved from this fury. Yet, that preservation is put at risk by the recalcitrant determination of the gentry to 'rowle themselves in envy'd leasure' in the town rather than discover 'more solid joyes, / More true contentment to the minde' in the country. Expressed thus, we can read the poem as evidence in the historians' debate concerning the origins of the Civil War. Fanshawe, an ardent royalist who, between 1644 and 1650 was to spend much of his time travelling in Britain and on the continent on royal business, nevertheless sees the decadent court culture as sapping (the plant metaphor is Fanshawe's own) the virility of the gentry who would be better employed spreading their 'quickning power' through the distant parts of the commonwealth. More than this, however, we can see how the poem's *generic* ancestry is rooted not only in the conventional Horatian theme of honest country life versus decadent town existence, but in a previous poem, written by the monarch himself, which functions as an ambivalent piece of quasi-executive command somewhat foreign to modern ears. Did the king's poem of 1622 contain the same force of command as was intended by the king's proclamation? What happens to the sovereign will, in other words, if it is expressed through the medium of poetic rather than proclamatory discourse?

It is this ability of the literary text to intervene in its own historical moment which is of concern here. Having placed the poem in that historical moment, and having uncovered its sources, have we explicated the history or the poem? We think not. Fanshawe's poem was first published in 1648 by which time its whole function, which we have just enshrined (as it were) in history, had radically altered. To put the question in the following Borgesian way seems helpful: is Fanshawe's 'Ode Upon His Majesties Proclamation' as written in 1630, the same poem as his 'Ode Upon his Majesties Proclamation' published in 1648? We would argue that it is clearly not the same. In 1630 the opening line of the poem 'Now warre is all the world about' served as a possibly anxious reminder that in other places life was not as comfortable as it was, for some, in Charles's England. But by 1648 the text has become an ironic commentary on the fact that war is now, quite definitely, all the world about. The irony is a product of the 'historicity' of the text.[6]

Poems, literary texts, clearly live and move in the history in which we place them. As our opening quotations illustrate, the past is re-made by the present, just as the present is fashioned by the past. The 1630 poem changes when it becomes the 1648 poem, and the experience of other wars and other texts serves continually to re-fashion past and present. At the same time, the relationship between reader and literary text is not constrained by that text's origins. This subtle relationship between the reader, the text, and historical process is what this collection sets out to explore.

II

The essays in this volume have been arranged to highlight five areas in which the debate between literature and history in the Civil War appear to be particularly significant. This topical arrangement is not designed to suggest that essays within each section are homogeneous in the interpretive strategies which they employ, nor are the groups exclusive in their concerns. By isolating these areas, though, we hope to show the ways in which civil war discourse operates across the more familiar boundaries of authors or genres. More than that, however, we hope that this arrangement will allow the reader to perceive the parameters of debate within the given areas of discussion. Few of the essays in this collection are in agreement with one another – though all of them establish points of contact which we believe are fruitful. In the remainder of this introduction we shall try and indicate some of the areas of agreement and disagreement.

Annabel Patterson's opening essay raises the central issue of how language is implicated in historical moments, an issue with which the volume as a whole is clearly concerned. What, in effect, are we to call the events which took place in England between 1640 and 1660? This question has been addressed more than once by historians, but it is one that tends to be evaded by those whose primary focus is the literature of the period. Paradoxically, it is the historian who has been most adept at, or at least most concerned about, attending to the nuances of language and terminology:

[The historian] can state without fear of contradiction that civil war broke out in England in 1642, but he cannot state categorically why, and even his choice of terms – whether he calls this event a rebellion or a revolution for instance – is often open to serious objections . . . Yet for want of anything better we have to go on using such terms, and other terms which would almost certainly have been meaningless to contemporaries . . . Any interpretation of the past is not only anachronistic but often written in anachronistic terminology.[7]

Thus J.P. Kenyon, who, like Clarendon, is in no doubt that what happened in the seventeenth century was a 'rebellion'. Kenyon's implied solution to the problem is that all would be well if we could only recover not just contemporary definitions of terms, but stable agreement (from the past and the present) as to both the denotative and connotative aspects of seventeenth-century writing. Patterson's essay takes this argument significantly further, raising both the historical and the theoretical question of naming. As she indicates, a current division amongst interpreters of the seventeenth century locates them either as historians of 'Order' or 'Disorder' – a categorisation which, she argues, can also be uncovered amongst those writing in the period itself. In the seventeenth century, just as much as today, the choice of a particular model with which to characterise events betrays often unvoiced political and social expectations. To assign a name is not simply a matter of clarification, or historical precision, but an ideological choice. Choices of vocabulary may either marginalise or centralise the issues from which we construct those interpretive stratagems by which we try to explain the past and the present. Patterson directs us to the affective component of history and the language of cultural memory, in the hope of isolating those cultural myths which operated in the civil war years.

Graham Parry continues this debate about names and definitions by examining a different set of myths. Parry looks at the ways in which the writings of Sir Richard Fanshawe, together with the work of other poets of the pre-civil war years, can be seen as attempting a 'recovery' of some form of political and ideological stability. If the 'Arcadia' of England has been violated by the present, then there exists the possibility of turning to the past in order to 'sustain a vision of the future that could overlap the calamities of the present'. Again, we sense how desperately important the past was to those who saw the nation drifting into what might now be termed a political crisis.

But which past was to be turned to? Was it a model of the past to be uncovered in the reading of Virgil, Tacitus and Seneca? Or was it, instead, a scriptural past, or even an anglo-saxon one, that could be refurbished and made to serve for the future? We might remind ourselves that it was in 1641 that Coke's *Institutes* were published by order of the Long Parliament, a decision which served to confirm that powerful historical myth of the supposedly pre-Norman origins of English law. Similarly, Gerrard Winstanley's understanding of the institution of private property also rooted itself in a historical argument.[8] In the two opening essays this struggle to name the present in terms of the past is highlighted, a topic to which several of the essays return.

An alternative was to avoid the problems of past, present and future altogether – to turn away from the world of messy political confrontation and create an idealised world of art or devotion. Whether such a retreat was possible (whether, indeed, it ever took place) is a theme of a number of the essays. It is the dominant concern of the second section of the book to investigate two very different forms of what have often been understood as escapism: devotional poetry and the masque. To link these two together might initially seem to be perverse. The masque is a determinedly public spectacle existing within the court culture. Devotional poetry, on the other hand, would seem to exist in total opposition to extravagant public utterance.

Yet, the juxtaposition of two very different sets of cultural vocabulary helps to illustrate the fracture which existed within aesthetic forms that, from the outside, appear self-enclosed, even resistant, to any form of self-scrutiny.[9] Both masque and devotional poem encode within their different structures a veiled commentary on the present. For Martin Butler the masque is not a representation of wilful escapism. Instead, it was an important means by which the king and his political elite could communicate with one another. In the moment of crisis of 1640, however, that possibility of communication had fallen apart. Davenant's *Salmacida Spolia*, far from being, in Butler's words, 'an attempt by an already superannuated monarchy to dazzle its sceptical audience into forgetting the problems of the moment' instead represents an attempt to 'intervene in events and construct a platform of confidence'. That project, we now know, was a failure, but it is a failure which can be investigated not only from the circumstances of the masque's production, but from within the structure of the masque itself.

Devotional poetry, on the other hand, does seem to signal a form of retreat, as Helen Wilcox argues. But what kind of retreat is possible? Here, Wilcox discovers a series of paradoxes which place the question of engagement or retreat into more complex configurations than those which have been proposed by modern commentators on seventeenth-century writing. It is all too easy to believe that devotional writing exists as no more than a form of recreational solace: an alternative form of literary disengagement from the present.[10] But powerlessness, passivity, weakness (terms invoked most frequently, though not exclusively, by the women poets whom Wilcox examines) may become in themselves articles of strength within a poetic which is struggling to find utterance in a time of confrontation. The result, Wilcox suggests, is a religious aesthetic of 'confinement' – one shared by both male and female devotional poets.

Confinement is a rather different proposition to disengagement. Confinement suggests that the war cannot be escaped, that it has intruded into individuals' experience not only of the world, but of themselves. The essays in the third section of the book carry this argument further. In the accounts of civil war writing offered by Francis Barker, Thomas Corns and Jonathan Sawday, the language of conflict and war seems to have entered the very structure of thought so that very little in the writer's experience can remain neutral, or even appear to be the product of a unified sensibility.

This sense of dislocation, explored in Wilcox's account and returned to in the context of women's writing in the penultimate essay in the collection, informs Sawday's account of that revolutionary 'madness' identified by Clarendon looking back on the war. Clarendon, however, was not alone in sensing that a profound psychological change had occurred in the war years. In Sawday's essay, the language of division, fragmentation and insanity is investigated in the context of seventeenth-century expressions of a wished-for psychological unity. An impossible ideal of wholeness, rooted in literary fables of self-completion, is opposed to the discovery that retirement into the psychological fortress of the mind may actually hasten that self-destructive moment which individuals, at a moment of profound political crisis, were set upon evading.

The essays in the central section of the book are concerned with registering the means whereby the war lies buried within the discourses available to the writer, sometimes hidden, but always inescapable. For Corns – taking Milton as his subject, and acknowledging that very few writers have been politically interrogated to the extent that Milton has – there is no single ideological position to which Milton can be consistently assigned. Instead, Corns argues, we are faced with a 'plurality' not just of ideologies, but of Miltons, writing in a diversity of genres each of which demands its own interpretive strategies, and each of which carries with it an ideological perspective which cannot be simply shunted aside. Corns' essay, therefore, returns us to that problem identified in the opening account – how can we begin the business of interpretation?

Barker also takes Milton's writings as his starting point, but juxtaposes his reading of Milton (specifically *Areopagitica*) with a reading of Thomas Hobbes who, like Milton, dominates our understanding of seventeenth-century writing. For Barker, Milton and Hobbes meet, or rather just fail to meet, in that vexed word: Truth. In Milton's writing, Barker argues,

Truth is embodied and given a concrete presence in tropes of militancy and war. Truth is associated with violence, with the armed female figure who, paradoxically, slips (or is pushed) into the position of victim of just that violence which Milton's text invokes. Where Milton's Truth and Hobbes's truth differ, crucially, is in the theory of discourse which underpins each account. In Milton, discourse rests upon struggle, almost as though the war being fought in England could be understood as fortuitously available to substantiate Milton's own evocation of knowledge as a species of armed struggle. In Hobbes's *Leviathan*, however, truth remains unbodied. It has no need of that process of figuration so insistently urged upon us in Milton's images. In part, this absence of embodiment can be ascribed to the fact that *Leviathan* itself demonstrates the procedures whereby the abstract commonwealth can become corporeal. More than this, however, is the vital part played by Hobbes's own theory of discourse. 'Rebellion', whether against power, reason or truth, becomes impossible, given the inter-linking of a theory of language and the theory of contract, because it involves a 'falling away from true language and even from language itself'. The whole endeavour of Hobbes's language is revealed as an attempt at keeping at bay the disruptive force of civil war through the demonstration that language and 'obedience' are indivisible.

Hobbes's concern with language and with a theory of discourse rooted in the war is a concern which has attracted some attention of late.[11] The link between language and rebellion, however, was an enduring concern of seventeenth-century writers. Milton's story of the tyrant Nimrod, punished by the confusion of language, finds its echo in other accounts of language in the period. The well-known passage on the 'abuse' of words in Thomas Sprat's *History of the Royal Society* of 1667 defines language as a 'Weapon . . . as easily procur'd by bad men as good' in the belief that '*eloquence* ought to be banish'd out of *civil societies* as a thing fatal to Peace and good Manners'.[12] For the war was a time of noise – a linguistic riot of conflicting sound. What Keith Lindley terms 'verbal outbursts and unorthodox conversations', the novelty of the woman preacher, 'tumultuous assemblies', petitions, and the spectacular outpouring of ballads, news-books and pamphlets particularly in the period 1642–7, substantiate the image of a conflict which was a matter of words as well as of pikes.[13]

Amidst the cacophony of sects, opinions and competing ideological and religious positions, it would not be surprising to encounter the urge to exert some form of interpretive control over discourse. Control – over interpretation, over history, over the moment of literary production, and, most importantly over territory and people – is the theme of the fourth section of this book. David Norbrook's discussion of Marvell's 'An Horatian Ode upon Cromwell's Return from Ireland' – takes as its starting point the suppression of the poem until 1776. That suppression, Norbrook argues, enabled subsequent generations to understand Marvell as a 'zealous protestant patriot' but not, significantly, as a spokesman for republicanism. In fact Marvell's disengagement from *any* form of political involvement is how generations of critics wanted to understand the author of some of the most politically motivated poetry in the language.[14] But, a republican culture is what the poem speaks to and for through its careful manipulation of generic expectations, and its sustained attempt at *revising* not only the politics of poetry but the politics of classical culture inherited by seventeenth-century readers. The result is an 'Ode' which sets out to defeat monarchism by defeating the rhetoric of monarchism by denying the reader's horizon of generic expectations. At the same time a further instance of the revolution's obsession with the past is underlined.

Texts and authors which out-trope their precursors – as Norbrook argues Marvell out-tropes Horace – and texts which call upon the 'horizon' of a reader's 'expectations' have, of course, become fascinating objects of contemporary theoretical study, whether concerned with a theory of literary production or interpretation.[15] But to place these activities of revision and denial within a precise historical moment (as opposed to the general Renaissance desire to recover classical texts) is a more difficult task. That writers and readers were caught up in such a revisionary struggle is suggested by Milton's sonnet 'When the assault was intended to the city'. Milton's poem foregrounds a *literary* past (were knights in arms really to be found facing the trained bands on Turnham Green in the winter of 1642?) which can be located generically (in Horace and Pindar), and in an idea of poetry which has emerged 'from the study and faces out into the street . . . ready to function as a counterforce to force'.[16]

At issue, then, is the extent to which seventeenth-century writers believed it possible to control the 'apophradic' (to adopt Harold Bloom's term) energy of literature. Past texts could return, or be summoned. Once recalled, as Richard Overton suggested, it might perhaps be a simple matter to extract from them a contemporary meaning: 'The figure is but the shell; will you not crack the shell to take out the kernel? Pass through the Parable to the Morall thereof?' But that was precisely the problem. For, as Overton continues, 'things (however in themselves) are to others as they are taken'.[17]

In Thomas Healy's essay, which takes Marvell's *Upon Appleton House* as its subject, the difficulties associated with controlling the past when it is summoned to do service for the present are highlighted. What are we to make, Healy asks, of the supremely unliterary crucifixion of a woman named Agnes Griffen who, so it was recorded in 1650, was forced to eat her own flesh? Here the past, specifically the scriptural past, has returned with a vengeance. For what is enacted, in this cruel account of suffering

– an account which reminds us that, despite the historical debate over how much or how little the people of England were affected by the war, some people suffered inconceivably[18] – is history as a bizarre manifestation of repetition. To understand the present as a fulfilment of the past is a variation on the pattern of return and re-enactment. But it is one that, given the understanding of the present as offering a form of completion of a scriptural and classical past, was peculiarly beguiling for a poet, such as Marvell, engaged in trying to make sense of what is happening around him. As Healy indicates through his discussion of the narrative frame within which *Upon Appleton House* operates, the problem is that the conflict of war could also suggest the breaking apart of just those patterns of historical repetition which might otherwise function as an aid to interpretation.

If classical or scriptural history and writing could be appealed to in an attempt to understand the conflict of the present, then so, too, could more recent events. The dramas and operas produced by Davenant in the restrictive conditions of theatre production prevailing in the 1650s are Susan Wiseman's subject, but her aim is to establish the extent (and the means whereby) an ostensibly de-politicised theatre participated in political debate. Davenant's 'operas', the only theatrical performances sanctioned during the Protectorate, are, Wiseman suggests, profoundly implicated in the attempt to construct a notion of 'Englishness' which might *appear* to transcend the actual divisions within the English polity. That effort of construction is conducted through the mobilisation of a set of mythologies which place old 'enemies' (the Spanish, the Turks) on the stage rather than present conflicts. As such, Davenant's dramas might be compared to that other attempt to intervene, through performance and spectacle, in political affairs which Butler's essay traces in its discussion of Davenant's masque.

But Wiseman's essay also raises the issue of interpretive licence, or the lack of it. Davenant's dramas represent an effort at stating what an 'English' (post-monarchical) culture might look like. But they are, at the same time, anxiously engaged in ensuring that their own interpretation is controlled. This is not so much a manifestation of overt censorship of a kind with which in Britain we are becoming increasingly familiar; rather it is the more insidious (and equally contemporary) presence of a degree of self-censorship. In Davenant's *The Cruelty of the Spaniards in Peru* this is illustrated by the endeavour to provide an unassailably 'non-political' frame of reference in which the audience is asked to locate what takes place before them.

Wiseman's essay on the drama – with its concentration on the definition of 'Englishness' determined by the presence of an alien, unknowable, foreign 'other' as the defining reference point – might remind the reader of the impeccably counter-revolutionary advice given by that reformed revolutionary, Henry Bolingbroke in *2 Henry IV*:

> Be it thy course to busy giddy minds
> With foreign quarrels, that action, hence born out,
> May waste the memory of the former days.   (*2 Henry IV* 4.v. 214–16)

To erase the immediate past in favour of a quarrel safely removed from the current sphere of action has often appealed to those in power. In seventeenth-century England there was one immediate source of 'foreign quarrel' which had the habit of domesticating itself within the English body politic. That quarrel, taking place in Ireland, is itself all too easily forgotten as Blair Worden (here in the context of the 1688 revolution and Ireland) has reminded us: 'A mature nation should be able to confront its past without recourse to institutionalised forgetting.'[19]

In terms of the literature of the civil war period, Ireland is chiefly remembered for having been the occasion of a poem commemorating a home-coming: a fact which Norbrook ironically records in his essay. Historical accounts of the Civil War have a tendency, if not to gloss over the events of October 1641, then certainly to understand the Irish uprising as no more than a contributing factor in what is essentially an English quarrel.[20] Cromwell's 1649 campaign usually receives even shorter shrift from literary historians who hurry through the matter of the Irish campaign in order to pursue their theme of civilised appreciation of Marvell's analytical detachment.[21]

In a similar fashion, it is sometimes forgotten that in the summer of 1649 there was not merely token or self-interested opposition to an Irish campaign.[22] Patricia Coughlan's closing essay to this section of the book acknowledges the domestic English dimension to Ireland, but its stated aim is to explore the prevailing discourses in which Ireland and the Irish were understood by England in the seventeenth century. As she argues, in the years before the outbreak of Civil War in England the predominating colonialist discourse of Ireland (comparable to that explored by Wiseman in her account of Davenant's drama) is one which is shaped by the remodelling of previous texts. Spenser's *The Faerie Queene* and *Short View of the Present State of Ireland*, though written at very different moments in time, are nevertheless made to function within the present historical context. Once more, we see how the 'historicity' of a text can operate. The *View* is a sixteenth-century account of Ireland, but its publication in 1633 enabled it to emerge as an authenticating vision against which post-1640 accounts (and actions) are to be measured.

English views of Ireland, determined as they may have been by Spenser's 'founding' texts were, nevertheless, not static. William Petty, in December 1654 appointed to carry out a survey of all those lands in Ireland which were to be forfeited by those defined as hostile to parliamentary forces, is a key figure in Coughlan's account. Petty's Baconian task was to limit the boundaries of land, and also to fix the geographical terrain in terms not only of ownership, but of identity: the very naming of the features of the land is encompassed in his task. The problematic process of naming – a traditional English concern in dealing with Ireland – completes that cycle of control which this section of the volume investigates.

The final section of the book is termed *Aftermaths*. The choice of such a title to this closing section is designed to indicate the ways in which individual experience was retrospectively fashioned by the turmoil of the revolutionary years. For some writers, and Pepys's description with which we opened this introduction might come to mind, the post-war period was a time of reflection and accommodation. Others chose a different route. Edward Chamberlayne's notorious *Angliae Notitia; or, The Present State of England* (1669), for example, is not dissimilar to that desire expressed in parliament's decision to exhume the past and set it marching once more. For Chamberlayne, and others of his persuasion, the events of the revolution are understood as marking a decisive break with the past. England before the revolution, he suggests, was an idyllic state. To recapture that Edenic moment, to return to the past, he realises, it would be necessary to embark on a policy of wholesale execution of those who have survived, rather than limiting revenge to the corpses of those who have died too soon. Such a policy, he concludes regretfully 'the clemency and meekness of the Protestant Religion seems to forbid'.[23]

N.H. Keeble's essay offers a different paradigm in which to understand the past. Lucy Hutchinson's *Memoirs of the Life of Colonel Hutchinson* were written in the 1660s. Her writings look back on the war, and on her husband's part in the Puritan cause prior to his death in 1644, in order to discover some pattern or meaning in what has happened in her life. But, as Keeble's discussion of Lucy Hutchinson's work demonstrates, the author of the *Memoirs* was no passive register of a male voice and authority. Instead, two Lucy Hutchinsons emerge from her act of pious remembrance. The one describes herself as a 'shadow' with no defined voice of her own. The other is, in Keeble's words, a 'creatively independent, defiant, and opinionated narrator' who speaks for the silent Lucy Hutchinson. These two voices represent two possible alternative models of female discourse. One can be located in Wilcox's description of female religious utterance in the period. The other speaks for (and of) those women for whom the war, in its disruptive challenge to the received, patriarchal structure of society, signalled a paradoxical, if momentary, freedom.[24]

The two voices discovered in Keeble's discussion of Lucy Hutchinson's writings find an echo in John Perrot's multiple voices struggling to find utterance. Nigel Smith's essay takes us out of the immediate frame of English political, social and cultural life in order to trace the strange story of Perrot, author of the Quaker visionary 'epic' poem *A Sea of the Seed's Sufferings* (1661). In Perrot's text we encounter the voices of seventeenth-century radical Nonconformism, seeking to define that conviction of 'inner light' so fundamental to certain forms of religious experience in the age.

What is also voiced in Perrot's text is the performance of suffering itself. A language of bodily gesture is called into being, where experience is inscribed on the complete physical identity of the individual. But Perrot's text and Perrot's story, though they appear to be two discrete phenomena, eventually merge into one another. The story of Perrot is comprised of an extraordinary blend of suffering, hardship and innocence culminating in the bathos of voluntary exile in Barbados and Jamaica where he was famous for sporting a very un-Quakerlike red velvet coat. Perrot's original undertaking was to journey with the avowed intention of taking his Quaker message to both the Pope and the Sultan of Turkey. Despite the missionary zeal of Perrot's travels to Livorno, and thence to Smyrna, Venice and Rome, in the hope of eventually reaching Jerusalem, the material destination of Perrot's wanderings hardly seems significant. Instead, what is of importance is the record of suffering itself. In the face of isolation and adversity it is Perrot's passivity which becomes a source of power. The remarkable experiences which produced Perrot's discordant and multiple voices are witnesses to the social, political, aesthetic and ideological fragmentation which was the English Revolution.

III

Roger Howell has told the story of how, in 1960, a proposal to name a street 'Cromwell Gardens' was banned by Wallingford Borough Council, with the comment that they had no wish to preserve the name of such a 'malefactor'.[25] As the commemorative occasion mentioned at the start of this introduction also suggests, the shock-waves of the conflict which took place in England in the seventeenth century can still be felt. The point is not to claim a timelessness for that conflict. On the contrary, wars inhabit geographical space and they take place in time, though their effects may linger. The essays in this collection are all determined to mark the moment of conflict in the literature which has come down to us from the seventeenth century. As such, they represent a clear statement that the historical moment matters in our understanding of all forms of writing. That moment does not inhere within the text, and neither does the text preserve its own moment of production as if it were a perfectly formed crystalline structure. A literary history which is alive to the past and, just as importantly, to the present, is what the editors of this collection believe is represented in these pages.

NOTES

The majority of the essays collected in this book are revised versions of papers originally given at a conference entitled 'Warre is all the World About: Literature and the English Civil War' held under the auspices of the Department of English at the University of Southampton in April 1987. A collection such as this is, to a greater or lesser extent, a collaborative project. However, we should like to thank all the contributors to this volume for their much-valued criticism, support and encouragement. We should also like to thank all those who participated in the Southampton conference.

1 Against Pepys' hesitant account of Parliament's decision to exhume the bodies of the regicides should be placed Marvell's almost casual reference to these events recorded in his letter of 4 December 1660. See H.M. Margoliouth, ed., *Poems and Letters of Andrew Marvell*, 2 vols. (3rd edition, Oxford, 1971), II, p. 7.

2 Edward Hyde, Earl of Clarendon, *Selections from 'The History of the Rebellion' and 'The Life by himself'*, ed. Hugh Trevor-Roper (London, 1978), pp. 1–2.

3 John Milton, *Paradise Lost*, ed. Alistair Fowler (London, 1968), V. 896–903.

4 See Sir Richard Fanshawe, *Shorter Poems and Translations*, ed. N.W. Bawcutt, English Reprints Series (Liverpool, 1964), pp. 88–9.

5 Fanshawe, *Shorter Poems and Translations*, p. 5.

6 So, John Frow proposes that every text is 'marked by a multiple temporality' along the lines that we have outlined for Fanshawe's poem. See John Frow, *Marxism and Literary History* (Oxford, 1986), p. 171. See also Janusz Stawinski's observation that 'a text's encounter with its first public is not to be identified with the irreversible "immobilization" of its semantics, or the preempting of its fate'. Janusz Stawinski, 'Reality and Reader in the Literary Historical Process' trans. Nina Taylor, *New Literary History* 19 (1988), p. 523.

7 J.P. Kenyon, *Stuart England* (Harmondsworth, 1978), pp. 11–12. See also Barry Coward, 'Was there an English Revolution in the Middle of the Seventeenth Century?' in C. Jones, M. Newitt and S. Roberts, eds., *Politics and People in Revolutionary England* (Oxford, 1986), pp. 9–39.

8 Christopher Hill, 'The Norman Yoke', *Puritanism and Revolution* (1958; rpt. Harmondsworth, 1986), pp. 58–125; F.D. Dow, *Radicalism in the English Revolution*, Historical Association Studies (Oxford, 1985), pp. 13–14, 76. Derek Hirst, *Authority and Conflict: England 1603–1658* (London, 1986), pp. 84–9.

9 On the 'cultural division', see P.W. Thomas, 'Two Cultures? Court and Country under Charles I' in Conrad Russell, ed., *The Origins of the English Civil War* (London, 1973), pp. 168–93. For a clear statement of the 'two cultures' argument see also Conrad Russell, *The Crisis of Parliaments: English History 1509–1660* (Oxford, 1971), pp. 178–9.

10 See, for example, Bruce King's observation that it was the pursuit of 'Royalists'

and 'moderates' to retire to the countryside to seek 'solace in writing satires, translations, and religious verse'. Bruce King, *Seventeenth-century English Literature* (London, 1982), p. 126.

11 See David Johnston, *The Rhetoric of Leviathan: Thomas Hobbes and the Politics of Cultural Transformation* (Princeton, NJ, 1987), pp. 64–5.

12 Thomas Sprat, *The History of the Royal Society*, ed. Jackson I. Cope and Harold Whitmore Jones (St Louis MS, 1958), p. 111.

13 Keith Lindley, 'London and Popular Freedom in the 1640s' in R.C. Richardson and G.M. Ridden, eds., *Freedom and the English Revolution: Essays in History and Literature* (Manchester, 1986), p. 133.

14 For example, Robert Ellrodt claimed that Marvell, even when involved in 'the world of action', always remained 'a detached observer of the social and political scene'. Robert Ellrodt, 'Marvell's Mind and Mystery' in C.A. Patrides, ed., *Approaches to Marvell: The York Tercentenary Lectures* (London, 1978), p. 230. This view is a variation on that offered by Douglas Bush, when he commented on Marvell's 'cool, analytical detachment' in the Horatian Ode. See Douglas Bush, 'Marvell's Horatian Ode', *Sewanee Review* 60 (1952), 336.

15 See, for example, Harold Bloom's notions of *apophrades* or 'the return of many poets dead and gone' in *A Map of Misreading* (New York, 1975; rpt. 1980), p. 129. The term 'Horizon of expectations' is of course culled from the call by Hans Robert Jauss to create a new form of literary historiography. See Hans Robert Jauss, *Toward an Aesthetic of Reception*, trans. Timothy Bahti (Minneapolis, 1982), pp. 3–45.

16 Janel M. Mueller, 'On Genesis in Genre' in Barbara Kiefer Lewalski, ed., *Renaissance Genres: Essays on Theory, History, and Interpretation*, Harvard English Studies 14 (Cambridge MA, 1986), p. 238.

17 Richard Overton, 'The Baiting of the Great Bull of Bashan' (1649) in Howard Erskine-Hill and Graham Storey, eds., *Revolutionary Prose of the English Civil War* (Cambridge, 1983), p. 147.

18 See Donald Pennington, 'The War and the People' in John Morrill, ed., *Reactions to the English Civil War 1642–1649* (London, 1982), pp. 115–35; Brian Manning, *The English People and the English Revolution* (Harmondsworth, 1978), pp. 181–248.

19 Blair Worden, 'Lawful Resistance', *London Review of Books* 10, 21 (24 November 1988), 5–6.

20 Lawrence Stone, for example, terms the 1641 uprising a 'chance event' comparable to the death of the Earl of Bedford. For Conrad Russell it is a 'crucial issue' which is, he admits, nevertheless absent from the collection of essays he edited on the origins of the Civil War. See Lawrence Stone, *The Causes of the English Revolution 1549–1642* (London, 1972; rpt. 1986), p. 137; Russell, ed., *Origins of the English Civil War*, p. 12.

21 Though Michael Wilding's account does confront the Irish perspective rather more squarely than has often been the case in the past. See Michael Wilding, *Dragons Teeth: Literature in the English Revolution* (Oxford, 1987), pp. 118–24.

22 For an account of this opposition, and the extent to which it was or was not motivated by principled objection to the prevailing English policy on Ireland, see Chris Durston, ' "Let Ireland Be Quiet": Opposition in England to the Cromwellian Conquest of Ireland', *History Workshop Journal* 21 (1986), 103–12.

23 For the full fury of Edward Chamberlayne's post-Restoration sentiments, see *Angliae Notitia: or, the Present State of England: Together with Divers Reflections upon the Antient State Thereof* (London, 1669), ch. 2.

24 On the notion of 'unruly women' and the possibility of a 'temporary release from the traditional and stable hierarchy' see Natalie Zemon Davies, 'Women on Top', *Society and Culture in Early Modern France* (Oxford, 1987), pp. 124–51.

25 Roger Howell, Jr, 'Cromwell and English Liberty' in Richardson and Ridden, *Freedom and the English Revolution*, p. 26.

PART I

Definitions and premonitions

1 The very name of the game: theories of order and disorder

AMONG THE Clarendon State Papers is a letter written from John Nicholas at The Hague to an English correspondent, dated 23 April 1654, four months after Cromwell was officially made Protector of the new English republic. It speaks, at first sight, merely of a piece of social or aesthetic gossip; but look more closely:

I doe not doubt but you heard of the great doings here at the Princesse Royalls Court, of a french and English play that her Gent[lemen] & Maydes of Honour are preparing to act before Whitsuntide and *the very name* of the English play seems to please many in that Court more then the play it selfe, it being soo juditious & discreetly chosen for these times; the name of it is *A King and Noe King*, but all loyall persons are astonished when they heard it named, & wonder more at it. I beleeve it will be shortly in the English prints, for the Dutch speake strangely of it, so that you may see its noe secrett thing, but you neede not to take notice from whom you have this advertisement.[1]

I have chosen this exhibit to begin with because it links my previous work on censorship and interpretation with the concerns of this chapter, which include historiography, political theory, and the now-imprecisely-named literary theory, omnivorous as it has become of other speculative systems. The link is made by way of the letter writer's keen recognition of the power of *names* to encapsulate entire programmes. In the recycling of Fletcher's tragicomedy, its title, which was once merely an irony at the expense of its flawed royal protagonist, has become re-ironised at the expense of Cromwell and *his* equivocal title of Protector, which makes him both king and no king, as was equally the condition of Charles II in political exile in France. The name of the play alone, 'soo juditious & discreetly chosen for these times', does the secret service that his sister's court, also in exile, required, carrying back to England an encoded message about royalist solidarity and constitutional inquiry. For the message to succeed it must be both obvious ('noe secrett thing') and incomplete, its name to be dispersed but not its source, who prefers to remain deep-throatedly anonymous.

The letter can therefore function not only as another proof-text of how the hermeneutics of censorship functioned during the Protectorate, but also as an introduction to a discussion, itself introductory, of the ideology of naming. There is a new nominalist controversy abroad among those who study seventeenth-century history and literature. I take it that the argument over names is actually a symptom of unspoken and perhaps unspeakable disagreements, the real issue being what *happened* in England between the death of Elizabeth I and the Restoration of Charles II and why it matters today. While the sequence of events is not in dispute, their constellated meaning is. We will begin with the problem of naming, and proceed to the subliminal struggles for control over the evidence.

There is a new version of logical positivism abroad in historiography, whereby, it is argued, we will not understand what we are talking about unless we use precisely the right words to denote it, and those must be only the words that were available or applicable at the time of the events in question. This movement is motivated by a desire for certainty in a discipline that has been destabilised by postmodernist theories of language and the loss of belief in objective historical knowledge. But it has produced an impasse for those who enter a classroom and wish to name what happened in England in the mid-seventeenth century. If 'Puritan' and 'revolution' are no longer, as some have asserted, legitimate terms, how else are we to name the extraordinary events that then occurred, still less explain their occurrence? The recent conference at Southampton University bowed to the new orthodoxy by naming its topic the 'English Civil War', a phrase that appears neutral, but that under scrutiny reveals meanings – of right on both sides, of *other* civil wars – that imply the exclusion of other interpretations, specifically those of definitive social change or ideological confrontation.

The argument most frequently heard against naming the events of 1640–60 revolutionary is that of linguistic anachronism. Consider, for instance, Ronald Paulson's *Representations of Revolutions*,[2] a powerful delineation of how the human imagination dealt with the experience of the French Revolution. No doubt unintentionally, Paulson shares with mainstream Marxist criticism the belief that the French Revolution was the first 'real' European revolution, that it constituted a definitive rupture in the structure of history, and was in that sense appallingly without precedent. This claim is made initially through naming, and so appears to be mandated by the history of our language. At the beginning of his book Paulson rehearses the familiar story that is held in common by the *Oxford English Dictionary* and Raymond Williams' *Keywords*,[3] of how in their own time the events of 1640 and 1660 were not *linguistically* apprehended as revolutionary, in the sense of achieving or attempting the restructuring of society. When they were named, it was, as Williams points out, by the republic's enemies, who called the experiment 'The Great Rebellion', a term crystallised in Clarendon's great but unmistakably royalist *History of the Rebellion and Civil Wars in England*. The word 'revolution', so goes the consensus, retained as its primary meaning the cyclical notion derived from its astronomical usage, and the first recorded political 'revolution' was therefore, ironically, the *restoration* in 1660 of the English monarchy. But it was 1789 that retrospectively invested 'revolution' with the political content it now bears.

It would be possible to question Paulson's theory of the unprecedented nature of the French Revolution merely by appeal to the cultural evidence adduced. He begins by showing how classical iconography, especially from the Roman republican period, and most brilliantly visible in the paintings of David, was used to legitimate the short-lived French Republic. One could easily demonstrate how the tropes and images of Roman history were also ubiquitous in the upheavals of 1640–60, and were patently being used as a language to render that earlier experience intelligible. Analogies to Roman history were not only drawn but wrestled for, as Marvell's 'Horatian Ode', or Cowley's *The Civil Wars*, to mention only familiar examples, testify. Not only was the cultural formation Paulson discovered in France anticipated in England a century and a half earlier, but in both periods of violent political disruption writers and artists turned to the ancient past for explanatory models, whose ideological import they fully understood.

For, as Thomas May observed in his *History of the Parliament of England* (1647), in the course of discussing the battle of Edgehill, 'there is nothing under the sun which is absolutely new':

Look upon the discourse of one historian in that subject, Dion Cassius . . . when he relates the last war about Roman liberty, which was the war of Brutus and Cassius against Caesar and Antony . . . although, saith Dion, before this war they had many civil wars, yet in others they fought who should oppress the Roman liberty; in this war, one side fought to vindicate liberty, the other, to bring in tyranny, yet the side of tyranny prevailed, and drew most to it. Of what quality they were, the same historian speaks also: the armies of Brutus and Cassius, that stood for liberty, consisted of the lower sort of people, and *ex subditis Romanorum;* the other, that stood for tyranny, consisted, saith he, *ex Romanis nobilibus et fortibus.* Brutus and Cassius . . . before the battle, making orations, encouraged them to fight for their ancient freedom and Roman laws. Caesar and Antony promised to their soldiers the estates of their enemies . . . and power to rule over their own countrymen; which proved, it seems, better oratory than the other, and more persuasive.

And, concluded Thomas May, 'Whether the parallel will in some measure fit this occasion or not, I leave it to the reader.'[4] The reader, even at the time, would have read the passage in the light of May's transfer of loyalty to the parliamentarians, a fact which, however reprehensible it may have appeared to some, at least lent some substance to the binary structure of opposed *sides*, whose agendas were structured by socio-economic difference, that May's analogy envisaged. For May, apparently, the term 'civil war' itself allowed of difference. Not all internecine contests were alike; at least one in the Roman past and its possible match in the English present were marked by class conflict – that element of revolutionary action that most historians have told us was not conceivable in the 1640s.

Hobbes makes the same point, but from the opposite position. When *Leviathan* appeared in 1651, it had four years' advantage over May's *History* in its perspective, which now included the king's deposition and execution. Part of Hobbes's project in re-laying the theoretical grounds for absolute sovereignty (while hedging his bets on who might most successfully embody it in England: Cromwell or Charles II) was an attack on the notion that history afforded an argument for republicanism. This attack came in two parts. On the one hand, Hobbes complained that rebellious and seditious ideas are fostered by the *misreading* 'of the books of Policy, and Histories of the antient Greeks, and Romans':

from which, young men, and all others that are unprovided of the Antidote of solid Reason, receiving a strong, and delightfull impression, of the great exploits of warre . . . receive withall a pleasing Idea, of all they have done besides; and imagine their great prosperity, not to have proceeded from the aemulation of particular men, but from the vertue of their popular forme of government: Not considering the frequent Seditions, and Civill warres, produced by the imperfection of their Policy. From the reading, I say, of such books, men have undertaken to kill their Kings.   (part 2, chapter 29)

In Hobbes's version of Roman history, all successes are explained by military leadership and heroic individualism. 'And therefore', he wrote in another section of *Leviathan*, 'he that hath the Sovereign Power is alwayes Generalissimo' (part 2, chapter 18). From such a perspective, Roman history between the expulsion of the Tarquins and the imperial era was an indistinguishable series of 'Civill warres' which in turn are indistinguishable from 'Seditions'.

Hobbes's other weapon against republican principles was also expressed as a matter of political semantics. He devoted himself to the task of trying to deracinate *theoretically* the idea of personal freedom, by transferring its name to the antithetical concept of state control. 'It is an easy thing', wrote Hobbes, 'for men to be deceived, by the *specious name of Libertie*; and for want of judgement to distinguish, mistake that for their Private Inheritance, and Birth right, which is the right of the Publique only' (part 2, chapter 21; italics mine). The linguistic trick attempted is to transfer the cultural power of the name of liberty from the individual to the state, in defiance of all previous authorities on history and political theory 'in these westerne parts of the world'. Every man in the state of nature (the only state in which equality has any meaning) has as much liberty as he chooses, argued Hobbes, to be at continual war with his neighbour; but as soon as he enters into the social contract that liberty is transferred to his representative, and changes into the liberty of the commonwealth 'to resist, or invade other people'. Again, there is a restriction of the concept to militarism, while sardonic aspersions are cast on the dream of a historically determined republican semantics:

There is written on the Turrets of the city of Luca in great characters at this day, the word LIBERTAS; yet no man can thence inferre, that a particular man has more Libertie, or Immunitie from the service of the Commonwealth there, than in Constantinople. Whether a Commonwealth be Monarchicall, or Popular, the Freedome is still the same. (part 2, chapter 21)

Given these principles, it is scarcely surprising that Hobbes (anticipating Althusser) consigns the whole of republican thought to the territory of ideological state apparatuses (the Athenians were taught that they were Freeman 'to keep them from desire of changing their Government'), and that he himself recommended a strong censorship to protect future English readers from contact with Aristotle, Cicero and the like. 'By reading of these Greek, and Latine Authors, men from their childhood have gotten a habit (under a false shew of Liberty,) of favouring tumults, and of licentious controlling the actions of their Soveraigns' (chapter 22). 'I cannot imagine, how anything can be more prejudiciall to a Monarchy, than the allowing of such books to be publikely read' (chapter 29).

The Roman historicists of seventeenth-century England may do more for us, however, than query the 'original' status of the French Revolution. They certainly indicate that observers of the 1640s and the 1790s shared a theory of history as continuous in 'these westerne parts of the world', and they may also cast doubts on the theory of anachronism in our own historical lexicon (a point to which I shall return). But what Thomas May and Thomas Hobbes have to tell us through the medium of Roman history has broader and deeper implications. Those two positions are early paradigms, of allegorical force, of the divisions in contemporary academic thought. My initial focus will be on how they have been re-enacted by British historians of the seventeenth century, and beyond that embattled arena loom contests and investments that surpass disciplinary quarrels.

Amongst scholars of seventeenth-century English history, there is almost absolute disagreement between a historian like Christopher Hill, committed to the occurrence of an 'English Revolution' and to the explanatory value of large-scale economic factors and class-consciousness and, on the other side of the discipline, a historian like John Morrill, who writes instead of *The Revolt of the Provinces*,[5] in which any theory of major unifying causes of the war or wars is replaced by the study of local interests and personal motive. Hill represents a certain style of Marxist historian, though modified (and here 'Marxist' must be added to our nominalist problematic) by his passionate commitment to the seventeenth century as distinct from periods more amenable to capital-centred analysis; while Morrill is a leader in the so-called revisionist history, whose agenda has been to question all holistic interpretations of the period by testing them against the mass of detail available in county records. While the *method* derives from the historiographical reforms inaugurated by the *Annales* school, the *consequences* of reading the political history of the seventeenth century as social history may actually be reactionary. Whereas Hill's contribution has been to render visible the activities of the sectarians and the Levellers, and so to draw attention to what Thomas May called 'the lower sort of people', Morrill's has been to focus on the provincial gentry on a case-by-case basis. As Hobbes had attempted to erase republican thought by rewriting Roman history as the story of heroic individuals, Morrill has eradicated both the Puritan revolution and any notion of class agendas by telling the stories of unheroic and essentially selfish persons.

Central to this project is the denial of political consciousness to his subjects. Taking as his exemplar William Davenport, whose commonplace book exists in the Chester public records, Morrill makes him 'typical of the upper gentry in knowing a good deal that was distasteful and unpleasant about the Court, but knowing and understanding less about the real constitutional issues, leaving that to the experts' (p. 23). The experts, on the other hand, are characterised as 'extremists', 'activists' or (in parenthesis) 'those who pushed themselves forward' (p. 47). Our choice is therefore between an uninformed, confused, if not actually stupid gentry (the majority) who fail to understand the constitutional issues underlying ship-money, and a minority of brash and dogmatic men like William Pym whose excesses in defining the constitutional issues eventually drove some of the passive majority into something resembling a position – namely, royalism. And Morrill concludes his study by citing the case of John Poyer, an early 'bullheaded' declarer for parliament who became entangled in local rivalries and ended his career by surrendering Pembroke Castle to Cromwell. 'Here was a man', Morrill sums up caustically (and it might be Hobbes speaking) 'praying that the "lawes of the land and the liberties of the people may be all established in their proper bounds." The great majority of Englishmen had never asked for any more and had yet to learn that a civil war can only protect such liberties by abrogating them' (p. 131).[6]

Such points are easy to make. And revisionist history of the events of the mid-seventeenth century has rendered itself vulnerable, as is already widely perceived, by ultimately depriving us of *any* explanation as to why the war between the king and his parliament began at all, or why it began when it did. But I want now to broaden the inquiry by focusing on Morrill's new interest, the phenomenon of popular protest. While at first sight the contemporary interest of historians in popular protest may seem a direct outgrowth of the *Annales* school mission to abandon the political history of elites, this approach actually permits conflicting interpretations and internal divisions that resemble, while not precisely matching, the ideological disparity between Thomas May and Thomas Hobbes. Yet to demonstrate this will take some patience. To begin with, it is impossible to focus on popular protest without invoking to some degree its entire history, beginning with the Peasants' Revolt of 1381. This is equally true of seventeenth- and twentieth-century perspectives. When Sir John Cole-pepper prepared for Charles I his Reply to Pym's Nineteen Propositions in June 1642, he was quick to observe the radical implications of Pym's decision to publish the Grand Remonstrance, and hence to appeal directly to popular sympathy for his reforms *before* attempting to negotiate them by parliamentary process. The people would soon realise, wrote Cole-pepper:

that all this was done by them, but not for them and grow weary of journey-work, and set up for themselves, call parity and independence liberty, devour that estate which had devoured the rest; destroy all rights and proprieties, all distinctions of families and merit, and by this means that splendid and excellently distinguished form of goverment end in a dark, equal chaos of confusion, and the long line of our many noble ancestors in a Jack Cade or a Wat Tyler.[7]

Colepepper thus invoked not only the Ricardian Peasants' Revolt, but Jack Cade's 1450 rebellion in the reign of Henry VI, as precedents to which the dangerous populist strategies of Pym were suggesting analogies.

A recent collection of essays from *Past and Present*, entitled *Rebellion, Popular Protest and the Social Order in Early Modern England*,[8] contains three essays on forms of popular protest in the 1640s; but it begins with the Pilgrimage of Grace (the Catholic uprising against Henry VIII's version of the Reformation), includes three essays on Robert Kett's rebellion in 1549 against Edward VI, and ends with the Sacheverell Riots in Hanoverian England. The chain of dates commemorating popular uprisings significant enough to have acquired the status of revolt or rebellion must also include the Northern Rebellion against Elizabeth (1569), which although led by aristocrats involved large numbers of the peasantry; the Essex rebellion (1601) which was popular in the sense that Essex (compared at the time to Wat Tyler) was the people's darling; possibly the Midland Rising of 1607 against enclosures at the beginning of James's reign; the rise of the Levellers and the Agreement of the People in 1648; Monmouth's rebellion against James II in 1686, which rallied popular support under a banner of Leveller green; and the London demonstrations in support of John Wilkes in 1768, which ended in the 'Massacre of St George's Fields'.

The effect of this vision – of a long line of popular protests in series – is ambiguous, and raises questions that are central to historiography and political theory alike. On the one hand, the chain of events suggests the continuity of popular unrest in England, and permits the thought that a tradition of radical political action has always existed – a thought reinforced by the references backwards, like Colepepper's, to earlier links in the chain. The history of popular protest is self-recapitulating; and it therefore operates much as we have seen was true for Roman history, as a distinct but parallel matrix of memorial analysis and political consciousness.

This is equally true, ironically, when the purpose of the reference back is to warn against repetition, or to deny to radicalism the privilege of continuity. In the same year that Colepepper identified Pym as a 1642 Wat Tyler there appeared an anonymous pamphlet, *The Just Reward of Rebels, or the life and death of Jacke Straw and Wat Tyler*, whose title sufficiently indicated its political forecast on current events, and whose brevity and crudity maintained that stance unequivocally. But in Elizabeth's reign there was published, and presumably acted, a dramatic representation of *The Life and Death of Jacke Strawe* (1593), perhaps by George Peele. This play may have been intended 'to demonstrate the dangers of popular rebellion', as Dobson claimed in his study of the Peasants' Revolt,[9] but if that was its mission it also inevitably reminded its audience of the central tropes of the originary peasant movement. In its quotation of the sermons of John Ball, the somewhat mysterious priest who had inspired the Ricardian uprising, the Elizabethan play passed on to another generation, in addition to emblematic names and dates, a crucial symbolic text:

> Neighbors, neighbors, the weakest now a dayes goes to the wall,
> But marke my words, and follow the counsell of John Ball,
> England is growne to such a passe of late,
> That rich men triumph to see the poore beg at their gate.
> But I am able by good scripture before you to prove,
> That God doth not this dealing allow nor love,
> But when Adam delved, and Eve span,
> Who was then a Gentleman.

Articulated here was an appeal to a principle of natural justice and equality, to a moral economy and a classless society, made memorable by an Edenic motto that, in the fifteenth century, had been passed by word of mouth around Europe. Wat Tyler's secular version of these principles included an appeal against villeinage and for the removal of all lords, whether secular or clerical, who would interfere between the peasants and their king, a position that has recently been identified as a coherent 'peasant ideology', involving 'local traditions of ancient rights' of mythical status, and associated, in a wonderful conflation of the recorded past with the apocalyptic future, with an appeal to the Domesday Book.[10]

In other words, popular protest in England was marked from the beginning by powerful cultural or symbolic formulas, equivalent in their economy of reference to the Roman and republican semantics of 'Libertas'. But the native tradition differed from the republican one in being, obviously, both Christian and grounded in issues of land ownership. Its effect was only increased, probably, by the manifest contradiction between Christian egalitarianism and the repressive behaviour of the church as a feudal landlord. The symbolic egalitarian core of the agenda survived when historical circumstances changed. When villeinage was merely residual, as in 1549 when Robert Kett led his Norfolk rising, the religious definition of freedom reappeared: 'We pray thatt all bonde men may be made ffre for god made all ffre wt his precious blode sheddyng.' John Ball's language was echoed again in the late 1640s by those who had begun to realise that the agrarian policy of neither the Long Parliament nor the army leaders included any redistribution of land across class boundaries. Fairfax might receive a very considerable estate as the result of sequestrations, but the Diggers were not to be allowed to till Saint George's Hill in Surrey. The question that Winstanley put to Fairfax (unsuccessfully) in 1649, in representing the Diggers, was 'whether the earth with her fruits, was made to be bought and sold from one to another? and whether one part of mankind was made Lord of the land, and another part a servant, by the law of Creation before the fall?'[11]

One of the most complicated witnesses to the concept of a continuous radical tradition was the ardent royalist John Cleveland, who in 1654 published *The Idol of the Clownes, or, Insurrection of Wat the Tyler, With his fellow Kings of the Commons*. Timed to appear in the first year of Cromwell's Protectorate,[12] Cleveland's history was also, patently, an extended allegory of contemporary events, enlivened by a topical lexicon of ideologically loaded names like 'malignants', 'Cavaliers', 'royalists', 'Commonswealth men'. Ball's Edenic motto is described as a 'lewd levelling Text', and his sermons are claimed to have argued that 'nothing but Independency was Divine' (p. 7). Yet if the Elizabethan play on this subject was, intentionally or not, complicit in making a famous radical agenda available to late sixteenth-century audiences, the mid-seventeenth-century history of Cleveland was equally compelled to articulate on behalf of John Ball and Wat Tyler the social and spiritual utopianism of their programme, along with its causes. So, writes Cleveland, speaking for Ball:

it was to be consequent, that as nature, and the Creation made no distinction, no more ought Lawes to make or suffer any; that servitude is the daughter of unjust oppression . . . That if it had pleased [God] to have created slaves, in the beginning hee would have chosen and marked out who should have beene the Lord, who the Vassall.   (p. 7)

And he also recounts in telling detail the extraordinary confrontation between the insurgents and the abbot of St Albans, in which a symbolic event of great power occurred, when the millstone that had been taken away from the villagers in token of the abbey's control over the rural economy, and set into the abbey's floor, was taken up, broken into pieces, and distributed by the rebels to each other 'as the sacred Bread is given in the Eucarist' (p. 86). While claiming from the beginning that 'Tyler had no brains' (A4v), and that the rebels were merely 'Sons of the Dragons teeth' (A4r), that is, sprung from the soil, Cleveland was *also*, as a historian, forced to acknowledge the rebels' capacity to engage in symbolic action. More telling still, he recounts the rebels' complaint against the abbot of St Albans, that he had wished to keep his villeins uneducated, and hence incapable of the self-consciousness that their action against him showed:

You have always kept us deprived, not onely of all meanes of learning or knowledge, but would willingly have taken away our very reason and common understanding.   (p. 83)

There is no doubt, finally, of Cleveland's agenda. He wishes his history of the late fourteenth century to remind his seventeenth-century readers of a distinctly Hobbesian message. 'Though the title of the Rebellion spoke faire' (A5r) in using the utopian names of liberty and equality, self-interest was the real motive in its leadership, and its consequences were failure:

Villeinage was not now abolished, though some think otherwise, but by degrees extinguished since the reigne . . . This I observe, to make it appeare, how little it is which the miserable common people . . . are gainers by any of their riots, or sedition, whatsoever the changes are; their condition is still the same or worse.
                                                                                                                      (pp. 141–2)

Yet he clearly fell into the representational dilemma that Pierre Macherey discovered in Balzac's *Les Paysans*, a novel committed to revealing 'the unceasing conspiracy' of the rural working class against the French bourgeois. Considering Balzac's unqualified hostility to the peasant, that 'indefatigable mole', 'who has made the ownership of land to be a thing that is, and that is not', Macherey noted that Balzac 'announces the advent of a *danger*':

In a single movement . . . the author intends to inform and to disquiet, The ideological proposition is . . . most apparent; but it is easy to reveal by its side,

as the condition of its realisation, the utterance of the fact which contests it . . .
If one is going to speak against the people, effectively, one must speak *of* the
people: they must be seen, given form, *allowed to speak.*[13]

There are other procedures for control than the attempt to draw explicit
moral or political lessons against the unruly. It is these that render the
recent explosion of interest so ambiguous. On the one hand, as the *Past
and Present* volume makes clear, the field was opened and some of its terms
established by the pioneering essay by E.P. Thompson in 1971, 'The
Moral Economy of the English Crowd in the Eighteenth Century', in
which he argued, characteristically, against the condescension with which
history has treated the popular uprising, especially the so-called 'food
riot', whose very naming Thompson begins by recognising as hidden
persuasion. The term, and the form of analysis associated with it, he
castigates as 'the spasmodic view of popular history', by which 'the
common people can scarcely be taken as historical agents before the
French Revolution'. Prior to that, their intrusions are seen as 'compulsive,
rather than self-conscious or self-activating: they are simple responses to
economic stimuli'.[14] And, in a brilliant phrase, he identifies this as the
theory of 'rebellions of the belly', with all of the irrational implications
that the hidden fable proposes. In place of this historiographical condescension, which is shared equally by many Marxist historians and their
opponents, Thompson proposed the view that food uprisings were 'a
highly-complex form of direct popular action, disciplined and with clear
objectives' (p. 78), those objectives being to retain a moral economy that
forbade over-pricing, food-hoarding, and food adulteration.

The subject is of more relevance to the larger historiographical questions than it might seem, since the history of early modern England is
scarred by a series of food protests that serve to punctuate the apparently
more political and more socially threatening uprisings. There were clusters of such events in 1527, 1551, 1586–7, 1594–8, 1605, 1608, 1614,
1622–3, 1629–31, 1647–8, 1662–3, 1674, 1681 and 1693–5, 1709, 1740,
1756–7, 1773, 1782, 1795, and 1800–1. One might assume that the protest
over food supplies was the primal form of popular action, and that therefore evidence of rational planning and social acuity on such occasions
could be extrapolated into a theory of a *self-consciously* continuous radical
tradition. Ironically, however, as an influence on the historiography of
seventeenth-century England, Thompson's approach has actually enabled
his successors to render the concept of popular protest politically neutral.
Against the notion of a continuous radical tradition is erected, firstly, the
ideal of particularism, in which no connections may be seen between the
agendas of protesters in different times and places. Another consoling
strategy is to claim that behind each popular uprising lies an educated,

upper-class leadership, as, for example, in the Sacheverell riots, where mysterious gentlemen disguising their fine dress under old cloaks could be seen inciting the artisans to their attack on nonconformist chapels. But more subtle in its larger implications is the claim (inherent in Thompson's own argument) that popular protest was by nature conservative, that it never envisaged or articulated widespread social change. So John Walter and Keith Wrightson, writing on 'Dearth and the Social Order in Early Modern England', conclude that the pattern of continuous food riots is reassuring:

What is significant is less that dearth in England provoked occasional outbreaks of disorder than that it led to so few. Seventeenth-century England was not capable of eliminating the spectre of dearth, but it was capable of interpreting and resisting this phenemonon in such a way as to preserve itself. Society emerged from the crisis intact, with its values and structure of authority reinforced, for dearth highlighted the former and enhanced the latter's legitimacy.[15]

John Walter has subsequently combined forces with John Morrill in an essay on 'Order and Disorder in the English Revolution',[16] in which they argue together that the story of a lower-class agenda has been greatly exaggerated. The new social history reveals less disorder than historians who rely solely on printed sources (a jibe at Hill) have concluded. There was no theoretical connection between the egalitarian programme that excited the Levellers and the issues of land ownership as the centre of a peasant ideology; rather, 'the tendency to equate the levelling of enclosures with the threat of levelling in society . . . reveals more about the propertied classes' fears than the rioters' intent' (p. 139). They argue that there were only two peaks of disruption, one in the early 1640s and one in the late 1640s, with no continuity between them (or, it goes without saying) with earlier insurrectionary moments. They point out that the Leveller programme was extinct by the 1650s, and replaced by the quietist Quakers; and they argue a version of the earlier thesis that food riots reinforce social consensus:

Economic change undoubtedly prompted greater popular discontent, but ultimately it created new structures which made possible the containment and even appeasement of that discontent.   (p. 150)

Significantly, the idea of 'containment' has simultaneously gained a certain attraction in New Historicist theories of the drama in this period; Stephen Greenblatt has led the way in suggesting that sixteenth- and seventeenth-century theatre was appropriated by society for its own self-conserving ends, and allowed to articulate in fictional forms a social and political criticism that only *seemed* subversive.[17]

The element of ritual in popular protest and the element of socio-political criticism in the public theatre make possible an anthropological approach to both that has proved exciting and fruitful. In the general ferment, other agendas, both spoken and unspoken, may be taking us where we do not all want to go. There is an interesting acknowledgement by Walter and Morrill that the story that historians tell not only depends on which archive they select for inspection but is also controlled in advance by their socio-political predilections. They define themselves *as the historians of order*, and distinguish themselves from those (unnamed) whom they recognise as *historians of disorder*. These terms, perhaps unwittingly, establish the terrain of English historiography today as one in which the conflict of 1640–60 is restaged; two secular ideologies, of more import for British politics and academic politics in the 1980s than the doctrine of historical objectivity would suggest, produce incompatible accounts of what happened in the past and imply incompatible theories of how 'society' is related to its members.

With this key in hand, we can better understand why still other 'histories' are somewhat uncertainly poised between the alternatives of order and disorder. Compare, for instance, the *textually* ambivalent history of John Cleveland in 1654 with Diarmaid MacCulloch's 1979 study of Robert Kett's 1549 uprising. For all his Thompsonian insistence that we must not underestimate the ability of Kett and his colleagues to have organised concurrent risings in Norfolk and Suffolk, MacCulloch concluded that the 1549 agenda was essentially conservative: 'They wished to recapture an imaginary past in which society had consisted of watertight compartments, each with its own functions and each interfering as little as possible with the others . . . It would have been a very tidy world, too tidy for the rebels' ultimate comfort, for the articles were heavy with disapproval of social mobility in any direction.'[18] In an attempt to explain this conservativism, MacCulloch suggests that 'the rebel leaders presumably lost sight of the implications of their demands in their concern to keep the company of gentlemen at arm's length' (p. 50); but he himself presumably lost sight of the implications of that most traditional of all insurrectionary demands, liberty, represented by that clause in the rebel's agenda: 'thatt all bonde men may be made ffre for god made all ffre wt his precious blode sheddyng'. Defining this as a 'puzzling anomaly', MacCulloch proceeds to explain its presence here *not* in symbolic terms, but as a local attack on Thomas Howard, Duke of Norfolk, whose family had been notorious for the retention of bondage on their estates. Whatever the validity of this explanation, it is worth asking whether an agenda that includes this clause is truly disapproving of social mobility in any direction; and whether McCulloch's account of Kett's rebellion is not, finally, to be best understood in terms of his *naming* of the event:

Despite . . . evidence of the rebellion's association with pre-existent radicalism, the general character of the Suffolk rising lends additional emphasis to Bindoff's remark on Kett's rebellion that 'no popular commotion was ever less like the conventional notion of a *jacquerie*'. It is a moot point, indeed, whether one should consider the affair a rebellion at all: if I have used the term 'rebel' it is merely as a form of shorthand.   (p. 53)

Surely it is necessary to distinguish the seemingly conservative clauses of any insurgent agenda from support of the system as such? The peasant revolts of the fourteenth century frequently expressed their appeal to natural justice in terms of a wished-for return of an earlier, semi-mythical era in which they would not have been subjected to unwarranted interference. Like all utopianism, the appeal was partly rhetorical. Calling for a return of the good old days *sounds* less alarming than calling for innovation. In Cade's rebellion the emphasis on the removal of court abuses and venal intermediaries between the young king and his people, in Kett's rebellion the same emphasis on loyalty and a desire for good government, were probably equally strategic, designed to hold off a military suppression of the uprising until its programme could be heard. And for the seventeenth century, we can recognise these same rhetorical and strategic features articulated in parliamentary records from the 1604 parliament onwards, more explicit now in the appeal to '*ancient* liberties'. It makes more sense to explore how political consciousness grows despite its own appeal to the past – how in fact we get from Adamic classlessness to constitutional theory – than to argue from the expression of conservative sentiments that nobody except a few extremists really wanted change. They may have talked backwards; but they must have thought forwards. For social change undeniably occurred, despite the touted failures of individual protests, and by and large in the direction that the protesters indicated, however fragmentarily, that they wished society to move.

It is worth comparing the implicit conclusions of recent historians of popular protest with Dobson's summation of the Peasants' Revolt as a *cultural* phenomenon:

Many civil rebellions in late medieval, Tudor and Stuart England certainly reflected several of the aspirations and grievances previously expressed in 1381; but these sometimes striking similarities were ones of which it seems certain that the later rebels were themselves largely unaware. When, as late as the summer of 1549, Robert Kett's Norfolk rebels demanded 'thatt all bonde men may be ffre for god made all ffre wt his precious blode sheddyng', they presumably had no conception that they were re-echoing the sentiments of John Ball's sermon. Post-medieval England experienced an important, and unjustly neglected, history of revolutionary movements, but not – as far as we can tell – an articulate revolutionary tradition.   (p. 30)

But how far can we tell? The central question that remains unanswered, or that seems presently even further from solution today than it once might have been, is why insurrections of varying scale occur when they do and not at other times – a classic dilemma of political theory since Hobbes. And this in turn reveals itself as part of a still larger theoretical problem, the relation of individual agency, or personal intentions, or political self-consciousness, to large patterns of historical change. The questions of agency that political theorists and historians ask restate in secular terms the questions of free will versus predestination that seventeenth-century thinkers at all economic and educational levels posed themselves. As Milton came eventually to see it in demonic terms, they 'reasoned high / Of Providence, Foreknowledge, Will, and Fate, / Fixt Fate, Free will, Foreknowledge absolute, / And found no end, in wand'ring mazes lost' (*Paradise Lost*, II. 558–61). The questions have become no more soluble for being desacralised. But it is a concern perhaps specific to our own cultural moment that today any theory of agency, or collective will – or, in my terms, radical agendas – runs into resistance from both ends of the ideological scale.

The two extreme positions, and their weaknesses, have been cogently identified by Perry Anderson.[19] He points to Talcott Parsons' *The Structure of Social Action* as a paradigmatic statement of what he calls the idealist solution, namely the positing of common norms and values that *normally* formed the social glue, a model that possibly explains order but not the occasional eruption of disorder. We should recognise the theories of Walter, Wrightson and Morrill, then, as versions of the idealist position. Conversely, the materialist position deriving ultimately from Hobbes possibly explains insurrection but not the intervening periods of stability. As Anderson put it: 'Why should the intersection of rival collective wills not produce the random chaos of an arbitrary, destructured log-jam? . . . How could the utilitarian model of conflicting rational interests ever found a coherent social order?' (p. 51). Nor does the structural Marxism of Anderson himself, or of Althusser, whom Anderson is here defending, make the materialist position more viable; for to deny the existence of general wills, and to declare that disorder is the involuntary and surface expression of the deep structure of conflict between antagonistic modes of production is merely to restate the problem in different language, without explaining why riots or risings or revolts or rebellions or revolutions occur *when they do*.

And even in its most sophisticated updatings, the Marxist denial of any self-conscious 'general will' for change produces the kind of condescension to early insurrectionists that E.P. Thompson has taught us to be wary of. According to Anderson, who is cautiously permissive of the causal value of class struggle in '*revolutionary* transformations' of society (by which he means transformations from one mode of production to another) this permission extends only to the history of fully developed capitalist societies: 'it is essential to remember the great distance between the relatively blind clashes of the immemorial past, and the recent – very uneven and imperfect – conversion of them into conscious contests in the 19th and 20th centuries' (p. 56). Yet what I trust this essay begins to show is that the past is by no means entirely blind or as inaccessible as 'immemorial' proposes. At least as indicated by the two separate but analogous structures we have been following, there *was* a continuous radical tradition available in the culture of earlier periods. Symbolic memories of Roman political history and of European popular insurrections ran stronger, deeper and more knowingly through the minds of people much like ourselves than either conservative historians or structural Marxists would have us believe. Perry Anderson regards any appeal to the 'roll-calls of past lives, as moral exemplars for present struggles or aspirations' as 'a very uncomplicated – indeed largely mythical – conception of historical time', and, as is typical of Marxist historiography, traces its origins to the 'romantic nationalism of mid-19th century'.[20] While I would agree with Anderson that the cultural memory functions with myths, historians and literary theorists who have fused their own work with anthropology are unlikely to accept that the study of cultural myths is uncomplicated, or inimical to the 'exacting sense of material care and measure' that Anderson wishes to claim for structural Marxism. Consequently, these controversies involve literature and literary theory. The question of how the cultural memory works, and of what explanatory force we should give to the *affective* component of history, may well be one that a newly historicised literary studies could take as its special province and in which it might make signal contributions. To look backwards and forwards simultaneously is also literature's prerogative, and the task of literary theory is to see it maintained.

NOTES

1 Clarendon State Papers, Clarendon MS 48, folio 136r.
2 Ronald Paulson, *Representations of Revolutions (1789–1820)* (New Haven and London, 1983).
3 Raymond Williams, *Keywords: A Vocabulary of Culture and Society* (Glasgow, 1976) pp. 226–9.
4 Thomas May, *The History of the Parliament of England,* (1647; Oxford, 1854), pp. 271–2.
5 John Morrill, *The Revolt of the Provinces: Conservatives and Radicals in the English Civil War 1630–1650* (London, 1976).
6 Little distinguishes such a statement from that of J.P. Kenyon, whose popular

history, *The Stuarts* (London, 1958; rev. ed. 1970) makes no secret of its conservative agenda. Not only does this study completely omit (as its monarchist focus might justify) the significantly named 'Interregnum', but its chapter on Charles I ends with his speech on the scaffold, defining the people's liberty as consisting in their 'having government, those laws by which their lives and goods may be most their own'. 'It is not their having a share in the government', insisted Charles (with nothing further to lose) 'that is nothing apperteining to them . . . Until . . . you put the people in that liberty [i.e. being governed], they will never enjoy themselves'. 'Such were the principles', concluded Kenyon, 'suitably modified, on which the gentry brought back his son in 1660' (pp. 98–9).

7 Quoted in Morrill, *The Revolt of the Provinces*, p. 34.
8 Paul Slack, ed., *Rebellion, Popular Protest and Social Order in Early Modern England* (New York, 1984).
9 R.B. Dobson, *The Peasants' Revolt of 1381* (London, 1970), p. 389.
10 See Rosamond Faith, 'The "Great Rumour" of 1377 and Peasant Ideology', in R.H. Hilton and T.H. Aston, eds., *The English Rising of 1381* (Cambridge 1984), pp. 63–4. Faith connects this belief to the legend of King Offa, who had once (*quondam*) granted the peasants liberties and privileges, as well as with the insistence of the 1381 insurgents against the abbot of St Albans that a 'charter of liberties' existed somewhere in the abbey.
11 Gerrard Winstanley, *Works . . . with an Appendix of Documents Relating to the Digger Movement*, ed. G.H. Sabine (Ithaca, 1941), pp. 289–91.
12 This was republished in 1658, as *The Rustic Rampant, or Rural Anarchy affronting Monarchy*.
13 Pierre Macherey, *A Theory of Literary Production*, trans. Geoffrey Wall (London, 1978), p. 265.
14 E.P. Thompson, 'The Moral Economy of the English Crowd in the Eighteenth Century', *Past and Present* 50 (Feb. 1971), pp. 76–136.
15 John Walter and Keith Wrightson, 'Dearth and the Social Order in Early Modern England', in *Rebellion, Popular Protest and the Social Order*, p. 128. First published in *Past and Present* 71 (May 1976).
16 In A. Fletcher and J. Stevenson, eds., *Order and Disorder in Early Modern England* (Cambridge, 1985), pp. 137–65.
17 See especially 'Invisible Bullets: Renaissance authority and its subversion, *Henry IV* and *Henry V*', in Jonathan Dollimore and Alan Sinfield, eds., *Political Shakespeare* (Ithaca and London, 1985), pp. 18–47.
18 Diarmaid MacCulloch, 'Kent's Rebellion in Context', in *Rebellion, Popular Protest and the Social Order in Early Modern England*, p. 50. First published in *Past and Present* 84 (August 1979).
19 Perry Anderson, 'Agency', *Arguments within English Marxism* (London, 1980), pp. 16–58.
20 Perry Anderson, *Arguments within English Marxism*, p. 87.

2   A troubled Arcadia

SIR RICHARD Fanshawe's Ode of 1630, 'Now warre is all the world about', with its remarkable panorama of European conflict from which Britain alone is exempt, is representative of a range of works celebrating the Caroline peace sustained by royal authority and love, yet hinting darkly through metaphor and allusion that the peace is fragile, and that the thunderclouds are already beginning to accumulate on the horizon. Despite the congratulatory tone of much court poetry of the 1630s, where England is made to seem a sanctuary for halcyons and a paradise for shepherds, there were many literary expressions of disquiet. Often the structure of a volume of poetry reveals tensions and fears that are not explicitly voiced, and further evidence of covert concern about the precarious condition of England can be gained from the currency of certain translations of the Caroline period. By looking at some volumes of Fanshawe, Davenant and Vaughan in particular, we can acquire a sense of how different poets anticipated the crisis of the times and responded to it.

Fanshawe provides a useful starting point, in that the contents of his *Poems*[1] extend from 1630, the beginning of Charles's personal rule, to 1648, when his fate had not been settled and when the future shape of English government was still an open question. When Fanshawe gathered together his work in 1648 he was able to structure it to record the vicissitudes of recent English history. The half-concealed anxieties and forebodings of the pre-war verse now appear to have been accurate premonitions, and this soundness of judgement helps to fortify the unexpected optimism with which the volume ends. In considering his poems, we should remember that Fanshawe (who was born in 1608) had been a courtier in the 1630s, had spent much time abroad in France and Spain, had been active in the King's service in the early 1640s, and had been appointed Secretary for War to Prince Charles in 1644.

At the head of his *Poems* of 1648 Fanshawe placed 'An Ode upon occasion of his Majesties Proclamation in the year 1630. Commanding the gentry to reside upon their Estates in the Country'. Here the familiar scenes of England as a island Arcadia are reviewed, and the Virgilian rhetoric of national congratulation is smoothly unfurled. England is 'A world without the world' (*Orbis divisus ab orbe*), a land set apart for a special destiny, enjoying the protection and blessings reserved by a watchful providence. Although the terrible conditions of the iron age have come to prevail over the greater part of the world, with wars and desolation everywhere, the golden age lingers on in England. The golden chain of Jove's concord is connected with the island, and holds Peace gently captive here:

> White Peace (the beautiful'st of things)
> Seemes here her everlasting rest
> To fix, and spreads her downy wings
> Over the nest.

Fanshawe's lines offer one of the most memorable evocations of the innocence and security of early Caroline England. Like clusters of ripe grapes, Fanshawe's verses suggest the pleasure and contentment that belonged to the golden world, inherited by this

> one blest Isle
> Which in a sea of plenty swamme
> And Turtles sang on ev'ry bowgh
> A safe retreat to all that came.

These are the commonplaces of Stuart panegyric, complimentary notions that had been gathered together by Jonson at the beginning of James's reign and repeated with ingenious variations through the masques and court poetry for the benefit of James and Charles. The assumption behind these images of the Fortunate Isles swimming in a sea of plenty, behind these themes of a revived golden age and of inviolable peace, is simple. All these blessings flow from heaven through the mediation of Stuart kings and their wise government. So it is natural for Fanshawe to turn to King Charles to affirm the wisdom of his rule when he sees signs of trouble in arcady. This magical peace, he reminds his reader, is royally maintained and royally dependent. It is the consequence of the king's wisdom and his absolute authority; this is: 'The peace hee made', 'His care preserves us from annoy.' We might remember that in the very year 1629–30 Charles was discussing with Rubens the subjects for the ceiling of the Banqueting House at Whitehall that would praise the benefits of King James's rule. The divinely inspired royal wisdom was one of them, the blessings of peace another. Charles's care is paternal too, for as 'pater patriae' – another familiar Stuart role – he acts as he thinks best for the nation, exercising his wisdom selflessly for the benefit of his people:

> Whilst hee proclaimes not his owne pleasure
> So much as theirs.

King Charles's prudence in ordering the gentry back to their estates in

1630 is part of a complex of values that are all perceived to be benevolent and enlightened. To resist that order is a kind of perversity on the part of those gentlemen who do not understand where their own good or the national good lie. Fanshawe strikes an ominous note when he suggests that if the gentry do not obey, the king may 'force us to enjoy / The peace hee made', and for a moment the power that lies behind the benevolence becomes visible. Fanshawe's poetry has a naturally optimistic character, but every now and then one can sense the pressure of hard truths on the verse. The king had proclaimed that the gentry should return to the country to look after their estates and not overload London with their presence. Charles's concern was obviously political, for the concentration of the gentry in the capital meant trouble for the king, as they were inclined to engage in political combination and grievances would gather to a head. The acrimony and strife of the 1629 parliamentary session lie unacknowledged in the background. Fanshawe glosses over the political issue, choosing instead to emphasise the dangers of the capital in terms that are recognisable as traditional Roman ones, warning of debt, the expense of fashion and the lures of lust. These are time-honoured devices to discredit the city and open the way to praise of the country life. If the gentry will recognise their true interests and return to their country pleasures and responsibilities, a pastoral serenity of a Virgilian order is promised by the poet, under the secure rule of King Charles: 'Th'Augustus of our world', the 'author of peace / And Halcyon dayes'.

Like many of Fanshawe's poems, the Ode is a poem of wise counsel, yet even as it takes a benign survey of the land, it acknowledges that there is the possibility of trouble in Arcadia. The lyrical language that sings so alluringly of country pleasures shows the strain of trying to maintain a confident, optimistic note. Image and metaphor disturb the peaceful scenes with fear and terror. The nightingale is 'harmelesse', but 'How prettily she tells a tale / Of rape and blood'. The making of fruit preserves seems a pleasurable if messy occupation, yet its description is ominously phrased:

> 'Tis innocence in the sweet blood
> Of Cherryes, Apricocks and Plummes
> To be imbru'd.

It is evident that Fanshawe has more serious things in mind than kitchen matters. The violence that is explicit in Europe, and described in the earlier stanzas of the poem, is latent in England, and its presence sends a cold wind through the calm landscape.

What might have seemed to be witty flourishes at the time of composition in 1630 could be read in 1648 as signs of a prophetic understanding of England's destiny. The double perspective in the Ode given by time and events made it a richer poem in 1648, and Fanshawe evidently felt it would serve well to introduce his verses and establish the theme of Arcadia despoiled that dominates the work he gathered together then as a commentary on the times.

The volume is dedicated to Prince Charles, to whom Fanshawe was both friend and mentor. Charles had been born in 1630, a detail that gives added point to the opening Ode, for Charles is by implication a child of the halcyon age whose fate has been to grow up in a time of storms. The strategy of the 1648 volume becomes clearer when we perceive that its principal reader is intended to be Prince Charles and that Fanshawe, by choosing to print some of his pre-war poems, adding a translation of Book IV of the *Aeneid*, and closing with a prose discourse on the Civil Wars of Rome, is offering a conspectus of events throughout the prince's lifetime, and figuring a role for the prince that will take him beyond the catastrophe of present fortunes into a scene of renewal. The poems have to be read too under the influence of Fanshawe's translation of Guarini's *Il Pastor Fido*, which he had first published in 1647, and which he reprinted in 1648 as the first half of the volume containing the *Poems*.

Fanshawe seems to have translated Guarini's pastoral drama in 1643–4, during the most bitter phase of the war, when he was based with the court at Oxford, serving as Secretary for War to the young Prince Charles. The play is set in Arcadia, and as the shepherds and shepherdesses engage in their delicate entanglements of love and disguise, the land is ravaged by a great boar and grows subject to violent disorders; those who should ensure the security of Arcadia are distracted, and the shepherd prince who should rule is lost. Fanshawe presses home the analogies with England's state in his dedication to Prince Charles:

Our author (exposing to ordinary view an Enterlude of Shepherds, their loves and other little concernments) . . . presents through the perspective of the Chorus, another and more suitable object to his Royall Spectators. He shows to them the image of a gasping State (once the most flourishing in the world): A Wild Boar (the sword) depopulating the Country: the Pestilence unpeopling the Towns: their gods themselves in the merciless humane Sacrifices exacting bloody contributions from both: and the Priests, (a third Estate of Misery) bearing the burthen of all in the Chorus, where they deplore their owne and the common Calamitie.[2]

As Fanshawe observes to the Prince: 'It seems to me (beholding it in the best light) a Lantskip of these Kingdoms (your Royal Patrimony) as well in their former flourishing, as the present distractions thereof.' In the play an auspicious destiny prevails: the boar is slain, the pestilence ceases, a marriage of noble shepherds takes place, and the final chorus prophesies that Arcadia will flourish again. 'So much depends on the marriages of Princes', Fanshawe pointedly remarks to Prince Charles, for Fanshawe looks with a wild optimism beyond the present catastrophe of royalist fortunes to a time when Charles will be an instrument of recovery. Nowhere does Fanshawe mention King Charles's plight in 1647–8; although the poet was deeply loyal to the king, his own hopes and fortunes rested with the prince. One may infer that he considered the king's cause to be hopeless and the king incapable of resolving the political crisis. Fanshawe encourages the prince to anticipate a glorious revival, and impolitic though it may have seemed to place one's hopes in pastoral fables, Fanshawe, improbably, was right.

This pastoral history is followed by two poems that urge Prince Charles to engage with the actualities of the contemporary political scene. The first, 'Presented to his Highness the Prince of Wales at his going into the West. Anno MDCXLV. Together with Caesar's Commentaries', reminds Charles that a prince, even a shepherd prince, may have to fight to regain his rightful kingdom, and when that necessity occurs he must fight in a magnanimous way, following the example Caesar set, 'mixing Terror with Love, Morals with Politicks'. The second, 'presented to his Highness, In the West. Anno Dom. 1646' reverts to the topic of the Arcadian prince whose duty is to recreate his country's happiness. The Stuart golden age of peace, unity and plenty has been interrupted by war, and its fulfilment postponed until Charles can restore it, just as in *Il Pastor Fido* the younger generation must repair the ruins of the failed Arcadia and bring it to a finer state.

> That Union, and that peacefull Golden Age
> Which to your Grandsire ancient Bards presage
> And we suppose fulfilled in Him, appears
> By Fate reserved for your riper years.

Prince Charles's destiny is confidently predicted: 'this Prince's Starrs / Promise an end to all our Civill Warrs'. The king his father is, as so often in Fanshawe's musings, written out of the picture as a man incapable of making his cause prevail. Fanshawe inhales his 'funerall odours' even in 1646, and gives all his attention to the Prince of Wales, exhorting him, as the dutiful counsellor should, to acquire those qualities that the noblest exponents of power should possess: self-discipline, charity, temperance and the love of those he governs.

> Let him believe
> 'Tis not so much both Indies to command
> As first to rule himself, and then a land.

So Prince Charles's future role as the healer of civil war and the agent of restoration is figured out. The other poems collected in the 1648 volume help in various ways to diversify these themes of war and restoration.[3]

The poem on the Escorial opens with the observation that this great palace was constructed as a replacement for a lesser building destroyed in war; war does create the occasion for greater achievements, in effect. The verses in honour of 'His Majesties Great Ship' praise the king's concern for the defence of the realm. A Latin poem that had recommended Thomas May's translation of Lucan's *Pharsalia* is reprinted (an item to which we shall return) and set against a poem that catches England on the brink of a similar catastrophe of civil war, 'On the Earl of Strafford's Tryall', composed between the earl's trial and execution. Strafford is presented as a noble sacrifice made by the king to prevent the outbreak of war, but his case is examined in a Roman context. He is hopefully compared to a Roman 'who gave his blood to quench a Civil War', yet ominously the poem concludes with the fear that the gathering momentum of the factions is uncontrollable, and that Strafford's downfall prefigures the disintegration of the state. The crisis recalls an ancient descent into war: 'So fell great Rome herself . . .'

Again Fanshawe sounds the theme that destruction is a prelude to reconstruction, for immediately there follows the most substantial piece in the volume, a translation of Book IV of the *Aeneid*, the episode of Dido and Aeneas. Virgil's works were commonly exploited for their political significance in the Renaissance, and Fanshawe's translation follows the general trend. Even the romantic scenes of Aeneas' infatuation can be turned to serve English affairs of state. Behind Aeneas is the experience of Troy destroyed; we know his future course, which will summon him on to the foundation of Rome. The present occasion dramatises the hero's determination to turn away from the seductions of love to realise some great destiny; the obligation to his public duty overcomes the impulse to pleasure. The application to contemporary affairs and to Prince Charles in particular is not hard to find, for Fanshawe, in a dark time, is attempting to assert an auspicious future by interpreting the Sibylline leaves of the *Aeneid*. A city or a state may be devastated, but a greater one awaits its creation. The prince, as fugitive hero, must not yield to the enervating temptations of love and ease, though his years dispose him in that way. Now is the time for resolution, the time to remember that his responsibilities lie in the future and concern the good of his people.

The insistent Roman references of the volume are reinforced by the translations of two odes of Horace, both of which deal with the dislocations of civil war. Ode III.xxiv (which is translated in the same measures as Marvell's 'Horatian Ode') arraigns the profiteers in time of war, and praises the virtue of the public man who preserves his integrity in evil times. A crisis in the state demands a strenuous response and rigorous commitment from those who aspire to master the times. Again, there is a veiled tutorly rebuke to the prince to make him respond to the seriousness of the occasion by disciplined application to the business of war. One can see that Fanshawe knows that the softer pleasures appeal strongly to Prince Charles, who, like Aeneas, has to be forced from amorous couches into the storms of war:

> And mould we our too plyant wills
> To rougher Arts: the Child
> Of noble Lineage cannot wield
> A bounding Horse of Warre.

Prepare for fierce action now, is Fanshawe's advice to the prince, or quit. The second translation, of Epode XVI, explores the alternative. Here Horace laments that Rome (like England), which had withstood the attack of many foreign powers, should now encompass its own destruction. The solution he suggests for those who despair of a satisfactory political accommodation at home is exile, but better still would be emigration to some unspoilt land: 'Let us seek those isles / Which swim in plenty, the blest soils' which effortlessly produce the fruit of the earth. The poem ends with a vision of a golden age attained by a passage to remote shores, where the ruined state can be forgotten and a new beginning made. Horace concludes with a promise of escape and renewal:

> aere, dehinc ferro duravit saecula, quorum
> piis secunda vate me datur fuga.

Fanshawe recasts this as:

> Now Iron reigns, I like a statue stand
> To point good men to a good land.

The prophetic nature of the conclusion links this poem with the destiny of Aeneas (for he too is moving to a fertile new land of hope), and relates further to the prospect of a restored golden age at the end of Il Pastor Fido. Fanshawe, by characterising himself as a figure of wise counsel and prophecy, may be putting before Prince Charles the possible course of redemptive emigration, but it remains, as in Horace's epode, only a possibility. The real thrust of the poem is an assertive optimism, the conviction that destiny does not desert men of resolution and virtue, even in iron times. The implication is that 'Pius Carolus' will have his sunlit day: his supporters will reach some fortunate shore.

Fanshawe wrote no poems directly on the events of the English Civil War. All of his approaches to the subject are made through the experience of the Roman conflicts where the pattern of finished action may be instructively contemplated. The final section of the 1648 volume is 'a summary discourse of the Civil Wars of Rome, extracted out of the best Latin writers in prose and verse. To the Prince his Highness, upon the occasion of the preceding odes.' This account offers an unadorned synopsis of the Roman civil wars, noting in passing Horace's involvement in them and his dismay at the strife, yet hinting at the happy outcome. Horace was a great survivor: 'This same despairing Horace did live to see, and particularly to enjoy, very different times', and it is evident that Fanshawe feels a close kinship with him. As he recapitulates the outlines of the Roman Civil War, Fanshawe does not labour comparisons between Rome and England. Only at the end does he introduce Augustus, the supreme beneficiary of fate, who fought through the civil wars and survived to heal the nation's wounds; the ruler in whom virtue, wisdom and strength were combined. Augustus was actual, not fabulous. The discourse modulates into verse, and a famous passage of the *Aeneid*, Book VI is laid before the prince, Fanshawe registering it thus:

> This is that Man of men, Augustus, he
> Whom (sprung from heaven) heaven hath promis'd thee,
> That man shall to Italy restore
> The Golden Age which Saturn gave before.
> And to the Parthians and the Inds extend
> His spacious Empire.

Thereafter, Augustus's name is translated directly as Charles, and past and future are conjoined. The design of the volume is now fully disclosed: contemporary affairs have been intermingled with pastoral, mythological and historical scenes, and a pattern of expectation has been established. Fanshawe secures his own place in the pattern as the faithful counsellor to the prince, as he unfolds his prophetic sense of restoration: 'I must confess, Sir, I am now where I would be, and from whence I would not be removed a great while.' His vast optimism would be vindicated in 1660, and his own reward would be to become a trusted diplomat in the king's service and ambassador to Portugal and Spain.

The materials of Fanshawe's work can hardly be considered novel. The eagerness to draw extensive Roman parallels and to elicit political fables from noted fictions, the tendency to discover in every Stuart a potential Augustus, the impulse to prophecy – all these were common literary habits of the time, when the pressure to comment on contemporary developments was irresistible, and when poets felt on their mettle to justify a reputation for prophecy which had survived from antiquity. Milton, Wither, Quarles, Davenant and Denham, all writing in the approaches to civil war, were doing comparable things. What distinguishes Fanshawe is his passionate belief in the ability of the royalist cause to recover, and his total identification of that recovery with a man of destiny, Prince Charles. In addition, the structure of this 1648 volume is designed in a more thoroughgoing way and the contents are more effectively inter-related than in any other contemporary volume of poetry, with the exception of Milton's *Poems* of 1645.

The presence of the poem commending Thomas May's translation of *Pharsalia* or *The Civil Warres of Rome* raises the issue of the political bearing of some of the classical translations in Charles I's reign. The choice of texts for translation from the great library of antiquity was presumably motivated by a sense of contemporary relevance. May's Lucan was first published in 1626, an enlarged version appeared in 1627, and there were several subsequent editions in the 1630s. This steady interest in it, indicated by its publishing history, conveys some idea of its timeliness. Although the dedication of the 1633 edition to King Charles includes a prayer to God 'long to establish your Majesties throne upon earth', the very subject of the book and the interest it excited suggest an undercurrent of anxiety running through the reign, and a doubt about the political stability of the nation. The possibility of civil war was not unimaginable, and the prevalence of May's Lucan fed such speculations. By including his minor commendatory poem in his post-war collection, Fanshawe evidently felt that the prominence of Lucan's epic had been a sign of the times.

Hobbes's Thucydides is another case in point. Given Hobbes's astuteness of political judgement, his choice of *The Peloponnesian War* for translation in the late 1620s invites enquiry. Hobbes considered Thucydides to be 'the most politique Historiographer that ever writ', and he undertook the work partly for the instruction of his friend and patron William Cavendish, second Earl of Devonshire, but also for the better political education of his more thoughtful countrymen. Diplomatic Cavendish relished 'History and Civil Knowledge', and Hobbes wrote of him after his death: 'For so he read, that the learning he took in by study, by judgement he digested, and converted into wisdom, and ability to benefit his country, to which also he applied himself with zeal, but such as took no fire, either from faction or ambition.'[4] Some themes in the history, then, have an evident application to English politics, the implication being that the potential for disaster within the state exists, but statesmanlike men may avert fatal errors by the wise reading of *The Peloponnesian War*. Hobbes reminds his readers of the practical use of his book, 'for the principall and proper worke of History, being to instruct and enable men, by the Knowledge of Actions past, to beare themselves prudently in the present, and providently towards the Future'.[5] Hobbes's fear, expressed in the Epistle, and in his Latin autobiography, was that the democratic tendencies in England would grow until they brought about the ruin of the state as they had done in Athens. He admired the firm rule of Pericles, whom he characterised as a *de facto* monarch, supported by a strong aristocracy. Populist politics and factions involving the *demos* cause the degeneration of a state. On the frontispiece, Hobbes included a vignette of *hoi polloi* being aroused by an orator who looks very like a Puritan preacher. Disorder threatens. When the translation was published in 1628, the king was already having trouble with parliament, and was under attack by the populist leaders Eliot and Pym. An English overseas expedition to relieve La Rochelle had just come to grief in 1627 and gave new significance to the Sicilian expedition of the Athenians. Parliament was trying to make the king accept a Petition of Right that would oblige him to respect 'the rights and liberties of the subject'. To Hobbes it was apparent that there was a weakening of monarchical rule in England and an emerging popular discontent. The lessons from Thucydides, if assimilated by the pro-royalist gentry, might prevent further unsettling of the state; publication of the work at this time was indicative of the disquiet that Hobbes felt about the direction of national events.[6]

A rather more ominous work of translation came from John Denham, who put Book II of Virgil's *Aeneid* into heroic couplets in 1636 and entitled it 'The Destruction of Troy'. The imaginative affinities between Troy and England had always been emphasised in Tudor and Stuart times, so that cross-referencing was inescapable. Denham's selection of the book in which Aeneas recounts to Dido the destruction of his homeland shows a strong sense of foresight. Again, there were enough signs of stress by the mid-1630s to cause alarm. With all the simmering hostility to the king's rule, it was not unimaginable that violence might flare up, in spite of all the assurances of security and peace that the court-associated artists and preachers delivered. Denham admits Virgil's relevance to contemporary affairs in the preface that he added to his translation, which appeared in print in 1656.[7] 'If Virgil must needs speak English, it were fit that he should speak not only as a man of this nation, but as a man of this age.' His premonitions of misfortune attain a fine accuracy in the description of the death of Priam, who is made a sacrifice for the sins of Troy. Priam dies:

> With such a signal and peculiar fate,
> Under so vast a ruin, not a grave,
> Nor in such flames a fun'ral fire to have.
> He whom such titles swell'd, such power made proud,
> To whom the sceptres of all Asia bow'd.
> On the cold earth lies the unregarded King.
> A headless carcase, and a nameless thing.

In the same year that Denham dated his translation of Virgil, 1636, a geographical *translatio* was proposed which had the air of a legendary adventure, a fabulous errand fit for chronicle or verse, which was in part a reaction to growing political stress. This was the conquest and plantation of Madagascar, a scheme first developed by Prince Rupert as an escape from his disappointments over the recovery of the Palatinate and as a redirection of his energies away from the depressing entanglements with English and European leaders who offered him no support for reclaiming his family's inheritance. The prospect of quitting the frustrations and corruptions of the old world to found a new state in some fertile island of the east seemed like a realisation of Horace's advice in Epode XVI, which we have already noted in Fanshawe's volume for Prince Charles: as the bronze age turns to iron, set sail for some unfallen land where the golden age still lingers. That was exactly how the expedition was celebrated by William Davenant, who appointed himself laureate of the venture, addressing his heroic poem 'Madagascar' to Prince Rupert as if the whole enterprise were already a *fait accompli*. Full of fancy and wit, the poem portrays the island as a lightly-guarded paradise, which Rupert and his colonists take possession of. The prince is imagined ruling already over his kingdom of delight:

> And here Chronologers pronounce thy style;
> The first true Monarch of the Golden Isle.

'But he in story only rules', for the expedition never set out and Rupert never knew if his eastern paradise would have the pearls and perfumes, silks and nectared fruits that Davenant promised. Opposition from the East India Company and difficulties in raising money caused the prince to abandon the scheme. (It was, however, seriously revived by the Earl of Arundel as his fortunes failed at the end of 1639. He had incurred a humiliating failure when the army he led against the covenanting Scots was forced to disband, he had very large debts, and he was depressed by the growing discontents in England. Madagascar seemed the solution to his problems. He commissioned Van Dyck to paint him and his Countess seated by a globe which shows the island to advantage in order to commemorate his decision. He too never left). Behind the Madagascar project there was a kind of desperation concealed by loudly expressed hopes of wealth, land, peacefulness and new authority. Davenant, in his volume *Madagascar; With Other Poems* (1638), works hard to keep up an optimistic pose, to such an extent that John Suckling, in one of the prefatory poems, laughs at him for having too facile an imagination in proclaiming Rupert's triumphs before he has even left port.

The collection as a whole is a good example of the social complimentary verse that kept up court spirits in the decade before the Civil War.[8] There is a 1630 ode here too, addressed to the king on New Year's Day, which shares some of the disquiet that Fanshawe had expressed in his veiled imagery. At first sight it seems an almost unruffled poem of contentment, breathing the air of the Caroline peace – a natural topic of praise at this time, for Charles had concluded treaties of peace with France and Spain in 1629, which helped justify the national mood of satisfaction at avoiding the conflicts of the continent. But there are shadows on the scene: parliament in particular, whose members in Davenant's view have an excessive opinion of their rights and powers, could be a source of trouble. His New Year wishes to the king include:

> A Session too, of such who can obey.
> As they were gather'd to consult, not sway:
> Who not rebell, in hope to git
> Some office to reclaime their wit:
> Let this yeare bring
> To Charles our King:
> To Charles; who is th' example and the Law,
> By whom the good are taught, not kept in awe.

The word 'rebell' lies there, like a worm within the oak, but its strength is softened by the buoyancy of the verse. In the event, Charles never summoned a parliament in 1630, so the threat of an unruly session was postponed, but the memory of the fractious parliament of 1629 gave observers some indication of difficulties ahead.

The other shadow is the continental war. The exploits of Gustavus Adolphus are glanced at, and one can tell from the tone that they make Davenant uncomfortable. The Swedish king aroused emotions of admiration and shame in English Protestants. He was heading the Protestant cause and now in 1630 he was about to lead his armies into Germany, while Charles kept out of the conflict and was reluctant to send men or money to help his sister Elizabeth, whose expulsion from Bohemia and the Palatinate had precipitated the Thirty Years War.[9] Davenant hopes that Charles will be persuaded to change his policies by

> Praetors, who will the publique cause defend,
> With timely gifts, not Speeches finely pend;
> To make the Northerne Victors Fame
> No more our envy, nor our shame.

There is a surprising amount of defensiveness in this congratulatory ode, and this defensive note helps to point up the ambivalent attitude towards the Caroline peace. It was blessed, enviable, Augustan, yet there was something faintly shameful about it, for it was achieved at the expense of what many held to be a national duty, the participation in the wars to restrain the Catholic advance in Europe. Knowledge of this widespread embarrassment at England's failure to do the honourable thing and support the Protestant cause makes it difficult to read the Madagascar poem of 1636 with unqualified approval for its engaging wit and fantasy. If its mood strikes one as falsely heroic, it is because one suspects that Prince

Rupert ought not to have been dreaming of eastern fantasies, but should have been engaged in the struggle in Europe with English support.

Most of the poems in the Madagascar volume are complimentary to the court and touch on a fairly conventional range of subject matter. There are poems of rapturous admiration to the queen, expressions of warm friendship to the courtier Endymion Porter, elegies on the untimely dead, and congratulations to the newly married. The prevailing tone is confident, with a succession of hopeful notes struck, with the result that the overall impression of the volume mutes the flickers of anxiety and doubt that we have noticed. Davenant's reservations about the integrity of the Caroline regime really came to the surface when he wrote the masque *Salmacida Spolia* for the king and queen in 1640, but by then the long-maintained professions of confidence and admiration were giving way to an acknowledged need to justify royal policy and to prevent opposition from getting out of hand. *Salmacida Spolia* has received much attention in recent years, and it is unnecessary to review it here, but we should notice that the fears of 1630 had been fully justified: what an ode had glanced at without undue concern now needed a masque to dispel, and a masque was hardly a sufficient instrument of state to combat the present discontents. Parliamentary opposition, Protestant distrust of royal intentions, doubts about the legality of Charles's law were all pushing people towards defiance and rebellion, and it would not be long before Prince Rupert would find a genuinely heroic mission in the king's service.

In the 1640s royalist poets needed large reserves of optimism, such as Fanshawe possessed, to sustain a vision of the future that could overleap the calamities of the present. A poet who well shows the difficulty of making sense of events as the country stumbled into war was Henry Vaughan. As a provincial poet enamoured of the Caroline court ethos that he had never known, he had futilely imitated the poetic gestures of the 1630s in the early forties when they had become empty and irrelevant. When he published his *Poems* in 1646, at the age of 24, he recognised his untimeliness in the preface, where he deprecated 'that courage that durst send me abroad so late, and revel it thus in the Dregs of an Age'. The Jonsonian verse compliments and the fascination with the outdated routines of platonic love relationships testify to the power that the refined gallantry of the Whitehall world possessed years after that world had been swept away – though no doubt the Civil Wars bred a nostalgia for those lost social graces. Vaughan relieves his discomfort at putting these effete preferences before the public by quoting a line from Persius as his epigram: 'Languescente seculo, liceat aegrotari' (When the age languishes, it is permissible to be sick). His self-diagnosis was quite accurate, for most of the poems here are fragile and thin. Appropriately, he concludes with a retirement poem, 'Upon the Priorie Grove', where he proposes to withdraw from the hostile scenes of the time in order to cultivate his delicate poetic fictions on the border of Wales. He faintly hopes that he may inhabit an unviolated sanctuary, an undiscovered pocket of Arcadia:

> Thou shalt stand
> A fresh grove in th' Elysian Land
> . . .
>
> So there again, thou'lt see us move
> In our first Innocence, and Love,
> And in our shades, as now, so then,
> We'll kisse and smile and walke agen.

The verses are mild, wan, and quite lacking in strength of conviction. Vaughan's hopes to live in some unnoticed colony of the Caroline pastoral world seem most unlikely to be realised. Their lack of credibility is immediately felt when one turns to the additional work that Vaughan printed with his English poems, a translation of Juvenal's Tenth Satire. That familiar sensation arises of being in the presence of a Roman poem which is commenting darkly on contemporary events. This is the Vanity of Human Wishes satire, full of lofty disillusion with the affairs of state. The long register of crime, disorder and war in Greece and Rome caused by restless ambition and the repeated failure of public men to impose their schemes of power, when read against recent history, makes English conflicts seem like one more convulsion of a political disease that is as old as mankind. We are not explicitly invited to see the fall of Sejanus as a parallel to Strafford's fall, but they belong to the same repeated pattern of failed hopes and uncompleted designs. Noble aspirations, military glory, desire for power upon power, the ambition to change the state or subvert it, all founder in misfortune. The wise man forsakes ambition and retires into the confines of his own self-sufficiency. Vaughan's translation is in some degree a ponderous justification of his own wish for retirement, but it also allows him to give large expression to a heart-felt pessimism about the nation's tribulations. It is a poem of displaced political emotion, and its long sonorous measures betray the despondency of a man who had no convincing imaginative resources to set against civil disorder.

The ineffectualness of his preferred pastoral retreat he confessed immediately in his next volume of verse, *Olor Iscanus* (which was ready for the press by the end of 1647, but not printed until 1651).[10] The title, 'The Swan of Usk', promises pastoral matters, and the opening poem on the river Usk evokes the scenes chosen for his retirement and shows him busily rearranging his landscape to make it a proper habitation for a rural poet. We see him settling in as the genius of the place, and walking the bounds of his Welsh Arcadia to secure them against misfortune:

> And what ever Fate
> Impose elsewhere . . .
>
>   . . .
>
>   . . . may those lowd anxious Cares
> For dead and dying things (the Common Wares
> And showes of time) ne'er break thy Peace, nor make
> Thy repos'd Armes to a new warre awake!
>   But Freedom, safety, joy and blisse,
>   United in one loving kisse
>   Surround thee quite, and stile thy borders
>   'The Land redeemed from all disorders.'
>   ('To the River Isca')

The redemptive power of poetry is not, however, as effective as Vaughan, in his more optimistic moods, would like to believe. The next poem, 'The Charnel House', immediately points up the fragility of his desire to escape the pressures of war and death. 'The Charnel House' deserves a fuller recognition than it has achieved, as a poem that registers the horror and desolation of death in language that plainly evokes the experience of the Civil Wars. After all the pastoral assurance of the 'River Isca' poem, in which he had pretended that his pastoral retreat was free from 'dead and dying things', the discovery of death's presence in the happy land comes as a most unpleasant shock. 'Blesse me! what damps are here? how stiffe an aire?' 'The Charnel House' is the equivalent of the tomb in Arcadia, but it is viewed in no Poussinesque mood of philosophic resignation: its foul odours and revolting display of bones terrify and unnerve the poet, and subdue all hope and ambition in him. This is not just the house of death, it is the place of communal death that inescapably reminds the reader of the human waste when 'Gun-powder blows up a land'. The description would fit the aftermath of a battle, 'where I can descrie / Fragments of men, Rags of Anatomie' in this 'leane, bloudless shamble'. After the storm 'whose tempest-wrath / Hath levelled Kings with slaves', death has piled up his trophies of the field 'in this Accumulat-ive Cell', to provide a chilling 'Display of ruin'd Man'. This is perhaps the one poem in Vaughan's work in which he fully admits the horror of the violent experiences of the war years. Though the poetic self of Henry Vaughan longs to live in fictional glades, he is honest enough to concede that nightmarish images of mutilation and death have had so powerful an effect on his imagination that they make his pastoral escapism seem a retreat into irresponsible ease.

The ordering of the contents of *Olor Iscanus* provides the volume with its own system of self-criticism. The jarring disharmony set off by the first two poems of the collection persists all the way through the book, as the poet's desire to retreat from life is frustrated by the claims of painful experience which must be faced, not evaded. Poems that attempt to maintain the contented equilibrium of retirement, poems of friendship, of the country life, of happy marriage, of nymphs 'exempt from common frailtie' are interrupted by elegies to the untimely dead: 'Mr. R.W. Slain in the late unfortunate differences at Rowton Heath, 1645', whose years 'could not be summed (alas) / To a full score'; 'Mr. R. Hall, slain at Pontefract 1648', who died 'the glory of the sword and gown'. Vaughan was a fine elegist. There is more judgement and maturity in his poem to R.W. than in anything he had written so far. His expression of measured grief conveys a poignant feeling of loss for a friend for whom he clearly had a deep affection. The language of familiarity develops a moving gravity as it restores the memory of a young and courageous man extinguished in some obscure skirmish. R.W. could stand for a generation whose promise had been lost in the war. Vaughan does not know where his friend is buried, and fears that he might lie anonymously in 'the Common Death' that he described in 'The Charnel House'.

A late addition to the collection, the epitaph to King Charles's daughter Elizabeth, records an ill-fated life and premature end which seems to sum up the violated innocence of the times:

> Thou seem'st a Rose-bud born in Snow
> A flowre of purpose sprung to bow
> To headless tempests, and the rage
> Of an incensed, stormie Age.

Vaughan then adds a number of translations from Ovid's *Tristia*, the poems of exile, a favourite text among royalists in the 1640s and 50s. The elegies of the *Tristia* express the sorrows of banishment and deprivation, but they demonstrate too the consolations that the writing of poetry provided in such circumstances. Modern poets, such as Vaughan in Wales or Herrick in Devonshire, were reconciled to their exile and remoteness from the cultural centre by remembering that Ovid had endured their lot and relieved it by writing poetry. Vaughan closes *Olor Iscanus* with two further groups of translations, poems by Boethius on the overcoming of ill fortune by stoical self-possession and calmness of spirit, and verses by the neo-Latin Polish poet Casimir on the pleasures of the rural life leavened by Christian resignation. As we reach the end of the collection, we have the sense that Vaughan is uncertain whether his chosen place of retreat has become an enforced exile; he seems aware too that his hope of projecting himself as a poet of rural contentment lacks credibility. The poetic refuge he has tried to construct for himself is quite inadequate and cannot keep out the violence and desolation generated in the Civil Wars. Vaughan comes across in his *Poems* and *Olor Iscanus* as a poet in confusion. He has a vocation but no certainty of direction, he is unsettled by the malignity of the age and has limited resources for dealing with disorder.

The way out of his impasse was shown him quite unexpectedly by an experience of conversion: a transformed sensibility, a sudden bright responsiveness to the divinity in nature, an understanding of the place of death within a Christian scheme, a high excitement at the prospect of an imminent revelation – all came together in the understanding and insight and hope of *Silex Scintillans*, enabling him to outsoar the darkness of the mortal night into a calmer region of divinity. There are no secular poems in *Silex*. Mourning and sorrow remain, but now there are reassurances that console, and secure expectations. The convictions of his faith caused him to find a resolution to the divisions of his age in an anticipation of divine intervention in history. His sense of distress and division would be ended by the personal rule of Christ and the melting of time into eternity.

As a poet, Vaughan, like Fanshawe, explored his experience of a violated Arcadia. For Vaughan, a retiring obscure man, the violation was of a personal sanctuary: his private tranquillity, his friendships, his poetic ambitions were all roughly broken by events, and his ultimate resource was religious consolation. Fanshawe, a prominent courtier and a politically conscious man, was concerned with the growth of violence in the public world and the destruction of a golden age. He too made an act of faith that a restoration of civil harmony and royal authority will occur. His hopes were public ones, and his knowledge of Roman history gave him confidence to see beyond the disastrous present. In addition, he found in pastoral fiction prophetic truths. No one could escape the tensions of the age, but poetry allowed men to express their anxieties, their distress and their victories of the spirit, and it took them through to a better world.

NOTES

1 The full title of the 1648 volume is *Il Pastor Fido. The Faithfull Shepherd with an Addition of divers other Poems.*
2 *A Critical Edition of Sir Richard Fanshawe's 1647 Translation of Giovanni Battista Guarini's Il Pastor Fido* ed. Walter F. Stanton Jr, and William E. Simione (Oxford 1964), p. xviii. It is worth remarking that this dedicatory letter of *Il Pastor Fido* might have provided Hobbes with the famous image that he used for the engraved title-page of *Leviathan*, 1651. Fanshawe describes a portrait of Richelieu in the Louvre 'presenting to the common Beholder a multitude of little faces, (the famous ancestors of that noble man), at the same time, to him that looks thru' a Perspective . . . there appears only a single portrait in great of the Chancellor himself'. Fanshawe praises this ingenious conceit as 'demonstrating how the Body Politick is composed of many Natural Ones' (1647 edition, A2c & A3). Hobbes was living in Paris while he was writing

Leviathan and may well have been acquainted with this picture, (which seems not to have survived), or he may have been struck by Fanshawe's description of it.

3 A modern edition of Fanshawe's poems with commentary has been undertaken by Peter Davidson: 'An Edition of the Poems of Richard Fanshawe', unpublished doctoral thesis, Cambridge, 1984.

4 Thomas Hobbes, *Eight Books of the Peloponnesian Warre*, 1634 edition, Epistle to William Cavendish, Earl of Devonshire.

5 *Ibid.*, To the Readers.

6 These points are made by Richard Peters in *Hobbes*, (Harmondsworth 1956; rpt. 1967), pp. 19–20.

7 Denham, incidentally, included a poem commending Fanshawe's translation of *Il Pastor Fido* in his collection.

8 Davenant's poems have been edited by A.M. Gibbs, *Sir William Davenant: The Shorter Poems, and Songs from the Plays and Masques*, (Oxford 1972).

9 The most familiar English response to Gustavus Adolphus in poetry is Thomas Carew's quasi-elegy at his death in 1632, in which he wilfully and perversely refuses to agree to mourn him. Though 'warre be all about', it is better to ignore it than to spoil the charmed peace of England.

> But let us that in myrtle bowers sit
> Under secure shades, use the benefit
> Of peace and plenty, which the blessed hand
> Of our good King gives this obdurate Land,
> Let us of Revels sing . . .
>
> . . .
>
> Tourneyes, Masques, Theaters, better become
> Our Halcyon dayes; what though the German Drum
> Bellow for freedome and revenge, the noyse
> Concernes not us, nor should divert our joyes;

But the German drum did concern England, and Carew knew that well enough. His provocative observations again serve to sound alarm while seeming to praise the arcadian peace of 'The Shepherd's Paradise'. The language of the lines quoted here chimes with the language of Fanshawe's 1630 Ode quite remarkably.

10 For possible reasons of delay, see *The Works of Henry Vaughan* ed. L.C. Martin (Oxford, second edition 1957), introduction, p. xviii.

PART II

Engagement or retreat?

3 Politics and the masque: *Salmacida Spolia*

WHILE IT IS only belatedly coming to be recognised that most
Renaissance literary forms were profoundly implicated in the social and
political changes of their day, and not merely passive reflectors of those
events, there has, traditionally, been no reluctance to perceive this dimension of the court masque. Indeed, the masque has come to be regarded as
having made only too significant a contribution to the crown's weakness
in 1640: it encouraged the king to take too optimistic a view of his political
resources – generating a misleading image of political harmony and insu-
lating the crown from the disquiet felt by many at royal policies – while
its expense engendered hostility among those without access to Whitehall
and so helped to accelerate the polarisation of attitudes in society in
general. The elitism of the masque, its esoteric symbols, its almost mystical ceremonial and its representation of the king as a god who effortlessly
reduces discord to harmony, are rightly supposed to have rendered the
form too narrow and inflexible a vehicle adequately to mediate between
the king's supporters and his critics. To those of us who understand the
political breakdown of 1642 as generated in part by a conflict within the
national culture, the masque goes a long way towards explaining why a
dynasty which had made such a substantial investment in artistic patronage of all kinds should at this crisis still seem to be isolated and remote
from the nation at large.[1]

In this essay I do not want substantially to challenge this view: it is self-
evident that the solutions proposed in masques of the late 1630s were
inadequate to the difficulty of the problems to which they were purport-
edly addressed. But it still seems to me that the current consensus on the
masque seriously underestimates the problematic nature of the form, and
overlooks the interplay of competing and contradictory pressures which
it was seeking to negotiate and which inevitably left their traces upon it.[2]
It has become habitual in writing about the masque to represent it as
ideologically and aesthetically unproblematic. To summarize briefly, the
form has commonly been represented as existing to legitimate royal
power and as speaking to and for a single-minded, monolithic court; in the
context of political failure this legitimation has been seen as increasingly a

matter of escapism, idealisation and wishful thinking. My contention, however, will be that the cultural and political situation of the masque was considerably more complex than it is typically represented, and that the statements which it can be construed as making are, correspondingly, dependent on our realising these complexities. Despite its narrow scope and seeming singularity of purpose, the masque, no less than other forms, articulated the discontinuities and contradictory imperatives of its moment of production.

In recent years, our picture of the early Stuart court has undergone considerable revision.[3] We no longer quite see the royal regime as teetering on the brink of inevitable collapse throughout the 1630s, though we do recognise its dangerously hand-to-mouth finances and radically divisive policies. We perceive that some sections of Charles's court were uneasy about his government or would have preferred to see a more parliamentary way of proceeding; and we no longer assume that in 1640 the gentry in parliament were bent on taking over executive power, though they were determined to force Charles to accept firm restraints. Against this background the masque can be read less as an attempt to stave off unwelcome nemesis than as part of the machinery of state through which a king intent on a particular programme of government sought to communicate with his political elites. The masques promulgated royal ideology; they advertised, authorised or outlawed values that defined the basis by which Charles deemed his power to subsist. Though it remains true that the masque was ultimately inadequate to the tasks assigned it, from this perspective the form looks less like a case of royal myopia than part of an ongoing political dialogue between the crown and its servants. And at times of crisis the masque potentially offered the king a means by which he could seek to negotiate his position, through acts of conciliation, rapprochement or appeasement.

It is one such moment of crisis that I want to address by examining Davenant's *Salmacida Spolia*, a masque danced early in the climactic year 1640. But as a way of raising some of the interpretative problems which have usually been marginalised in writing about the masque, I would like to dwell first on three aspects of the genre which have, I believe, been habitually underemphasised. The first concerns the extent to which masquing could be taken for granted by contemporaries as a legitimate part of court pleasures. From the point of view of William Prynne, indulgence in frivolous masques was only to be expected from a court that had neglected its duties to international Protestantism, sought Spanish alliances and suppressed godly preachers, and Prynne's uncompromising attack on court masquing reflects not only his cultural preferences but his disapproval of the political and religious positions which court culture was being used to underwrite. But, as David Norbrook has argued, this means that if court masques had voiced the political attitudes of the anti-Spanish militants, they might well have aroused less criticism among the court's Puritan observers; after all, the godly citizens were themselves happy to promote pageantry with a strongly Protestant flavour on the annual occasion of the Lord Mayor's procession.[4] And though the court provoked criticisms from observers upset by Charles's willingness to watch plays on Sundays,[5] it was as the official historian of the Long Parliament that, in 1647, Tom May wrote:

The example of the Court, where Playes were usually presented on Sundaies, did not so much draw the Country to imitation, as reflect with disadvantage upon the Court it selfe, and sowre those other Court pastimes and jollities, which would have relished better without that, in the eyes of all the people, as things ever allowed to the delights of great Princes.[6]

May seems to mean that had Charles kept the Sabbath holy his revels would have been more readily tolerated as part of the necessary spectacle of the early modern state; or, as Samuel Daniel had put it, 'these ornaments and delights of peace . . . deserve to be made memorable as well as the graver actions, both of them concurring to the decking and furnishing of glory and majesty, as the necessary complements requisite for state and greatness'.[7] Cromwell would discover in the 1650s that masques were as needful as state banquets, audiences and other kinds of political ceremonial. Staged in the presence of foreign ambassadors expert in the forms of European pageantry, they asserted the strength of the nation and its claim to international credibility and competence. Masques had political functions that went beyond that of flattery of the monarch.

My second point concerns the kinds of political statement that were possible in the masque. Masques were performed before tiny audiences drawn from the social elites, and as one of Beaumont's characters says, they were 'tied to rules of flattery';[8] given these conditions, the range of sentiments that they could accommodate was severely restricted. When the masque was presented *to* the king, as usually happened before 1625, advice or limited criticism *could* code itself as praise; the king could be tactfully admonished with an image which represented him as the ideal ruler he ought to be. Under Charles and Henrietta Maria, who liked to dance in their masques, this limited freedom of manoeuvre became narrower still: nevertheless, it still seems that conditions could exist within which the masque might attempt to do more than merely reaffirm the king's point of view. For example, the masques associated with Prince Henry were significantly different in form and content from those written for his father, while during the period of the Palatine marriage, several masques took the opportunity of hinting at hopes of a change of direction on foreign affairs.[9] So too Ben Jonson's middle masques, though they celebrate the court during the period of the Howard and Villiers ascendancies, occasionally register something of Jonson's personal unease about being 'tied to rules of flattery'. Some take account of objections to the masque, though with a view to evading or discrediting them,[10] and the *Masque of Metamorphosed Gipsies* has a current of private irony that disturbs modern readers, even if it was all but invisible to the aristocrats dancing in it.[11] Rather more suggestive are those masques of the 1630s which, within the limits of compliment, unmistakably take issue with favourite policies of the crown. When the Inns of Court presented Charles with *The Triumph of Peace* in 1634 they praised his regime but seized this chance of reflecting on his manipulation of the law to raise finance without parliament, and two years later, during the visit to England of the exiled Palatine Prince, Henrietta Maria herself sanctioned by her presence a masque, *The Triumphs of the Prince d'Amour*, expressing the readiness of her subjects to fight in the Protestant cause.[12] Masques were primarily expressions of policy sponsored by the king, but they could be used to address the king in his own language; the direction of meaning did not have to be only one-way.

Davenant's *Triumphs of the Prince d'Amour* brings me to my third point, which is that it has always been very readily assumed that every participant in the masque thought the same way as the king; yet it seems self-evident that as well as representing the court's image to the world at large, the masque must also have had to mediate between rival factions competing *within* the court for influence over the making of policy. For example, in the hiatus that descended on royal policy following the collapse of the Spanish match, Charles and Buckingham seem to have promoted *Neptune's Triumph for the Return of Albion* as a means of representing their now anti-Spanish policy to the firmly pro-Spanish King James. In this instance the masque could not be performed, owing to James's fear of offending the Spaniards. Similarly, it was well known that for much of the 1630s Henrietta Maria was at odds with her husband concerning his foreign alliances and was prepared to promote a significantly more aggressive line on Europe than his.[13] Contemporaries who watched masques praising the loving identity of purpose between king and queen would not have naively understood them to be empty of ideological implication. Even more remarkable is the presence in masques of the 1630s of courtiers whose future careers would lead them into postures of hostility or even resistance to the king. Certainly most masquers dancing with Charles in the 1630s were courtiers of a stamp such as we might expect, but a remarkable minority were men who, when it came to a divide, chose either to be neutral or to fight that king in whose entertainments, in less polarised times, they had been prepared to participate.

One striking case is the Earl of Holland, who danced in all the main masques from 1632 to 1634, *Love's Triumph Through Callipolis, Albion's*

Triumph, *Tempe Restored* and *Coelum Britannicum*. Brother to the Puritan Earl of Warwick, Holland was closely associated in the 1630s with the queen's circle, and he operated from within the court as a bitter opponent of Weston, Laud and Strafford (at whose trial he would give evidence for the prosecution). Increasingly remote from the king in 1640–1, he consorted with people 'to whom the court was obnoxious', though his aims seem to have been to find a composing middle way between king and parliament. Amongst the peace party in the Lords in 1643, he finally went to the king in August, but was frostily received and returned almost at once to Westminster. Thereafter he was distrusted by both sides, but his hesitation between equally unpalatable alternatives speaks eloquently of the difficulties of a courtier for whom participation in masques did not mean uncritical support of the king.[14] Even more remarkable is the case of Philip, Lord Wharton, variously known as the Good Lord Wharton or as Sawpit Wharton, following a slander that he ran away from the battle of Edgehill and took refuge in a sawpit. Wharton was among the minority of lords in the Short Parliament that voted against the court's demand that money should be advanced before grievances were debated, and he was personally rebuked by Charles during the Second Bishops' War for opposing billetting in Yorkshire; Strafford said he should have been shot as a sower of sedition. In the Long Parliament he quickly emerged as a leading ally of the radicals, he commanded a regiment of foot under Essex at Edgehill and Kidderminster, and he continued to be energetic on committees until Pride's Purge in December 1648. He refused Cromwell's invitations to sit on the Council of State but remained in friendly communication with him; yet this man danced in the 1630s in *Albion's Triumph*, *Coelum Britannicum* and in that masque exceptionally offensive to Puritan sentiment, *Britannia Triumphans*.[15]

How much weight should be given to the presence of such masquers? In his personal memoir, Wharton tried to imply that he had no option but to obey the royal will: in 1631, he wrote, I 'was *commanded* by the King to present myself at the customary masque, in which he, like others, always took part', but thereafter he retired to the country, 'living there continuously except when the King *commanded* me to bear a part in a similar masque, as he did every year till the beginning . . . of the troubles in Scotland'.[16] Yet Wharton may well have been laundering his memory for the sake of retrospective consistency, since it *was* possible to refuse to co-operate, as for example the Countess of Carlisle had done in 1635 when she declined to dance in *The Temple of Love*, apparently out of rivalry with the queen.[17] Furthermore, despite his later allegiances, Wharton happily involved himself in other kinds of courtly culture in the 1630s: Van Dyck painted elegant portraits of him, his wife and children, placing Wharton himself in Arcadian setting, complete with sheep-hook.[18] The examples of Holland and Wharton suggest that although the crisis of 1642 was cultural as well as political, the lines of cultural preference were not determined by political allegiances but were frequently crossed by them. Even more important, the participation of such men in Charles's masques is a measure of the survival of the middle ground between the king and his future critics. As long as Charles could continue to attract the co-operation of men like these, his government would be a long way from confrontation or collapse; with such men dancing, the performance would be an act of propaganda but also an attempt at political bridge-building.

The building of bridges is, I want to argue, what *Salmacida Spolia* endeavours but finally fails to achieve. Traditionally, this masque has been presented as an attempt by an already superannuated monarchy to dazzle its sceptical audience into forgetting the problems of the moment; in a famous and evocative essay, Veronica Wedgwood describes the event as epitomising this evanescent dynasty, dancing elegantly but ironically on the very edge of collapse.[19] Yet late in 1639 Charles's options, though substantially reduced, were not without some room for manoeuvre. Opportunities for accommodation were still available which were conspicuous by their absence six months later, when Charles found himself without the support of those moderates, such as Holland, on whom he had hitherto been able to depend. The turning point was the failure of the Short Parliament of 1640, the forfeiture of moderate confidence which that entailed being a crucial step in the process towards his isolation in November 1640. Clarendon was later to represent the Short Parliament as the squandering of an ideal moment for achieving a settlement. He would emphasise the conciliatory temper of the Commons, writing that 'it could never be hoped that more sober and dispassioned men would ever meet together in that place, or fewer who brought ill purposes with them', and he recounted his shock at hearing the pleasure taken in the premature dissolution by Oliver St John, who said that 'this Parliament would never have done what was necessary to be done'.[20] The language and iconography of *Salmacida Spolia* interact at every point with the proceedings of these months; I intend to read it as an attempt to initiate an understanding with the moderates, though one which simultaneously discloses the seeds of its own failure.

The parliament was forced onto Charles by his inability to suppress the revolt that followed his imposition of the prayer book onto the Kirk. At Berwick he had been obliged to accept a bloodless but humiliating peace, and he returned home determined forcibly to reduce the Scots to obedience. The recall of parliament was first discussed by privy councillors in November 1639; a second campaign needed money, but the lords, said the Earl of Northumberland, 'found themselues so pusseld that they knew not where to begin'.[21] Having decided all irregular ways to be inadequate,

Charles was reduced to 'makeing Tryall of his People in Parlament, before he used any way of Power'.[22] Thus the failure of Scottish policy forced Charles into attempting a new understanding with an English parliament, the advantage being, said Secretary Windebank, that this way[23]

he might leave his people without excuse, and have wherewithal to justify himself to God and the world, that in his own inclination he desired the old way; but that if his people should not cheerfully (according to their duties) meet him in that, especially in this exigent, when his Kingdoms and person are in apparent danger, the world might see he is forced, contrary to his own inclination, to use extra-ordinary means, rather than by the peevishness of some few factious spirits to suffer his State and Government to be lost.

Just the same uneasy tension that characterised the Council's deliberations, between loving gestures for English subjects and sabre-rattling for the Scots, was to mark the text of *Salmacida Spolia*, the inception of which coincided exactly with the summoning of parliament: the day before the decision was communicated to the Council, Charles was reported to have begun practising his dance-steps.[24] It was perhaps no accident that when Secretary Vane reported the king's unusual intention of dancing two per-formances of the masque (a decision which itself implies Charles was seeking to reach an audience larger than normal), his letter mentioned in the immediately preceding sentence Charles's continuing commitment to the new parliament:[25]

Although it may seem there are many reasons which might threaten some rubs and difficulties in the desired success of his Majesty's gracious resolution . . . yet there is great hope that *by his wisdom* all shall be overcome and carried so that so happy a meeting may be followed by a like conclusion, to the contentment and satisfaction both of the King and his subjects.

Charles's secret wisdom is precisely that attribute which in *Salmacida Spolia* is represented as effortlessly overcoming his enemies (line 11).[26]

The particularly remarkable feature of *Salmacida Spolia* is its unusually high proportion of masquers known to have held reservations about Charles's policies: almost two-thirds of the male masquers were either moderate critics or future opponents of the king. Several, including Lord Paget and the Earls of Newport and Andover, were courtiers who were unfriendly to Strafford and Laud and favoured an accommodation with parliament but who underwent changes of heart as events polarised. Of these three, Andover was basically a loyal man caught momentarily on the wrong side,[27] but Newport was a court office-holder who nonetheless was at odds with Charles on religion and who disgraced himself by his hostility to Strafford,[28] and Paget was a strong advocate of a parliamentary way who was said to be one of the 'great contrivers' in November 1640.[29] Both of these fought for Charles in 1642, though Paget remained a 'waverer' and Newport finally chose to surrender to Fairfax rather than to hold out needlessly against him.[30] Two more masquers were sons of the Earl of Bedford who, as a popular nobleman trusted by both sides, was probably the single most important aristocratic moderate of 1640–1. His death in 1641 disappointed many hopes of an accommodation, and his masquing son and heir, Lord Russell, fought for parliament in the west, went with Holland to the king in 1643 and like him returned immediately after to Westminster, claiming he had hoped 'to procure his majesty to comply with his parliament' but found him deaf to such advice.[31] A sixth masquer, Lord Herbert, was a son of the strongly parliamentarian Earl of Pembroke and a future member of Cromwell's Council of State; his sister created problems for *Salmacida Spolia* by refusing to dance on a Sunday.[32] Finally, a seventh masquer was Basil, Lord Feilding, who distressed his otherwise firmly royalist family by siding actively with parliament, campaigning in the Midlands and sitting on Cromwell's Council of State.[33]

All of these men had danced with Charles in earlier masques, usually repeatedly, but their combined presence makes *Salmacida Spolia* look rather different from the standard court entertainment. And this impression is strengthened by the fact that the masque's form was not the usual exchange of compliments between king and queen, since both Charles and Henrietta Maria participated. The guest of honour and principal spectator was the queen's mother, but it is tempting to suppose that the real audience was the political nation whom Charles needed to convince of his goodwill in the approach to the new parliament. The spectacle of king and queen dancing among courtiers who favoured accommodation and a parliamentary way was calculated not as an exorcism of political difficulties but as a gesture of royal willingness to build bridges to moderate opinion, the support of which Charles badly needed.

The masque's commitment to appeasement was signalled in a Latin adage over the stage, explaining that *Salmacida Spolia*, the spoils of Salmacis, are the fruits of a victory won by persuasion, without bloodshed or sweat. The fable to which it alludes tells of the Salmacian spring near the Greek colony of Halicarnassus; the indigenous barbarian tribes who were drawn to drink at the spring had their fierceness gradually moderated, by their contact with the settlers, to a Grecian civility. This myth of the harmonising power of civilisation has direct applicability to Charles's relations with the Scots: it states his intention of subduing them, but represents it as coming about through peaceable rather than warlike means. A second adage warned of the dangers of Cadmian victories, alluding to the story of the siege of Thebes, in which the city was won only at the expense of catastrophic losses on both sides. Allegorical figures

on the proscaenium symbolised Affection to the Country and Forgetfulness of Injuries (lines 49–52).

Charles himself performed as Philogenes, lover of the people, which in
itself was a remarkable transformation as typically he danced in masques
as a triumphant Hercules. The confident hero had been reworked into a
role that struck a political pose, emphasising his attitude of constructive
conciliation. The masque opened with a storm scene, in which a Fury
expressed envy at Britain's peaceful appearance from afar and threatened
to create her own tempests of humours; in the second scene, a peaceful
landscape, the Good Genius of Great Britain pleaded in song with the
figure of Concord, who was threatening to depart (it is significant that
this figure should represent *Great Britain*, rather than just England). He
urged Concord to remain, if only 'to please / The great and wise Philogenes' (lines 160–1), whose virtues are the forbearance with which he
endures his people's ingratitude, and his commitment to achieving a settlement through the difficult ways of peace rather than the easy ones of force.
They sang together:

> O who but he could thus endure
>   To live and govern in a sullen age,
> When it is harder far to cure
>   The People's folly than resist their rage?   (lines 176–9)

Curing the people's folly rather than resisting their rage expresses not
so much wish-fulfilment as good intentions towards the forthcoming
parliament; the twenty grotesque antimasques which then followed
included two comic doctors, antitypes of the royal physician, and dancers
representing each of Charles's three kingdoms.

This insistence on Charles's commitment to following avenues which
are troublesome but finally beneficial rather than a simple resort to force
was reiterated in the third scene which depicted '*the difficult way which
heroes are to pass ere they come to the Throne of Honour*' (lines 284–5). Here
Charles was revealed in the distance, enthroned amidst his lords, but
before him was a craggy landscape, symbolic of his chosen difficult path,
and here the Chorus sang of that patience which prefers endurance to
conquest:

> If it be kingly patience to outlast
>   Those storms the people's giddy fury raise
> Till like fantastic winds themselves they waste,
>   The wisdom of that patience is thy praise.   (lines 345–8)

Charles was represented as conciliating rather than avenging: 'Nor would
your valour, when it might subdue, / Be hindered of the pleasure to *for-
give*' (lines 357–8). The final scene, a great imperial city surmounted with

crowds of deities, depicted the accomplishment of this civilising ideal. Given the concerns of the moment and the known political attitudes of the lords with whom Charles was masquing, it seems almost inevitable to me that when he was discovered with his lords in the Throne of Honour spectators would have read it as an allusion to one of two things: either the united front which it was necessary to achieve towards the Scots, or the understanding with the political elites in parliament through which that would come about. John Peacock points out to me that in Inigo Jones's design for the final scene, dominated as it is by a bridge carrying people across a great river, the connection is represented as already achieved.[34]

So *Salmacida Spolia* attempts to make a remarkable adjustment, both in the typical form and content of the court masque. The price, however, is disruption, contradiction and evasion, since even as the text advances a line of appeasement it tries to find space for attitudes which are in open competition with it. These radical tensions in the text expose the deep contradictions in Charles's position: the concessionary pose which he adopts is directly in conflict with the limitations that he simultaneously places on accommodation.

These limits are signalled pretty clearly, for example, in the treatment of the antimasques. There are two sets of antimasques: the furies who attack the nation from without, and the twenty entries in scene two which embody the nation's inner ills. Or so they *should* do – but where other masques use the antimasques to allude to socio-economic problems in need of reform, the internal problems in *Salmacida Spolia* are represented merely as grotesques and follies, with no socio-economic analysis whatever, nor are they allowed to speak but only to dance. Furthermore, the arrival of the Good Genius and Concord earlier in this scene means that these follies do not embody a real threat that has to be overcome but are already contained within the masque's structures of reassurance. Nor do the remedies on offer promise any far-reaching social reform, as Concord and the Genius promise they will '*incite the beloved people to honest pleasures and recreations*' (lines 173–4): it is the Book of Sports, that depressingly inadequate Stuart social programme, all over again. As for Philogenes, it is repeatedly emphasised that while he loves his people he also knows better than they do what is good for them, and that when placed in the Throne of Honour he will be surrounded by his lords but will still rule alone:

> Since strength of virtues gain'd you Honour's throne,
>   Accept our wonder and enjoy your praise;
> He's fit to govern there and *rule alone*
>   Whom inward helps, not outward force, doth raise.   (lines 361–4)

Charles may be preparing for his first parliament in eleven years, but it is hardly power-sharing that he has in mind, and it is the significantly named Chorus of the Beloved People from whom the hymns to the wisdom of his government come.

It is particularly interesting, therefore, that immediately before the discovery of the king amidst his masquers, some doubts about his intentions were admitted into the text (if not into the performance). At this point the text prints some lines '*Inviting the King's Appearance in the Throne of Honour*' which, rather than praising him, urge him to have the confidence to put his professions into practice and press on the difficult road. They hint at his reluctance, and encourage him to ignore the 'o'er-weening priests' who claim to have a wisdom superior to his (line 321), which could equally well be an allusion to the Covenanters or to Archbishop Laud. These lines were directed '*To be printed, not sung*' (line 309) and they were probably distributed before the performance.[35] The problem is, of course, knowing whether or not they were authorised by the king, but their lack of performance would seem to imply that they did not fully attune with the king's consciously presented point of view. Written as advice rather than congratulation, they suggest that Davenant, or even some of the masquers, were conscious of hesitations about the king's intentions which could not openly be admitted in the performance. The court is seen to celebrate the love of Philogenes, but plainly even within this circle some of his subjects had inadmissible reservations of their own. Their presence and their verses admit into the masque a current of scepticism significantly divergent from the views of the king by whom the masque is sponsored.

What decisively disrupts the masque, however, is its insistence on the king's military and political resolve, which everywhere hedges around the pose of conciliation. On the proscaenium Forgetfulness of Injuries jostled for place with the figure of Resolution, a woman bearing a sword wreathed with a serpent, while elsewhere three cherubs symbolised Intellectual Light consorting with Doctrine and Discipline, patently in allusion to Charles's religious disagreements with the Scots: plainly there was no room for manoeuvre over the Kirk. And while the king was represented as passive, his was the iron passivity of control. The queen's mother was hailed as a fount of royal valour, Henrietta Maria descended from the heavens dressed as an Amazon, and though Charles sat among his moderate lords, beneath him '*lay captives bound, in several postures, lying on trophies of armours, shields, and antique weapons*' (lines 333–4). The ambiguities expressed by these images repeatedly spill into the masque's language, especially in the final song, which seems uncertain whether to praise Charles for bringing civilisation or repression:

All that are harsh, all that are rude,
Are by your harmony subdued;
Yet so into obedience wrought,
As if not forc'd to it, but taught.   (lines 455–8)

The devastating concessions in Davenant's syntax ('so into obedience wrought, / As if not forc'd to it, but taught'), and the confusions in his vocabulary, as he hesitates between rival languages of educational harmony, and discipline, suppression and control, exactly embody the radically ambiguous programme of the masque: the appeasement on offer is everywhere subverted by the need to reassert the king's inviolable authority.

The consequence of this impossible enterprise is a breakdown in the form of the masque as a whole. In effect, there are here two incompatible structures competing for control of a single text. The overt conciliatory programme is as I have described it, and from this point of view the turning point is, as in all other masques, the moment of the king's revelation, here seated with his moderate lords in the Throne of Honour. But in the account of the masque which prefaces the printed text, this discovery, and the antimasques which precede it, are passed over lightly, and the central moment is said to be the defeat of the malicious furies by their intimations of the king's 'secret wisdom', which translates their tempest into a serene calm (lines 1–18) – in which case the difficulties symbolised by the grotesque antimasques and especially by the Throne of Honour become merely incidental obstacles for the king's all-competent heroism.[36] It is difficult not to feel that the masque's contradictory objectives generate a fundamental formal incoherence: Charles's rule is said to be perfect yet also to be troubled, England is both a serene landscape and a rocky defile, harmony is to arrive by patience but also to be compelled, peace is affirmed in military gestures, dances become Amazonian triumphs – the masque is torn between affirming that Charles is and is not a good king, and between urging him to be more resolute and to be more conciliatory. It is profoundly implicated in the rival initiatives of a moment of crisis, and can accommodate only with extreme difficulty the contradictory positions which it is seeking to bridge. Its affirmations of Charles's godlike control are on every level disrupted by intimations of strain and tensions which the text is unable effectively to marginalise.

Two months after the masque's second performance, Charles's parliament finally met, to be opened with a speech by the Lord Keeper, on behalf of the crown, that reads virtually like a paraphrase of the argument of *Salmacida Spolia*. In the space remaining, there is room to do little more than gesture towards the remarkable correspondences between the Short Parliament's proceedings and the sentiments of the masque. Lord Keeper

Finch's appeal for speedy co-operation exhibited precisely the same tensions which I have been describing in the masque as he endeavoured – heroically but unsuccessfully – to reassure parliament that despite his warlike intentions the king really had paternal generosity at heart:[37]

out of his Piety and Clemency [his Majesty] chose rather to pass by [the Scots'] former miscarriages, upon their humble protestations of future Loyalty and Obedience, than by just vengeance to punish their Rebellions . . . It is a course his Majesty takes no delight in, but is forced unto it; for such is his Majesties grace and Goodness to all his Subjects, and such it is and will be to them (how undutifull and rebellious soever they now are) that if they put themselves into a way of humility becoming to them, his Majesties Piety and Clemency will soon appear to all the World.

Finch's hesitations between promises of forbearance and a bullish insistence on the duty of suppressing rebellion damningly expose the confusions of royal policy: Charles cannot pose at one and the same time as forgiving father *and* as bringer of political retribution. For their part, the Lords and Commons professed their willingness to serve the king but remained reluctant to advance money before they had discussed grievances. They politely but firmly declined Charles's suggestion (sent again through the hapless Lord Keeper) that they should vote him money first in order to discover how accommodating he would be in return: 'you cannot express so much dutiful Affection . . . as He will requite and reward with Graciousness'.[38] Increasingly the debates came to turn on what I have been arguing was centrally at issue in the masque, the question of trust; messages from the king pleaded, 'If they will not trust Me first, all My Business this Summer will be lost, and, before the Year goeth about, I must be trusted at last', but as Sir Francis Seymour for one put his reply, 'if hee had sattisfaction for shipp money hee should trust the King with the rest'.[39] Charles proved to be singularly lacking in that patience of which the masque had boasted and dissolved the parliament after only three weeks. In a declaration published shortly after, he complained that he had approached the Commons 'with all the expressions of grace and goodness which could possibly come from him', and reiterated that he needed no other mediator for the Scots than 'the tender affection he hath ever born to that his native Kingdom'.[40]

However, the failure of confidence, and the limitations of royal patience, had already been adumbrated in that last masque. *Salmacida Spolia* does not merely reflect the strains and contradictions of a moment of crisis, but directly participates in them. It is an attempt to intervene in events and construct a platform of confidence which instead exposes the deeply ambivalent and untrustworthy nature of Charles's protestations. In failing to find a stronger point of contact with the moderates, it actively contributed to the weakness of the court's position: the accommodation to which it gestures it simultaneously reveals as deeply compromised, and the changes it makes to the form of the masque are inadequate to contain the ideological gaps which are opening up. This conclusion is perhaps only to be expected of a masque performed at a moment of crisis, but the larger general conclusion which it serves is that as a genre the masque has tended to receive a less discriminating hermeneutics than it demands. The siting of the masque in relation to its political context, and the appropriation of its meanings even within the relatively circumscribed circle of the court, is much more problematic than it has generally been taken to be. *Salmacida Spolia* is a masque that is saying different things to those involved in it, those watching it, and those reading it after the event. The failure of Charles to communicate even with his traditional masque audience is one of the main pointers that tells us we are at a moment of profound political and cultural collapse.

NOTES

I am very grateful to David Lindley for his criticism and encouragement of an earlier version of this chapter.

1 For an important analysis of this paradox, see R.M. Smuts, 'The Political Failure of early Stuart Cultural Patronage', in G.F. Lytle and S. Orgel, eds, *Patronage in the Renaissance* (Princeton, 1981), pp. 165–87. See also Judith Richards, ' "His nowe Majestie" and the English Monarchy: the Kingship of Charles I before 1640', *Past and Present* 113 (November 1986), pp. 70–96.

2 Two notable exceptions to this generalisation are D. Norbrook, 'The Reformation of the Masque', in D. Lindley, ed., *The Court Masque* (Manchester, 1984); and D. Lindley, 'Embarrassing Ben: The Masques for Frances Howard', *English Literary Renaissance* 16 (1986), 343–59.

3 For two recent and conflicting assessments, see H. Tomlinson, ed. *Before the English Civil War* (London, 1983); and D. Hirst, *Authority and Conflict: England 1603–1658* (London, 1985).

4 Norbrook, 'The Reformation of the Masque', p. 98.

5 See my *Theatre and Crisis 1632–1642* (Cambridge, 1984), p. 97.

6 T. May, *History of the Long Parliament of England* (London, 1647), part 2, p. 27.

7 S. Daniel, *Complete Works* ed. A.B. Grosart (London, 1885), III, p. 187.

8 F. Beaumont and J. Fletcher, *The Maid's Tragedy*, I.i.10–11.

9 See D.G. Gordon, 'Chapman's "Memorable Masque" ' in *The Renaissance Imagination* ed. S. Orgel (Berkeley, 1975), pp. 194–202; and D. Norbrook, ' "The Masque of Truth": Court entertainments and international Protestant Politics in the early Stuart period', *The Seventeenth Century* 1 (1986), 81–110.

10 L.S. Marcus, 'Masquing Occasions and Masquing Structures', *Research Opportunities in Renaissance Drama* 24 (1981), 7–16. The most openly ambivalent masques are *Love Restored* and *Pleasure Reconciled to Virtue*.

11 See D.B.J. Randall, *Jonson's Gipsies Unmasked* (Durham NC, 1975).

12 See my 'Politics and the Masque; *The Triumph of Peace*', *The Seventeenth Cen-*

tury 2 (1987); and 'Entertaining the Palatine Prince: Plays on Foreign Affairs 1635–37', *English Literary Renaissance* 13 (1983), 319–44.

13 R.M. Smuts, 'The Puritan Followers of Henrietta Maria in the 1630s', *The English Historical Review* 93 (1978) 26–45; and C. Hibbard, *Charles I and the Popish Plot* (Chapel Hill NC, 1983).

14 B. Donagan, 'A Courtier's Progress: Greed and Consistency in the Life of the Earl of Holland', *The Historical Journal* 19 (1976), 317–53; B. Manning, 'The Aristocracy and the Downfall of Charles I' in *Politics, Religion and the English Civil War* (London, 1973), pp. 35–80.

15 B. Dale, *The Good Lord Wharton* (London, 1901); and G.F.T. Jones, *Saw-pit Wharton* (Sydney, 1967). See also E. Hyde, *The History of the Rebellion* ed. W.D. Macray, 6 vols (Oxford, 1988), I, pp. 244, 263; II, pp. 70, 356, 377; and A. Fletcher, *The Outbreak of the English Civil War* (London, 1981), pp. 75–6, 79, 88, 117, 170, 244.

16 Jones, *Saw-pit Wharton*, p. 19. My italics.

17 G.E. Bentley, *The Jacobean and Caroline Stage* (Oxford, 1956), III, p. 217; Butler, *Theatre and Crisis*, pp. 29–30.

18 O. Millar, *Van Dyck in England* (London, 1983), pp. 92–3, 45–6.

19 C.V. Wedgwood, 'The Last Masque' in *Truth and Opinion* (London, 1970), pp. 139–56.

20 Hyde, *History of the Rebellion*, I, p. 183.

21 A. Collins, *Letters and Memorials of State*, 2 vols (London, 1746), II, p. 623; R. Scrope, ed. *State Papers Collected by Edward, Earl of Clarendon*, (Oxford, 1773) II, p. 81.

22 Collins, *Letters and Memorials*, II, p. 623.

23 Scrope, *Clarendon State Papers*, II, p. 81. I have added some punctuation to this passage as an aid to comprehension.

24 Collins, *Letters and Memorials*, II, p. 621.

25 *Calendar of State Papers, Domestic*, 1639–1640, p. 459.

26 All citations are to the text edited by T.J.B. Spencer in *A Book of Masques in Honour of Allardyce Nicoll* ed. T.J.B. Spencer and S.W. Wells (Cambridge, 1967).

27 Hyde, *History of the Rebellion*, I, p. 244. Anthony Fletcher, *Outbreak of the English Civil War*, pp. 96–7, 276.

28 Hibbard, *Charles I and the Popish Plot*, p. 55; Fletcher, *Outbreak of the English Civil War*, p. 117. For his role as a potential 'bridge appointment' between court and parliament, see Manning, 'The Aristocracy and the Downfall of Charles I', pp. 71–2. He was rumoured to be among the radicals meeting secretly during the recess in summer 1641 (see V.F. Snow, *Essex the Rebel* (Lincoln NE, 1970), p. 276). For his full career, see *DNB*.

29 Hyde, *History of the Rebellion* I, p. 24; II, pp. 181–2; Fletcher, *Outbreak of the English Civil War*, pp. 38, 75, 108, 188. See also Scrope, *Clarendon State Papers*, I, p. 204.

30 'Waverer' is Fletcher's term for Paget's later career (*Outbreak of the English Civil War*, pp. 348, 351, 363).

31 The quotation is from the *Lord's Journals*, VI, p. 356. See *DNB*; Hyde, *History of the Rebellion*, II, pp. 299, 317, 355–7; III, pp. 146–52, 156, 200; Scrope, *Clarendon State Papers*, II, p. 94; O. Ogle and W.H. Bliss, eds, *Calendar of the Clarendon State Papers* (Oxford, 1872), I, p. 203; Snow, *Essex the Rebel*, p. 224. Lord Russell's brother Francis, who also danced in *Salmacida Spolia*, died in 1641, though it may not be irrelevant that he was son-in-law to another parlia-

mentarian peer, William Baron Grey of Warke, future Commander-in-Chief of forces raised for parliament in the eastern counties (Dec. 1642), Speaker of the House of Lords (1643), and a Commissioner of the Great Seal (1648). Baron Grey did not concur in Charles's execution, and though nominated to Cromwell's Council of State, he did not take his seat. Professor Conrad Russell kindly informs me that there are extracts from *Salmacida Spolia* among the private papers of the Earl of Bedford.

32 Lord Herbert took over his father's seat in the Commons in 1650. His sister married a zealous king's man, but her scruples about dancing on Sundays may indicate that her outlook was coloured by her father's sympathies. See Collins, *Letters and Memorials*, II, p. 621.

33 See *DNB*; Hyde, *History of the Rebellion*, II, p. 356, III, pp. 469, 496; Snow, *Essex the Rebel*, pp. 276, 397; Cecilia, Countess of Denbigh, *Royalist Father and Roundhead Son* (London, 1915).

34 The design is reproduced in Spencer and Wells, eds., *A Book of Masques*.

35 The practice of distributing printed summaries of material too complex to communicate in performance goes back to the Elizabethan tilts; see R. Strong, *The Cult of Elizabeth* (London, 1977), pp. 145–6. For Stuart instances, see Jonson, *Neptune's Triumph*, lines 6–7, 125–6; Carew, *Poems* ed. R. Dunlap, 1949, pp. 274–5; and (possibly) Townshend's 'Antemasques' for *Florimene*, printed as a small pamphlet. Some kind of printed help must have been distributed for audiences of *Salmacida Spolia* as the recondite meaning of the title and the significance of the first antimasque (explained in the text, lines 182–216, though not in performance) would need explaining, beside this speech 'to be printed, not sung'.

36 It should be noticed that though Davenant wrote the songs, the preface and narrative were by Inigo Jones, and this may well have contributed to the text's differences of emphasis.

37 J. Rushworth, *Historical Collections* (London, 1680), II, pp. 1116–17.

38 *Lord's Journals*, IV, p. 63.

39 E.S. Cope and W.H. Coates, eds., *Proceedings of the Short Parliament, 1640*, Camden Society Publications, 4th Series, 19 (London, 1977), p. 189.

40 *His Majesty's Declaration to all his loving Subjects of the Causes which moved Him to Dissolve the last Parliament* (London, 1610), p. 7–8. It may also be worth bringing Davenant's story down to 1642. In November 1640, on the eve of the Long Parliament, he addressed a poem to Henrietta Maria, urging her to become the 'Peoples Advocate' and act as a channel of mediation between the nation and the king. The poem criticises Charles for being 'obdurate', and advises Henrietta Maria to 'cure this high obnoxious singleness' by persuading the king to respect the rule of law and by bringing his perogative to a 'yielding-ness' which may include, he darkly hints, the throwing over of Strafford as a sop to parliament (see my *Theatre and Crisis*, pp. 58–9; and Manning, 'The aristocracy and the downfall of Charles I', pp. 52–4). Six months later, with Strafford condemned against the king's wishes, Davenant switched horses and became involved in the Army Plot, an attempt to rescue Strafford from the Tower which went badly wrong and seriously damaged royal credibility. Davenant fled and was arrested in Kent; in a petition to parliament he subsequently claimed that in writing and speech he had 'often extold the naturall necessity of Parliaments here, with extreme scorne upon the incapacity of any that should perswade the King he could be fortunate without them' (Butler, *Theatre and Crisis*, p. 59).

4   Exploring the language of devotion in the English Revolution

THE ENGLISH Revolution – by which I mean roughly the years 1630 to 1660 – was a time when the English language took on an intensely religious tenor. An observer like Nehemiah Wallington was happy to talk of 'God's providence in guiding of bullets', and Elizabeth Major felt that she was living in the 'worst of ages', defined as an era when 'England sure doth *Sodom* pass in sins'.[1] These are just two instances of a prevailing mode of expression, found in diaries, speeches and everyday discourse as well as works of literature during this period. Given such a context of widespread religious consciousness, it seemed to me pertinent to enquire what happened to specifically devotional language at the time of the revolution. I shall be concentrating almost entirely on devotional poetry, though I trust that my observations will carry implications for devotional writing of all kinds during the period.

This chapter is particularly conscious of the term 'exploring' it adopts in the title. This is intended to imply not only a necessary modesty on my part – aware as I am of the enormous output of devotional works at the time of the Civil War and its aftermath – but also a necessary experimentation, an 'exploration' of the possibilities of devotional writing, by the writers themselves. Further, literary historians have always had difficulty maintaining continuity in accounts of the religious lyric from the metaphysical mode to the beginnings of Augustanism, and so there is something of a sense of entering a vacuum when attempting to 'explore' the devotional poetry of the mid-seventeenth century. Can it really be true, as one critic has maintained, that during the period of the English Revolution 'the rich tradition of the Renaissance lyric was almost completely spent'?[2] And if this is indeed the case, why should this decline have occurred at a time when religion was so centrally on the agenda of national and personal life?

Setting out from this point, then, in an exploration of devotional language in mid-seventeenth-century poetry, it would be all too easy to concentrate on the religious equivalent of 'poems on the affairs of state' – that is, to focus simply on the explicit links between text and

context. It is not difficult, for example, to find instances of the direct
influence of historical events on devotional poets, infiltrating collections
of overtly religious verse or, more subtly, substituting devotional
instincts with political anxieties. We might note, for instance, the
inclusion in An Collins's *Divine Songs and Meditacions* (1653) of a 'Song
composed in time of Civill Warr, when the wicked did much insult
over the godly' (pp. 63–6). We might examine the tendency towards
elegy, a prevailing tone of lament, in collections of devotional verse,
citing Vaughan's *Silex Scintillans* (1650 and 1655) as a typical case. But
this model of the poets' relation to contemporary events is not my
main concern: I am more interested in tracing the continuing tradition
of strictly devotional writing than in examining overt poetic discussions
of the immediate issues of the revolution. Abraham Cowley expressed
this distinction well in the preface to his *Works* (1656), when he wrote
that 'a warlike, various, and a tragical age is best to write of, but worst
to write in' (p. xx). My question is: how did religious writers cope
with writing *in* such a time? How did their poetic conversations with
God change, if at all?

My explorations in the devotional poetry of this turbulent time have
revealed five major features of poetic language and writing experience.
The first – and this could perhaps be regarded as an indirect influence
of context on text – involves the destabilisation of the function of
metaphors in these poems. It is clear, for example, that metaphors
consistently appear in a close and ambivalent relation to the real. An
Collins, seeking in one of her 'Songs' for expressions of harmonious
existence, writes of 'union' as 'one Family / Of one mind and communion' (p. 36) – metaphoric vocabulary which is inevitably coloured by
the events of the Civil War in which both 'family' and 'communion'
were sites of dissention and disruption. Later in the same poem, Collins
speaks of one who finds his 'household mates / To be his greatest foes'.
Is this a continuation of the metaphor, or has it become a factual
comment? It is, surely, both at once. In the uncertainty of this mutual
reference, the stable relation between metaphoric and non-metaphoric
is undermined. Similarly, when the Jesuit poet John Abbot Rivers
writes in his *Devout Rhapsodies* (1647) using political metaphors to
describe the ideal 'state' of heaven, he idealises the 'countless multitude'
as:

> deeply learned, having for their book,
> Even God himselfe, on whom they daily look.   (p. 50)

When he contrasts this multitude with the ignorant and dangerous
people of contemporary England, the safely metaphoric is threatened

by the disruptive intrusions of the all too real. In these instances the metaphoric is drawn closer to real events, so that it becomes unclear which is more real. The conventional relationship between statement and metaphoric expansion, opinion and illustration, is elided in these texts; thus the apparently immediate – 'family', 'communion', 'household', 'state', 'multitude' – can become the politically loaded metaphor for a *more* immediate devotional mood. Events themselves become translatable into the metaphoric, as in Thomas Washbourne's meditation on Ecclesiastes 12:7 found in his *Divine Poems* (1654). The poem opens:

> Our famous *Harvey* hath made good
> The circulation of the blood,
> And what was paradox; we know
> To be a demonstration now.
> The like in bodies doth befall
> Civil as well as Natural.
> Such revolutions in them found,
> That they are alwaies turning round.
> We knew a kingdome which of late
> Converted was into a State;
> And from the hands of many men,
> That State devolv'd to one agen.
> We know that wealth, which now doth flow
> I'th' City veins did lately grow
> I'th' Country furrowes, and the same
> Soon runs to th' place from whence it came.
> We know our bodies frame of dust
> At first created was, and must
> Crumble to dust ere long; we see
> Not one from Dissolution free. (pp. 27–8)

This contemplation of the turning circles of mortality and eternity absorbs within itself (punningly) the 'revolution' and its brevity and futility. It makes a political point and goes on to contrast the transient 'state' with the 'state pacifical' to which our souls will ultimately return. But the notable feature of the poem is the way that experience becomes an *exemplum*, part of a sequence of metaphors ranging from contemporary science to, later, the archetypal patterns of the seasons. Through the operation of metaphor in these examples from Collins, Rivers and Washbourne, we see both the politicising of the language of devotion – opening it up to the disturbance of the real – and at the same time the defusing of the contemporary by absorption into the metaphoric mode.

This double operation in the interplay of the contemporary and the eternal may also be seen in the reworking of biblical language in the poems. When a people is going through the 'land of darkness, and the shadow of death' (Job 10: 21) – whether metaphorically or practically – then biblical language will, of course, form a vital element in devotion. It can be handy in its equivocal reference. When Vaughan commands his God to 'Arise, and let thine enemies be scattered', the passion is clear but the object safely unspecified.[3] However, what is especially significant about biblical metaphors in the poetry of this period is the balance created between scriptural text and poetic gloss, and the consequent blurring of one into the other. Washbourne's poem on Psalm 80: 12–14, the text in which the 'vine' is being torn up by the 'wild boar out of the wood', develops into a meditation on the current state of the English church and the vulnerability of sacramental 'grapes' to the destructive beasts (pp. 17–18). Here the biblical language is almost overwhelmed by contemporary implications, so that the two are subsequently inseparable. A similarly unsettling mix of biblical and present experience may be found in Cardell Goodman's description of 'affliction', which is said, with psalm-like overtones, to 'nip the over-forward spring' but yet to form 'Physic for a King'.[4] Once again the scriptural source merges with seventeenth-century political commentary. Which reading should be given priority? Biblical language has, of course, always been accessible to this kind of interpretative usage and typological reading – the text as mirror of the times – but the strange balance between scriptural and contemporary is particularly striking in the devotional poetry of this period. As with the metaphors of family and kingdom which we looked at earlier, there is a blurring of fact and fable, individual and type; and this deliberate equilibrium of reference has, paradoxically, a destabilising effect on poetic text and reader.

This particular placing of metaphors, general and biblical, in relation to 'the real' is the first of the five notable aspects of devotional verse in the mid-seventeenth century with which this chapter is concerned. The second is a remarkable absence of major differences between the poets' devotional language on the grounds of their doctrinal affiliation. This may be illustrated in the feature we have just been considering – the use of biblical language. There is common ground between the poets, not only in their fondness for typological expression of the present, but even to the extent of their use of certain recurring favourites among the biblical 'types', including David (popular for his combination of song, comfort, aggression and lament) and Jonah (central to explorations of sin and the response to guilt). Certain key clusters of biblical metaphors also seem to have had a special relevance to the poets despite the doctrinal differences between individual writers. Could it be that in the Civil War context the reassurance of the 'rock' in the 'desert', and the appeal to the 'cross' as fact and metaphor, were such as to over-ride the detail of controversy? Of course, it would be misleading to deny the presence of partisan moments and moods in devotional poetry, whether overtly declared or more subtly coded, as in Vaughan's use of the palm tree emblem which also featured in the frontispiece to *Eikon Basilike* ('The Palm-tree'; p. 490). However, in my reading of devotional verse from this period, what has struck me most forcibly is not the difference but the similarities between poets. Remarkable evidence of this perception of common ground in devotion may be found in the work of John Abbot Rivers, whose *Devout Rhapsodies* – themselves treating the shared territory of the 'Excellencie of Divine Scriptures', as the title-page announces – were written while he was imprisoned at Newgate. In his preface he explains that, though the poems were written partly for diversion from 'too serious thoughts of publick and private calamities', yet in addition 'some part of my study and care, in the prosecution of it, hath been as to offend no Religion, so no Person' (sig. A3). In the religiously self-conscious and divided 1640s, to read such a profession from the pen of an English Jesuit is notable indeed. The shared spiritual purpose, often in spite of differences in religious or political ideology, may be seen in the converging of devotional language used by poets, towards similarities which might be gathered under the term conservatism. An element of retrenchment in verse style is perhaps not surprising given the exciting developments in prose writing during this period, in which controversy, and the invention and immediacy it generated, were transformed into prose and action itself. Devotional poetry was, as it were, left with the business of contemplation, highlighting continuity and tradition.

One aspect of this 'conservatism' is the continuing attraction of several kinds of highly structural verse. These include those forms structured from outside – such as the tradition of emblem poems, appealing to Jesuits and Puritans alike – and internally patterned poems, such as dialogues or echo poems, the latter being particularly popular in this period. There was also a marked interest in expressiveness through more than one dimension. This may be seen in 'shaped' verses, and exercises in word-play such as acrostics and anagrams, revealing truths hidden within the word itself – showing 'Heav'n in a little frame' as Goodman said of the name Jesus (p. 47). All of these forms and features combine the attraction of established styles with the need for considerable qualities of invention on the part of the individual poet. Thus the term 'conservatism' immediately requires qualification, since the poets were, in these highly structured forms, paradoxically containing experimentation within tradition. A striking example of this combination is to be found in Elizabeth Major's 'Author's Prayer':

O my blessed Lord and Saviour Jesus Christ, have mercy on thy poor hand-maid, Elizabeth Major.

O	Gracious God, inhabiting	E	ternity
My	Blest redeemer, that hast	L	ovingly
Bless'd	me with hope, a kingdom to	I	nherit,
Lord	of thy mercy give an humble	S	pirit,
And	grant I pray, I may my life	A	mend:
Savior	tis thou that canst my soul	B	efriend.
Jesus	with grace my guilty soul	E	ndue
Christ	promis'd grace, and thou, O Lord, art	T	rue;
Have	care of me, deal out with thine own	H	and
Mercy	to my poor soul, thou canst com-	M	and
On	me a shower of grace, sin to	A	void,
Thy	praise to sing, my tongue shall be	I	mploy'd;
Poor	Lord I am, with fear and care	O	press'd,
Handmaid	to thee I am, in thee I'le	R	est.

(p. 191)

Here the author manages to combine the text of her prayer and the letters of her name to form a substantial individual devotion. She exploits the expressiveness of the word and the alphabet within the rules of a traditional rhetoric, yet with personal creativity and a symbolic affirmation of self. More importantly, her private devotion is framed (almost literally) in the comfort and safety of pattern and tradition.

A further aspect of this shared 'conservatism', this common ground of stylistic continuity despite theological differences, is a marked tradition of imitation of George Herbert among devotional poets of the civil war era.[5] All the poets considered in this chapter, and many more besides, owed poetic or spiritual allegiance to Herbert, a loyalty (and debt) revealed in borrowed phrases, conscious or distant echoes, tonal similarity to the poems from *The Temple*, and that rich Herbertian mixture of homeliness of metaphor with complexity of lyric structure. Herbert's influence was rarely kept secret: many poets made open proclamations of imitation or respect, including, as Washbourne did in his *Divine Poems*, putting a quotation from Herbert on his title-page in place of a biblical epigraph. Cardell Goodman's preface to *Beawty in Raggs* declared that he wished his poems to be regarded as an 'echo' of his 'Leader', otherwise termed his 'Example' and 'Pattern'. He counted it a privilege to have 'so fair a Coppy' on which to base his own devotions (p. xiv). While Washbourne and Goodman, both Anglicans, might have been expected to respect the poetic 'Country Parson', it is more surprising to trace the line of influence in the work of, for example, that 'honest injudicious Zealot of Wales',[6] the Fifth-Monarchist poet Vavasor Powell. The lyric conversation, tone and imagery of Herbert's *Temple*, particularly 'Love (III)', are all found in the gentle interrogation of man by Christ in Powell's *Bird in the Cage*:

C.   I see thou art my *Creature Man*, Come in,
M.   *Ah Lord no man! unless a man of sin.*
C.   Poor *Wretch* thou wast not made *sin*, but *I* was,
        And of us *two*, which was in the worst case?
M.   *I Lord, full of all sin but thou had'st none.*
C.   *I* had sins of Millions, *thou* but of one.
M.   *But my sins were mine own, so were not thine.*
C.   *Yet thine and* theirs were *really made* mine.[7]

We might well ask why the Anglican poet of the 1630s appealed so profoundly to poets across so wide a spectrum, and one element would seem to be nostalgia, both for the 'good old days' of the Church of England, and more generally for an era noted for the expression of private spirituality. As Baxter wrote in his analysis of Herbert's greatness, this poet spoke to God as 'one whose business in the world is most with God'.[8] To the devotional poets of the English Revolution of all persuasions, there was no doubt safety in an achieved language for conversation with God. Their poetry represented one possible strand of continuity amidst controversy and change.

Does this mean, then, that devotional poetry in this period was in retreat from immediate events, from stylistic development, and from theological debate? To a certain extent the answer must be 'yes', though this would be misleading if retreat were taken to imply simply a kind of escapism.[9] It would be more accurate to interpret this by reference to the prevailing devotional focus on 'last things'; that is, a quieter equivalent of the apocalyptic strain found in doctrinal emphases of the time. 'Watchfulness' is the key to the mood of mid-century devotional verse; the term comes from Vaughan's poem 'The Constellation', where 'Silence, and light, and watchfulnes' are the qualities of the stars that he envies (p. 469). This 'watchfulnes', this anticipation of the second coming within 'moneths or years' (Major, p. 185), was of course linked to the sense that the time of the Civil War was 'the last and worst Age' (Washbourne, p. 17) or 'last and lewdest Age' (Vaughan, 'White Sunday', p. 486). The poets looked eagerly for release from this 'Age', but watched rather for signs of the promised coming than for a negative escape. The refrains of devotional verse very frequently take the form of a plea, as in Washbourne's:

    Come, O come Lord Jesus,
    Quickly come and ease us.   (p. 16)

or Powell's more positive variant:

    Come quickly, come Lord Jesus Christ,
    Thy Saints do waite and stay
    To see thy kingdom here on earth
    And to behold thine eyes.[10]

Paradoxically, the poets' awareness of current events – a kind of implied worldliness – is thus expressed by means of an increased otherworldliness in the poetry. Poetic focus on heavenly matters only intensifies the desire for a divine kingdom on earth.

This element of apparent retreat in the verse, a significant intensification of an existing aspect of the genre of devotional poetry, also reveals itself in the increased isolation of the speaker. In Goodman's poem entitled simply 'Musique', for example, he seeks the 'sweet consent' of true music but finds the search a fruitless one:

> Where shall I find thee O thou sweet Concent?
> I sought thee on each stringed Instrument:
>   And mett with something there
>   Which charmd my listning eare:
>   Butt now a string did crack,
>   And then another was to slack;
> In tuning, fretting, so much time was lost,
> I thought the musique would not quitt the cost.
>
> With that another calld mee to a place,
> Where I beheld a most harmonious face;
>   The musique of each glaunce
>   Did cause my heart to dance;
>   There I resolved to stay,
>   Thought it no loss to spend the day;
> Butt, as, with full desire, I neerer came,
> The musique vanisht in a wanton flame.
>   (p. 21).

In subsequent stanzas the speaker is frustrated by the music of friendship – ending in a 'mournfull close' with a 'parting knell' – and disappointed by the 'discord' of the church, where 'this perfect Harmony' should have been found. Finally he discovers peace in the 'feast continuall' provided by the individual conscience:

> Peace in the Conscience, in the mind faire weather,
> Is a brave feast, and Musique both together.
>   (p. 22)

In a poem by Herbert – whose influence this lyric undoubtedly demonstrates – the conclusion would more likely have been the safety of the church's harmonious worship. In a poem written in a more confident era, the final feast might have been heavenly. But here, in this practical version of otherworldliness, it is the poet's own conscience which plays the right notes – a testament to self-reliance and individuality. It is common in the devotional poems of this era to find a turning to conscience, a reference to the individual as spiritual arbiter. Washbourne's poems, for instance, include an echo-verse in which the echo is the 'voice of a good Conscience' (p. 83). The poems collectively express mistrust of community and find consolation in the individual solving of problems or, dialogue with God. Although most of the verse is not outspoken, it has implicitly the aim of the lone voice of the prophet. Elizabeth Major's 'humble suit' in her poems was to 'purge this Age' (p. 207), but the method and expression was always in terms of the self, the private conscience and consciousness. So, this third feature of the devotional verse may be summed up as an element of retreat into anticipation and individuation.

Such a statement might be thought to imply that the poets had a consistent individuality into which to retreat. However, one of the most fascinating aspects of the poems is that, while they reflect remarkably little division among the writers on grounds of church allegiance, they do reveal divisions within the individual selves of the poets. This splitting of self as seen in the language of devotional experience is the fourth feature I wish to consider. It may first be perceived in the extremes of mood between which the poems swing. The most common topic is misery – 'affliction', the multiple variants of that 'luckless apple' as Marvell encapsulates the bitter experience.[11] Washbourne's poetic invitation is to:

> heavy souls, opprest that are,
> With doubts, and fears, and carking care
> (p. 75)

urging them to 'Lay all your burthens down'. The acknowledgement of oppression and despair would be unremarkable in a body of devotional writing, if it were not for the simultaneous presence of the opposite extreme – a joy striking in its intensity, as typified by Vaughan's ecstatic 'much gladnesse' which is all the greater because of the 'sadnesse' he has undergone ('Chearfulness' p. 428). The writers are themselves aware of their 'fickle and inconstant mind' – Goodman likens the ups and downs in human life to the nature of mixed cloth or 'linsey – wolsey' (p. 28) – and the division of their work and selves into such extremes is a fundamental aspect of existence to these poets in their particular historical setting. The biblical text lying behind their dilemma (the very verse placed on the title page of Major's *Honey on the Rod*) is the apocalyptic Romans 8:18: 'I consider that the sufferings of this present time are not worth comparing with the glory that is to be revealed to us'. The text acknowledges the two extremes of spiritual experience – 'sufferings' and 'glory' – but puts them together only to deny the usefulness of comparing them. Poems, and persons, who indeed combine despair and joy are compelled to express both and yet to see them in a negative relation to one another, co-existent but divided.

There is, therefore, a profound division within the devotional self here, desiring to express extremes of affliction, perceiving in them also the anticipation of ecstasy, yet by biblical precedent urged not to see the two parts of their experience as comparable. When Goodman's voice of Christ advises the poet in 'The Dialogue', the observed truth is that 'Thy heart not Broken, but Devided is' (p. 66). In this split self we see an interesting example of the displaced language of conflict: an apparent conversation with God is often in fact an attempt to find a mediating language between parts of the self – sinner/saint, afflicted/ecstatic being. This phenomenon may well help to explain the popularity of dialogues and echo poems noted earlier. The most basic division, and attempted dialogue, is between the devotional individual and his/her poetic self. During this period we find a deepening of the fundamental dilemma of religious writing – the need to write is constantly challenged by the doubt that spiritual experience can ever be adequately expressed. This split is present in the work of all the writers discussed here – most notably in Collins's verse – but also, of course, famously in Marvell's 'The Coronet'. However, few are as intense as Vaughan in this perplexity of self-division and self-doubt:

> My God and King! to thee
> I bow my knee,
> I bow my troubled soul, and greet
> With my foul heart thy holy feet.
> Cast it, or tread it! It shall do
> Even what thou wilt, and praise thee too.
>
> My God, could I weep blood,
> Gladly I would;
> Or if thou wilt give me that Art,
> Which through the eyes pours out the hart,
> I will exhaust it all, and make
> My self all tears, a weeping lake.
>
> O! 'tis an easie thing
> To write and sing;
> But to write true, unfeigned verse
> Is very hard! O God, disperse
> These weights, and give my spirit leave
> To act as well as to conceive!
>
> O my God, hear my cry;
> Or let me dye! –
>
> ('Anguish', p. 526)

Vaughan goes further, in his daring ending, than most of his contemporaries. Herbert and his other 'followers' always finished their poems on the impossibility of matching their 'utmost art' to God's,[12] but Vaughan appears to give up here, following the despairing logic to its end. The extremes taken in devotional language at this time, then, were not just despair and joy, but 'tears' and 'praise', the capacity to 'conceive' and 'to act' – ultimately, art or silence.

It remains to explore the implications of another fundamental divide in language and devotional experience – that of gender. I raise it at this point because the doubting of one's capacity to write, as well as being part of the rhetoric of devotional verse, is a classic feature of writing by women – questioning their right, and their skill, to express themselves. The two women in my group of poets – Collins and Major – are no exception to this. In her poetic preface, Collins begins by stating the reasons for publishing her work:

> Being through weakness to the house confin'd,
> My mentall powers seeming long to sleep,
> Were summond up, by want of wakeing mind
> Their wonted course of exercise to keep,
> And not to waste themselves in slumber deep;
> Though no work can bee so from error kept
> But some against it boldly will except:
>
> Yet sith it was my morning exercise
> The fruit of intellectuals to vent,
> In Songs or counterfets of Poesies,
> And haveing therein found no small content,
> To keep that course my thoughts are therfore bent,
> And rather former workes to vindicate
> Than any new concepcion to relate.
>
> Our glorious God his creatures weaknesse sees,
> And therefore deales with them accordingly,
> Giveing the meanes of knowledg by degrees,
> Vnfoulding more and more the Mystery,
> And opening the Seales successively,
> So of his goodness gives forth demonstracions,
> To his Elect in divers Dispensacions.
> (*Divine Songs and Meditations*, sig, A3)

She acknowledges that her poems are 'counterfets' but later adds that she cannot suppose them to be 'worthlesse quite, whilst they with Truth agree' (sig. A4v). Elizabeth Major equally confessed artistic 'ignorance' but trusted that 'Truth and plainness' would commend the work to the reader (sig. A3v). Collins asserts that her poems stem from 'weakness', written from a position of 'confinement' to the house, and therefore 'homely' in nature and skill, yet they are justified by God's actions on her helplessness: 'what God still for my Soule hath wrought' (sig. A4v). As we read on in these verse collections, it is tempting to fall for superficial differences which are clearly gender related. For example, male and female poets use the same biblical metaphors in distinctive ways; the Song of Songs was much favoured by both Vaughan and Collins, but 'inhabited' quite differently according to gender. The relationship of writer to work also varies according to gender: can it be coincidence that to Collins, Major and other women writers of the period, their poems are 'offspring' of the 'mind' (Collins sig. A4v) or 'babes' (Major sig. h3v), whereas to Vaughan, Goodman and others (and of course to Herbert before them), they were holy 'ejaculations'?

Intriguing and genuine though these differences may be, I would contend that the more important gender issue here is the sense that devotional writing in this period draws closer to a female aesthetic: in its self-doubt, its uncertainty, its extremes, its retreat – in fact, in virtually all the features that I have explored so far. As Vaughan's 'Anguish' makes uncomfortably clear, the devotional poet's world is not that of action – not the sword (in all its masculinity) but the word. Similarly An Collins writes of 'taking words' (p. 35) as though speaking of a substitute for taking arms. However, a civil war ballad reminds us that

> Small power the Word has, and can afford us
> Not half so many Priviledges as the Sword has.[13]

Devotional poetry which proclaims no warlike message but in fact upholds the 'Word' in all its meanings must come to terms with powerlessness, stemming as it does from a world of acknowledged weakness and a conscious withdrawal from events, a 'confinement' as it were. The male poets were well aware of their marginality as 'poor harmless Doves'[14] and enacted it by their distance from the war, whether imposed (Powell and Rivers both wrote from the physical confines of prison) or chosen (as in Vaughan's retreat to the Usk Valley). The word 'weakness' occurs not only in Collins's prefatory poem, but repeatedly in prefaces and texts by male devotional poets, much more often than the conventional protestations required. The focus of the poems, too, is passivity; their subject is God's action on the world, and in or on the poems. The only activity permitted to the poet, other than with the 'word', is the 'Rhet'rick of a tear',[15] the emotional mood found also in Vaughan's 'Anguish', though normally associated with femininity.

Another common aspect of the female aesthetic which is found in the devotional writing of the English Revolution is the absence of debate and controversy, the competitive poetic drive. Instead of justifying the writing by triumph in argument, the poets are at pains to proclaim its healing function, bringing 'Honey' to the 'Rod' of suffering. However, there is one notable difference between this devotional femininity and the general mood of women's secular writing. The devotional writing of males and females in this period is, paradoxically, strengthened by its sense of 'weakness'. The state is perceived to be transient, and there are positive benefits to be gained from retreat and in passivity before God.

It is clear, then, that the vitality and variety of devotional poetry at the time of the English Revolution belie the idea noted earlier that the lyric tradition was in decline by this period. However, my purpose has been less one of evaluation than of exploration into the kinds of language found by religious poets to be appropriate to that 'war-like, various' and 'tragical age' of the mid-seventeenth century. These may be summarised in terms of a series of paradoxes. First, looking at the shift in the use of metaphors, we find a blurring of the inter-relation of the real and the imaginary, a destabilising of metaphorical usage; and this is partly a result of accepting the political even in the act of neutralising it. Secondly, the poets achieved a new and striking unity of mode through a common reference to, and even reverence for, poetic tradition. Thirdly, they expressed intensity of involvement through retreat, and created a kind of community through isolation of voice and conscience. Fourthly, their work is characterised by irresolvable internal divisions, in extremism of mood – notably self-doubt and joy – which yet find a middle way in agonised expressiveness. Finally, the poetry reveals gender distinctions which are themselves subsumed in the general prevalence of a female aesthetic. Faced with these paradoxes, we might finally ask what drove the poets to keep writing at all in the circumstances of the English Revolution. Their ultimate common ground must surely be that they perceived the need, and desire, to praise God, in spite of (or indeed because of) the events of the revolution. The particular vocation of the devotional poet in such an era is itself a frequent theme among the poets, but is most clearly expressed by Collins, who asserts that devotional verse continues despite all. For, even though the 'beauty of the Land' has been destroyed in war, and people have lost homes, friends, community, even the 'fabricks of Art' in the nation – yet:

> from those storms hath God preserved
> A people to record his praise.
>
> (p. 69)

NOTES

I am grateful to the editors, and other members of the conference on Literature and the English Civil War, April 1987 (particularly Lois Potter, Lucy Gent, Nigel Smith and Warren Chernaik) for constructive discussion of the ideas in this paper.

1 Paul S. Seaver, *Wallington's World: A Puritan Artisan in Seventeenth-Century London* (Stanford, California, 1985), p. 3; Elizabeth Major, *Honey on the Rod* (London, 1656), pp. 187, 175.
2 Lawrence A. Sasek, *The Literary Temper of the English Puritans* (Louisiana, 1961), p. 12.
3 Henry Vaughan, *The Mount of Olives* (1652), in *Works*, ed. L.C. Martin (Oxford, 1957), p. 166. All citations are from this edition.
4 Cardell Goodman, *Beawty in Raggs* (*c.* 1648), ed. R.J. Roberts (Reading, 1958), p. 62.
5 See Helen Wilcox, ' "Something Understood": The Reputation and Influence of George Herbert to 1715', unpublished D. Phil. thesis, Oxford, 1984, and Robert H. Ray, *The Herbert Allusion Book: Allusions to George Herbert in the Seventeenth Century*, (*SP*, 83, 4, Chapel Hill, 1986).
6 Richard Baxter, *Reliquiae Baxterianae*, ed. M. Sylvester (1691), III, 72.
7 Vavasor Powell, *The Bird in the Cage* (1661), 'A true Christians Spiritual Pilgrimage', p. 37.
8 Richard Baxter, *Poetical Fragments* (1681), A7v.
9 See Leah S. Marcus, *Childhood and Cultural Despair: A Theme and Variations in Seventeenth-Century Literature* (Pittsburgh, 1978), pp. 94–152.
10 Vavasor Powell, *Three Hymnes, or Certain Excellent new Psalmes composed by those three Reverend, and learned Divines Mr. Goodwin, Mr. Powel and Mr. Appletree* (1650), p. 7.
11 Andrew Marvell 'Upon Appleton House', *Complete Poems*, ed. E. Story Donno (Harmondsworth, 1972), p. 85.
12 George Herbert, *Works*, ed. F.E. Hutchinson (Oxford, 1941), p. 146.
13 'The Power of the Sword', in *Rump: or an Exact Collection of the Choycest Poems and Songs relating to the Late Times* (1662), p. 333.
14 *The Life and Death of Mr. Vavasor Powell* (1671), p. 103.
15 John Collop, *Poems*, ed. Conrad Hilberry (Madison, Wisconsin, 1962), p. 153.

PART III

Truth and the self

5 In the wars of truth: violence, true knowledge and power in Milton and Hobbes

I believe that it is not to the great model of signs and language [*la langue*] that reference should be made, but to war and battle. The history which bears and determines us is war-like, not language-like. Relations of power, not relations of sense. History has no "sense", which is not to say that it is absurd or incoherent. On the contrary, it is intelligible and should be able to be analysed down to the slightest detail: but according to the intelligibility of struggles, of strategies and tactics.[1]

I philosophise only in *terror* . . .[2]

I

THE TEXTS I shall be addressing, Milton's *Areopagitica* and, all too briefly for such a monument, Hobbes's *Leviathan*, clearly have the Civil War as their historical context. Each is concerned, if in rather different ways, with the pressingly contemporary question of power, with the form and function of the state, and with the problems (thrown up in the last analysis by the revolutionary struggle itself) of the production, circulation and control of discourse. But it is appropriate first to reflect on what sort of relationship between writing and history will be implicitly at work in my own text, and in particular to try to specify something of the theoretical profile of my approach to our topic of literature, or as I prefer, discourse, and the Civil War.

The invitation to relocate these texts in the political – and as we now know, decisively historical – engagements of their day seems inescapable for any analysis tempted to claim a certain materialism for itself. And with such a project, expressed in these general terms, I have no quarrel. On the contrary, to do anything else would seem to me an intellectual and political dereliction of some proportion. But even to begin to put matters in the language of text and context is perhaps unwittingly to summon up a form of the historical study of writing which, while not without its own radical history and potential, may be too easily content with an empiricism of the 'text-and-background' kind. One, which in the very attempt to return to a real history text hypostatised by the traditional fragmentation of the academic disciplines and the inherent and systematic tendency of the disciplines to idealise their own materials, nonetheless retains a fore-grounding of literature in a way which remains quite acceptable to the methodological assumptions – although often not the explicit politics – of traditional study. The limit case is the move too directly to history 'itself' which in reversing the received hierarchy leaves it in place. I am at least as concerned to challenge such assumptions as I am with appropriating them. Perhaps this sounds as if I simply eschew what have been called 'real historical' positions? Sceptical as I am about the pursuit of history 'itself', I think the matter of historicity is a little more complicated than that.

In practice my aim is to combine some description, in Milton and Hobbes, of the tropes of true discourse or Truth and the warlike violence with which they are associated, with some reflection on the theory of discourse today. But in the combination I hope – by a kind of dialectical parallax – to avoid two strategies which seem to offer a way out of the text-and-background trap, but do so only at the cost of other problems presenting themselves. They are the twin phenomena of what is some-times called 'historicism' on the one hand, and 'theoreticism' on the other, errors in my view, as much political as theoretical or methodological. They are both very much available today, and in very clear form in mod-ern Renaissance and seventeenth-century studies. An academic movement of increasing popularity, even authority, announces itself more or less unashamedly to be a new historicism; while few critical schools can have been more assiduous in their espousal of 'theory' – sometimes to the point of ostentatious formalism – than deconstruction.

Where for an older historicism the background provided at least a chronological locality and at best an explanatory ground, for the new variety, refusing the metaphor of foreground and background and empha-sising the historicity of the texts themselves, the erstwhile 'background' becomes a network of discourses and symbolic practices, parallel, analo-gous or even intercalated with the textual materials under discussion. In its best versions the New Historicism possesses an impressive although unfetishised scholarship which has considerably widened the scope of texts normally thought relevant, an advanced, theoretically informed con-ceptual framework, and a pertinent insistence that it is cultural production and cultural power that should really be at stake. It is possible to have much sympathy with this insistence, but also a number of reservations about the politics of the characteristic New Historicist model of slippage and cultural containment. It seems to me that there are dangers in the approach of appearing to seek out what is oppositional or resistant in the text while actually incorporating that into the functioning of the culture at large and so producing what amounts to a spectatorial passivity in respect of power. Within and among the discourses in play there are seen to be slippages and discontinuities to which older historicisms were far from alert, but these are often resolved in practice into a higher functional unity behind a tendency for history to be grasped – anti-empirically, but in my view rather simply – as other texts. At worst the anecdote is raised to a methodological level. Certainly when slippage becomes 'subversion' – a key word for such studies, and one which has its uses, to be sure – the conceptual language of New Historicism risks familiarity with discourses on the right that seek to empower and legitimate domination by a deviant rather than oppositional naming of those who resist its effects. Even on the left, subversion may be a poor name or a poor thing where in reality revolutionary perspectives are either meant or needed. At the very least I should want to measure what real distance there is (and there is some) between the demonisation of subversion in order to justify and maintain domination, and the ultimate lack – inherent in the incorporation of subversion into power – of a thoroughgoing critique of domination. I suspect that the latter tends to offer the political effect of leaving everything as it is, when it doesn't actually debilitate the very idea of opposition in the name of all subversion being a necessary condition of the functioning of power as such. The result is often, in the name of studying the poetics of power, a practical denial of the fact and poignancy of domination, substituting notions of circulation for those of oppression, anxiety for terror.

But if New Historicism is in any sense new, this must partly be because it is willing to attend to history again 'after' the resolutely anti-historical cast of theoreticism in its by now familiar deconstructionist form. Characterised by a tendency to identify in the texts of the Renaissance and the seventeenth century the linguistic phenomena and rhetorical practices which are essentially those of its own contemporary modernism or postmodernism, deconstruction, in the name often of engaging the *aporias* where cultural authority is not at one with itself, can also threaten a debilitating fatalism; either in the complacent form of the play of textual power (where it is not mere play in the weak sense) being seen to be egregiously self-subverting and therefore in need of no transformation other than that which it works upon itself by virtue of its nature as textuality; or by way of the pessimistic and radical scepticism that will interminably question as metaphysical all positive strategies. Its political limitations lie in its circularity, in precisely the theoreticism that in reducing all not simply to language but to a theory of the text tends to mistake the problem for the solution, seeing difference as ultimately endemic rather than fully critical.

In practice the boundaries between historicist and theoreticist approaches are not distinct. On the contrary, and despite their logical and philosophical incompatibility with each other, they are frequently combined. The New Historicism has little hesitation in adopting to its own uses a variety of postmodernist interpretative strategies, although usually without thinking through the problems raised by the historical character – even the historical time – of such strategies themselves. Deconstructive readers, while analysing avowedly historical texts, seem equally well able to abolish historical difference in the name of generalised textuality, without perceiving any problem of theory or method. A certain Foucault and a certain Derrida gazing into the mirror of each other's eyes, with, I imagine, some incomprehension.

What, then, is to be done? As a contribution to the formulation of a strategy in respect of all this I wish to offer the following exploration of a different way of approaching the relationship between writing and the Civil War, one which will involve discourse or writing and the war in a certain interiority with each other. While, in particular, I want to evade the received hierarchisation of literature and background, I don't in any sense wish, in the name of either 'circulation' or 'the play of the text', to lose sight of other hierarchisations of discourse, whose description should continue to allow the discussion and apprehension of the (traces of) structures and practices of domination and resistance.

II

In terms of contextualisation *Areopagitica* is not without its own pointers as to the correct background against which it ought to be set. Passages like the following suggest the immediacy of the Civil War as the significant environment of discourse:

> Behold now this vast City: a city of refuge, the mansion house of liberty, encompassed and surrounded with His protection; the shop of war hath not there more anvils and hammers waking, to fashion out the plates and instruments of armed Justice in defence of beleaguered Truth, than there be pens and heads there, sitting by their studious lamps, musing, searching, revolving new notions and ideas wherewith to present, as with their homage and their fealty, the approaching Reformation: others as fast reading, trying all things, assenting to the force of reason and convincement.[3]   (p. 177)

In the light of this invocation of the city at war, a certain kind of historicism might well attempt to dislocate Milton's text from its traditional setting, whether that be, say, a place in the history of English prose style or in the universality of some discussion of supposedly fundamental rights and liberties, and refer it to the immediate context of the Civil War as the real ground, or at least the most politically interesting content, of its representations. But this is not the kind of locatedness I wish to examine here. I prefer over too swift a resort to the text's evocation of a real London embattled by royalist forces, the less empirical address to context inherent in the passage's association with each other of figurations of warfare and of discursive practice. Counter to traditionally liberal versions of the relative value of violence on the one hand, and literature on the other, here the material preparation for battle and the forging of the ideological weapons of the approaching Reformation, the coming revolution, run parallel to each other. If the armouries and the munitions factories are self-evidently necessary for the advancement of Justice in defence of Truth, no less so, in the rhetoric of Milton's argument for free debate unhindered by licensing, is the discursive struggle, itself mobilising the *force* of reason and convincement. It is this association of discourse and violence, as likes rather than opposites, which will become the main thematic component of what I have to say.

The powerfully warlike character of discourse strikes an early and key note in Milton's text. In a famous passage, usually taken to be a rhetorical sop to the parliamentary supporters of a reinstituted censorship replacing that of the crown which had fallen with Star Chamber, Milton grants the need for a police of discourse in terms that infuse the latter with a danger-ous criminality and a potential for militant, transgressive if not actually rebellious, violence:

I deny not, but that it is of greatest concernment in the Church and Common-wealth, to have a vigilant eye how books demean themselves as well as men; and thereafter to confine, imprison, and do sharpest justice on them as malefactors. For books are not absolutely dead things, but do contain a potency of life in them to be as active as that soul was whose progeny they are; nay, they do preserve as in a vial the purest efficacy and extraction of that living intellect that bred them. I know they are as lively, and as vigorously productive, as those fabulous dragon's teeth; and being sown up and down, may chance to spring up armed men.

(p. 149)

The necessity is conceded of church and state regarding books as potential malefactors and suborning them to a justice that is seen clearly as state power, even if, as it later becomes clear, Milton intends this action to be after the event of transgression, contrary to the Star Chamber practice of pre-publication licensing. And the positive – vigorous and productive – danger represented by books, the dragon's teeth that spring up armed men, can be measured in the extremism of its antidote as the passage turns rhetorically back on itself to emphasise the value of books – in an anti-humanism not of the theoretical kind – above the value of individual men, or even life itself:

And yet, on the other hand, unless wariness be used, as good almost kill a man as kill a good book. Who kills a man kills a reasonable creature, God's image; but he who destroys a good book, kills reason itself, kills the image of God, as it were in the eye. Many a man lives a burden to the earth; but a good book is the precious life-blood of a master spirit, embalmed and treasured up on purpose to a life beyond life. 'Tis true, no age can restore a life, whereof perhaps there is no great loss; and revolutions of ages do not oft recover the loss of a rejected truth, for the want of which whole nations fare the worse.   (pp. 149–50)

Together with the casual disposal of the many who are a burden to the earth, the remarkable insistence of this language of killing, blood and death, connected with a significantly bodily discourse of 'progeny', 'the potency of life' and the notion of literary production as 'breeding', escalates to the point where only mass slaughter will have the required rhetorical effect:

We should be wary therefore what persecutions we raise against the living labours of public men, how we spill that seasoned life of man, preserved and stored up in books; since we see a kind of homicide may thus be committed, sometimes a martyrdom, and if it extend to the whole impression, a kind of massacre; whereof the execution ends not in the slaying of an elemental life, but strikes at that ethereal and fifth essence, the breath of reason itself, slays an immortality rather than a life.   (p. 150)

The massacre envisaged reaches out to a death beyond death, to the decease of immortality itself. These early passages are shot through with a violence of, or against, discursive practice that offers little to ideal accounts of writing as expression, transcription or aesthetic value. Discourse and violence go, implicitly and explicitly, together in this text, whether one be the object of the other or rather its active perpetrator. We are more or less forced to encounter in the very language of the text a conception of discourse as struggle and battle, in contradistinction to so many texts, or so many readings, which will neutralise the political register of textuality in the name either of some anodyne meaning, or, to pick up the language of one of my epigraphs, 'sense'.

But if discourse, and above all true discourse, is inlaid with violence, it is important to notice, however, the discrepancy among the forms of this imbrication. There are principally two quite differently inflected figurations of Truth in *Areopagitica* and I shall briefly describe the positivity of each of them. The first is of true discourse as a warrior. In the following passage, for example, the militancy of the personification of Truth enables a series of military metaphors for what would otherwise be conceivable only as the ideal (non)practice of discourse:

And though all the winds of doctrine were let loose to play upon the earth, so Truth be in the field, we do injuriously, by licensing and prohibiting, to misdoubt her strength. Let her and Falsehood grapple; who ever knew Truth put to the worse, in a free and open encounter? Her confuting is the best and surest suppressing . . . When a man hath been labouring the hardest labour in the deep mines of knowledge; hath furnished out his findings in all their equipage; drawn forth his reasons as it were a battle ranged; scattered and defeated all objections in his way; calls out his adversary into the plain, offers him the advantage of wind and sun, if he please, only that he may try the matter by dint of argument: for his opponents then to skulk, to lay ambushments, to keep a narrow bridge of licensing where the challenger should pass, though it be valour enough in soldiership, is but weakness and cowardice in the wars of Truth. (p. 181)

The extraordinary extension of the military metaphor – amounting to something like prose conceit – and the detail of its internal differentiation, between the honourable encounter in open battle as against the skulking unworthiness of guerilla tactics, again contains a charge of force which outpaces normal assessments of discourse as in some sense the opposite of violence. Discursive practice is here distinctly practice, and practice of a very practical kind. The strength, the sureness of her victory, carries over from the figuration of Truth as a warrior in the field of war grappling with Falsehood, into the account of learning as battle in such a way as to construct what is valued in the practice of knowledge as not so much the knowledge itself but its deployment. The argument here is again one for open debate rather than pre-emptive licensing: but the discourse is one of strategy and tactics in – precisely – the wars of truth.

Although it is men who do the labouring in 'the deep mines of knowledge', (and knowledge is at once abstract and a matter of deployment), Truth in this passage, and in others like it, is personified as a woman. The same gendering, which I shall return to below, also inflects the other principal figuration of Truth at work in *Areopagitica*, where true discourse is figured not as a militant activist, the subject of a certain force, but in its potential for becoming the object-victim of a definite violence. In contrast to the image of Truth who is 'strong next to the Almighty', who 'needs no policies, nor stratagems, nor licensings to make her victorious' for 'those are the shifts and the defences that error uses, against her power' (p. 181), there is another insistent set of references not to a heroic Truth in triumph over the forces of the adversary falsehood but rather to 'those dissevered pieces which are yet wanting to the body of Truth' (p. 176). For example:

Truth indeed came once into the world with her Divine Master, and was a perfect shape most glorious to look on: but when He ascended, and His Apostles after Him were laid asleep, then straight arose a wicked race of deceivers, who, as the story goes of the Egyptian Typhoon with his conspirators, how they dealt with the good Osiris, took the virgin Truth, hewed her lovely form into a thousand pieces, and scattered them to the four winds. From that time ever since, the sad friends of Truth, such as durst appear, imitating the careful search that Isis made for the mangled body of Osiris, went up and down gathering up limb by limb, still as they could find them. We have not yet found them all, Lords and Commons, nor ever shall do, till her Master's second coming; He shall bring together every joint and member, and shall mould them into an immortal feature of loveliness and perfection.   (p. 175)

This, of course, is of one the passages that are usually thought of as arguments for religious toleration. But in any case I am less concerned here with the notion that the truth may consist of separate elements, the total of which is in the possession of no single person or group, than with what is manifested in the trope of truth as a mangled body, where two things are important: that it is a trope of the body, and that it is a dismembered and female body which is at stake. Although this is, as it were, a 'positive' figuration, Truth, in this version, is the absent object – victimised cruelly in the torn and scattered corporeality of 'joint and member', 'limb by limb' – of what is elsewhere described as 'one general and brotherly search' (p. 177) but whose gender and corporal disruption give a new inflection to such otherwise unremarkable idioms. Would 'we' (and we are assumed to be males) be any the 'less knowing, less eagerly pursuing of the truth' (p. 180) if the precise character of what we are enjoined to pursue were at every moment as explicit as it is here? Perhaps it will not be stretching the point to suggest that what I shall soon call an economy of truth is equally an erotics of the figurations of truth? Certainly when we are invited not merely to 'do our obsequies to the torn body of our martyred saint' (p. 175), but to 'See the ingenuity of Truth, who, when she gets a free and willing hand, opens herself faster than the pace of method and discourse can overtake her' (p. 161), it is hard not to sense a sexual charging in the metaphor, even if there is no hint of rape. And the gentleness of the search at one moment, or that ardour of the pursuit at another, is surely over-determined by the violence that has already been done elsewhere to the object of these desires.

But this is apparently paradoxical because against this violence of the body, the phrase 'method and discourse' ought to bring to mind that other great seventeenth-century philosopher of the truth, Descartes, who thought, or thought that he thought, that the only way to a truthful certainty was by, precisely, method and discourse. Is there not a tension between the scientistic procedure of discourse and method which is depassionated (to recall an ugly word) and disembodied, and the investment of sexual violence in the Miltonic figuration of Truth-as-victim? It is not that Milton is antipathetic to procedure, to 'method and discourse'. On the contrary there is that persistent emphasis on reason, especially as the measured exercise of judgement by the individual, which is intellectually cognate with Cartesian method, and theologically coherent with a Protestant emphasis on the unmediated activity of the individual conscience, in contradistinction to ecclesiastical authority, which Descartes would have been able to recognise. But in the figures I have been discussing here there is a sense of truth having an availability which outstrips discourse and method, which offers a faster access by different, somehow more transcendental but at the same time more bodily means. And the crucial point is that these means are articulated in a metaphor which is specifically sexually inflected.

At one level Brian Easlea's account of the gendering both of Nature and of scientific enquiry in the seventeenth century may help to reduce this tension, and in any case provides an essential context for the Miltonic use of apparently conventional metaphor by which truth becomes figured as a sexually available woman opening herself to male entry.[4] Easlea detects in the discourses of the 'scientific revolution' of the period, an insistent complex of metaphors for nature as veiled but penetrable woman and for the masculinity of knowledge which enters her mystery, which he is able to trace through to the epistemo-erotics of the production and use of nuclear weapons. Easlea's account of the masculinity of bourgeois scientific discourse would suggest that the procedures of reason and those at work so far in the Miltonic text may not be that distant from each other. There is indeed a sexual charging in both, even if reason dominantly represses its own bodily violence (if it is not actually constituted by that repression) while in the figures of Truth as object-woman, or even as female militant, the violence, the corporeality and the desire of true discourse remain more overt. But nonetheless the forms do differ from each other, and differ in the mode of their different representational weighting of the sexed violence of true discourse on the one hand and impersonal and bodiless method on the other. There is clearly a more than problematic dimension to the text when the drive towards the invisible because intellectual and – from the point of view of power, systemic – mastery of 'nature' inaugurated in the Cartesian initiative, and the positive figuration of embodied Truth whether militant or victimised, negotiate uneasily and unknown to each other. And there is much more to be said here, particularly concerning precise political interpretation of the different figurations of Truth, and their historical locations in a pattern of what, using a language with which I am not entirely happy, I would have to call residual and emergent components of the text.

For the moment, however, having established, albeit only descriptively, that Milton's figurations of Truth or true discourse are variable and varied within a text that eroticises even its abstractions, I want to move on now at another level to abstraction itself and suggest that in addition to these two positive tropes that I have been discussing – Truth as militant warrior, Truth as pursued victim – there is indeed a third discourse of the truth which can only be referred to loosely as figuration. In fact it consists in a systemic organisation of the place, function and supports of true discourse that does belong properly on the Cartesian threshold of emergent modernity, aspects of which I have discussed elsewhere.[5] In arguing for the shift in the moment of censorship from prepublication licensing to post-publication intervention by the state, Milton begins to construct, in design at least, the lineaments of the modern situation in which the great caesura between the public and the private is inscribed in the general form of social organisation, and the private citizen is constituted in reason and judgement as a self-policing entity, free in the sense of being free to transgress and to be punished for transgression, but unfree by virtue of pre-constitution in docility. Now this structure cannot be positively figured. Precisely in as much as it is a structure or a structuration it escapes positive depiction, and precisely because of this achieves its power. It organises, almost pre-cognitively, true discourse as that uttered by a properly self-disciplined subject, in whom the erstwhile authorisation of state licensing has been internalised and transformed into a quasi-critical, quasi-psychological restraint. This structure, as I have indicated, is different in kind from the positive depictions of truth which I have been discussing, but it is also at odds with them in terms of its political and historical strategy. The essential political sobriety, and above all the incorporeality, of this structural principle of true discourse sits very uneasily with truth as militant combatant with its amalgam of classical amazon, Renaissance republicanism, and puritan valour, and is hardly more consonant with truth as eroticised but mutilated victim. Disappearing from the view of figuration is an ever more powerfully coercive, invisible – inscribed – domination infiltrated behind the text's otherwise more politically overt discursive figures.

There is an important argument to be had about whether the power of this process is a result of the difference between structure and metaphor, between the politics of organisation and that of positively figured discourse. It would probably be an argument tending not to celebrate the literary as narrowly and traditionally received, and certainly one whose historical basis would have to be in a very full discussion of a general movement in the seventeenth century from performance to text. But that being for the present assumed, the two positive figurations of Truth – taken together with the systemic framework I have just invoked – do turn the text into a quite complex and dynamic economy of truth. The tropes of true discourse do not exactly circulate (as the fashionable word has it) in the text, but certainly they take discrepant forms and positions within the text's organisation of various sets of eroticised relations among its uttering subject or subjects, the reading subject, the overt and virtual addressees, objective thirds, and so on. Indeed, the critique of writing could be taken still further in order to think the text not as a univocal tract but as something more like a theatre of discourses and positionalities. But in any case what we encounter here is the mode of the text's lack of complete resolution into the modern regime of discourse that it nonetheless prefigures. A bourgeois text it is, and in its structure tends towards a post-revolutionary discursivity of apparently depoliticised private utterance. But it contains still – at least in the Truth-as-militant trope – a revolutionary figuration of true discourse not yet willing to surrender itself to private obscurity. Equally in the other positive figuration of Truth, is there not a sign, even in its condition of victimisation, of a certain bodily excess of structure, if not actually the site of a resistance? Not that it is now possible to 'side' with one or the other, as if a 'return' to these discursive events were available; or that it would be appropriate to identify with an early bourgeois heroism of the truth – and still less with female mutilation and dismemberment – as models of appropriate political and epistemological value. I take it that the point of historical study is not such 'nostalgia', formal or positive, as if even a full body (which would have to be regarded as wholly imaginary in any case) could somehow stand against the system of subjection emerging here. The point is rather to deploy what could be called the parallax of historical difference which will want to apprehend *at the same time* the 'slippage' in the text as an arena of struggle among different figurations and strategies, and also the degree of ideological fixation that secures this instability by tactics of hierarchisation and writing in a degree of stasis. The text is not a monolith, nor is it a free indeterminacy, but rather a precise, and precisely historical, event. But if the event secures a dominant, it is not without traces of the violence of its institution (or even in some cases glimpses, however utopian, of alternative possibilities) remaining a trouble to it. It is that potential for the discovery of a limit to the dominant that both constitutes and makes valuable for us the historicity of the text.

III

I want to turn now to another text in which tropes of war and truth are imbricated with each other, and one also pre-eminently a police of discourse. The composition of Hobbes's *Leviathan* spans the civil war period and in that sense is contemporary with *Areopagitica*. It too, is not without its own – although curiously attenuated – gesture to the war as its context. Milton's references to the war are explicit, and Hobbes too, while for the main part apparently far less topical and immediately conjunctural in his preoccupations, is nonetheless prepared to define the purpose of his work in *Leviathan* as the avoidance of the kind of conflict in which his compatriots are currently engaged. His conclusion states at last a project:

And thus I have brought to an end my Discourse of Civill and Ecclesiasticall Government, occasioned by the disorders of the present time, without partiality, without application, and without other designe, than to set before mens eyes the mutuall Relation between Protection and Obedience; of which the condition of Humane Nature, and the Laws Divine, (both Naturall and Positive) require an inviolable observation.[6]   (p. 728)

But the attenuation of the contextual placing is somehow typical of the discourse if not of Thomas Hobbes, at least of the persona that utters the text. The disclaimer of direct interest in the war that nonetheless occasions the text acutely reflects in content and tone that mixture of intellectual arrogance and timorousness in the face both of constituted authority in particular and all external conditions in general, that otherwise permeates the work. The relative abstraction of 'the mutuall Relation between Protection and Obedience', of natural and positive laws which require an inviolable observation, both reveals and disavows the political objectives of a text at once wholly committed to domination, yet simultaneously couched in terms that tempt me to designate the text and its author-function paranoic to a degree. Hobbes is pre-eminently the philosopher of and in terror.

If only in respect of these different degrees and kinds of self-contextualisation, it is clear that in turning from *Areopagitica* to *Leviathan* we are dealing with texts apparently very different in kind. And in contradistinction to the 'slippage' I have illustrated in the Miltonic text, *Leviathan* is normally regarded as enjoying a very high degree of closure indeed. But the closure is not as total as is usually thought, and I shall try to demonstrate this by identifying a certain fissuring of the apparently monolithic, absolute and closed character of the text. At the risk of some reduction, the discussion will concentrate on one well-known area of what is technically a very complex theory, although one not particularly obscure in its political objectives. I have in mind the famous discussion in chapter 13 of the state of nature as a state of war, and the issues it raises in respect of power and the power of true discourse.

It is of course commonplace to remark that Hobbes's account of the state of nature (its speculative archaism on the one hand and its appeal to contemporary America on the other notwithstanding) depends equally if implicitly on the immediate environment of the Civil War and, less directly but probably more profoundly, on the extant social conditions of revolutionary and pre-revolutionary England in general. Not surprisingly, then, chapter 13 is in at least two important ways the linchpin of the theorisation of power. Most frequently noticed is the manner in which

Hobbes's description of the state of nature picks up the theory of desire from chapter 11 in order to legitimate dominion as the overcoming of its own founding naturalism. Because, the deadly but not unfamiliar logic goes, desire is like this:

Nor can a man any more live, whose Desires are at an end, than he, whose Senses and Imagination are at a stand. Felicity is a continuall progresse of the desire, from one object to another; the attaining of the former, being still but the way to the later. The cause whereof is, That the object of mans desire, is not to enjoy once onely, and for one instant of time; but to assure for ever, the way of his future desire . . .

So that in the first place, I put for a generall inclination of all mankind, a perpetuall and restlesse desire of Power after power, that ceaseth onely in Death.

(pp. 160–1)

Nature is therefore like this:

Hereby it is manifest, that during the time men live without a common Power to keep them all in awe, they are in that condition which is called Warre; and such a warre, as is of every man, against every man. For Warre, consisteth not in Battell onely, or in the act of fighting; but in a tract of time, wherein the Will to contend by Battell is sufficiently known: and therefore the notion of *Time*, is to be considered in the nature of Warre; as it is in the nature of Weather. For as the nature of Foule weather, lyeth not in a showre or two of rain; but in an inclination thereto of many dayes together: So the nature of War, consisteth not in actuall fighting; but in the known disposition thereto, during all the time there is no assurance to the contrary. All other time is Peace. (pp. 185–6)

And the only way of securing that peace, of abating the natural war engendered by desire, is indeed the constitution of a sovereign power keeping all in awe. I shall return to that sovereignty later. But the other reason why this area of Hobbes is fundamental, and this is less usually commented on in relation to 'the nature of War', is the significance of what apparently escapes, or at least stands outside, the system of desire and power. In chapter 13 it is science; or rather 'that skill of proceeding upon generall, and infallible rules, called Science' is used to stand for what Hobbes calls 'the arts grounded upon words', and which he insists on 'setting aside' from the faculties and capacities which in general men have naturally and more or less equally (p. 183). The setting aside is important because it does indeed tend to disengage science and, if we take Hobbes at the letter of his text here, all discursive practice, from the formations of power and desire. The most graphic, and the one which Hobbes takes to be the most politically neutral version possible of this improbable but necessary strategy that seeks to construct a discursive space where interest and power are held to be least at stake, is the example of geometry:

the doctrine of Right and Wrong, is perpetually disputed, both by the Pen and the Sword: Whereas the doctrine of Lines, and Figures, is not so; because men care not, in that subject what be truth, as a thing that crosses no mans ambition, profit, or lust. For I doubt not, but if it had been a thing contrary to any mans right of dominion, or to the interest of men that have dominion, *That the three Angles of a Triangle should be equall to two Angles of a Square*; that doctrine should have been, if not disputed, yet by the burning of all books of Geometry, suppressed, as farre as he whom it concerned was able.   (p. 166)

The segregation of geometry, standing here for science in a much broader sense – closer to rational discourse as such – to a place outside sociality and the desires and dominions in which it consists, is both essential to Hobbes's analysis and at the same time 'subversive' of it. Given the two epistemic models offered by Foucault in the passage I have quoted as an epigraph – the model of language on the one hand and the intelligibility of struggles on the other – it would seem obvious that despite its thematics of war and objective of domination, Hobbes's discourse appeals wholly to the former, to a manipulation of what Foucault calls the great model of signs and language. *Leviathan* begins not with a discussion of power or right, but with a theory of discourse, of signs and representation, which only subsequently provides the foundation for the emphasis on proper definitions and, ultimately, the language of contract, which are then central to Hobbes's account of power and language alike. The effect of this sequence from representation to the propriety of the submissive contract under which the members of any given society supposedly agree together to establish a power over themselves, is that of an ever-pre-constitution of a – highly political – 'truth' concealed in the very structure of what counts as 'sense' or 'intelligibility' itself. The fabulous contract itself is then subsequent to and consequent upon the language in which it can be conceived and framed: the discourse which is outside power constitutes an absolute power. It is not simply that mathematical and geometrical science (or the deployments of Hobbes's own reasoning which he would have be of a similar order) represent but another mode of discourse from that either of the natural passions or of the laws of any duly-constituted commonwealth after the event of its constitution (for these are then explicitly the discourse of the sovereign power and need have no reason in them), but rather that the science of the text, in its very character as that discourse which is not involved in power, tends implicitly thus ever to pre-empt the possibility of civil conflict, because such would entail an unthinkable falling away from true language and even from language itself. I have mentioned how the persona of the utterance disassociates itself from faction, from explicit political engagement; but this can now be read not merely as a psychology effect, or even in this case a censorship effect. It is simply impossible to discourse properly or truthfully and rebel. This contrasts markedly with the positive figurations of Truth in Milton.

If there we saw an interiority to each other of truth and violence or, to put it at its weakest, a parallel between the warlikeness of discourse and the warlikeness of the war itself, in Hobbes true discourse is wholly a shore against civil war. The implicitude (if there is such a word) of this in Hobbes is analogous, rather, with what in Milton I have called the 'systemic', the *regime* of discourse, and similarly produces a coercive theoretical –juridical or power effect by writerly structuration. In Hobbes, with the exception of one major qualification that I shall come to, truth is not figured, personified or embodied, and not then also caught up in the drama of political and gender violence. This is not because his text is 'philosophical' rather than 'literary' – and how, precisely, would we characterise Milton's text in any case? – but because of the 'abstract' pregivenness in proper language of inescapable, even 'involuntary' – or, as he says, 'inviolable' – obedience.

In Milton there are residual figurations of truth and war and an emergent structuration which dispenses with those figurations in favour of a more ineluctable, systemic domination. In the case of the Hobbesian non-figurative pre-constitution of obedience and truth, by contrast, we seem to be already wholly within structure, within an abstract discourse, implicative and reasoned and in that sense politically unnegotiable. But there is, as I mentioned earlier, at least one rent in this near-seamless, near-invisible closure. It involves that paradoxical way in which truth and power, or the effectivity of truth in power, *are* embodied or 'figured' in the sense in which I have been using the word, in the double person of the sovereign whose artificial rather than natural body is the commonwealth itself. Although it is not as rich in empirical detail, not as fully dramatised as, say, the sacred person of the Shakespearean monarch, and if it is figured, it is so in the abstract, non-depictive form seemingly appropriate to philosophical and juridicial discourse, the figure of the Sovereign in *Leviathan* is nonetheless much closer to, say, 'The Lord's annointed Temple' which in *Macbeth* 'Most sacreligious Murther hath broke ope' (II.iii.66–7) than it is to the regime of discourse and subjection we see emerging in *Areopagitica*. Or again, although the symbolic register has been somewhat flattened since Shakespeare – there is little finally that is both sacred and fundamental in Hobbes – the paramount role in the polity of the monarch (which is how Hobbes thinks of the sovereign in all of his routine appellations and inadvertent examples despite the fact that theoretically, if half-heartedly, he allows for the possibility of other forms of sovereignty), belongs more to the erstwhile fantasy of a full kingship than to the implicative manipulation of true discourse that characterises the dominant strategy of Hobbes's text itself.

But the matter is complicated, for the Sovereign has a very curious textual existence in *Leviathan*, double not only in body of course, but in positionality with respect to the commonwealth. This has nothing to do with any sacred mystery of the royal person so much as a slippage in the theory itself, or rather, since it is not ultimately a philosophical critique of Hobbes I am conducting, in the textual deployment of the theory. The problem is that the sovereign is both inside and outside the commonwealth. Like science which is set aside from interest and conflict and yet yields the true discourse that legitimates power, the sovereign is outside of sociality as such. But if discourse is in its most fundamental sense contractual and subjecting, the sovereign, with whom in Hobbes it is axiomatically impossible to make a contract, is not subjected and the war continues: the sovereign remains in a state of nature in respect of other sovereigns and their commonwealths, but also in respect of its own, carrying, in effect, the war that sovereignty is designed to quell into the commonwealth itself (an act, by the way, of aggression against its own body which is strictly unthinkable in Hobbes because of the primitive and fundamental right of self-defence, to which I shall return in a moment). Or, unless mediated by the textual no-place to which are consigned the trueness of true language and all that goes with it in Hobbes's 'great model of signs', empowering as it ought the dominion of the sovereign and the ever-pre-constitutedness of obedience, war and nature and the commonwealth are actually internal to each other; language doesn't succeed as a prophylaxis against violence and desire, and the whole system breaks down under its own absurdity, as peace becomes war and war peace.

This critical, unstable slipping of the categories around the duplicity of the figure of the sovereign is instanced again in the impossibility of Hobbes fully theorising the prohibition of resistance to sovereign power which is otherwise one of the text's major objectives. The one natural right reserved to the subject, the only one which is inalienable in Hobbes, which cannot be contracted away and for the alienation of which there simply cannot be therefore any true sign or discourse is that of self-preservation. This is famously never reconciled in Hobbes in the discussion of punishment where the power of the sovereign comes up against the limit of the subject's right to resist. In fact it would even be possible to fabricate from Hobbes's account of the subject a theory – a somewhat individualistic one, no doubt – of revolution which would be consonant with Hobbes's general position on nature and power, but quite at odds with his project of obedience. Hobbes is simply and symptomatically evasive and eventually silent on the question of resistance to punishment, because it becomes a sign of profound contradiction where the inalienable nature on which his theory is founded there confronts itself as an opposite. If the sovereign carries the war into the commonwealth by violence against his subjects then in such a case the individual must resist by nature. But if such resistance is not naturally given then the theory which empowered the sovereign in the first place is fatally flawed. The problem is that Hobbes doesn't really have a model of subjection at his disposal, which is clear enough from the way in which private belief or mere opinion in Hobbes remain truly private, an ineffable, unconstituted area where dominion does not run. And this in turn is because, as I suppose Foucault would have said, he hasn't – he has no desire to – cut off the king's head *in theory*. Or rather, his text hasn't become writerly or written enough. The violence of nature fails to be contained by the very theorisation of sovereignty it was supposed to underwrite. The slippage is in the terror, by which, through a whole series of points of fracture in the Hobbesian text where implicitude fails quite to achieve an adequate dispersal of power throughout the system, domination remains the external offer of the threat of a performable violence, rather than, as Hobbes would rather have had it, inevitable and 'acceptable' correlative of true discourse.

IV

I began by drawing attention to what I see as problems in the nature of contextualisation and in the dilemma offered by the notions of textual indeterminacy, of slippage, limitless semiosis, free circulation or play on the one hand and the closure of historicisation on the other. This needs, I think, to be brought into contact with the seventeenth century's own movement from transactions of discourse and violence to the essentially ideal epistemological models that we dominantly inherit but in respect of which Foucault's reference to the intelligibility of struggles should offer a kind of critical limit. It should also prompt some discussion of whether it wouldn't be better to attempt to evade altogether this binary opposition given in theory in favour of an emphasis on the degree to which patterns of closure and slippage are themselves textually intrinsic and, above all, historically determinate and historically variable. I have tried to offer contemporary examples in Milton and Hobbes where different degrees of closure or of slippage and fracture correspond to the texts' different political strategies, among which definite organisations of both hierarchisation and play are detectable. The main traditions of reading have – no doubt for ideological reasons – preferred the dominant discourses of these texts at the expense of what in them tends to 'subvert' the hierarchy. That is understandable of course. But only if the subversion is not in fact 'contained' (in the sense of forming a constitutive moment of what it apparently subverts), but rather remains in the historical time of the text unreconciled with and even critical of the dominating discursive strategies. The aggravation of that precision of difference would seem much to the point if, under newer forms of reading, it is indeed criticism in which we are interested.

Finally, having apparently eschewed earlier what have been called real-historical positions, I would like now to emphasise what in fact I take to be the 'real-world' character of the understanding of discourse I am trying to elaborate. Just as my sense of the right context is not that which appeals to the empirical content of the text's representations, but rather to the problematic of representation itself, so my sense of the 'real-worldness' of discursive practice is linked entirely to its political function. In fact it is as much from the texts of the seventeenth century where we can detect a movement from figurations of true discourse as political action to writerly and epistemic structures of a coercive truth, as from contemporary theory, that I gain, by that parallax effect of historical difference, an understanding of discourse as anything but ideal transcription. On the contrary, there is quite a strong, and fully political sense, which it would be well to infuse into our discourse today – even our academic and literary discourse – of powerful *inscription*, of real things thus at stake: positions being marked out, enabled or prevented, and advances, even victories, being gained, or not.

And after all, it matters which, in as much as 'Warre' – and not just the war of epistemology – truly is 'all the world about'.

NOTES

The text is that of a lecture which was given in an early version to the annual conference of the Australia and New Zealand Association for Medieval and Renaissance Studies held at the University of Melbourne, August 1986. A subsequent version was delivered to the conference, 'Warre is all the World About: Literature and the English Civil War', on which the present volume is based and published in *Southern Review* 20 (1987), pp. 111–25. It has been revised again for publication here.

1 Michel Foucault, 'Power and Truth', in Meaghan Morris and Paul Patton, eds., *Michel Foucault: Power, Truth, Strategy* (Sydney, 1979), p. 33.
2 Jacques Derrida, 'Cogito and the History of Madness', *Writing and Difference*, trans. Alan Bass (London, 1978), p. 62.
3 All quotations from *Milton's Prose Writings*, introd. K.M. Burton (London, 1958).
4 See Brian Easlea, *Fathering the Unthinkable: Masculinity, Scientists and the Nuclear Arms Race* (London, 1983).
5 The discussion addressed the constitution of the historical structure which gives the basis to that well-known Althusserian pun by which, according to Althusser's theorisation of the subjection of the concrete individual, the subject conceived in the philosophical or psychological register is also, implicitly and

inescapably, the subject of a definite regime – both, I would want to suggest, in the narrowly political sense and in the Foucauldian understanding of a regime of discourse. See Francis Barker, *The Tremulous Private Body: Essays on Subjection* (London and New York, 1984), pp. 41–52 and *passim*; Louis Althusser, 'Ideology and Ideological State Apparatuses', *Lenin and Philosophy and Other Essays* trans. Ben Brewster (London, 1971), pp. 123–73.

6 All quotations from Thomas Hobbes, *Leviathan*, ed. C.B. Macpherson (Harmondsworth, 1981).

THOMAS N. CORNS

6 'Some rousing motions': the plurality of Miltonic ideology

I TAKE MY title from the words with which Milton's Samson announces the restoration of the divine afflatus:

> Be of good courage, I begin to feel
> Some rousing motions in me which dispose
> To something extraordinary my thoughts.   (lines 1381–3)[1]

I begin with Samson, a figure whose ambiguous status is familiar to us moderns: Samson, the Israelites' freedom-fighter and the Philistines' terrorist. My interest in him, for the moment, resides simply in the plurality of his expression, 'Some rousing motion*s*.' A plurality which perhaps matches the complexities of Milton's own political thought and expression rather better than the murderous single-mindedness of his hero. My contention is that the ideological implications of the Milton *oeuvre* are convoluted, ambivalent, and internally contradictory to an extent that has not hitherto been appreciated. Other critics have attempted to reconcile such contradictions and to reduce to unity a position which is genuinely fissured, and through this unifying, synthesising impulse have perhaps falsified the nature of his writing, which manifests ambivalences and contradictions produced by clusters of factors. Some of these relate to the psychology of political commitment, some to the exigencies of the shifting polemical situation in which he operated, of the debates in which he participated, and some to questions of genre, to the kinds of writing he adopts and, at times, to the very literariness of literature.

Milton's politics have been more persistently engaged by the critical tradition than those of any other English writer. Of course, in part the reasons lies in his political prominence – few poets have stood so close to the seat of power – and to the large body of political writing which at once invites analysis and encourages the extension of a political reading into the more obviously creative areas of the *oeuvre*. The title *Political Shakespeare*[2] may occasion a ripple of mild disquiet: the title *Political Milton* would not – nor would it ever have aroused surprise or unease, for, from his own day onwards, Milton's political commitments and his readers' perception of them have shaped responses to his writing.[3] A factor which has stimulated such interest in the development of political readings and has perhaps made matters seem simpler and such enquiry more attractive is the mass of information at our disposal. More is known about Milton than about any earlier canonical writer. Among his younger contemporaries, we find Marvell, a figure in public life for several decades, but his biography is much less well documented. Compared with Milton, John Dryden seems a ghostly shadow. Probably not until Swift do we find a major writer in English about whom we have so much information. Moreover, the information is perhaps uniquely available for interpretation. Much is there in Masson's masterly *Life*, completed in seven volumes in the 1880s. In the 1950s, French, in a singularly open and helpful way produced his five large volumes of *Life Records*, noting nearly every contemporary reference that he could find relating to Milton and much that relates to his immediate family. Parker's biography of the 1960s has in its second volume a package of meticulous documentation available for interpretation. Fletcher's ambitious *Intellectual Development of John Milton* attempts to list almost every book Milton may have encountered in his education and much he would have come across later.[4] In one sense, it is easy to write about Milton. All one requires is freely available in the chronicling of earlier investigators. The pieces stand ready for the game. And many have played, producing a multiplicity of Miltons, each profoundly reflective of the cultural and political assumptions of the interpreter. Let me briefly consider three.

First, Parker's view in the interpretative rather than documentary components of his *Milton: A Biography*, which foregrounds Milton the European humanist, making little of his connections with the native, radical milieu. Parker steadfastly resists a detailed political reading of the major poems. On Parker's account, Milton's biography is a near tragedy, averted narrowly by the *felix culpa* of the Restoration, 'the most fortunate single event in [his] life' (I, 589). Milton is represented (reasonably enough) as a consummate artist, but one afflicted with the terrible flaw of intellectual pugnacity, an aggression which came close to seducing him from what is of abiding worth (writing *Paradise Lost*) to what is marginal and transitory (engagement with the political life of seventeenth-century England). With an unconcealed impatience that is remarkable in one who toiled so long and so fruitfully in research into civil war polemic, Parker offers Milton's prose to us as a digression from his destiny: 'Today [we are] no longer much interested in ecclesiastical controversy of the seventeenth century' (I, 195); 'To modern taste the *Eikonoklastes* is a meticulous, often tiresome piece' (I, 364); 'Today no one cares' (about the scholarship displayed in *Pro Populo Anglicano Defensio*) (I, 383); etc. It is a critical stratagem which perhaps concedes too much too soon to sophomoric ennui. Parker charts the curious course of his hero, drawn persistently off-course into the wandering rocks of radical polemic, charmed by the siren song of neo-Latin controversial prose, saved by the fortuitous shipwreck of the Restoration. For Parker, Milton's prose, 'a chip on [its] sturdy shoulder', discloses 'a nature over-strong in combativeness' (I, 589), a kind of perverse predilection so close to precipitating a real tragedy. Milton belongs as an artist among artists: his polemic constitutes an explicable but regrettable falling off. The periods when Milton functioned primarily as a prose polemicist were not, Parker concedes, 'wasted years', for they contributed, in ways he cares not to specify, 'to the wisdom and artistry of his final creations' (I, 589). Poetic transcendence soars far above the mundane for Milton and the fit audience. Probably Parker's most distinctive single contribution to Milton studies, his (in my view, dubious) dating of *Samson Agonistes* as a work composed in the mid-1640s, serves *inter alia* to strip the poem of its post-Restoration political resonance (I, 317–18).

Secondly, Christopher Hill's critical biography, *Milton and the English Revolution*, offers a Milton in whom Parker's emphases are inverted.[5] Instead of the European humanist straying into polemic, Milton appears rather as one whose mature writings all reflect a profound engagement with a native radical tradition. Hill's view, of course, reflects a value system at some remove from Parker's. For Hill, radical politics of the mid-seventeenth century are not an issue which, as Parker might have put it, we don't much care about today. Nor is Hill's commitment simply a product of academic curiosity. Plainly, for him, as for many historians of the period from throughout the political spectrum, the issues which brought Englishmen in arms to Burford and to Marston Moor still reverberate in British political life. But Hill also differs from Parker in his broad conception of the man. His Milton does not blunder into politics. Instead, a progressive perception so shapes his way of regarding the world that all his mature work, in verse and prose, projects a radical dimension. Hill's readings of the major poems, the subject of the sixth and longest section of his book, see them as a working out, in a different mode, of his political concerns of the mid-century. For Hill, Milton numbers among the angels of progress. We should see him not as a Leveller or Ranter but as an unorthodox thinker 'living in a state of permanent dialogue with radical views he could not wholly accept, yet some of which greatly attracted him' (pp. 113–14).

Thirdly, Andrew Milner's *John Milton and the English Revolution* shares Hill's notion of the centrality of Milton's political activism, but he locates him rather differently within the mid-century political spectrum.[6] Far from fruitfully relating to Hill's third-culture radicals, Milner's Milton works as 'as theorist affiliated to a political party locked in mortal combat with the Levellers' (p. 106). In Milner's account, Hill has sentimentalised Milton, and in so doing has marginalised him, placing him as a quirky progressive neither unequivocally engaged with revolutionary independency nor distinct from more extreme groups. Milner responds:

Once we dispense with Hill's notion of a unitary third culture and substitute for it the notion of a class conflict between bourgeois Independents and petty bourgeois Levellers, Milton's own precise social and political location becomes much easier to situate. He is, in fact, an Independent pure and simple. (p. 199)

Perhaps fortunately, little about Milton and his *oeuvre* really is pure and simple. Nor should we be surprised or alarmed at such interpretative diversity. Each perspective is produced, among other things, by the cultural and political predilections of its authors, and it would be naive to expect anything other. However, what is most striking about Milton criticism is not only the diversity but the plausibility of the alternatives. Each in its way produces a version of Milton which is richly documented and substantiated from the text. This is not surprising given the richness and diversity of the Milton *oeuvre* and the availability and copiousness of information relating to his social, cultural and political circumstances. Each substantially unified vision has been achieved through the seemingly defensible procedures of selection and simplification. The disparities have arisen in the foregrounding (for reasons which relate to the politics of criticism) of those elements which best match the aspirations and preconceptions of the critic. Each version has been achieved at the expense of silence about that which is adverse and contradictory.

The alternative is not to hunt out yet another image of Milton, but to adopt an interpretative strategy that matches the complexities of the problems, and which reads the Milton *oeuvre* with a proper sense of its diversity and the diversity of its contexts. Mine is an argument for an opener, looser, more sceptical reading which admits the coexistence of contradictions, originating in the complexities of registral and political situations Milton negotiated and in the complexities of political psychology.

Milton's writings belong to a huge range of genres: masques, lyric poems, Latin and vernacular panegyric, classical exercises, pastoral, formal exegesis, polemic, history, drama, epic, and more – each requiring its own interpretative strategy. Different literary discourses have inscribed in them certain ideological values which cannot easily be put aside. For example, once the late Jacobean student had agreed, as Milton did, to write a panegyric in praise of the king in the form of a poem on the fifth of November, certain attitudes and postures implied in the conventions of praise were accepted as concomitants of the genre. Again, when Milton undertook, for whatever reason, to provide material for the masque to be presented at Ludlow Castle in celebration of the installation of the Earl of Bridgewater as President of the Council of Wales, certain generic assump-

tions were unavoidable. A masque which is not a celebration of courtly
virtues and the values of aristocratic society is inconceivable. David Norbrook observes that masque could retain 'a certain margin for critical
comment' (and *Comus* itself criticises a certain 'aristocratic assumption'),
yet like all Stuart masques it too celebrates 'the incarnation of divine
qualities in the persons of the courtiers'.[7] The opportunities for alternative
or subversive messages are strictly circumscribed, though we should be
alert to significant silences.

The opportunities for alternative messages are further manifest when
we come to look at the autobiographical component in Milton's writings.
Often, it seems, both in poetry and prose, he addresses his readers *in
propria persona*. However, contrary to that liberal, sympathetic interpretation we encounter in critics like Parker, we should beware of regarding
Milton's autobiographical utterances as those of some transcendent figure,
who regards clear-eyed and dispassionately the progress of world history
and articulates truths of an eternal validity. Instead, Milton's own comments are articulated in precisely determined contexts and with respect
for the inhibitions and requirements of his circumstances. As Hill has
observed, Milton works over his personal biography as assiduously as a
twentieth-century civil servant gardening the public records before exposing them to scrutiny.[8] One occasion may demand an englobing of his
own stance within a broad Puritan position; another may require an attack
on Presbyterianism in defence of the sectional interests of independency.
Then he may have needed to rest silent on third-culture radicals. Now he
wants to distance himself from any taint of proletarianism or hostility to
property.

Nor should we ignore the complexities of political psychology. Those
who attempt to develop a unifying thesis about the Milton *oeuvre* attribute
to him a degree of single-mindedness which is probably alien to most
people at most times. Fantasy and a fierce pragmatism, a romantic affection for past struggle or present ideals, personal admiration or friendship
towards people with whose politics he may disagree sharply, and conflicting polemical imperatives – all may coexist. Milton, as a major apologist
for a political tendency, as an original and heterodox exegete, and as
the towering literary figure of the period, marches – sometimes almost
simultaneously – to such different tunes that his political gait is eccentric
and his direction difficult to discern.

Conflicts of interests and situation become apparent when we attempt
the reconciliation of certain closely contemporary works. For example,
let me take the seemingly simple question that has attracted its share of
critical consideration: what did Milton think of the English working
classes in the mid-1640s? I start at *Colasterion*, a pamphlet which modern
Miltonists tend to avoid and which Hill mentions just three times, never

really giving a proper indication of its content.[9] Milton issued it in 1644 as stern punishment to the only writer who had made a book-length response to his first divorce tract. *An Answer to a Book, Intituled, The Doctrine and Discipline of Divorce* (London, 1644), published anonymously, had called Milton blasphemer, had associated him with low-class antinomianism, had criticised his use of English, and had commended his work to the hangman's fire. But in comparison with the treatment Milton received at the hands of an earlier adversary – the author of the *Modest Confutation of a Slanderous and Scurrilouss Libell, Entituled, Animadversions* (London, 1642) – this attack was almost deferential. *An Answer* acknowledged Milton's status as a prose stylist, and suggested that he had erred in his thesis about divorce because he had started from too high a notion of human nature and its potential.[10]

Milton's response to the anonymous refutation, though savage and vituperative, was not wild anger, but rather the measured cruelty of the skilled executioner. Moreover, what he has to say has considerable implications for our understanding of Milton's social assumptions and his perception of, and complicity with, his readership's preconceptions. *Colasterion* asserts the discovery that his opponent is a serving man turned solicitor, a 'fact', if such it was, which informs the whole strategy:

the chief [opponent] . . . was intimated to mee, and since ratifi'd to bee no other, if any can hold laughter, and I am sure none will guess him lower, then an actual Serving-man. This creature, for the Story must on, (and what though hee bee the lowest person of an interlude, hee may deserv a canvassing,) transplanted himself, and to the improvement of his wages, and your better notice of his capacity, turn'd Sollicter. (*CPW*, II, 726–7)

Did Olympian Milton really laugh that a working-man thought about controversial theology? Whether he did or not, the posture of amused disdain shapes his whole strategy. Note especially the way in which Milton invites his reader to share a joke among gentlemen at the expense of 'an actual Serving-man', as he calls him, a 'Servingman both by nature and function' (p. 741). Perhaps his most shocking flourish is at working-class sexual mores. His attacker had made the sober and reasonable point that Milton's divorce tract has not envisaged the need for providing for children conceived before separation but born afterwards. Milton responds that it must be a surprising development for servant girls that serving men have become solicitous for the offspring they promiscuously engender upon them: 'good news for Chamber-maids, to hear a Servingman grown so provident for great bellies' (p. 734). Milton imperiously excludes the proletariat from political or ethical debate: 'this is not for an unbutton'd fellow to discuss in the Garret, at his tressle' (p. 746), a phrase which unsqueamishly foregrounds the physical circumstances of impoverishment as if excluding the poor from political consciousness; whereas, he concludes, 'To men of quality I have said anough' (p. 742).

I had formerly regarded the evidence of *Colasterion* as a useful and perhaps even definitive index of Milton's class-consciousness and of his hostility to working men, a point I have developed elsewhere.[11] More recently, Michael Wilding, in a brilliantly argued account of *Areopagitica*, has addressed my argument and caused me to reconsider.[12] For example, Wilding examines the following passage in which Milton, who has a number of contradictory and at times rather riddling things to say about the sectaries, discusses in wholly sympathetic terms their role in perfecting the Reformation in England:

> Yet these are the men cry'd out against for schismaticks and sectaries; as if, while the Temple of the Lord was building, some cutting, some squaring the marble, others hewing the cedars, there should be a sort of irrationall men who could not consider there must be many schisms and many dissections made in the quarry and in the timber, ere the house of God can be built. And when every stone is laid artfully together, it cannot be united into a continuity, it can but be contiguous in this world; neither can every peece of the building be of one form; nay rather the perfection consists in this, that out of many moderat varieties and brotherly dissimilitudes that are not vastly disproportionall arises the goodly and the gracefull symmetry that commends the whole pile and structure. (p. 555)

Wilding comments:

> The class implications are unmistakable. A clue was given in 'we rather should rejoyce at' men reassuming the 'care of their Religion into their own hands again' [quoted from a little earlier in *Areopagitica*]; it is not aristocrats or bishops or business men who take things 'into their own hands': there is a powerful respect here for manual labourers. This is made quite explicit in the unambiguously mechanical trades that are specified in the building of the temple; people are shown cutting, squaring, hewing. These are all manual activities; there is 'spiritual architecture' . . . but no architect, only 'builders' [quoted from an adjacent passage]. The physical labours of the common people are here properly presented as dignified, noble, beautiful. (p. 16)

Colasterion had antedated *Areopagitica* by only a few weeks. I had wondered how to respond to Wilding's argument, but on reflection it became clear that, while each Miltonic exposition is capable of explanation and interpretation, neither can be demonstrated to have a transcendent validity as an expression of Milton's position on class. The contradiction is determined by a combination of factors. These in part are registral. *Colasterion* is a brutal sort of writing, a point-by-point refutation, a work of insult and invective. *Areopagitica*, which Milton rather grandly subtitles 'A Speech . . . to the Parlament of England', works persistently to elevate and transform the participants in a local and mundane political struggle to figures of heroic proportion locked in epic combat. That sectarian fellow-travellers as well as heterodox intellectuals should be thus meta-morphosed is perhaps unsurprising. Moreover, *Areopagitica* as a whole is, within the Milton canon, remarkably free from narrow and local ani-mosities of a transparent kind – though its negative subtext is there for the cognoscenti to read. Again, despite the approximate synchronism of their composition, each pamphlet meets radically different polemical requirements. In *Colasterion*, Milton is meeting the attacks of Presbyter-ians and others on more radical Puritans: attacks which sought to suggest that the radicals especially were beyond the pale of what was to be toler-ated because of their loose sexual morality and because they were not really gentlemen with a legitimate stake in the political life of the nation. Presbyterians and their allies persistently identified all independents and radical or heterodox Puritans with the fringe groups of the lower orders, equating them with Familists and Anabaptists and, rather later, with Ran-ters.[13] Milton in *Colasterion* slips that trap by rounding on a probably Presbyterian apologist and denouncing him in those same class terms which were used to traduce Milton's own position. In the case of *Areopagi-tica*, different imperatives produce a different strategy. As Wilding notes, Milton skilfully deprecates his enemies by suggesting that the difference between the orthodox and the heterodox is that the former are otiose and undynamic. This manoeuvre meshes with his argument that the English clergy, with their privileged learning ill-applied, are easily suborned and potentially treacherous. By contrast the radicals, though some indeed may be working men, are purposeful, dynamic and constructive. *Areopagitica* is ultimately a plea to be allowed to get on with the work of reformation, at least till useful lines of thought can be distinguished from hopeless ones. Milton would find it difficult to argue for his own freedom from interference without similarly pleading a toleration for others whom his enemies sought to suppress, whatever their social status. Again, the con-tradictory perspectives assumed in *Colasterion* may be explained in terms of political psychology. Milton would not be the only British radical to approve of the proletariat in the abstract and at a remove, while invoking all the privileges of class and culture to dismiss any particular working man who crossed him.

The second problem I should like to consider raises a different set of issues. As Carey notes, the following poem appears in the Trinity MS in a fair copy in the hand of an amanuensis under the heading 'On his door when the City expected an assault', which title is crossed through and 'When the assault was intended to the City' substituted in Milton's own hand, with the date, '1642', later deleted (*Poems*, pp. 284–5):

Captain or colonel, or knight in arms,
   Whose chance on these defenceless doors may seize,
   If deed of honour did thee ever please,
   Guard them, and him within protect from harms,
He can requite thee, for he knows the charms
   That call fame on such gentle acts as these,
   And he can spread thy name o'er lands and seas,
   Whatever clime the sun's bright circle warms.
Lift not thy spear against the muses' bower,
   The great Emathian conqueror bid spare
   The house of Pindarus, when temple and tower
Went to the ground: and the repeated air
   Of sad Electra's poet had the power
   To save the Athenian walls from ruin bare.

When Milton first published it, in October 1645, in *The Poems of Mr John Milton Both English and Latin*, it appeared merely headed with the roman numeral VIII as part of a series of sonnets (*Poems*, pp. 284–5).

The poem well illustrates the ideological instability of Milton's political utterances. It simulates the form of an address to royalist commanders. Plainly, it cannot refer to parliamentary troops since there is a scheme of opposition between Milton, Pindar and Euripides ('sad Electra's poet') as poets associated with beleaguered cities; and royalists, Alexander ('The great Emathian conqueror'); and Spartans as attackers (*Poems*, p. 285nn.). The argument of the poem is premised on the assumption that royalist commanders are capable of response to appeals to their sense of culture and can translate this response into control over their troops. Milton, of course, had friends and relatives in arms for the king.[14] He was, moreover, right in his seeming respect for the conduct of royalist troops, which was, for the most part, somewhat better than that of the parliamentary forces in the opening years of the war.[15] So perhaps we are to applaud a refreshing freedom from easy stereotyping on Milton's part. Yet, the poem sits uncomfortably in the Milton *oeuvre*. It is explicitly written in response to the royalist advance on London after the battle of Edgehill, a thrust that was halted when the royalists decided against engaging the London trained bands drawn up on Turnham Green in November 1642. From May 1641 through to May 1642 Milton had produced a series of antiprelatical pamphlets calling for the radical extirpation of the ecclesiastical hierarchy and the immediate reformation of the Church of England on militantly and uncompromisingly Puritan lines. It was that kind of intransigence, a hard line which he had consistently promoted, which precipitated the spiral down into civil war. Now, with the king's army outside his house, Milton declares himself Cinna the poet, not Cinna the conspirator. How may we interpret this reverse? We need not, I think, attribute it to simple pusillanimity. Fairly obviously, the social and political context of the poem is more complex than its earlier headings suggest. No-one but a fool would pin such a poem to his door in a beleaguered city, and certainly not in a city as intolerant of dissent as London had become.[16]

Instead, we must, in part, invoke some concept of literariness. Here, a lyric poem explores a binary opposition of war and the arts, resolving it in the potential of the arts for conferring immortality, rehearsing a version of the familiar topoi of the relationship of the artist to the world and to time. We should not underestimate the limitations which the imperatives of genre place upon lyric poets. But 'Captain or colonel, or knight in arms' nevertheless fits very strangely alongside what Milton had been writing and what he says later about the king and his followers. For example, in *Eikonoklastes*, he describes the men at arms who had accompanied Charles in his attempt on the five members as 'the ragged Infantrie of Stewes and Brothels; the spawn and shipwrack of Taverns and Dicing Houses' (*CPW*, III, 381–2), thus invoking the usual parliamentarian stereotype of the royalists as ill-disciplined, pox-ridden drunkards.[17]

While the dating of the poem in the context of 1642 has its own significance, what concerns me here is its ideological implications at the point at which Milton placed it before the reading public in 1645. Suppose we set it alongside his comments published in *Areopagitica* shortly before the collection of his poems, in the November of 1644:

Behold now this vast City; a city of refuge, the mansion house of liberty, encompast and surrounded with his protection. The shop of warre hath not there more anvils and hammers waking to fashion out the plates and instruments of armed Justice in defence of beleaguer'd Truth, then there be pens and heads there, sitting by their studious lamps, musing, searching, revolving new notions and idea's wherewith to present, as with their homage and their fealty, the approaching Reformation: others as fast reading, trying all things, assenting to the force of reason and convincement. What could a man require more from a Nation so pliant and so prone to seek after knowledge. What wants there to such a towardly and pregnant soile, but wise and faithfull labourers, to make a knowing people, a Nation of Prophets, of Sages, and Worthies. We reck'n no more than five months yet to harvest; there need not be five weeks, had we but eyes to lift up, the fields are white already.   (*CPW*, II, 553–4)

This is a stunning image of the comradely linking of ideologue and revolutionary fighter and of London as bastion of revolutionary fervour. So evidently Milton says rather different things at different times – albeit times that are fairly close together. But different media carry different ideological messages. In the poem, he rehearses the traditional advantages to the poet of the passive life and remarks on the transcendence of art. In the tract, he glorifies the militancy and commitment of the controversialist. Yet, the issues are still more convoluted. Milton's collection of poems appeared right at the end of the long series of pamphlets he wrote to defend his heterodox notions about divorce at will – notions which, as we have seen, occasioned his targetting by the Presbyterians and their allies as the embodiment of the sexual laxity implicit in the sects and in independency. His collection of poems relate in at least two ways to the controversies of 1643–5. Like the sonnet, it could mark an envoi, albeit temporarily, to the distasteful business of prose polemic – a business particularly distasteful to Milton, once more apparently on the losing side. Alternatively, we may relate the 1645 anthology to the problem of autobiographical image-making. As in *Colasterion*, Milton may well be constructing a self-image remote from the easy stereotyping of his enemies. All but a handful of the poems in the collection had been written quite some time before, and many express sentiments which seem curious in terms of Milton's writing of the mid-1640s. Several praise deceased bishops, for example – and not simply because they are deceased: though by 1641 and *Of Reformation* it is clear enough that for Milton the only good bishop *is* a dead bishop (*CPW*, I, 616–17). Yet, paradoxically, the collection still serves the polemical purposes of the moment. Once more, Milton offers an image of himself, as cultured humanist and timeless artist, which distinguishes him from the scruffy alternative into which his enemies laboured to compress him.

Finally, let me consider the political implications of some of Milton's publications of the early 1670s, *Samson Agonistes* and *Paradise Regained* (published together in 1671), and *Of True Religion, Heresie, Schism, Toleration, And what best means may be us'd against the growth of Popery* (published in the spring of 1673). The last is, of course, straightforwardly a political pamphlet, though one which has attracted little critical attention.[18] *Paradise Regained* and, in particular, *Samson Agonistes* have received in recent decades many subtle and intelligent readings which have been alert, among other things, to their ideological implications.[19] But I wish to examine one important area of political consideration within the texts: the question of the appropriate nature of political action for the warfaring/ wayfaring true believer in the decades of eclipse following the Restoration.

Both the poems seem to counsel a species of patience, of waiting for and reacting to events. *Samson Agonistes* assumes that previous opportunities have been squandered. Samson, recollecting past victories of an active, military kind, chides the Chorus of Danites thus:

> Had Judah that day joined, or one whole tribe,
> They had by this possessed the towers of Gath,
> And lorded over them whom now they serve;
> But what more oft in nations grown corrupt,
> And by their vices brought to servitude,
> Than to love bondage more than liberty,

> Bondage with ease than strenuous liberty;
> And to despise, or envy, or suspect
> Whom God hath of his special favour raised
> As their deliverer; if he aught begin,
> How frequent to desert him, and at last
> To heap ingratitude on worthiest deeds.   (lines 265–76)

Whatever date of composition we choose to postulate, interpretation of such sentiments from the acknowledged publication of a notorious republican must inevitably have assumed a political direction. Perhaps a trifle sulkily, the defeated criticises those who stood by and let defeat occur. 'Special favour' as an explanation of the success of the parliamentary and subsequently the republican cause recurs *ad nauseam* in the polemic of the 1640s and 1650s – as royalists on occasion remarked with chagrin.[20] Furthermore 'To heap ingratitude' understates the horrific punishment inflicted upon those regicides selected for execution at the Restoration. Among Samson's principal self-reproaches is his recognition that he has devalued the argument that God's favour is manifest in the military success of his people. He has brought 'diffidence of God, and doubt / In feeble hearts, propense enough before / To waver' (lines 454–6). At no time does Samson claim a mandate for the war he wages against the ungodly, save that of the particular imperatives of God himself, and he shows, too, a thoroughly republican indifference to any concept of the will of the people. Choric scorn for 'of men the common rout . . . Heads without name' (lines 674–9) echoes similar elitist sentiments in Milton's own republican writing (*CPW*, VII, 388). Nor does the lack of popular endorsement bother Samson, or, by implication, Milton:

> I was no private but a person raised
> With strength sufficient and command from heaven
> To free my country; if their servile minds
> Me their deliverer sent would not receive,
> But to their masters gave me up for nought,
> The unworthier they; whence to this day they serve.   (lines 1211–16)

The political action of *Samson Agonistes* is twofold, consisting in the hero's persistence in his defeated godliness – he will not accept the comfortable compromises of wife or father – and in his final murderous act. He procedes with stealth and dissimulation, acceding to the charge of the Philistian officer that he should go to the festival with the equivocal 'Masters' commands come with a power resistless / To such as owe them absolute subjection' (lines 1404–5): Samson, and Milton for that matter, owed absolute subjection to only one master. Once at the feast, Samson fakes his way into the best position to do the most damage, exploiting the 'unsuspicious' and humanitarian nature of his guards (line 1635).

The Chorus, while celebrating the victory and accepting that, were it endorsed by similar acts by other Israelites, it would lead to 'freedom' (line 1715), yet recognise the unprogrammatic nature of Samson's actions. Unpremeditated (at least by Samson), the action does not necessarily produce political change. It is, rather, 'dearly-bought revenge, yet glorious,' (line 1660) – what the rhetoric of terrorists in a later age might call 'an act of revolutionary justice'. Gloatingly, the Semichorus notes the Philistians were 'only set on sport and play' (line 1679). How would an old republican read this text? Surely, the advice would seem to be: lie low, seem reconciled to the monarchy, wait till they trust you, then kill as many as possible. While it is certainly true that the opportunities for republican insurrection or even outrages were severely circumscribed, Clark has noted: 'The impression they made was exaggerated by the romancing of secret agents and by the general nervousness of the public',[21] though not until the Rye House Plot of 1683 did former parliamentary troops intent at least on kidnapping get close to the king himself. The sort of political action that *Samson Agonistes* seems to validate is direct and unconstitutional – anything to take the shine off royalist triumphalism. It is not based on any optimistic assessment of the present position, save that God will not always permit the godly to be mocked.

The ideological orientation of *Paradise Regained* is not hard to discover. Kingship deserves less credit than does the integrity of the true believer: 'he who reigns within himself, and rules / Passions, desires, and fears, is more a king; / Which every wise and virtuous man attains' (II. 466–8), a classical sentiment, but one not ill-fitting the English republican. Milton's Christ shares the familiar Independent reservations about the validity of popular sentiment, dismissing as unworthy the praise of the 'herd confused, / A miscellaneous rabble' (III. 49–50). Milton confidently lets Satan speak – unchallenged by Christ – the most eloquent condemnation of the clergy, observing that God permits 'the hypocrite or atheous priest / To tread his sacred courts' (I. 486–7). *Paradise Regained* exhibits many of the political values and assumptions of *Samson Agonistes*. Its principal points of contradiction would seem to be the obvious ones that, whereas the play celebrates political activism of the directest kind, the brief epic appears a pacific poem. Christ has considered and rejected, as an adolescent fantasy, the resort to arms, (I. 214–26), and dismisses 'that cumbersome / Luggage of war' as 'argument / Of human weakness rather than of strength' (III. 400–2). In terms of Christ's transcendence, military victory is puny, even irrelevant. Appropriate political action consists of retaining an ethical and intellectual resolve.

Yet in a subtler and more important way *Paradise Regained* develops a position on the nature of the political task which distinguishes it from *Samson Agonistes*. The latter assumes that opportunity has been lost but,

through cunning and fortitude and with God's providence, it can be rediscovered. *Paradise Regained*, however, develops the idea that the real victory
may already have been won, with the implication that the position of the
revolutionaries in the 1670s should be more optimistically interpreted.
Consider all the episodes in the life of Christ in which Milton could have
located his victory and the regaining of Paradise. It is not the spectacularly
predicted and celestially acclaimed incarnation he selects – though that
had been the theme of his 'On the Morning of Christ's Nativity'. Nor the
triumph of the Resurrection. Nor, save most obliquely, the Last Judgement. Rather, the victory occurs in private, in debate, and is known
only to Christ and Satan, 'deeds / Above heroic, though in secret done'
(I. 14–15), and, on Milton's account, unrehearsed by previous Christian
poets. When Christ leaves the wilderness, Satan knows he is beaten,
though neither knows the timetable for his final overthrow. Time is much
an issue in the brief epic. The word 'time' occurs 25 times (compared with
3 times in *Comus*, 5 times in *Samson Agonistes*, and 38 times in the whole
of *Paradise Lost*).[22] The frequency largely reflects Satan's anxieties and
Christ's indifference to the final schedule: as Satan puts it, 'no man knows
when, / For both the when and how is nowhere told' (IV. 471–2). The
theological implications for the godly in the 1670s are clear. Christian
patience is the best resolve – victory is assured – and a strident millenarian-
ism perhaps no longer recommends itself. Only Satan is really worried
about the when and how.[23]

There are political implications too. If the role of the wayfaring/warfar-
ing Christian is in part an *imitatio Christi*, then *Paradise Regained* would
seem to offer a radically different imperative from *Samson Agonistes*. From
the latter, a pessimistic construction, comes the sanction for terroristic
outrage in an epoch of defeat. From the epic comes an alternative interpretation: that the victories which count are intellectual, spiritual and ethical,
and they have already been achieved. By resisting Satan and his cohorts
in one's own private life (and politically this must mean by refusing, in
one's heart, to accept the Restoration) the godly revolutionary has already
won the cardinal victory, though its material manifestation is nowhere to
be seen. Retaining the honest radical consciousness, without compromise,
is presented as a finer victory than slaughtering a few of the enemy.

Two years later, Milton is back to pamphleteering, offering not an
assured reserve but rather a tactical shrewdness. *Of True Religion* is Milton's contribution to the vexed and complex issues which troubled parliament and king in the opening years of the 1670s. The possibility of some
measure of toleration for dissenting Protestants had arisen as a concomitant of Charles's manoeuvres to secure a similar toleration of Catholicism.
'The Author *J. M.*', as the titlepage to the pamphlet terms him, responds
with a guilefulness redolent of his subtler works of the 1640s, briskly

redefining the eccelesiastical configuration in terms convenient to his polemical objectives. All Protestants are in some senses brothers:

> But some will say . . . God hath promis'd by his Spirit to teach all things. True, all things absolutely necessary to salvation: But the hottest disputes among Protestants calmly and charitably enquir'd into, will be found less then such. The Lutheran holds Consubstantiation . . . The Calvinist is taxt with Predestination . . . The Anabaptist is accus'd of Denying Infants their right to Baptism . . . The Arian and Socinian are charg'd to dispute against the Trinity.
>
> (*CPW*, VIII, 424)

The listing suggests a parity between the more orthodox wings of Protestantism and heterodox factions, and slides over the author's own partialities in these issues. Persistently, Milton works to speak for all Protestants: the language of 'we' and 'us' pervades, and it is a pronominalisation which englobes all non-Catholic Englishmen.[24] Milton is here assuming a rather different perspective on political action. *Of True Religion* is itself a political act, and it is one in which Milton opens up a dialogue with all Protestants, in particular those controlling the important political institutions of the 1670s. No talk now of the hypocrite or atheous priest serving at the altars of Restoration Anglicanism. More subtly comes a call to unite the broadest spectrum of Protestant belief in face of the threats of Catholicism through 'mutual forbearance and charity one towards the other, though dissenting in some opinions' (*CPW*, VIII, 435).

Milton's publications of the 1670s illustrate my thesis about the indeterminacy of his ideology. In *Samson Agonistes* and *Paradise Regained*, despite the simultaneity of their issue, we find radically different perspectives on the nature of political action and by implication on the problems facing the godly in the Restoration. One, almost wholly pessimistic, looks for the simpler rewards of revolutionary justice or terrorist outrage; the other, transcendentally, assumes the major victory to be in heart and mind and that it has already been accomplished. A little later, Milton is to be found using his old polemical skills to exploit the political moment in the interests of an immediate and relatively narrow objective. To do so, he reopens a dialogue with men whose religion he can scarcely have liked any more than he did when he savaged them in the 1640s.

NOTES

1 All references to Milton's poetry are to the *Poems of John Milton*, ed. John Carey and Alastair Fowler (London, 1968), hereafter *Poems*; references to the prose are to the *Complete Prose Works of John Milton*, ed. Don M. Wolfe *et al.* (New Haven, 1953–83), hereafter *CPW*.

2 *Political Shakespeare: New Essays in Cultural Materialism*, ed. Jonathan Dollimore and Alan Sinfield (Manchester, 1985).

3 See, for example, G.A. Sensabaugh, *The Great Whig Milton* (Stanford, 1952).

4 David Masson, *The Life of John Milton* (London, 1859–80); J. Milton French, *The Life Records of John Milton* (New Brunswick, 1949–58); W.R. Parker, *Milton: A Biography* (Oxford, 1968). Harris F. Fletcher, *The Intellectual Development of John Milton* (Urbana, 1956–61).

5 Christopher Hill, *Milton and the English Revolution* (London, 1977).

6 Andrew Milner, *John Milton and the English Revolution* (London and Basingstoke, 1981).

7 David Norbrook, 'The Reformation of the masque', in *The Court Masque*, ed. David Lindley (Manchester, 1984), p. 104; *Poetry and Politics in the English Renaissance* (London, 1984), pp. 264–5.

8 Hill, *Milton and the English Revolution*, p. 9.

9 *Ibid.*, pp. 109, 125, 133.

10 *An Answer*, pp. 14, 16, 17, 31; for the sternest criticism, see pp. 18, 28, 36–37, 41.

11 Thomas N. Corns, 'Milton's Quest for Respectability', *Modern Language Review*, 77 (1982), 769–79.

12 Michael Wilding, 'Milton's *Areopagitica*: Liberty for the Sects', *Prose Studies* 9,2 (1986), 16; rpt. *The Literature of Controversy: Polemical Strategy from Milton to Junius*, ed. Thomas N. Corns (London, 1987), p. 16.

13 Corns, 'Quest', pp. 770–2.

14 His brother Christopher was entered on the muster-roll of the royalist garrison at Reading and his in-laws were supporters of the king (*Milton Encyclopedia*, V, 135; VI, 212).

15 See, for example, C.H. Firth, *Cromwell's Army* (third edition, London, 1921), pp. 294–5, for an account of the plundering of the Reading garrison.

16 For the difficulties of London royalists in 1642, see Valerie Pearl, *London and the Outbreak of the Puritan Revolution* (Oxford, 1961), p. 7.

17 T.N. Corns, W.A. Speck and J.A. Downie, 'Archetypal Mystification: Polemic and Reality in English Political Writing, 1640–1750', *Eighteenth-Century Life* 7 (1982), 1–27.

18 See, however, Reuben Marquez Sanchez, Jr, ' "The Worst of Superstitions": Milton's *Of True Religion* and the Issue of Religious Tolerance', *Prose Studies* 9 (1986), 21–38.

19 For example, Mary Ann Radzinowicz, *Towards Samson Agonistes: The Growth of Milton's Mind* (Princeton, 1978) and Joseph Wittreich, *Interpreting Samson Agonistes* (Princeton, 1986); William Empson has a classic discussion of the ethical structure of *Samson Agonistes* in *Milton's God* (London, 1961), especially chapter 6; Hill and Milner vigorously debate the political aspects of both poems.

20 For example, Lady Halkett's comments in *The Memoirs of Anne, Lady Halkett and Ann, Lady Fanshawe*, ed. John Loftis (Oxford, 1979), p. 60.

21 Sir George Clark, *The Later Stuarts 1660–1714* (second edition, Oxford, 1955), p. 57.

22 *A Concordance to Milton's English Poetry*, ed. William Ingram and Kathleen Swaim (Oxford, 1972), s. v. 'Time'.

23 For a pertinent discussion see Michael Fixler, *Milton and the Kingdoms of God* (London, 1964), especially chapter 6.

24 Consider: 'Shall we condescend to dispute with them [i.e., Catholics]?'; 'To

save our selves therefore, and resist the common enemy, it concerns us mainly to agree within our selves, that with joynt forces we may not only hold our own, but get ground; and why should we not?'; 'This is the direct way to bring in that Papistical implicit faith which we all disclaim'; etc. (*CPW*, VIII, pp. 432, 436, 437).

7 'Mysteriously divided': Civil War, madness and the divided self

The self is a text – it has to be deciphered . . . the self is a project, something to be built.
                                                            Susan Sontag, *Under the Sign of Saturn*

I

AT THE TIME of the army's occupation of London, in August 1647, a pamphlet appeared in the guise of a petition to parliament. Entitled *Englands Mad Petition* it claims to represent 'above 12 millions of well-affected (before so ill-distracted) people of all sorts, Ages, Sexes, and Sises'. The purpose of the pamphlet was to achieve the 'enlargement of Bedlam, and other respective places in the cities of *London* and *Westminster*, with other cities, Towns, and Boroughs, throughout the kingdom'. Why, amidst the political tumult of the summer of 1647, should it have been thought necessary to present such a request? The pamphlet explains. England has been transformed into a national mad-house. The ties of 'Proximity, Consanguinity, Affinity, Alliance, Christianity, Vicinity, or Naturall Affections' have been destroyed. Instead, 'an (almost) universall lunacie and apostasie from God and our Kinge' has taken place. The only remedy, the pamphlet continues, is to turn the lunatics out of Bedlam and admit the genuinely insane – the English nation.[1]

Englands Mad Petition is no more than one of any number of such documents which have come down to us from the revolutionary period. It deals with a theme familiar to any political propagandist. Behind the mask of facetious parody, it presents an image of a nation caught up in a kind of mass-suicide, intent on self-destruction. The anonymous author adopts the pose of the voice of reason struggling to be heard amidst the cacophony of contending faction. It is not, it need hardly be said, evidence for a widely held belief that, in the summer of 1647, England had, in reality, gone mad.

Yet, this mock-petition highlights certain themes which are the concerns of this chapter. It hints at the way in which the language of madness or un-reason can be located within the political discourse of the period. Madness can be associated with opposition to the king, itself a form of irreligion. The petition illustrates, too, how the actual processes of civil war, the denial of seemingly natural affiliations such as the claims of neighbourhood, local allegiance, or familial relationships, can be easily assimilated under the general heading of 'lunacie'. Finally, it establishes with heavy-handed irony a figure with which we are familiar in the literature of the period – the figure of the sane individual who seeks to reatreat from a world of chaos and disorder.

In exploring these themes I hope to keep in mind the idea of the political dimension to the charge of insanity. Historians of psychiatry have become increasingly aware of such a dimension, in part as a reaction against (though on occasion in favour of) the work of Foucault, specifically his *Madness and Civilization*. As Roy Porter and others have noted:

The history of madness is now self-consciously being written not just as the history of disease or affliction, but as the story of power relationships – paternalistic, legal, institutional, therapeutic, commercial.[2]

Or, as Klaus Doerner writes of the later seventeenth century:

Insanity . . . must unquestionably be seen as a political issue in the broadest sense of the word . . . contemporary medical approaches and practitioners were strongly influenced by the concepts of the emergent bourgeoisie.[3]

To that bourgeoisie, in the late summer and autumn of 1647, it may well have seemed that the charge of insanity was an appropriate response to the ideological turmoil which was to produce *An Agreement of the People*, and, in October, the Putney Debates.

The language of madness in the seventeenth century is, though, double-edged. To accuse an individual or a group of being 'mad' is, as Fiona Godlee has noted in the context of Quakerism, to 'disqualify and invalidate their claims' to be heard.[4] Conversely, to speak with the voice of madness, to adopt the pose of insanity, is to speak from a privileged position, one we might associate with Edgar in *King Lear*. Christianity itself has long countenanced the belief that certain types of madness represent a peculiar form of grace. As Screech has observed, Erasmus, in translating Matthew 11:25 and Luke 10:21, has Jesus thanking the Father for revealing the mysteries of faith not to *nēpiois* (infants) but to *stulti* (fools). The idea of a 'holy madness' presents particular problems to the Renaissance psychiatrist. 'Any christian doctor' Screech continues:

treating what he took to be madness had to take great care to ensure that he was not resisting the spirit: that he was not, that is, treating as organically mad an enraptured lover of the living God.[5]

Two discourses of madness, both of which have political implications, are thus available. In one form the charge of madness acts to silence the deviant or aberrant voice. In the other, paradoxically, madness is discovered as a means of investing the word with divine authority and power. We can see these two contrasting discourses of madness struggling with one another in the revolutionary period, reflecting the ideological confrontations of the war itself. John Taylor, for example, the royalist 'water poet' discovered in madness what he termed an 'emblem of these times' when, in 1642, he published his *Mad Fashions*, a popular wood-cut showing a series of images which reverse the natural order of experience (rats chase cats, horses whip carts, etc.). Such images, he claims, 'plainly doth declare / This Land (Quite out of Order) out of Square'.[6] In 1644 Taylor characterised the war itself as 'the maddest mad rebellion, / That ever story told'.[7] The theme of national madness is taken up in another pamphlet, published in 1647, under the title *Universall Madnesse*, composed, so the anonymous author claims, specifically for London but which 'may generally serve for the use of the whole kingdom'.[8] The imprisoned royalist Sir Francis Wortley, however, adopted that other discourse of madness when, in 1648 he adopted the role of Mad Tom and wrote a twelve stanza royalist ballad praying for 'distracted England's restauration to her wits again'.[9] The news-sheets, too, frequently resorted to the familiar theme of lunacy. *Mercuricus Melancholius* for the last week in October 1647, for example, claims that he has been woken by the babble of 'fooles and madmen' roaming the streets, whilst *Mercurius Democritus*, as late as August 1653, claims to bring news from the 'Antipodes, Manggy-land, Tenebris, Faery-Land, Green-land, and other adjacent countries' to the 'right understanding of all the Mad-merry people of Great Bedlam'.[10]

The other, privileged form of mad discourse, one that Christopher Hill has termed 'radical madness', might be represented by the anonymous author of *Divinity and Philosophy Dissected and Set Forth by A Mad Man* published, supposedly, at Amsterdam in 1644.[11] Here madness acts as a liberating voice: To be a 'fool and mad-man to the world' is yet to be 'in my wits and right mind to God' (Sig A2v). More famous is William Erbury's *The Mad Mans Plea* of 1653, an attack on the Baptist minister Edmund Chillenden. Erbury's mocking voice adopts the mask of madness not, I think, as Hill suggests of this and similar texts, in order to 'express dangerous thoughts under cover of insanity or delusions' (Hill, p. 282). The disguise is too easily pierced. Instead these texts remind their audience of the truly radical Christian tradition of 'Holy foolishness'. 'Not onely *Paul*' writes Erbury, 'but *Christ* was counted *mad* . . . the reason is the wisdom of God is Foolishness with men. 1 *Cor*. 1: 18. *Act*. 26: 25.'[12]

What picture can we now construct from this babble of mad discourse? Hill offers a literal possibility of 'mental breakdown' as a 'form of social protest'. Again, that some of those who wrote as lunatics were genuinely insane is possible, though I find it rather more doubtful to believe that it was 'the effort to grasp new truths' which sent them mad (Hill, p. 279). Michael MacDonald's influential work, *Mystical Bedlam*, on the other hand, offers a perhaps more convincing account of madness in the seventeenth century, and one which attends more completely to the language of madness. 'By the early seventeenth century' MacDonald writes, 'the language of madness had become rich and pervasive; words and phrases about insanity were part of the common coinage of everyday speech and thought'.[13] The discourse of madness is thus readily available, waiting to achieve its fullest expression in the confrontation of the war itself. After the war a new attitude to madness, in England, becomes apparent. 'Secular interpretations of the signs of insanity' begin to emerge and 'lunatics lost their places as members of a household and aquired new identities as the victims of mental diseases' (MacDonald, p. 2). The war thus stands as the climax and the watershed of lunacy. John Aubrey, looking back to the 1640s, remembers that vast numbers of 'Abram-men' or 'Toms O'bedlam' (the patients discharged from Bethlem hospital and licensed to beg) were a common sight 'Till the breaking out of the Civil Warres'.[14]

II

To speak of the language of madness is, inevitably, to invoke the language of contemporary psychoanalytic theory. Psychoanalytic ideas of fragmentation, division, and dislocation may prove helpful in understanding the 'mad discourse' of the revolution, though they are terms with which historians have, traditionally, remained uncomfortable.[15] Writing in the late 1950s, R.D. Laing's still influential account of the self encountered in schizophrenia provides a useful point of departure. Laing claimed that any idea of the self possessed by the subject is not 'an inviolable strong-hold against ontological doubts and uncertainties'. He continued:

If the whole of the individual's being cannot be defended, the individual retracts his line of defence until he withdraws within an inner citadel. He is prepared to write off everything he is except his 'self'. But the tragic paradox is that the more the self is defended in this way, the more it is destroyed. The apparent eventual destruction and dissolution of the self in schizophrenic conditions is accomplished not by external attacks from the enemy (actual or supposed) . . . but by the devastation caused by the inner defensive manoeuvres themselves.[16]

Tempting as it is to adopt this description of the self caught up in the process of dissolution as a metaphor for the body-politic in England in the 1640s, it is Laing's discussion of the idea of a withdrawal to protect the self which actually hastens the self-destructive movement with which

I am here concerned. In Lacan's terms, a withdrawal into the self is not only self-defensive, but central to our thinking about the 'self' as a subject. Lacan uses the image of a fortress, encountered in dreams, as fundamental to the symbolic formation of the 'I'. Within this architectural structure, the subject 'flounders' in quest of a 'lofty remote inner castle'.[17] Such a quest may also be thought of as an attempt at escaping from surfaces which are unstable only to encounter fragmentation at a deeper level. So, Deleuze, describing schizophrenia and language, recalls how Freud, in *Metapsychology*, emphasised the 'schizophrenic aptitude for perceiving the surface and skin as if each were pierced by an infinite number of little holes'. 'From this' Deleuze writes:

comes the schizophrenic way of living contradictions: either in the deep cleavage that traverses the body, or in the fragmented parts of the body which are nested in each other and whirl about. Body-sieve, fragmented body, and dissociated body form the first three dimensions of the schizophrenic body – they give evidence of the general breakdown of surfaces.[18]

The breaking apart, or breaking down, of surfaces might present itself as a means of describing the ideological crisis of the civil war period, or, indeed, the general 'crisis of order' which, as David Underdown has sought to demonstrate, can be traced back to the early seventeenth century.[19] But I have in mind here Stephen Greenblatt's analysis of late Renaissance culture as being informed by what he terms a 'virtually fetishistic emphasis on manner' which helps to create 'an integrated rhetoric of the self'.[20] To say of this sense of identity that it is challenged under the conditions of civil war might seem axiomatic. Yet, the psychoanalytic model suggests that it is not so much what happens outside the subject which precipitates breakdown (e.g. Hill's pressure of radically unthinkable ideas), so much as it is the very processes of retreat into an internal world in an endeavour to preserve a unified sense of selfhood which brings about the crisis.

We are familiar with the idea of a retreat into the self as it is encountered in the poetry of Marvell and his contemporaries. Indeed, Marvell's 'The Garden' might stand as paradigmatic of the poetry of retreat and withdrawal. The mind, in Marvell's poem, 'withdraws into its happiness' – a happiness which involves the annihilation of all external reality. For Marvell's contemporary, the Laudian royalist divine Joseph Beaumont, the Civil War is also a period of retreat. Exiled from Cambridge by what he calls the 'turbulence of these times' the withdrawal results in him writing one of the longest poems in the English language – the twenty-canto *Psyche* – as a remedy for 'meer idleness'. But it is also a remedy for that kind of retreat into defensive architectural structures which is encountered in his short poem entitled, simply, 'Home':[21]

> observe thy breast
> There alone dwells solid rest.
> That's a close immured Tower
> Which can mock all hostile power.[22]

The mind may become, as Lacan suggests, a fortress, fixed in a world of drifting co-ordinates, but the act of entrenching the mind within the fortifications of self may, paradoxically, hasten the very dissolution which the self is struggling to evade. Knowing yourself, to adopt the familiar Renaissance adage, might entail destroying yourself.

For evidence of this self-destructive inwardness, I would point to a poem such as Lovelace's 'The Snail', where the snail is held up to be a 'sage' and 'wise emblem' of the political world because it possesses the ability to be within its own 'self curl'd'.[23] But the snail's retreat fails utterly to preserve itself from dissolution. Nature shrinks from it, familial relations are confused by it, as are questions of gender and origin: 'Thou thine own daughter then, and Sire' Lovelace writes:

> That son and mother art intire,
> That big still with thy self dost go,
> And liv'st an aged embryo;   (p. 136)

Unable to give birth or be born, the snail's dwelling becomes its 'tomb' within which its 'dark contemplation' of the outside world ends only in its final dissolution into 'jelly'. The 'analys'd king' who appeared to be both church and state has become a substance whose surface is viscous and unsettled – a dissociated body.

Lovelace's posthumous volume of poems *Lucasta* of 1659 abounds in images of self-dissolution, fragmentation, and penetration. The erotic 'In allusion to the *French-Song N'entendez vous pas ce langue*', for example, concludes with a stanza which manages to combine all three dimensions of Deleuze's schizophrenic body:

> Know then I would melt,
> On every limb I felt,
> And on each naked part
> Spread my expanded Heart,
> That not a vein of thee,
> But should be fill'd with mee.
> Whil'st on thine own Down, I
> Would tumble, pant, and dye.   (p. 125)

Whilst the poem entitled 'To Lucasta' imagines, in conclusion, a self-fragmentation which metonymically preserves only one organ:

> Then let me be
> Thy cut Anatomie,
> And in each mangled part my heart you'l see.   (p. 132)

In the song 'In mine own Monument', a disembodied retreat into the self, not unlike that of the snail, is imagined:

> In mine own Monument I lye,
>   And in my Self am buried;
> Sure the quick Lightning of her Eye
>   Melted my Soul ith'Scabberd, dead;
> And now like some pale ghost I walk,
> And with anothers Spirit talk.
>
> (p. 149)

The soul, resting in the body like a sword in the scabbard, or like the self buried in the self, is melted and dissolved. The poem 'The Duell', which imagines the poet and Love in aristocratic combat, opens with a strange evocation of the body and the self divided from one another: 'Love drunk the other day, knockt at my brest, / But I, alas! was not within'. Discovering the body to be empty, Love proceeds to vandalise it, an outrage which the self discovers on returning, informed by 'My man, My Ear'. Fragmented body and absent self gather together in order to fight Love, but even once this recompaction has been effected, the poem is still caught up in exploring images of airy dissolution. Stabbing at Love, Lovelace writes, 'I nothing touch'd but a fantastick flame'. The more directly political 'Mock-Song', which evokes the ultimate image of cleavage in the 1640s, that which took place in Whitehall in the January of 1649, imagines the universe itself has undergone a transformation:

> Now the *Sun* is unarm'd,
> And the *Moon* by us charm'd,
> All the *Stars* dissolv'd to a Jelly;
>
> (p. 155)

and the body politic, like the body of the king, is metamorphosed into a structure which has lost its organic integrity:

> Now the *Thighs* of the Crown,
> And the *Arms* are lopp'd down,
> And the *Body* is all but a belly.
>
> (p. 155)

It is, however, to 'The Snail' that we must return in order to investigate further the political dimensions of 'mad discourse'.

III

'The Snail' alerts us to another aspect of the divided or fragmented self which has important psychological and political implications. For in confusing familial relations, the snail has, in seventeenth-century terms, failed to pass the first test of sanity. The inability to recognise parents, family, near kin, was taken as being a clear sign of lunacy. A further sign of mental abnormality was the failure to acknowledge 'superiors', a failure which the Quakers, in their refusal to doff the hat, and in their adoption of the familiar 'thou' form in dealing with social superiors, were accused of.[24] 'Rebelliousness', Michael MacDonald writes, was taken as 'a clear sign of mental disturbance' (MacDonald, p. 126). Such a sign should not, perhaps, be surprising in the context of a society in which the patriarchal authority of the king is reflected in the patriarchal hierarchy of the family.[25] To refuse to acknowledge one's father is but a short step from refusing to acknowledge the king.

The language with which insanity is described is, in the seventeenth century, a consciously political language. A treatise on suicide (or to use the preferred seventeenth-century term, self-murder) published in 1637, opens with a dedicatory verse which expresses a wished-for psychological and political unity: 'From *Albion* (whence now we *all* be *one*)'. But such unity is challenged by the very idea of self-murder which the author of the treatise, John Sym, describes in the following way:

If *parricide* be a *grievous Sinne*, as wilfully to kill our own *parents*, children, wives, husbands, etc. who are distinct *persons* from *ourselves* much more is *self-murder* abhominable. For, by *unitie*, things are preserved; and individuals are principally *one*: and therefore if individuals be divided against themselves, the world cannot stand . . . things shall cease to be true.[26]

Self-murder challenges the very concept of a unified subject or, politically, body of subjects. It entails a splitting in two of that which, in the naturall order of things, should be indivisible. The subject, Sym continues, becomes 'both . . . active and passive . . . and so a mans *Selfe* becomes his own executioner'. It was the absence of doctrinal unity, according to one pamphleteer, which drove John Hobson, at one time Prebend of Ely Cathedral, to suicide. Hobson's choice was to halt 'between two religions, the Protestants and the Papists' from whence he 'fell headlong into dispair', and killed himself. Hobson is cited by the author (one T. S.) as an example of 'distractions' caused 'by the copiousnesse of sects'.[27]

Suicide in the seventeenth century was not, however, seen as necessarily an act of insanity. It was, also, a civil and religious crime. Penalties were exacted from both the living and the dead. The suicide was tried posthumously, declared a felon, and moveable goods forfeited to the king's almoner (MacDonald, p. 132). As a crime it existed within a political context. This is made clear in Sir Mathew Hale's *Historia Placitorum Coronae – The History of the Pleas of the Crown*. Hale, Lord Chief Justice of the Court of the King's Bench until shortly before his death in 1676, left a manuscript of his *History of the Pleas of the Crown* which, though it was not published until 1736, contains a clear statement of seventeenth-century legal *practice* in relation to madness, lunacy and idiocy.[28] Suicide, or 'self-killing or felo de se' is defined as a crime 'where there is no other offender but the sufferer'. Two types of suicide can be identified: 'felony of a man's self' and 'pure accident'. The first kind, 'felo de se' is: 'where a man of the age of discretion, and *compos mentis* voluntarily kills himself by stabbing, poison, or any other way'. It is defined as a felony, because, Hale continues:

No man hath the absolute interest of himself, but 1. God almighty hath an interest and propriety in him, and therefore self-murder is a sin against God. 2. The king hath an interest in him, and therefore the inquisition in case of self-murder is *felonicè et voluntariè seipsum inter-fecit et murderavit contra pacem domini regis.*[29]

Suicide, in other words, disturbs the king's peace, and, at the same time robs the king of his interest in the body of his subject. Hence the confiscation of the suicide's material goods – a recompense exacted by the wronged monarch.

Suicide can be thought of as the most extreme form of self-division which theologians had identified. The idea of a double or divided self was by no means foreign to mid-seventeenth-century writers. For the popular Puritan divine, Richard Sibbs, writing in 1635, self-division is the rule rather than the exception. 'We carry that within ourselves that, if it be let loose will trouble us more than all the world besides.' Each individual is thus in a state of potential rebellion against unified authority. Human nature itself is Janus-like:

we must conceive . . . a double self, one which must be denied, the other which must denie; one that breeds all disquiet, and another that stilleth what the other hath raised.[30]

'Everyone feels that he is a single person' Descartes wrote in 1643, but to the theologians the divided individual was the rule.[31] Pierre Charron, in *De La Sagesse* (1601) had argued that man is a creature 'made of parts quite contrary and enemies to themselves'.[32] Similarly, Thomas Brightman, the Puritan Divine who claimed to have written his commentary on the Apocalypse under divine inspiration, argued in his posthumous *The Arte of Self-Deniall* (1646) that the individual must always be on guard against him/herself.[33] The independent divine, Thomas Goodwin, who attended Cromwell on his deathbed, saw the self as actively pursuing a species of interior dialogue with itself. Thoughts, he wrote in 1643, are 'those talkings of our mindes with the things wee know . . . those same parleys, enterviews, chattings, the mind hath with the things let into it'.[34] The anonymous *Treatise of Self-Denyall* which appeared in 1646 takes the problem into the realms of speculative theology. Taking the text of Matthew 16: 24 ('If any one will come after me, let him deny himselfe') the author endeavours to define what 'selfhood' amounts to. Only God, it is concluded, has genuine selfhood: '*God* is *of* and *by Himselfe* . . . Therefore that *He alone* claims Selfnesse (as I may terme it) to himselfe'. For the human being there exists 'no such thing in *rerum natura* . . . but onely in *corrupt opinion* and *desire*'. Instead, humanity is plagued with a 'double self to be deny'd of us; one *absolutely Evill*, and ever to be *Deny'd*; the other Evil only in some cases'.[35]

For Richard Sibbs, the existence of the double self engages each individual in violent confrontation with him/herself. In an endeavour to recapture the unified subject, Sibbs proposes violent ideological struggle. We cannot form any kind of accommodation with the rebellious self, or 'parlie with it and devide government for peace sake'. Instead we must 'strive against it, not with subtlety and discourse, so much as with peremptory violence silence it' (Sibbs, 143–4). In the divided self, only one part may speak, and discourse with the rebellious self give way to the violent assertion of hierarchy whose end is 'silence'.

As Andrew Wear has noted, the workings of the mind were of intense interest to Puritans in particular, given what he terms the 'institutionalization' of the believer's 'inner anxiety' under Calvin.[36] But to see this discourse with the self resulting in 'silence', as Sibbs argues, is, perhaps, a rather more unfamiliar manifestation of Puritanism. Silence was, of course, to become of importance to later Quaker practices, but, as Gillian Alexander says, it is more normal, now, to think of the period of the revolution as a 'time of noise'.[37] Yet, Sibbs's violent struggle with the self, a struggle which can admit of no form of accommodation or compromise, was to find its poetic equivalent in a poem of the 1640s already alluded to – Joseph Beaumont's *Psyche*.

Psyche, composed during Beaumont's enforced absence from Cambridge following the Earl of Manchester's visitation of the university in 1644, was published in 1648. In the poem, the overt political confrontations of the 1640s are transformed into an internalised drama of the human soul.[38] Psyche's realm, the personality, is in disarray. Her kingdom has become 'shapeless'. Disruptive rebellious forces, stemming from within, have been allowed to overthrow reason, encourage the rebellion of the will, and capture Psyche's one ally: *logos* or the word.

But the greatest of all Psyche's *political* errors, her own grand self-betrayal, is to parley with the rebels. She seeks a compromise with the disruptive forces of the personality, and she is left deluded. From this delusion she must be rescued by heavenly intervention, the 'soul-subduing art' of true (that is, Laudian) religious practice. It is this intervention which is the poem's main theme. However, when we recall the date of the poem's composition (between 1645 and the spring of 1648), it is not difficult to read the text as offering an overt political warning to Charles I.

In the poem, the 'great deceit' of Love is to persuade Psyche to accept compromise: to 'divide government'. This compromise sets the seal to Psyche's misery:

> Laws and Sovereignty, the Life and Health
> Of every Heav'n-descended State, must bow
> Unto Plebian wills: (V. 164)

Compromise and negotiation – of the kind which had been fruitlessly entertained at Uxbridge in 1644–5, at Newcastle in June 1646, and which Cromwell and Ireton had hoped to achieve in late 1647 based on the *Heads of the Proposals* – represent, for Beaumont, a defeat of the state whose ultimate sanction is divine rather than human.

It is not so much the political allegory of *Psyche* which concerns me here, however, as it is the transformation of political confrontation and conflict into an internal conflict within the human personality. Psyche's realm is not just a divided kingdom, but rather it is a representation of the state or personality fractured into multiple factions. The integrity of the individual has been destroyed from within to produce what the poem terms a 'monstrous *Hydra's* shape' – a formless reversal of creation which 'throws the world back to its Breeding heap' (V. 165). As Sibbs had observed some ten years earlier: 'We carry that within ourselves that, if it be let loose, will trrouble us more than all the world besides'. Rebellion, we might conclude, may take place internally as well as in the external world of affairs, as the great self-divided figure of Milton's Satan was to discover in 1667.

IV

The theme of the double-self, and the image of the monstrous creation which is the result of the inability to keep in check the potentially disruptive forces of the personality are to be found repeatedly in royalist poetry of the period. In Lovelace's second poem on the snail, entitled 'Another', a procession of mythical double figures is introduced into the poem – the centaur, the siren, the 'mixed sphynx', the 'renown'd Hermaphrodite' – before the snail is, once more, fixed upon as the double figure, and a sick one at that:

> Yet the Authentick do beleeve,
> Who keep their Judgement in their Sleeve,
> That he is his own Double man,
> And sick, still carries his Sedan: (p. 138)

For John Cleveland, defender of Newark against the Scots in 1646, double figures and what Parfitt terms 'monstrous unities' exerted a strange

kind of fascination.[39] His poem 'Upon an Hermaphrodite' (one of two
poems Cleveland was to compose on such a theme), struggles to uncover
in the hermaphrodite a 'perfect Dialogue', a unified discourse informing
every 'heteroclite part'. But, writes Cleveland, 'Ravel thy body, and I
find':

> In every limb a double kind.
> Who would not think that head a pair
> That breeds such factions in the hair?[40]

In the second hermaphrodite poem 'The Authors Hermaphrodite', Cleveland imagines that his verse is hermaphroditic, but the mixing of forms
does not produce anything other than a superficial unity. The hermaphrodite is 'I'th body joyn'd, but parted in the head' (*Poems*, p. 17).

That the English body-politic should be 'joyn'd' but was, in reality,
'parted in the head' represented for Lovelace, Cleveland and Beaumont,
that 'aggressive disintegration of the individual' described since by Lacan,
but enacted, for them, on the political level. Such a disintegration, on
the psychological level, Lacan has suggested, is manifested in dreams of
'disjointed limbs . . . organs represented in exoscopy, growing wings and
taking up arms for intestinal persecutions' (Lacan, p. 4). For the royalist
writers of the 1640s the taking up of arms for 'intestinal persecutions' was
a dream that had become reality. Such a disintegration of the seventeenth-
century polity was to become the theme of Cowley's abandoned epic, *The
Civil War*, the text with which I should like to conclude this discussion.

After the war, when Cowley looked back on the events which had
taken place, and on his own attempts to transform them into the matter
of epic, he discovered that 'silence', of the kind recommended by Sibbs,
was the appropriate response. The preface to the 1656 edition of Cowley's
Poems describes the abandoned project in language which accords with
Laing's modern description of the self in a schizophrenic condition,
though its subject is political and intellectual surrender. Cowley acknowledges that 'we have submitted to the conditions of the *Conqueror*' and the
task is now to:

lay down our *Pens* as well as our *Arms*, we must *march* out of our *Cause* itself, and
dismantle that, as well as our *Towns* and *Castles*, of all the *works* and *fortifications* of
Wit and *Reason* by which we defended it.[41]

The mind's retreat into architectural structures must be terminated if any
kind of political or psychological unity is to be rediscovered. Cowley's
own attempt at recovering such a unity is represented by his decision to
'burn the very copies' of his poem which sought to memorialise the war.
Political expediency? Perhaps, but his own term for this act of destruction
is 'punishment'. This punishment involves a double erasure, since it was

the poem's endeavour to erase all memory of that rebel-self which, for Cowley, was plaguing England. The irony, in 1656, would appear to be that the rebel-self is the force which has triumphed, and forced Cowley into 'silence'.

This effort at erasure is in keeping with the text's situation of the conflict before the battle of Newbury in September 1643 (the point at which the poem abruptly ends) within a rhetoric of madness and self-division. The poem opens:

> What rage does England from it selfe divide
> More than seas doe from all the world beside?[42]   (I. 1–2)

Geographically divided from the world, and psychologically self-divided, England's 'rage' can be understood as a distinct form of madness. 'Rage' – a 'brevis furor' – was held to be worse than ordinary madness since it was a passion entered into 'wittinglye and willinglye'.[43] The rage of civil war, then, is a peculiar form of frenzy, one that is a species of voluntary madness or, as Cowley writes 'Into war we scared ourselves' (I. 123).

The conflict of war is also a conflict between psychological models. One model is unified, integrated and royalist, the other disjointed, factionalist and republican. A rhetoric of unity is thus opposed to a rhetoric of division, an opposition made clear in the king's speech before the battle of Newbury: 'Yow all one Church binds close' Charles says to his troops, but 'More Sects then Squadrons fill their spotted host' (III. 295–6). The 'spotted Host' (spotted with what? disease? sin? party-coloured factionalism?) are an opposition of monstrous and divided figures, carefully listed in all their variety by the text. Indeed the length of this description (some 120 lines of text in Book III) is an index, drawn from the tradition of the epic catalogue, of the anti-royalists' variegated natures. They are monstrous and divided figures motivated by images of rebellion which 'Softly, as Dreames . . . steale into every head' (III. 10). Dreams and sickness confront health and self-knowledge, as the king, again, tries to indicate:

> They for wild dreams which from sick fancies flow
> Which may they o'recome, if yet themselves doe know.   (III. 293–4)

The monarch, here, is appealing to an ideal of wholeness and sanity which places the ensuing conflict on a psychological plane. Not only must the Battle of Newbury be fought and won, but a battle in the heart and mind of each rebel-self must also be won if the nation is to be restored to psychological as well as political health.

In Cowley's text, though rebellion is enacted within each individual rebel, the origins of rebellion are to be located in the influence of the spirit Alecto, an inhabitant of hell. Alecto is a divided figure, androgynously both male and female, she/he possesses a double-face, one 'virgin-like' the other 'grisly black of hew' (II. 404–5). Alecto can be identified with the Fury of that name, a daughter of Zeus, who, in the *Aeneid* (VIII. 323ff.) is a protean figure, able to drive individuals insane. In the *Iliad* (XIX. 91–4) she is Atē, described by Homer as 'flitting through mens heads', and she reappears in Book IV of *The Faerie Queene* as 'mother of debate' that 'many a publicke state / And many a priuate oft doth ouerthrow' (IV. 1. 19). In Spenser's account her double nature and figure are pains-takingly described. She has a 'lying tongue' which is 'in two parts divided' so that her speech is always bifurcated. Her heart, similarly, is 'doubly' guided, as are her senses. Her physical configuration is 'unequall' and 'deformed'. She is, in other words, a traditional epic figure, but one whose form is culled from the language of dreams of self-disintegration.

'If individuals be divided against themselves, the world cannot stand' wrote John Sym. In 1646, the playwright James Shirley, protégée of the Earl of Newcastle, and habitué of court circles, saw his re-telling of the Narcissus myth which had been published as *Echo; or the Unfortunate Lovers* in 1618, re-published under the title *Narcissus, or the Self Lover*. It is not, I think, mere coincidence that, in 1646, the emphasis should shift from Echo to the figure of Narcissus. For Narcissus is the counter-part of Alecto/Atē. Lost, he is 'endeavouring my selfe to finde' a quest which ends only in the discovery of 'the shadow of my selfe' which leaves him 'Mysteriously divided . . . / Halfe in the water, halfe upon the land' – a true amphibian.[44]

In the period of the Civil War, to be mysteriously divided is to see one's sense of selfhood under threat both externally and internally. The war becomes a psychological as well as a political confrontation, and the lan-guage of self-division is appropriated in order to explore that confron-tation. These texts also indicate the ways in which those who witnessed or took part in that war sought to understand it as being more than a break-down in the institutions of government. In exploring this language of self-division they also are seeking to find causes for the conflict which lie within their own individual psyches. The opposition of armies, factions, regions, ideologies, theologies, classes and literary texts, has been and will continue to be the chief means by which we comprehend the events of the mid-seventeenth century. But an investigation of the psychological dimensions of the revolution begins to uncover, paradoxically, a political reality which each generation has to re-learn. There is no retreat (*pace* Marvell's green thoughts in green shades) from the world into another world of the mind's making. The self is no place to hide.

NOTES

1 Anon., *Englands Mad Petition* (London, 1647), title-page and p.3 BL TT, E. 404 (30).
2 W.F. Bynum, Roy Porter, Michael Shepherd, eds., *The Anatomy of Madness: Essays in the History of Psychiatry*, 2 vols. (London and New York, 1985), I, p. 2.
3 Klaus Dorner, *Madmen and the Bourgeoisie: A Social History of Insanity and Psychiatry*, trans. Joachim Neugroschel and Jean Steinberg (Oxford, 1981), p. 24.
4 Fiona Godlee, 'Aspects of Non-conformity: Quakers and the Lunatic Fringe', in Bynum *et al.*, *The Anatomy of Madness*, II, p. 80.
5 M.A. Screech, 'Good Madness in Christendom', *ibid.*, II, p. 34.
6 John Taylor, *Mad Fashions, Old Fashions, All out of Fashions* (London, 1642) sig. A2. BL TT, E. 138 (30). The illustration is the familiar wood-cut *The World Turned Upside Down* (London, 1647), BL TT, E. 372 (19).
7 John Taylor, *Mad Verse, Sad Verse, Glad Verse, and Bad Verse*, (London, n.d.), BL TT, E. 46 (13). A note in Thomason's hand records the date as 10 May 1644.
8 Anon., *Universall Madnesse: Or A New Merry Letany* (London, 1647), title-page, BL TT, E. 412 (14).
9 Sir Francis Wortley, *Mad TOM a Bedlams desires of Peace* (London, 1648), title-page, BL TT, 669 f (12) 59.
10 *Mercuricus Melancholicus* 9 (Saturday 23 Oct. – Saturday 30 Oct. 1647) sig. A2. BL TT, E. 412 (13); *Mercurius Democritus* 68 (Wednesday 10 Aug. – Wednesday 17 Aug. 1653), title-page, BL TT, E. 711 (3).
11 Christopher Hill, *The World Turned Upside Down: Radical Ideas During the English Revolution* (Harmondsworth, 1972, rpt. 1978), p. 282.
12 W. Erbury, *The Mad Mans Plea* (1653), p. 2. On the idea of 'Christian madness' see Screech, 'Good Madness in Christendom'; George Rosen, *Madness in Society: Chapters in the Historical Sociology of Mental Illness* (London, 1968), p. 155.
13 Michael MacDonald, *Mystical Bedlam: Madness, Anxiety, and Healing in Seventeenth Century England* (Cambridge, 1981), p. 123. For further discussion of madness in the early modern period see: V. Skultans, *English Madness: Ideas of Insanity 1580–1890* (London, 1979), ch. 2; John G. Howells, ed., *World History of Psychiatry* (London, 1975), pp. 184–9; Michael MacDonald, 'Religion, Social Change, and Psychological Healing in England 1600–1800', in W.J. Sheils, ed., *The Church and Healing* (Oxford, 1982), pp. 101–25.
14 John Aubrey, *Naturall History of Wiltshire* (Wiltshire Topographical Society, 1848), p. 89, cited in Rosen, p. 153.
15 See Peter Gay, *Freud for Historians* (New York and Oxford, 1985), pp. 6–41.
16 R.D. Laing, *The Divided Self: An Existential Study in Sanity and Madness* (Harmondsworth, 1965, rpt. 1984), p. 77.
17 Jacques Lacan, 'The Mirror Stage as Formative of the Function of the I as Revealed in Psychoanalytic Experience', *Ecrits*, trans. Alan Sheridan (London, 1977), p. 5.
18 Gilles Deleuze, 'The Schizophrenic and Language: Surface and Depth in Lewis Carroll and Antonin Artaud', in Josué V. Harari, ed., *Textual Strategies: Perspectives in Post-structuralist Criticism* (London, 1970), pp. 286–7.

19 David Underdown, *Revel, Riot, and Rebellion: Popular Politics and Culture in England 1603–1660* (Oxford and New York, 1987), pp. 40–3.

20 Stephen Greenblatt, *Renaissance Self-fashioning: From More to Shakespeare* (Chicago and London, 1980), p. 162.

21 Beaumont's autobiographical comments can be found in Joseph Beaumont, *Psyche: or Loves Mysterie* (London, 1648), 'The author to the Reader' sig. A4. References to the poem are to this edition.

22 Joseph Beaumont, *Original Poems in English and Latin* (Cambridge, 1749) p. 8.

23 References to Lovelace's poetry are to C.H. Wilkinson, ed., *The Poems of Richard Lovelace* (Oxford, 1930).

24 Godlee, 'Aspects of Non-conformity', p. 77–8; Hill, *The World Turned Upside Down*, p. 283.

25 Lawrence Stone, *The Family, Sex and Marriage in England 1500–1800* (Harmondsworth, 1979) pp. 109–45; Jonathan Goldberg, 'Fatherly Authority: The Politics of Stuart Family Images', in Margaret W. Ferguson, Maureen Quilligan, Nancy J. Vickers, eds., *Rewriting the Renaissance: The Discourses of Sexual Difference in Early Modern Europe* (Chicago and London, 1986), pp. 3–32.

26 John Sym, *Lifes Preservative Against Self-killing* (London, 1637), p. 54.

27 T.S., *The Arminian Haltered* (London, 1641), p. 1 BL TT, E. 166 (9).

28 For a discussion of Hale's work see Nigel Walker, *Crime and Insanity in England*, 2 vols. (Edinburgh, 1968), I, pp. 35–6.

29 Sir Mathew Hale, *Historia Placitorum Coronae: The History of the Pleas of the Crown*, 2 vols. (London, 1736), I, pp. 411–12.

30 Richard Sibbs, *The Soules Conflict with Itself and Victory over Itselfe by Faith* (London, 1635), p. 143. Passages from this work can be found in Richard Hunter and Ida Macalpine, eds., *Three Hundred Years of Psychiatry 1535–1860* (London, 1963).

31 Letter to Princess Elizabeth of Bohemia, 28 June 1643, in Descartes, *Philosophical Letters*, ed. Anthony Kenny (Oxford, 1981), p. 142.

32 Cited by Kitty Scoular Datta, 'New Light on Marvell's "A Dialogue Between the Soule and the Body" ', *Renaissance Quarterly* 22 (1969), 254–5.

33 Thomas Brightman, *The Art of Self-Deniall: or, A Christian's First Lesson* (London, 1646), p. 13 BL TT, E. 1203 (1).

34 Thomas Goodwin, *The Vanity of Thoughts Discovered with their Danger and Cure* (London, 1646), p. 5 BL TT, E. 57 (4).

35 Anon., *Heutonparnumenos or A Treatise of Self-Denyall* (London, 1646), p. 25 BL TT, E. 336 (8).

36 Andrew Wear, 'Puritan Perceptions of Illness in Seventeenth Century England', in Roy Porter, ed., *Lay Perceptions of Medicine in Pre-Industriall Society* (Cambridge, 1985), pp. 56–7.

37 Gillian Alexander, 'Politics of the Pronoun in the Literature of the English Revolution', in Ronald Carter, ed., *Language and Literature: An Introductory Reader in Stylistics* (London, 1982), p. 218.

38 On the circumstances in which *Psyche* was published, see P.G. Stanwood, 'Joseph Beaumont – A Portrait of Stuart Orthodoxy', *Church Quarterly Review* 165 (1964), pp. 27–39.

39 George Parfitt, *English Poetry of the Seventeenth Century* (London, 1985), p. 130.

40 John Cleveland, *Poems* (1653), p. 13.

41 Abraham Cowley, *Poems* (London, 1656), sig. A4.

42 Abraham Cowley, *The Civil War*, ed. Alan Pritchard (Toronto, 1973). All references to the poem are to this edition.

43 John Downame, *Spiritual Physicke to Cure the Diseases of the Soule* (1606) in Hunter and Macalpine, *Three Hundred years of Psychiatry*, p. 56. For Renaissance classifications of the kinds of madness, see Andrew Boorde, *Brevary of Health* (London, 1557), fols. 75–92; Philip Barrough, *The Method of Physick* (London, 1596) chs. XV and XXVII.
44 James Shirley, *Narcissus, or the Self Lover* (London, 1646), p. 14 (st. 53), p. 26 (st. 99), p. 26 (st. 101).

PART IV

Interpreting the present

8 Marvell's 'Horatian Ode' and the politics of genre

'AN HORATIAN Ode upon Cromwell's Return from Ireland' has played a central part in twentieth-century discussions of the relationship between poetry and politics. The poem has often been applauded for avoiding political partisanship, for maintaining an equal balance between Charles and Cromwell, between the arts of peace and war, between feudal and bourgeois orders, and so on.[1] But as critics have begun to situate the poem more closely in its historical context, that 'balance' has become harder and harder to locate. The 'Ode' is grim, witty, exuberant, explosive, savage, elliptical, elegiac, apocalyptic, but not balanced and transcendent. It is a poem urgent with the pressure of a particular moment in Marvell's life and in English history, a moment when the future seemed to lie not with monarchy but with a republic. As Blair Worden has shown, this was a Machiavellian moment: the fledgling republic was in danger, and it was essential to seize the occasion of decisive action or the cause would be lost.[2]

It is because, in the end, the cause was lost that the Ode's political complexion has often been misread. Jerome McGann has argued that 'all literary works . . . are inhabited by lost and invisibilised agencies', and that 'one of the chief functions of criticism is to remember the works which have been torn and distorted by those losses'.[3] Interpretations of Marvell's Ode, and, indeed of the Revolution itself, have exemplified such losses.[4] From the right, it has often been argued that the foundation of the republic was an aberration from a monarchism otherwise naturally ingrained in the English people – the term 'interregnum' represents the events as standing quite outside the normal temporality of British history. From the left, the revolution has been seen as installing a regime of ruthlessly competitive bourgeois individualism and the internal repression of the bourgeois subject.[5] But the political and discursive regimes installed after 1660, with their renewed aristocratic ethos, were not quite those the Revolution had fought for, with long-standing consequences for British culture.[6]

If that is so, then we should be wary of reading the Ode as simply poised between old and new orders, and should be alert to ways in which the failure to establish a distinctive republican culture in Britain may have distorted its reception. For reasons that will be discussed later, the Ode does not seem to have been published in 1650. After the Restoration, Marvell, like so many public figures, was anxious to minimise the degree of his involvement with the Commonwealth; it was in their interest to present themselves as motivated by a pragmatic loyalism rather than anything as doctrinaire as republicanism. For a brief moment the Ode again seemed about to become timely at the time of the exclusion crisis in the early 1680s, when Marvell's poems were posthumously printed. The publisher, Robert Boulter, allegedly 'did not question to see the monarchy reduced into a commonwealth and very speedily'; but he apparently changed his mind over whether this would happen speedily enough for it to be safe to print the Cromwell poems, and they were dropped.[7] Thus for a century and a quarter after the poem's composition, Marvell's image as a zealous Protestant patriot was untarnished by republicanism. The Cromwell poems were not published until the auspicious republican year of 1776, when James Barry issued an engraving showing Marvell, Milton and other patriots saluting the phoenix of liberty arising across the Atlantic.[8] But by this time the tradition of Marvell the unwavering monarchist was so strong that it could be used by a circular process to read back into the Ode itself.

And by then the tradition of public poetry and political rhetoric that went back to the early Renaissance was nearing a climacteric that was also to lead to its eclipse, in the reaction against the French Revolution. That reaction, which has moulded the idiom of modern literary studies, involved a reaction against rhetoric, against public political poetry in the name of inner integrity. The long-term result was the privileging of Marvell's lyrics over his public poetry and prose. Equally significantly for the interpretation of the Ode, the Romantic period saw also the eclipse of the idea of genre, of poetry as performing a particular kind of public action, and the emergence of the notion of the poem as a timeless artefact standing above the debased world, and expressing an individual sensibility that would be repressed by strict generic categories. Charles himself, the royal actor, becomes in this tradition an emblem of the lost autonomy of the artefact. Hazlitt, knowing the poem only by report, thought of it as an elegy for Charles, while Hartley Coleridge, initiating the tradition of balanced opposites, said that the poem could be either a satire or a eulogy of Cromwell.[9]

In the heyday of the New Criticism such 'balanced' readings were to become the norm. There have always been dissenting voices, especially from historians; Christopher Hill long ago argued that the poem enacted a move towards Cromwell rather than contemplative neutrality.[10] Such interpretations, however, have been liable to criticism as historical readings which fail to take account of the poem's literary qualities. The terms of that antithesis need challenging: it is precisely by sharpening the analysis of the poem's formal properties beyond a narrow conception of the 'literary' that it becomes possible to return it to history. Recent scholarship, in regaining an understanding of rhetoric and genre, has become better equipped to understand the links between poetry and politics.[11] Rather than seeing the Ode as pure literature, and Marvell as an isolated genius transcending lesser poets who wrote mere propaganda, it becomes possible to recover the role of the poem's generic acts in a far wider cultural movement. In the analysis of the poem as act, many questions remain to be answered: Marvell's own personal allegiances and the circumstances of the poem's production and reception remain obscure. I believe, however, that the hypothesis of the Ode as radically revisionary opens the way to making more sense both of the poem and of its context.

Both parts of the poem's title arouse royalist expectations. In giving the bald generic characterisation 'Horatian Ode' – as far as I know uniquely – Marvell evoked the royalist admiration of Horace, with his cult of peace under a worthy emperor. In an Ode of 1630 Sir Richard Fanshawe celebrated Charles's preservation of the peace while 'warre is all the world about'.[12] Marvell himself had written a monarchist Horatian Ode, a close imitation of the second ode of the first book which he contributed to a volume of panegyrics in 1637.[13] In the aftermath of the Second Civil War there had been a resurgence of royalist Horatianism, and Fanshawe's Ode was one of many ceremonial poems from the 1630s which were published as a loyal gesture in the period leading up to the regicide. The other element in the title, the reference to a return, is also a strong generic signal. Renaissance rhetoric recognised a distinct kind of demonstrative or panegyrical oration, a celebration of a hero's return, a *prosphonetikon* or *epibaterion*.[14] Horace's odes were regularly classified in Renaissance edition according to panegyrical genres: for example, the fourth ode of the fourth book, long recognised as one of Marvell's chief models for his Ode, was classed as a *prosphonetikon*.[15] The second and third decades of the seventeenth century saw a proliferation of poems in this genre: Oxford and Cambridge were issuing more and more volumes of commendatory verse to commemorate royal births and also royal returns: Charles's return from Spain in 1623 and his returns from Scotland in 1633 and 1641.[16] The word 'return' appeared prominently in such volumes; and it took on broader significances, as the king was hailed as returning or restoring the realm to a lost golden age.

Some critics have taken this use of royalist forms to indicate that Marvell is balancing royalist poetry against Puritan politics; or, more radically, that he is using the Horatian echoes to undermine and obliquely satirise

Cromwell.[17] It is often assumed that Marvell began as a royalist and remained sympathetic to that position down to 'Tom May's Death'; Wallace argues that he was consistent to the end in preferring government with a monarchical element. But we need to be wary about constructing an unproblematic grand narrative of Marvell's career: in a period of massive political upheaval, major discontinuities may have marked personal and poetic histories.[18] If the Ode evokes royalist genres, it is in order to subvert them, to return English poetry to a truer course. For the 'balanced' or royalist readings tend to take at face value the claim that Renaissance culture was essentially royalist and centre on whether he is vindicating that culture against Cromwellian anarchy or saying a sad farewell to it. But it all depends what is meant by the Renaissance, and by culture.

Renaissance humanism centred on the recovery of classical texts; and deeply engrained in some of the most prestigious texts was an enthusiasm for republican liberty and a disdain for monarchy as a primitive and superstitious form of government. For the more radical humanists, then, the restoration of classical culture was not a narrowly literary matter. Roman eloquence had reached its height with Cicero the defender of the republic, and under the Empire it had become flabby and ornamental, debased by courtly flattery.[19] In the *First Defence of the English People* Milton immodestly compared himself to Cicero and pointed out that he had the advantage of a happier theme for his eloquence: whereas Cicero's story had ended tragically, with the senate disregarding his warnings against rule by one man, the English had been able to reverse this outcome and move from monarchy to republican liberty. A *Tragedy of Cicero*, published in 1651, pitted a virtuous Cicero against a corrupt and devious Octavius.[20] Machiavelli had linked this decline with larger social causes; the selfishness of the nobility which grabbed more and more land, leading to a polarisation between an easily manipulated propertyless multitude and an idle nobility which had bartered political liberty for a luxurious life on its country estates. As J.G.A. Pocock has shown, the Machiavellian analysis was developed in the 1650s both by Harrington and, in a very radical direction, in the newspaper *Mercurius Politicus*. It was symptomatic of the thinking in this period that Harrington, in his translation of Virgil's eclogues, should have taken for granted a rudimentary sociology of literature, pointing out that the changes in land-holding alluded to in the first eclogue were to lead directly to the establishment of the debilitating feudal order which must now be swept away.[21] Maecenas after all earned much of the enormous wealth which he consumed so conspicuously from confiscations from defeated republicans, the kind of confiscation to which Horace owed the substantial estate he liked to present as a modest country farm.

In the context of Marvell's Ode, it is particularly interesting that the politician who did most to win poets to the republic, Henry Marten, should have attempted to revise the cult of Horace. It was Marten who gave a classical cast to the iconography of the new republic, proposing that before the statues of the king were taken down their heads should be struck off in imitation of Brutus's mutilation of the images of Tarquin, and devising the aggressively final inscription 'Exit Tyrannus Regum Ultimus'. A more thoroughgoing republican than the Levellers, Marten risked their hostility in 1649 to support Cromwell as the only effective agent for getting rid of the monarchy. He remained suspicious of Cromwell's ambitions, however, and in 1653, when Cromwell dissolved the Long Parliament, Marten wrote a poem in protest. His 'Antepod[um] Horatian[um]' was a direct inversion of Horace's most celebrated epode, the second, 'Beatus ille qui procul negotiis', which had been translated by Jonson and echoed by innumerable cavalier poets. Horace praises the life of rural retirement; Marten inverts Horace's opening to attack retirement as a cowardly shunning of public business:

> Ignavus ille qui sepultus ocio
> (Vt bruta gens animalium)
> Materna bobus rura vexat pigrior,
> Inhians decuplo foenori
> Rostris ineptus, impar et se iudice
> Civis, cliensq[ue] civium.[22]

(Cowardly, slothful is he who buried in leisure, like the brute race of animals, more sluggish than his oxen, vexes his mother lands, gaping for tenfold increase, unfitted for the rostra, even in his own judgement unequal to a citizen, and a dependent of citizens.) This poem turns upside down the values of aristocratic Horatianism in the name of civic humanism: Marten entitled it 'Vitae civicae laudes'.[23]

For classical republicans, in fact, the problem with Renaissance culture was that it had not yet happened, in the sense that there had not been a full return to the central principles of the Roman republic; instead, there had been various botched compromises with feudal institutions and monarchical superstition. It was the commonwealth, not the monarchy, that permitted a true return to the golden age, a true renaissance, a true restoration. Marten seems to have been responsible for the inscription on the Commonwealth's seal: 'in the first year of freedom by God's blessing restored'. All these words overlap with the term 'revolution', which also had the sense of returning to origins, of restoring. But there was an important difference between restoring a recent status quo and restoring some very distant and half-mythical era: in that sense, the word 'revolution' was already acquiring its modern connotations.[24] There was even talk of reforming the entire calendar, in anticipation of the French revolutionary regime, and some books were dated according to the years of the restoration of liberty.[25] When taxed in parliament with the outrageousness of presenting the abolition of the monarchy as a 'restoration', Marten cheekily replied that 'there was a text had much troubled his spirit for severall dayes and nights of the man that was blind from his mother's womb whose sight was restored at last'.[26]

Marten urged the new regime to recruit writers who would disseminate this view of a possible cultural revolution and to show clemency for former royalist poets who might be won round. This campaign was at its height at the moment when Marvell was probably writing his Ode, in June 1650, when Marchamont Nedham started the aggressively republican journal *Mercurius Politicus*. The recruitment of prominent writers was important for the regime's national and international prestige. It is true that the number of committed republicans was small, but hindsight has tended to diminish the degree of support the new regime could begin to muster. Amongst those who rallied to the cause was the veteran Spenserian George Wither; interestingly, in January 1651 he directly recalled Caroline *prosphonetika* in a collection of poems celebrating the regicide:

> It fareth, now with me, as on that *morning*
> Which, first, inform'd us, of his *safe returning*

– that is, Charles's return from Spain in 1623.[27] Payne Fisher wrote several volumes of pompous neo-Latin panegyrics.[28] A far more prestigious champion for the new regime was John Milton; and his example would have been most significant for Marvell, whose early verse is full of echoes of the 1645 *Poems*. Milton had recently glorified the regicide, Cromwell, and the Irish campaign in his *Observations upon the Articles of Peace* (published in May 1649), polemically contrasting the language of republican 'fortitude and Magnanimity' with courtly flattery.[29] Not only the political content but the form of Marvell's poem has Miltonic analogues: for Milton too was experimenting with revisions of Horatian poetic models. He ended his *Second Defence* with a quotation from the last ode of the third book, adapting Horace's claims for the immortality of his odes to his own panegyric of the republic, whose foundation in his view surpassed any of the political feats Horace had celebrated. Milton's sonnets of the 1640s and 1650s adapt the Horatian ethos to new political circumstances.[30] And Milton seems to have seen the odes through the eyes of didactically minded critics who presented him as a *sacerdos*, a poet-priest who summons readers to civic virtue and whose own linguistic skill is a pattern of the discipline demanded of the citizen.[31] Marvell's Ode needs to be seen in the context of these attempts at a radical rethinking of the politics of poetry and of classical culture; its tone is not that of a merely pragmatic loyalism. Marvell's title has complex associations: he both criticises royalist Horatianism as falling short of classical standards of public responsibility and to some extent criticises Horace himself and revises him in a republican direction.

To illustrate this point it will be necessary to analyse Marvell's inversion of the generic expectations raised by the title in five main areas. Generic patterns were never rigid, and a considerable degree of deviation from the norms laid down in rhetorical handbooks was expected; but the norms of the *prosphonetikon* had been made particularly prominent by the orchestrated chorus of adulatory verse in the first part of the century.

The revision begins very strikingly with the opening, the *exordium*. In an extreme literalisation of the conventional declaration of modesty, the poet presents the very writing of his own poem as a deviation from the political imperatives of the moment. In Horace's *prosphonetika*, and still more in Caroline panegyric, the hero's return is normally a signal for conflict to end and the arts of peace to revive. In direct contrast, Marvell's forward youth is urged to turn from the shadows, from 'Numbers languishing'.[32] As A. J. N. Wilson has pointed out, Roman poets in militaristic vein often censured the shadowy 'vita umbratilis'.[33] 'Languish' was a potent term in republican vocabulary, going back to Cicero and associated with the opposition between republican activism and monarchical lethargy.[34] John Hall, an ambitious young poet who went to Scotland in the summer of 1650 to support Cromwell's campaign, warned recalcitrant Scots monarchists that despite its superficial peace and elegance Caroline society had been rotten at the core: courtiers knew how to lull the people asleep 'with some smal continuance of peace (be it never so unjust, unsound, or dangerous) as if the body politick could not languish of an internal disease, whilst its complexion is fresh and chearful'.[35] Before Marvell's triumphal poem has begun the youth is already setting off, so that the *prosphonetikon* turns into a *propemptikon* for Cromwell's departure to Scotland. It is only at the very end of the poem, when Cromwell is imagined as setting off, that the poet addresses him directly. This is in the first instance an *occasional* poem, responding to a particular, and very real, crisis: Charles was on his way to Scotland, and if his alliance with the presbyterians succeeded the republic would be in grave danger. Marvell is not necessarily making a general claim that war is superior to peace, but he is appealing to the Machiavellian idea of the armed citizen (Marten had raised his own force during the Second Civil War without consulting parliament). When liberty is in danger, retirement is irresponsible.

After the *exordium*, the *prosphonetikon* would be expected to continue with an analysis of the hero's birth, education and character. In his portrait of Cromwell, Marvell radically revises the kind of idealised image of authority to be found in Caroline panegyric: indeed, by inserting a portrait of Charles, Marvell heightens the contrast between monarchical man and republican man. Caroline panegyric idealised the figure of the monarch, making him a living embodiment of transcendental justice and of the unity of the body politic; Caroline odes and masques constantly identify the royal family with mythological figures. This idealisation goes with a strong sense of social as well as aesthetic decorum. Marvell presents Charles in such terms – he is comely, he fastidiously disdains the vulgar, the common, the mean. By contrast, Marvell emphasises that Cromwell climbs up from a relatively modest position – though he confutes royalist attacks on him as base-born by placing him in a gentlemanly garden. For the socially conservative, 'industrious' was a condescending term; but Blair Worden has pointed out that 'industrious Valour' might be a translation of Machiavelli's *industria* and *virtù* and the Machiavellian usage may lie behind the prominence Marvell gives in his poem to the simple word 'man': 'Much to the Man is due', 'So much one Man can do'.[36] Whereas monarchs rely on the ornamentation of high rank to beautify their actions, Cromwell is all the more impressive because he draws on elemental human qualities. This fact is heightened by a very striking absence: there is no classical mythology. Of course Cromwell is not presented in merely human terms, he fulfils a divine will, but it is made clear that he does so by opening himself to a mysterious and transcendent force rather than by occupying a traditional divinely sanctioned role: he is a bolt flung from above, the force of angry heaven's flame.

In human terms, however, Cromwell emerges as someone far from the conventional panegyrical frame of reference. Some writers have tried to fit the praise of Cromwell into the conventional encomiastic categories of the four cardinal virtues, but it takes a struggle.[37] He is valiant in war, but in the context of Caroline panegyric, to value military courage so highly as to describe the arts of peace as 'inglorious' would have come as a shock. His prudence amounts to deviousness, 'wiser Art': Marvell accepts the claim put about by royalists that he deliberately manipulated Charles's escape. His temperance is pushed to the point of being 'reserved and austere', terms which in royalist discourse would have connotations of puritanical preciseness. And justice, the final cardinal virtue, is made to plead against Cromwell. Some critics therefore see the poem as ambivalent, or as a satire on Cromwell the Machiavel.

Such readings, however, take it too easily for granted that Marvell would reject a Machiavellian frame of reference. One royalist described Marvell as a notable English Italo-Machiavellian, and Worden has shown that it is worth taking this description seriously. While most defenders of the republic couched their argument in merely pragmatic terms, a few, recognising that the legality of the regicide was highly dubious, argued that a radical revision of conventional political categories was necessary, that an orthodox moral vocabulary was often no more than a mask for social conservatism. Marvell makes Cromwell break out of the frame of conventional panegyric, of the rhetoric of praise and blame: as Patterson emphasises, it is in the context of a panegyric that we are told that it would be madness to blame him.[38] Hall similarly revises traditional language in *The Advancement of Learning* (1649):

For discomposition of the present frame, may not, I pray this be a Topicke for any Government, though never so ill grounded, never so irregular, or never so Tyrannicall? Should we sit still, and expect that those in whose hands it is, should quietly resigne it, or new-mould it themselves, or some fine chance should do it to our hands? or should we not out of this very reason, if our houses were all untiled and obvious to all injuries of the weather, forbeare to pull them down or mend them, because we would make no alteration, and so continue in our miserable patience, because we feare a change and some trouble . . . or should we expect that some Deity, or unthought of influence would rescue us from these inconveniences which we saw, but would not remove? I am afraid whether any can be serious upon this question: For as happinesse is the reward of courage and industry; so what ever people ever yet obtained any Reformation without sweat or wounds, and a just violence to the over-ruling power; just I say, though it clashed with the letter of some *Positive* Law for with the *Fundamentall* and true ends of government it could not. But there is no need in this case to urge this so hard to you [Parliament], who so nobly brake through this objection, and redeemed the supreme power.[39]

Hall uses one particular significant word of the new regime: he says that it nurtures 'men of sublime mindes'.[40] In 1652 Hall published the first English translation of Longinus's late-classical treatise on the sublime. In his dedication to Bulstrode Whitelocke, a patron of Davenant's 'reformed' drama, he reminds him that Longinus discusses the theory that rhetoric flourishes best in conditions of political liberty. Though he concedes that 'the corruption of time hath diseas'd most Governments into Monarchies', Hall implies that the republican sublime may revive under the commonwealth.[41] Hall believed that what he called 'this turne of time' was capable of a 'noble alteration': the 'highest spirits' were 'pregnant with great matters . . . labouring with somewhat, the greatnesse of which they themselves cannot tell'. This 'great and . . . restlesse Genius' of the time would bring forth many a 'sublime and elevated spirit'.[42] Longinus makes a central distinction between artistic effects which are merely skilful and competent on the one hand and the magnanimous or sublime on the other: sublimity, he declares, 'wheresoever it *seasonably* breaks forth, bears down all before it like a whirlwind'; sublime poets '*burn* up all before them'; Demosthenes '*thunder-strikes* and in a manner *enlightens* the Oratours of all ages'.[43] Marvell's portrayal of Cromwell burning through the air aims at this kind of sublimity – a height, indeed, somewhat above Horace himself. This notion of the English Revolution as something sublime, something that transcends conventional modes of expression, was widespread: in his *Second Defence of the English People* Milton says that the establishment of the republic transcends all the deeds of the ancients even if he is not able to find the words fit to describe it.[44] Learning after the Restoration that Milton had written some 'admirable panegyricks, as to sublimitie of wit', on Cromwell and Fairfax, John Aubrey eagerly sought them out: even if they were in praise of the devil, "tis the *hypsos* [sublime] that I looke after'.[45]

Marvell heightens this sense of Cromwell as a force that can scarcely be contained within conventional forms by his use of metre. Renaissance humanists tended to regard rhyme as one of the feudal barbarisms which they wanted to abolish, and made some vain attempts to restore the classical metres of unrhymed quantitative verse. Rhyme became a symbol of the courtly corruption of language under the later Empire, tinkling sound as opposed to moral sense. Milton, who denounced rhyme as a symbol of bondage in a prefatory note to *Paradise Lost*, had as a young man attempted an unrhymed translation of a Horatian ode. Marvell admits rhyme, but his metre is nonetheless exceptionally terse, particularly because the semantic level accentuates the impression of the necessary rigours imposed by the form. Cromwell is consistently seen as breaking out of closed spaces: nature must make room for him, he casts kingdoms into a new mould. At times his energy makes the syntax break down altogether: 'And with such to inclose Is more then to oppose'. Marvell keeps in reserve until line 114 the longest word in the poem, 'indefatigably', which almost fills up its line. And there is a pointed contrast with Charles, who *can* be contained within his form: Cromwell, with his net, chases him into Carisbrooke's narrow case, and Charles, in an almost languishing gesture, bows down in those short couplets that end his life, as if upon a bed. Charles may seem to be identified with the arts of peace, Cromwell with the arts of war, but in fact Cromwell, who can know as well as act, is constantly associated with artistic emulation: he blasts Caesar through his laurels, stages Charles's performance on the tragic scaffold, he is the bold architect of the new state. If Cromwell is the republican sublime, Charles is the courtly beautiful; Marvell is establishing a similar relationship between his forebears the cavalier poets and the new and more innovative genre of poetry he is now founding.[46] In this sense, it could be argued that by giving a favourable portrait of Charles, Marvell makes his poem more rather than less radical: monarchical culture is weighed at its own highest self-valuation, as the source of grace, decorum, elegance, exclusiveness, and found beautiful but limited.

The poem thus rejects the Caroline aestheticisation of politics. But may not the celebration of Cromwell's sublimity be merely a new and potentially just as authoritarian aestheticisation, reducing the complex forms of political agency to a cult of personality? As Wilding points out, Marvell plays down the Leveller viewpoint. All the same, he goes into more considerable constitutional detail than would be expected in an encomium. Horace had left the precise relations between Augustus and the senate discreetly vague, but Marvell insists that Cromwell is concerned not with his own glory but only with the state's: he presents to the Commons not only the kingdom of Ireland but also his own fame, and his campaign is shown as a firmly republican one. The more conservative members of the Rump were indeed hesitant about using the word 'republic' and preferred the blander 'commonwealth'; Cromwell himself had long hesitated before deciding that the king must die. But Marvell insists on the way in which the traditional political order has been overturned. Machiavelli had argued (*Discourses*, I,9) that only a single decisive individual could achieve radical constitutional change. Having arranged the decapitation of the king, the head of the body politic in the old political language, Cromwell lays a kingdom at the feet of the Commons, the 'feet' who have now abolished their monarchical 'head'. The prominently placed word '*Republick*' is reinforced by '*Publick*' eight lines later. Cromwell has left his 'private Gardens' to serve the public; but it will be necessary for the public to exercise their political responsibility, ensuring that he does not continue to pursue his private interests now that he exercises such influence, growing 'stiffer with Command'.

This context gives an unconventional edge to the old maxim:

> How fit he is to sway
> That can so well obey.

These lines can be taken as proposing that Cromwell should run for king. But the conventional maxim gains a new, paradoxical force in a republican context: the more prince-like he is, the more virtue resides in renouncing kingship and serving the republic. This idea is reinforced by the falcon analogy. Earlier in the poem Cromwell had been the hunter, Charles the hunted animal; now the republic is the hunter, Cromwell its tame falcon. Falcons are not always so easy to lure back: one could read the word 'sure' at line 96 in a number of tones. The analogy condenses the uneasy respect with which republicans viewed Cromwell at this stage.

That unease is also, perhaps, reinforced by the poem's unusual metrical tensions, which function as an analogue of the necessary tensions that maintain republican liberty. Machiavelli had argued that a certain element of disorder strengthened a state, that Rome had been greater when there was an element of popular participation and unrest and declined into lethargy when this challenge was lost. John Hall argued against the idea that monarchy was the best form of government because most unified: in a republic, 'among many joynt Causes, there may be some jarring, yet like cross wheels in an Engine, they tend to the regulation of the whole'.[47] Even when celebrating Cromwell more unequivocally in *The First Anniversary*, Marvell was to retain this emphasis on structural tension, contrasting the republican 'resistance of opposed Minds' with the authoritarian unity aimed at by conservative monarchs, more 'slow and brittle then the *China* clay'.[48] If Cromwell's sublime energy resists the confining forms of an older and more conservative poetry, Marvell's metrical austerity, the counter-pull of the terse six-syllable couplets, implies the need for a severe counter-discipline to resist energies that may potentially become dangerous to the state.[49]

Such implicit reservations should not be overplayed, however. The poem is an encomium and its heroic mode prevails over the caricature of Cromwell as a monomaniacal social climber which had been propagated by royalists and was being taken up by the Levellers. The fact that Marvell nonetheless feels it necessary in the name of this new republican ethos to engage with opposing views may explain why as far as we know the poem was not published in 1650. It gives too much credit to Cromwell to please many parliamentarians and radicals, but is too Machiavellian and republican to please Cromwell. And before long Marvell was to enter the service of Fairfax, who had opposed the Scottish war, so that he would have had little incentive to publish it: the poem's moment was a very brief one.

The next section of the *prosphonetikon* would conventionally be an analysis of the deeds of the returning hero. But Marvell's narration is highly unconventional. He plunges into the narrative:

> So restless *Cromwel* could not cease
> In the inglorious Arts of peace
>   But through adventurous War
>   Urged his active star.

The account of what he actually did, however, is oblique in the extreme: scholars still dispute the exact meaning of the densely metaphorical description of the lightning breaking through the clouds. The lightning metaphor is then continued to give an indirect description of the regicide at lines 23–4. The poem then turns back on itself to describe Cromwell's life before he became a soldier, but this retreat is used to point the contrast with the speed and force of his emergence, and we move again to the regicide at lines 34–6. Then we move back again to a narrative of the civil war campaigns, before turning yet again to the events leading up to the regicide; and here Marvell makes a striking concession to royalists by suggesting that Cromwell deliberately engineered Charles's escape from Carisbrooke. It is as if the regicide is a topic that keeps breaking through the muffled syntax that seems to obscure it. In rhetorical terms, however, the poem is not an equal balance between Cromwell and Charles: syntactically and structurally, the description of the regicide is a digression. The poem could certainly have glided over the event as the most desperately controversial and perhaps unpopular act of the new regime, and turned pragmatically to the Irish conquests as something that would unify a broad section of English opinion; instead, Marvell enacts a process of facing up to difficult and perhaps unpalatable truths even in an encomium. We are made to sympathise with the doomed king: the infinitely regressive pain of

> with his keener Eye
> The Axes edge did try

is terrifying. But the poem gives the reader the impression of facing the fact of regicide coolly and unflinchingly, after earlier evasion, and this comes as a kind of emotional release, a surge of energy as the poem moves on, having been able to accommodate the tragic within the panegyrical.

The main event marked by the poem, the Irish campaign, formed a striking contrast with the triumphal returns of Charles I, particularly his return from Scotland in 1641. On that occasion rebellion had just broken out in Ireland. Many recent historians have argued that the panic over the 1641 Irish rebellion, fuelled by Pym, was the leading factor in precipitating political disputes into open war. But the university panegyrics for Charles's return blandly ignored the scale of the crisis: the poets prophesied that the king would bring peace like Venus from the Irish seas and even suggested that the rebellion was to be welcomed as a recreation which would allow Charles to keep his sword free from rust.[50] Cromwell's situation in 1650 turned Charles's situation in 1641 upside down: where Charles was returning from an ill-managed expedition to Scotland to try to confront an Irish crisis he was accused of having fomented, Cromwell was returning from a decisive campaign in Ireland and about to take on the Scots. Where the Caroline panegyrists had lavished hyperboles on Charles's non-existent victories, Marvell's poem is strikingly subdued in what it says about Cromwell's victories, enacting a contrast between empty words and decisive actions.

It is disturbing to find a poem that celebrates national emancipation simultaneously endorsing Cromwell's brutal repression of Irish resistance, and some critics have argued that in putting praise of Cromwell in the mouths of the Irish Marvell was being ironic at his expense. It is certainly not true to say that all seventeenth-century Englishmen were indifferent to Irish interests. Cromwell had crushed at Burford a mutiny by Levellers who resisted the campaign; Marten, too, had spoken up for the Irish.[51] But there were tactical reasons for the campaign, and Marten came round to supporting Cromwell's mission, though he gave it an ideological cast by proposing that it be funded with the sale of the regalia. Ireland had long been a source of difficulty for English governments, and now it threatened to become a base for a restoration; some republicans urged the most drastic possible measures. In an earlier moment of comparable crisis, Spenser had called for Irish traditions to be rooted up, for the entire political and social structure of the island to be transformed, and had quoted Machiavelli's *Discourses* in support of the appointment of a strong military leader; similar plans were being floated in the 1650s. On Cromwell's departure a newsletter declared that 'on the event of this they vary their conjectures whither ever there shall be a King of England again or not'.[52] Later in the year William Hickman insisted to Cromwell that the Irish campaign must be the basis for radical political change: 'hetherto in the chandge of our Government nothinge materiall as yet hath bin done, but a takinge of the head of monarchy and placing uppon the body or trunck of it, the name or title of a Commonwealth, a name aplicable to all forms of Government, and contained under the former'. The new republic was 'not to be pattern'd by any Commonwealth auncient or moderne'.[53] In a similar vein, Marvell stresses the ideological, republican elements of the campaign. The Irish praise of Cromwell has a generic precedent in Hannibal's praise of the Romans in the fourth ode of Horace's fourth book; Marvell was to make foreign princes praise Cromwell in *The First Anniversary*. If there is a grim wit in lines 73–80, it lies in making the defeated conservatives adopt a mode of praise more conventional than the iconoclastic spirit of the rest of the poem: it is the Irish who use the language of conventional, non-Machiavellian panegyric.

If the Irish are presented, albeit ironically, as exquisitely courteous, no holds are barred in ethnic stereotyping of the Scots. Fairfax and the presbyterians doubted the legality of the Scottish campaign; its most vehement supporters used a cheekily anti-monarchical rhetoric. For example, in trying to woo the Scots from their allegiance to the young Charles II, John Hall drew on the radical tradition in Scots historiography, rushing through the chronicle of rebellions, depositions and regicides so quickly that he turned it into a grotesque black comedy, implying that only a perverse political masochism would have kept the Scots faithful to their kings.[54] Marvell's portrayal of Cromwell hunting the Scots (lines 105–12) shares this ideologically charged aggression.

Having sketched the actions and character of the returning hero, the *prosphonetikon* would be expected to describe the celebrations marking his return. Aristotle declared (*Rhetoric*, I, 3) that epideictic rhetoric was especially concerned with the present tense, and 'now' is the key word of the *prosphonetikon*: Horace's 'nunc est bibendum' (I, 37). Here as so often Marvell departs from Caroline conventions just where he seems about to conform completely: 'now' appears in the second line, but the ode immediately looks to the future; rather than writing poetry the youth must be prepared to ward off the Scottish enemy. We do not return to the present tense until the 'now' of line 73, and any expectation that after the long narration there will be time for festivities is frustrated: the 'yet' and 'still' of lines 81–2 look to future possibilities before Cromwell's present actions have been fully described. Marvell's 'now' could perhaps be linked with a portrait of Marten by Lely which has 'now' inscribed on it: this seems to have been a Machiavellian injunction to decisive action, to seize the *occasione*, perhaps linked with the regicide.[55] Marvell lays all the emphasis on Cromwell's humility, on his readiness to abnegate praise and honour; and nothing at all is said of the republic's response. It is in fact true that Cromwell discouraged elaborate preparations for his return. The pamphlet describing his arrival at Windsor struck a somewhat unfestive note by remarking that Cromwell had been less seasick on the way back than on the voyage out to Dublin.[56]

The festivities in classical poetry often included a sacrifice, and the cavalier poets adapted the pagan symbolism of sacrifice to their own panegyrics.[57] Here Marvell's inversion of the conventions is at its most grimly witty. There is a sacrifice at the centre of the poem: the king himself. The famous lines about Charles on the scaffold have often been detached from their context. Certainly they do arouse sympathy for the king at his moment of death. But in formal terms this is a digression – Horace was celebrated for his digressions[58] – and Marvell meshes his account of the regicide in with his narration, beginning with a 'that' taking up from Cromwell's actions and ending with a 'So' emerging as the first term in a comparison:

> So when they did design
> The *Capitols* first Line,
> A bleeding Head where they begun
> Did fright the Architects to run;
> And yet in that the *State*
> Foresaw it's happy Fate.

The architectural metaphor is Marvell's addition to the Roman legend; this, and the fact that the head is bleeding, enable him to tie in the regicide to the theme of sacrifice, to modulate from the tragic to the conventions of the *prosphonetikon*. Cromwell's victories in Ireland do not require any new sacrifice to be made, for they were implicit in the original sacrifice that formed the new republic.

The symbolism of founding a republic on the basis of sacrifice was widely diffused in the Renaissance, and appears in several defences of the regicide.[59] Writing of the death of Tarquin, the last Roman king, Machiavelli argued, in a *reductio ad absurdum* of traditional monarchist imagery of the body politic, that the founders of the Roman republic were wise in cutting off the sick head when the body was healthy.[60] It was perhaps in Machiavelli's admired Livy that Marvell found the story of the head whose discovery gave new hope to the builders of the Temple of Jupiter. His analogy of the frightened architects presents accurately enough the reaction of many members of the Rump Parliament who were backing away from the radical implications of the regicide. Cromwell, by contrast, is someone who does not fall back on a familiar model but has the boldness to push on with a new one which will be more securely founded than the elegant but brittle world of the Caroline court. If Caroline panegyric tended to gloss over violence and seek to contain political conflict within the mythological structures of the masque, the new, republican panegyric is prepared to persevere in the face of uncomfortable facts. The leading republicans took pride in the fact that, as Thomas Harrison declared on the scaffold, the regicide 'was not a thing done in a corner'. Wither boasted that whereas tyrants had often been removed secretly,

> we, with *open face*;
> By *Publick Justice*; in a *Publick place*;
> In presence, of his *friends*, and, in despight
> Of all our *foes*, and ev'ry opposite,
> *Try'd, Judg'd*, and *Executed*, without fear;
> The greatest *Tyrant*, ever reigning here.[61]

Marvell, in much more circumspect terms, makes the regime acknowledge the blood on its hands. Cromwell lays the foundation even though its line runs through the king's neck; similarly, Marvell celebrates the new state and makes his own line decapitate the king: the moment when the king's eye tries the axe is the exact mid-point. If the poem's first sixty lines embody in their form the 'memorable Hour' of the execution, the Ode moves on to a new political world: its structure is centrifugal, not symmetrical, moving out both at the beginning and end from the encomiastic present to the uncertain but urgent future.[62] On the scaffold Charles had called on God, declaring that if he failed to make a speech he would be conceding his guilt; Marvell's silent king refuses to call on God to vindicate his right. In the context of 1650, what is most remarkable about the poem is its complete silence about the young Charles II. What royalists in 1650s were eager to celebrate was not Cromwell's return from Ireland but the young prince's return from exile to avenge his father's death and turn the world the right way up again. But at the centre of his poem, Marvell maintains an eloquent silence: the Stuart dynasty is charming but irrelevant.

The final expected element of a *prosphonetikon* would be a conclusion often involving a prophecy. The jingoism of Marvell's finale has often disconcerted critics. And certainly it is yet another drastic revision of Caroline *prosphonetika* which regularly ended with praise of the peace enjoyed by Britain while war raged elsewhere. Up to a point it can be said that Marvell is here going back more rigorously than the Carolines to the Horatian model; for many of Horace's poems of return ended with prophesies of future campaigns, notably the poem that is Marvell's closest model, the fourth ode of the fourth book. In Sir Richard Fanshawe's translation:

> What is't but *Neros* can effect,
> Whom Heav'ns with prosperous Stars protect,
> And their own prudent care
> Clews through the Maze of War.[63]

The parallel here of divine aid and 'curae sagaces', prudent care, is very close to Marvell's concluding antithesis between divine aid for Cromwell and the secular arts of tactical skill that he will need on the coming mission:

> And for the last effect
> Still keep thy Sword erect:
> Besides the force it has to fright
> The Spirits of the shady Night,
> The same *Arts* that did *gain*
> A *Pow'r* must it *maintain*.[64]

Where Marvell's poem differs from Horace's is in its much more radically ideological character. Where Horace celebrates campaigns that will consolidate the power of Augustus' dynasty against the remaining institutions of the Roman republic, Marvell celebrates wars that are specifically directed by the newly-founded republic against monarchies and in defence of republican values. As Christopher Hill has pointed out, there had indeed been anti-monarchical risings in many parts of Europe which lent at least some plausibility to such prophecies.[65] Italy, the heartland first of Roman and then of Renaissance republicanism, showed signs of throwing off the Spanish absolutist yoke.

There is a further twist in that many of Horace's poems prophesy victories against the Britons. Patriotic translators took issue with this: in his 1649 translation of the twenty-first ode of the first book, which ends with a plea that plague and famine will light on the Britons, John Smith writes, 'Avertat omen *Britannis*'.[66] Fanshawe comments on the ninth epode that Britain is '[u]nconquered, though twice attempted by the rude Courtship of *Julius Caesar*'.[67] To seventeenth-century Protestants, modern Rome was the inheritor of the worst aspects of ancient Rome, its imperial authoritarianism and idolatry. To the confident Counter-Reformation culture of seventeenth-century Italy, the heretical Britons were seditious inhabitants of a remote and backward region. Many critics have seen the fact that Caesar is Charles at the beginning of the poem, Cromwell at the end as a sign of ambivalence or satire against Cromwell; but such readings miss another stroke of grim wit. The question of genre needs to be considered: an encomium was expected near the end to have a section of comparisons. And it was normal to compare on the basis of very specific attributes. In fact a whole host of panegyrics directed to Cromwell without any apparent ironic intent – including a report on his departure to Ireland – compare him both to Caesar and to Hannibal.[68] The point is that each of these comparisons is qualified by restricting it to a particular place or time: Caesar when he conquered Gaul but not when he threatened liberty, and so on. Marvell specifies that his Cromwell is a Caesar in relation to Gaul, but he also inverts the situation at the end of Horace's odes, making Cromwell a Caesar who attacks Gaul not from the south on his way to Britain but from the north on his way to an apocalyptic assault on Rome. The apparently peripheral culture of Protestant England which in fact is closer to the true spirit of Roman greatness and generosity will triumph over the decadent imperial centre.

This is not say that some ambiguity does not play over the end of the poem: as before, there is always the possibility that Cromwell the defender of liberty, but also a Nimrodian '*Hunter*' (line 110), may himself endanger it.[69] The words 'force' and '*Pow'r*' of the last stanza recall the earlier 'forced Pow'r'; is the power here the new republic as a whole or simply Cromwell's personal authority? In 1650 these things were very hard to disentangle, for the one depended on the other. Marvell's ode is not unequivocally triumphal: it sees immense possibilities in the revolution, but is also aware of the deep-seated irony in the fact that its greatest defender and its destroyer might be one and the same man:

> The same *Arts* that did *gain*
> A *Pow'r* must it *maintain*.

The poem's wit is both youthfully irreverent and nightmarishly grim. All the same, there is an affirmative note: *if* the forward youths of the realm rally behind the young republic's campaigns, there is a world to win. And in writing the poem, Marvell had already gained one kind of victory for republican culture. The English revolution had turned upside down the monarchical order to return to republican origins; Marvell's out-troping poem of return turns royalist Horatianism, and Horace's own monarchism, upside down.

NOTES

Research for this paper was aided by a term at the Folger Shakespeare Library with financial support from the British Academy and the English-Speaking Union; I am very grateful to all at the Library. A fuller version will appear in the *Proceedings of the Folger Institute Centre for the History of British Political Thought*. I have benefited from discussion with Boyd Berry, Conal Condren, William Lamont, Nancy Klein Maguire, Annabel Patterson and J.G.A. Pocock. Jeremy Maule, Brian Vickers and Blair Worden have also provided helpful comments.

1 The classic 'balanced' reading, widely influential beyond seventeenth-century studies, is Cleanth Brooks, 'Marvell's *Horatian Ode*', *English Institute Essays, 1946* (New York, 1947), pp. 127–58.

2 Blair Worden, 'Andrew Marvell, Oliver Cromwell, and the Horatian Ode', in Kevin Sharpe and Steven N. Zwicker, eds., *Politics of Discourse: The Literature and History of Seventeenth-Century England* (Berkeley, 1987), pp. 147–80; see also Worden's 'Classical Republicanism and the Puritan Revolution', in *History and Imagination: Essays in Honour of H.R. Trevor-Roper*, ed. H. Lloyd-Jones, V. Pearl and B. Worden (London, 1981), pp. 182–200.

3 Jerome J. McGann, *Social Values and Poetic Acts: The Historical Judgment of Literary Work* (Cambridge MA and London, 1988), p. 6.

4 I am primarily concerned here with the political revolution of 1648–9, the foundation of the republic.

5 But see Francis Barker's 'In the Wars of Truth', chapter 5 above, for differences between the 'revolutionary bourgeois' discursive regime of *Areopagitica*, with its insistence on public participation in the discovery of truth, and in warfare, and the subsequent order, with its more rigid public/private distinctions.

6 On the absence of a republican culture in Britain see Tom Nairn, *The Enchanted Glass: Britain and its Monarchy* (London, 1988).

7 *The Poems and Letters of Andrew Marvell*, ed. H.M. Margoliouth, third edition, revised by Pierre Legouis with the collaboration of E.E. Duncan-Jones, 2 vols. (Oxford, 1971), I, 241.

8 William L. Pressly, *James Barry: The Artist as Hero* (London, 1983), pp. 73–5.

9 Elizabeth Story Donno, ed., *Andrew Marvell: The Critical Heritage* (London, 1978), pp. 133, 159n.

10 Christopher Hill, 'Society and Andrew Marvell', in *Puritanism and Revolution* (corrected edition, Harmondsworth, 1986), pp. 324–50. John M. Wallace, *Destiny His Choice: the Loyalism of Andrew Marvell* (Cambridge, 1968), pp. 69–105, and Michael Wilding, *Dragons Teeth: Literature in the English Revolution* (Oxford, 1987), pp. 114–37, see the poem as firmly endorsing Cromwell but resisting more radical republican or Leveller viewpoints. See also Judith Richards, 'Literary Criticism and the Historian: Towards Reconstructing Marvell's Meaning in "An Horatian Ode" ', *Literature and History* 7 (1981), 25–47.

11 Wallace, *Destiny His Choice*, pp. 100ff, touches on generic factors; Annabel Patterson relates genres more closely to republican ideas in *Marvell and the Civic Crown* (Princeton, 1978), pp. 59–68.

12 Sir Richard Fanshawe, *Shorter Poems and Translations*, ed. N.W. Bawcutt (Liverpool, 1964), p. 5.

13 Marvell, *Poems and Letters*, I, pp. 1–2.

14 Francis Cairns discusses the related terms *prosphonetikon*, *epibaterion*, and *apoba-*

terion in *Generic Composition in Greek and Roman Poetry* (Edinburgh, 1972), pp. 18–24; for Renaissance classifications see Julius Caesar Scaliger, *Poetices libri septem* (Lyon, 1561), pp. 158–9.

15 *Bernardi Parthenii . . . in Q. Horatii Flacci carmina atq. epodos commentarii* (Venice, 1584), fols. 142–5, 117v.

16 For discussion see Raymond A. Anselment, 'The Oxford University Poets and Caroline Panegyric', *John Donne Journal* 3 (1984), 181–201.

17 See R.H. Syfret, 'Marvell's "Horatian Ode" ', *Review of English Studies* n.s. 12 (1961), 160–72; John S. Coolidge, 'Marvell and Horace', *Modern Philology* 63 (1965–6), 111–20; R.I.V. Hodge, *Foreshortened Time: Andrew Marvell and Seventeenth-Century Revolutions* (Cambridge, 1978), pp. 118–31; Barbara Everett, 'The Shooting of the Bears', in *Andrew Marvell: Essays on the Tercentenary of his Death*, ed. R.L. Brett (Oxford, 1979), pp. 62–103; Margarita Stocker, *Apocalyptic Marvell: The Second Coming in Seventeenth Century Poetry* (Brighton, 1986), pp. 257–305 (Stocker brings out the important apocalyptic elements).

18 On problems in the dating, interpretation and attribution of the earlier poems, see Nicholas Guild, 'The Contexts of Marvell's Early "Royalist" Poems', *Studies in English Literature* 20 (1980), 126–36, and Gerard Reedy, S.J., ' "An Horatian Ode" and "Tom May's Death" ', *ibid.*, 137–51.

19 For this 'anti-Augustan' perspective, see Howard D. Weinbrot, *Augustus Caesar in 'Augustan' England: The Decline of a Classical Norm* (Princeton NJ, 1978).

20 Milton, *Complete Prose Works*, gen. ed. Don M. Wolfe, 7 vols. (New Haven; 1953–82), IV, pp. 536, 332; Anon., *The Tragedy of That Famous Roman Oratour Marcus Tullius Cicero* (London, 1651), sigs. C3v–4r, E4r.

21 J.G.A. Pocock's introduction to *The Political Works of James Harrington* (Cambridge, 1977), gives an important survey of republican thought; on Virgil, see pp. 579–81.

22 Cited by kind permission of the Brotherton Collection, University of Leeds (Marten-Loder papers, ML78, fol. 4v). I am indebted for this reference to C.M. Williams, 'The political career of Henry Marten with special reference to the origins of republicanism in the Long Parliament', unpublished D.Phil. thesis, Oxford, 1954, p. 217. For 'Rostris' Marten had first written 'Foris'.

23 The temperamental affinities between Marten and Marvell were noted by the last poet in the neo-Latin republican tradition, Walter Savage Landor: see 'Andrew Marvel [sic] and Henry Marten', in John Forster, *Walter Savage Landor: A Biography*, 2 vols. (London, 1869), II, 584–6.

24 Cf. Christopher Hill, 'The Word "Revolution" in Seventeenth-Century England', in *For Veronica Wedgwood These: Studies in English SeventeenthCentury History*, ed. Richard Ollard and Pamela Tudor-Craig (London, 1986), pp. 134–51.

25 David Underdown, *Pride's Purge: Politics in the Puritan Revolution* (Oxford, 1971), p. 260. Payne Fisher's volume of neo-Latin panegyrics to the republic's leaders, *Irenodia Gratulatoria* (London, 1652), is dated in the 'Aera' both 'Salutis Humanae MDCLII' and 'Libertatis Angliae IIII'.

26 John Aubrey, *Brief Lives*, ed. Andrew Clark, 2 vols. (Oxford, 1898), II, p. 47 (the allusion is to John 9: 2, 19).

27. George Wither, *The British Appeals* (London, 1651), p. 4. Published as a public rejoicing on the anniversary of the king's execution, the volume ends with a series of odes and a defence of such genres against the attacks of more radical

brethren. Contemporary satirists linked Wither with Marten, who is definitely known to have helped Waller and Davenant.

28 Fisher's *Irenodia Gratulatoria* (1652) contained an Ode to Cromwell and a *propemptikon* for Edmund Ludlow's departure to Ireland.

29 Milton, *Complete Prose Works*, III, pp. 311, 333; I am grateful to Dr. T.N. Corns for showing me his forthcoming article on this work.

30 On Milton's Horatianism see John H. Finley, Jr, 'Milton and Horace', *Harvard Studies in Classical Philology* 48 (1937), 29–74; cf. *Complete Prose Works*, IV, p. 682. For the possibility that Marvell may already have been in contact with Milton at the time he wrote the 'Ode', see Christopher Hill, 'John Milton and Andrew Marvell', in *Writing and Revolution in Seventeenth-Century England: The Collected Essays of Christopher Hill, Volume One* (Brighton, 1985), pp. 160–1.

31 See for example the heavily didactic edition by Daniel Heinsius, Leiden, 1612, fols. 7v–8v, lines 139–51.

32 For 'forward' in the context of a dual revival of military and intellectual arts, cf. Milton's celebration of the 'pious forwardnes' of free England in *Areopagitica*, *Complete Prose Works*, II, p. 554.

33 A.J.N. Wilson, 'Andrew Marvell: "An Horatian Ode upon Cromwell's Return from Ireland": The Thread of the Poem and its Use of Classical Allusion', *Critical Quarterly* 11 (1969), 325–41 (328–9). The fullest study of the poem in the light of seventeenth-century classical studies, which concludes that the poem is fundamentally pro-Cromwell, is Joanna Martindale, 'The response to Horace in the seventeenth century (with special reference to the *Odes* and to the period 1600–1660)', unpublished D. Phil. thesis, Oxford 1977, pp. 298ff; I am grateful to Dr. Martindale for allowing me to cite her thesis.

34 For political languor in Cicero see *Academicus*, 2.2.6, *De natura deorum*, I.iv.7, *De officiis*, 3.1.3, *In Pisonem*, 33.82, *Orator*, 2.6; for a catalogue of royalist languor see Worden, 'Marvell, Cromwell, and the Horatian Ode', pp. 167–8.

35 J.[ohn] H.[all], *The Grounds and Reasons of Monarchy, Considered and Exemplified out of the Scottish History* (Edinburgh, 1651), p. 5.

36 Worden, 'Marvell, Cromwell, and the Horatian Ode', p. 165.

37 Wallace, *Destiny his Choice*, p. 75.

38 Patterson, *Marvell and the Civic Crown*, p. 63.

39 John Hall, *The Advancement of Learning*, ed. A.K. Croston (Liverpool, 1953), p. 20.

40 *Ibid.*, p. 15.

41 J.[ohn] H.[all], *Peri Hypsous, or Dionysius Longinus of the Height of Excellence* (London, 1652), sig. A8r, pp. 78–9. Hall states that the translation had been completed some years before its publication. The idea of the Revolution as sublime was passed down in the English republican tradition: e.g. Catharine Macaulay on the foundation of the Republic, *The History of England from the Accession of James I to the Elevation of the House of Hanover*, V (London, 1771), p. 19.

42 Hall, *The Advancement of Learning*, pp. 21–2.

43 Hall, *Peri Hypsous*, sigs. C2r, F7b, F8b.

44 Milton, *Complete Prose Works*, IV, p. 554.

45 Aubrey, *Brief Lives*, II, p. 70.

46 On comparable contrasts between revolutionary sublime and monarchist beautiful in the French Revolutionary period see Ronald Paulson, *Representations of Revolution 1789–1820* (New Haven and London, 1983), pp. 57ff.

47 *Ibid.*, pp. 20–1.

48 Marvell, *Poems and Letters*, I, p. 111.
49 Compare Hall's distinction between the need for one man to predominate in war, where 'the ferocity of daring spirits, can hardly be bounded', and civil rule where a poise and balance of opposing factions is better than rule by one: *The Grounds and Reasons of Monarchy*, pp. 9–10.
50 *Eucharistica Oxoniensia* (Oxford, 1641), sigs. B1r–v.
51 Wilding, *Dragons Teeth*, pp. 120–4, argues that lines 13–20 celebrate Cromwell's crushing of the Levellers. For Marten's position on Ireland see Williams, 'The political career of Henry Marten', pp. 44, 344, 509ff.
52 *The Kingdomes Weekly Intelligencer*, no. 323 (31 July 1649), p. 1449.
53 John Nickolls, Jr, ed., *Original Letters and Papers of State, Addressed to Oliver Cromwell* (London, 1743), pp. 31ff.
54 Hall, *The Grounds and Reasons of Monarchy*, pp. 24ff, 45. On the Scottish historians see my '*Macbeth* and the Politics of Historiography', in Sharpe and Zwicker, eds., *Politics of Discourse*, pp. 78–116.
55 Reproduced in Oliver Millar, *The Age of Charles I: Painting in England 1620–1649* (London, 1972), p. 108, this portrait is now in the National Portrait Gallery.
56 *A Speech or Declaration of the Declared King of Scots . . . Also some Excellent Passages Concerning the Lord generall Cromwell, his entertainments at Windsor Castle* (London, 1650), p. 5. Note the subordination of Cromwell's return to the Scots crisis in the title.
57 E.g. Robert Herrick, 'To the King, upon his welcome to *Hampton-Court*', *The Poetical Works of Robert Herrick*, ed. L.C. Martin (Oxford, 1956), p. 300.
58 Cf. Parthenio's commentary on *Odes*, II, i, fol. 67r.
59 E.g. [Henry Robinson], *A Short Discourse Between Monarchical and Aristocratical Government* (London, 1649), p. 7; Wither, *The British Appeals*, p. 2, compares the publication of his poem in praise of the regicide to the raising of a stone for the temple of Jerusalem. For an interesting critical analysis of the sacrificial motif see Hannah Arendt, *On Revolution* (revised edition, Harmondsworth, 1973), pp. 208ff.
60 *Machiauels Discourses*, trans. E. D[acres]. (London, 1636), p. 88 [I.17].
61 Wither, *The British Appeals*, p. 29.
62 Alastair Fowler, *Triumphal Forms: Structural Patterns in Elizabethan Poetry* (Cambridge, 1970), pp. 78–81.
63 [Sir Richard Fanshawe], *Selected Parts of Horace, Prince of Lyricks* (London, 1652), pp. 54–5 (as has often been noted, Fanshawe may have invented the stanza-form Marvell uses for his ode).
64 Cf. *Poems and Letters*, II, p. 324, letter of 9 August 1671: 'in this World a good Cause signifys little, unless it be as well defended'.
65 Christopher Hill, 'The English Revolution and the Brotherhood of Man', in *Puritanism and Revolution*, pp. 126–53; see also Worden, 'Marvell, Cromwell, and the Horatian Ode', pp. 160–2.
66 J[ohn]. S[mith]., *The Lyrick Poet. Odes and Satyres translated out of Horace into English Verse* (London, 1649), p. 22.
67 Fanshawe, *Selected Parts of Horace*, p. 65.
68 E.g. Fisher, *Irenodia Gratulatoria*, translated by T. Manley as *Veni, Vidi, Vici* (London, 1652), pp. 10, 26–7, 71–2; *The Moderate Intelligencer*, 28 June – 5 July 1649, fol. 10R1r. There was a tradition of poetry supporting such Protestant expansionism in the face of monarchical resistance: Fulke Greville's *Life of Sidney*, finally published in 1652, called on Protestant leaders to emulate Hanni-

bal in marching on Rome (Worden, 'Marvell, Cromwell, and the Horatian Ode', p. 161).

69 On Nimrod and other possible ambivalences see Worden, 'Marvell, Cromwell, and the Horatian Ode', p. 176.

9 'Dark all without it knits': vision and authority in Marvell's *Upon Appleton House*

THE OSTENSIBLE literary culture in which Marvell's civil war poems seem to participate is a conventional Renaissance one, characterised by the idealisation of the poet in 'Tom May's Death':

> When the Sword glitters ore the Judges head,
> And fear has Coward Churchman silenced,
> Then is the Poet's time, 'tis then he drawes,
> And single fights forsaken Vertues cause.
> He when the wheel of Empire whirleth back,
> And though the World's disjointed Axle crack,
> Sings still of ancient Rights and better Times,
> Seeks Wretched good, arraigns successful Crimes.[1]

Despite the smooth progress of time being broken, the poet is presented as a figure who stands out from the discord of the age. His role, in fact, is to restore a sense of concord, recalling successes of the past and, through them, to look forward as a *vates* to the glory which will be restored. The perspective of past and future come to be linked, presenting an explanation of present events by indicating their position in the wider scheme of things. The past provides a model through which current events (even disruptive and apparently chaotic ones) may be organised and made comprehensible, and through which the future may be fathomed. The unease engendered by the execution of Charles in 'An Horatian Ode' is transformed by seeing it as the same type of unease experienced by the founders of the Roman temple of Jupiter Capitolium (lines 68–72). The beheading becomes a symbol pointing towards a happy and glorious fate, a vision of the future whose authority rests upon the past.

Yet Marvell's poetry rarely confidently reflects the idealism it attempts to celebrate. A playful, self-ironic exposure always seems to lie behind his most ardent praise. The lines above apparently adopt a royalist voice with their presentation of the old world compromised by the sword, where judges and churchmen are silenced, leaving only the poet. But, in a contemporary context, what is noticeable is the way royalist poets did not readily continue the battle as poetic knight-errants, the role Marvell's lines offer them. Such images are actually out of keeping with royalist poetic strategies, which largely depend on withdrawal and retreat rather than confrontation. 'Ancient Rights and better times' are commonly recalled from the safety of pastoral enclosures or other places of refuge and confinement. The poem's supposed condemnation of the parliamentarian May's prostitution of poetic high ideals backfires, exposing the absence of active engagement in royalist circles. Similarly, Marvell notes in his poem prefacing Richard Lovelace's *Lucasta* collection (1649) that 'our times are much degenerate', and that poets, along with all others, fall victim to the times' 'infections' ('To his Noble Friend Mr. Richard Lovelace'). Here, too, implications are not straightforward. The initial insinuation that Lovelace belongs to an older order which has avoided the age's disease is quickly compromised by a reading of *Lucasta*, revealing most of the contents dating from the infected civil war period.[2] Marvell's own appearance in this poem, indeed, is shown wanting in relation to the initial heroic postures he apparently celebrates. He begins by seemingly taking a brave stand against the hostility displayed towards Lovelace by parliamentarian 'barbed censurs', and what their actions imply about Puritan culture (lines 17–32). He concludes, though, by blunting his attack, suggesting Lovelace's poems are merely love-lyrics most staunchly defended by 'beauteous ladies' who admire Lovelace's amatory charms, physical as well as poetic. Marvell's Lovelace is certainly not the poet who provides a powerful moral or heroic force to confront the age's supposed decay. Instead we are reminded of the amatory frivolity (and the associated effeminacy and licentiousness) which parliamentarians liked to portray their royalist opponents possessing.[3]

Marvell's exposures are not only directed at the royalists. Even the later lauding of Cromwell's participation in a heavenly order and pattern of apocalyptic fulfilment in *The First Anniversary of the Government under his Highness the Lord Protector, 1655* restrains the extent of Marvell's conviction by proposing the limitations of his vision: 'That tis the most which we determine can, / If these the Times, then this must be the Man' (lines 143–4). It is hard, too, not to read this poem's hyperbolic elaborations on Cromwell's overturned coach in Hyde Park (lines 175–214) as a burlesque on the exaggerated poetry of praise and deliverance recalled from earlier Caroline celebrations. Cromwell may not be guilty of such posturing, but his poetic recorder is.

I propose that we accept, with Louis Montrose, that there is a 'historicity of texts', a specific cultural and social embodiment to the texts we examine; and, further, a 'textuality of history', a mediation by these texts of the lived histories they embody.[4] These two aspects seem closely intertwined and interdependent, and to understand the first we must have some inkling of the latter. This seems particularly important for our understanding of civil war texts, because they frequently are extremely conscious of their own processes of historical textualisation. The problematic procedures by which poets during the Civil War came to construe their times, and the resources they deployed to draw attention to their constructions of 'historical texts', seem one of the most complex and yet most distinctive features of the period's writing. This is particularly true of Marvell. He appears most aware of the civil war poets' paradoxical position: that they live in a time which demands a convincing projection of current events within poetry's traditional idealistic models, and that the nature of the times are such that these ideals are engulfed by historical experience.

I wish to explore the implications of this paradoxical position in Marvell's longest and most difficult civil war poem, *Upon Appleton House*. The poem explores the unease generated by contemporary history, but, more precisely, it details an unease about the poet's role as historical explicator and projector of the future. Although, throughout the poem, Marvell's poetic persona attempts to offer a privileged vision of a world destined to undergo regeneration, restoration, and reparation (interestingly, according to norms commonly employed in royalist poetry), it is, as Peter Schwenger has noted, composed of an artistic mode that both creates its vision and opposes it.[5] Marvell constantly subverts his poetic narrator's vision, intruding into the text to render its organisation unstable and suspect. The poem provides little reassurance for Fairfax in his 'retirement' from Cromwellian dominated public life, but it provides even less reassurance for readers who seek to find in it a poetically formed ideal place. Its poetic enclosures are as fragile as any in England erected to shut out the consequences of the Civil War.

As is being increasingly well documented, throughout the civil war period writers of a variety of political, social and religious orientations characterised the events of their own period as part of a historical fulfilment based, usually, on either biblical or classical patterns.[6] History was perceived as a *consummatum*, a confirmation of a plan. Contemporary events were not viewed as original but as reproductions, erected and enacted according to plans set forth in Scripture or other perceived repetitive temporal cycles. This style of historiography was employed by both royalist and parliamentarian supporters, and the impetus to use it was manifestly attractive. It allowed either side to characterise their position as participating in long-regarded patterns revealed in scripture or antiquity, and not as suspiciously innovatory. It enabled factions to organise current history so that its events became both comprehensible and helped fulfil their endeavours. Thus, during uneasy times (and we are increasingly discovering how, for all sides in the conflicts of the 1640s and 1650s, there was continuous and acute concern about the immediate future) literary texts could present current history as possessing a more stable and ordered character than was experienced.

It was just this experience of civil war, however, which exposed the fallacy of the comprehensive prescriptions offered by literary texts. Fragmentation and faction at the centre rather than at the margins characterised social and political life.[7] It became difficult for a writer (whether enthusiastically embracing or, more reluctantly, forced into supporting a particular side) to sustain an absolute conviction in his or her organisation and justification of recent events as being the only proper one. This is especially so when writers of other factions employed the same models to argue different organisations and justifications, and both contending visions were, on the whole, available to the same readership. Cowley's 'Preface' to the 1656 edition of his poems drew attention to an alteration in the perception of the poet's role:

Yet when the event of battle and the unaccountable *Will* of *God* has determined the controversie, and that we have submitted to the conditions of the *Conqueror*, we must lay down our *Pens* as well as *Arms*, we must march out of our *Cause* it self, and dismantle that, as well as our *Towns* and *Castles*, of all the *Works* and *Fortifications* of *Wit* and *Reason* by which we defended it.[8]

Cowley does not reject the notion of a God-given order, he merely places it beyond the poet's understanding. He views poetry as engaged in the defence of a faction's cause rather than aligned to universal truth and some notion of absolute validity. The success of the poem is dependent on the victory of the faction. The poetic fortifications Cowley built for himself in the royalist cause had been shown by 1656 to be far from impregnable. Unlike Marvell's orthodox idealisation of the true poet in 'Tom's May's Death' as a figure placed above his age, inhabiting a universal and perhaps omni-temporal sphere, Cowley proposes that the poet's authority rests on the recognition of more powerful contemporary authorities.

During the Civil War a realisation developed which perceived writing as not only organising and explaining the character of its period, but as being itself a reflection of the period, and thus subject to the dictates of the victorious and the powerful. In the Putney Debates of 1647 Sir John Wildman, for example, attacked the validity of defending ancient laws by reference to chronicles: 'I conceive that there is no credit to be given to any of them; and the reason is because those that were our lords . . . would suffer nothing else to be chronicled'.[9] Similarly, William Walwyn writing in *The Compassionate Samaritane* (1644) demonstrates a clear awareness of the politics of writing in support of factional interest:

> And past all question, if the King should thrive in this unnatural war,
> the Parliament should, in their [i.e. royalist] court histories, not only be
> called Anabaptists, but branded also to all posterity with that
> opinion . . . that they were enemies to the government, and went about
> to bring all to confusion.[10]

Imposing a character upon history, providing a narrative for its interpretation in poetry or prose, is recognised as fulfilling the needs of the writer's
own historical moment, and of the factional requirement with which the
writer's allegiance lay. Some writers, of course, remained blind to this,
or happily accepted the obligation, believing in its necessity. Others, and
Marvell is one, remain anxious or sceptical about their position. Indications multiply within their texts which pose alternatives, seeking to
disrupt the dominant account in which events are written. That which in
previous eras might be discovered only submerged or repressed within the
text now seeks to contend openly with the text's apparent interpretation.

In *Upon Appleton House* Marvell's poetic narrator constantly attempts
to focus his interpretation on images he believes signal a positive future.
These images attempt to explain current decline and destruction as a mere
episode anticipating greater things. The narrator's celebration of the Fairfax family, and the reading of signs invested in the house and surrounding
landscape, are ostensibly designed to reveal how family and environment
are a unified text which inscribes a pattern of providential hope and
renewal. Illustrations of this pattern are easily found. Appleton House
is compared to Romulus's cell (lines 33–40), implying that, as with the
Romans, a great race and future empire will emerge from the Veres and
Fairfaxes. Fairfax's humility in accepting the confines of Appleton House
and in following the will of God presents him as a memorial of Christ,
indicating how a new life and possible salvation will arise from him
(lines 49–64). In the family's overthrow of the false religion represented
by the Roman Catholic nuns, we observe the Fairfaxes actively involved
in a process of Reformation (lines 225–80) – a process which continues,
even if, as in the case of the nuns, it involves a destructive demolishing of
the old order. In the scenes where the mowers, the villagers' cattle, and
finally the flood apparently reduce the landscape to a topsy-turvy chaos
(lines 377–480), the process is also celebrated as a refertilisation similar to
the Nile's annual deluge (lines 625–32). The apparent destruction is part
of a cycle which offers regeneration. During the flood the poet retreats to
a wood which is an ark in which to survive the world's transformations,
creating the expectation of a new covenant between God and man based
on the Fairfaxes (lines 481–8). Finally, Maria Fairfax appears as a memorial
of the Virgin, both classical Astraea and Christian Mary, supplying the
means of returning mankind to a greater Eden (lines 649–768).[11] A complete, if at times seemingly contradictory, range of positive possibilities

to the envisaged future is defended. *Upon Appleton House* employs the rewriting of a scriptural narrative and a Virgilian reconstruction of heroic development, both of which are designed to assert glorious, if perhaps different, convictions about the future's direction.

Against this confident celebration of a providential scenario to contemporary events, the poem continuously introduces devices which contend with and subvert this interpretation. The authority of the narrator's vision is questioned. The poetic penetration and understanding brought to the interpretation of signs is rendered suspect. Previous interpretive patterns in the poem challenge rather than harmonise with later ones, causing the narrator's pattern to be disrupted and made unstable. The artifice used in the construction of the text is made deliberately manifest. Other alternative interpretations assert themselves and usurp the narrator's control over his images.[12]

In each case these disruptions appear as part of Marvell's design in the poem. The exposure of the poetic narrator's limitation is carefully crafted to have the reader perceive the humour generated by the narrator's naivety and clumsiness in handling his providential projections for the Fairfaxes. Parodic imitation of poetic styles and manners was a widely utilised and well-regarded weapon which civil war poets employed against writers of opposing factions.[13] Marvell, as I have indicated above, may well have been exposing royalist ideals in poems which seem to celebrate their poets' endeavours. Certainly, *Upon Appleton House* uses parodic elements in exposing the narrator's overly idealistic vision. The whole basis of the poem's argument in projecting a retreat to an enclosed space as a positive virtue, an idea pursued by many royalist writers, may well have been designed to give Fairfax cause for alarm. Part of the poem's concerns can be seen as Marvell offering criticism to, and warning, his employer. Fairfax's leaving of active public life in 1650 placed him in a dubious relation with the state's dominant forces. The poem makes him, like Prince Charles, an expected force of restoration, when the controlling political direction of the country is forcefully pursuing a new order. As Marvell shows, aspects of that new order (and aspects which should not encourage Fairfax in his choice of retirement) intrude into the poem and appear out of either Fairfax's or the poetic narrator's control. Trusting in the narrator's vision, the poem seems to suggest to Fairfax, is like trusting in the visions offered by royalist projections (some of which Fairfax's previous actions on behalf of parliament had been instrumental in proving wrong). The verse may be charged, but its real effect is impotent.

Marvell, though, is not contemptuous of his narrator. The laughter stirred by his narrator's inadequate attempts to control his poetic vision is one neither of derision nor dismissal. Rather, like that provoked by the salmon-fishers at the poem's conclusion (lines 769–76), it is unsettling.

The revelation that the poetic narrator may mistake the signs, or force them into artificial patterns, leaves a future and a present which threaten by becoming unknown. If the narrator tries to create a poetic ark for Fairfax, it is a structure which leaves the outside: 'Dark all without' (line 505).

The apparent confidence of sanctuary offered by the wood (lines 481–624) with its trees: 'How safe, methinks, and strong' (line 601), provides a good example of the poem's organised subversion of its narrator. It is evident the woodland is far more the narrator's construction than the Fairfaxes' planting; but, even though the result of his own generation, the narrator's interpretive abilities are betrayed. He believes he distinguishes signs among the trees and birds which provide assurance, allowing him to play the *'easie philosopher'* (line 561), while 'languishing with ease' (line 593). Yet, his happiness, founded on his supposed ability to read in 'Nature's mystick book' (line 584), is revealed as based on a limited perception and understanding of the images which confront him:

> Dark all without it knits; within
> It opens passable and thin;
> And in as loose an order grows,
> As the *Corinthean Porticoes.*
> The arching Boughs unite between
> The columns of the Temple green;
> And underneath the winged Quires
> Echo about their tuned Fires.
>
> The *Nightingale* does here make choice
> To sing the Tryals of her Voice.
> Low Shrubs she sits in, and adorns
> With Musick high the squatted Thorns.
> But highest Oakes stoop down to hear,
> And listening elders prick the Ear.
> The Thorn, lest it should hurt her, draws
> Within the Skin its shrunken claws.
>
> But I have for my Musick found
> A Sadder, yet more pleasing sound:
> The *Stock-doves*, whose fair necks are graced
> With Nuptial Rings; their ensigns Chaste;
> Yet always, for some Cause unknown,
> Sad pair unto the Elms they moan.
> O why should such a Couple mourn,
> That in so equal Flames do burn. (lines 505–28)

In each one of these stanzas, whether we focus on classical or Christian symbolism, uneasy and destructive aspects of the images are asserted. The elaboration of the Corinthean porticoes propose that this may be a temple of Venus worshipped through erotic rites at Corinth, or the columns of a Laudian church.[14] The birds' fires may be the consuming passions of erotic love which cannot be satisfied, (doves were traditionally harnessed to Venus's chariot). In classical reference the nightingale is the metamorphosised Philomela, a victim of a cruel rape and mutilation resulting from the passion of Tereus.[15] The Christian and scriptural terms of reference provide even less satisfaction to an easy philosopher. The 'tuned fires' which the winged choirs echo suggest the imagery of Isaiah 24:14–23 where the inhabitants of the earth attempt to 'sing for the Lord in Majesty' and 'glorify ye the Lord in the fires'. This is part of a prophetic vision of the end of the world. Isaiah develops the vision to show that those (like the narrator) who have attempted to flee the destruction will find no escape:

The earth is utterly broken down, the earth is clean dissolved, the earth is moved exceedingly. The earth shall reel to and fro like a drunkard and shall be removed like a cottage; and the transgression thereof shall be heavy upon it, and it shall fall and not rise again.   (24:19–20)

The prospect of imminent destruction is amplified by the nightingale and stock-doves. The nightingale was traditionally associated with Christ and its song with Christ's lament for his unseen death.[16] The stock-doves amplify this foreshadowing of destruction through further associations with Christ. They are the sacrificial victims at the Presentation of the Temple (Luke 2:22–24) and as such prefigure Christ's own sacrifice. Further, the doves being 'graced with nuptial rings; their ensigns chaste' extends the sacrifice to the martyrs, whose choice of chaste marriage with Christ is made at the cost of their lives. Birds, of course, are employed by augurs to fathom the future. In each case the images the narrator presents as ostensibly suggesting the peace and security offered within the wood possess alternative threatening implications.

The erotic undercurrents to the green temples of the narrator's wood also help direct attention to the strange parallels which develop with the false religious buildings in which the nuns attempted to seduce Elizabeth Thwaites earlier in the poem (lines 89–200). There the '*Subtle Nuns*' (line 94) argue that the convent is not a limited enclosed place, rather the opposite:

> These Walls restrain the World without
> But hedge our Liberty about.
> These Bars inclose that wider Den
> Of those wild Creatures Called Men   (lines 99–102)

The poetic narrator argues with similar subtlety. Despite the enclosed space of the woodland retreat, he presents it as a liberating, bountiful place which lacks nothing: 'What *Rome, Greece, Palestine* ere said / I in this light Mosaick read' (lines 581–2). He even adopts a similar use of the nuns' 'hedge'. The trees grow so closely together: 'As if the Night within were hedg'd' – the night is knitted without while the woods open 'passable and thin' (lines 504–6). The narrator is attempting to propose a gloomier world hedged outside the wood. He later announces: 'Oh what a Pleasure 'tis to hedge / My Temples here with heavy sedge' (lines 641–2), celebrating the 'naturalisation' of his devotions, but also revealing the way the structures he worships are protected and cut off from a more threatening world. The narrator becomes suspiciously identified with the protection of an existing order, not the creation of a new one, applying his poetic skills to create a web of deceitful images in the manner of the smooth-tongued nuns.

This is reinforced by considering the circumstances of the narrator's retirement to the wood. The immediate occasion is the flood, but the flood is the conclusion of a sequence of events (ironically and fatuously called 'pleasant acts') which show the Fairfax estate disrupted. These other 'acts' are the pillaging of the rails and grass by the mowers, and the further decimation caused by the local villagers' cattle, whose activities resemble the Levellers (lines 449–54). The introduction of Levellers into the poem had especial significance for Fairfax.[17] He had shown little sympathy with the Levellers during the St George's Hill experiment in 1649. Gerrard Winstanley had tried to persuade Fairfax of the righteousness of the Leveller's project, had met with him and addressed a number of pamphlets directly to Fairfax. In 1650 Winstanley defended the Levellers in a further tract entitled *A New-Year's Gift for the Parliament and the Army* in which he asserted:

And all this falling out or quarrelling among mankind is about the earth, who shall and who shall not enjoy it, when indeed it is the portion of everyone and ought not to be striven for, nor bought, nor sold, whereby some are hedged in, and others hedged out. For better not to have had a body, then to be debarred the fruit of the earth to feed and clothe it.[18]

The woodland in *Upon Appleton House* certainly appears to provide bounty for the narrator (he can carelessly tread on strawberries, while herons willingly offer Fairfax their young, line 529–36). It also clothes him (providing 'an antic cope', line 591). But, while the Fairfax estate may allow its owner and his circle to 'hedge out' the darkness in the Lord General's retirement, they are able to do so only by excluding those who believed they too were fighting against darkness in order to regain their ancient rights to common land. Fairfax had played a prominent part in both the rigorous suppression of Leveller mutineers at Burford in 1648 and their colony on St George's Hill in 1649–50. In *Upon Appleton House* the narrator tries to present the village 'Levellers' as unthreatening, pursuing pastoral activities. Yet, he once again does not succeed. Their cattle are also 'razing' the estate, the pillaging initiated by the mowers continues. Further, the line: 'Is pinched yet nearer by the beast' (line 454), with its apocalyptic overtones of the beast of Revelations, presents an image which purposes the ostensibly harmless pursuits of the villagers as unnerving.

Finally, in relation to the poem's posing of alternatives to the narrator's celebration of retirement to the wood, we should note that the world which he experiences in the wood is decadent and corrupt. As Brian Vickers has noted, retirement in the style of the narrator was usually viewed as *inertia* and *luxuria* by the classical world – vices rather than virtues. Further, being 'careless' (line 529) in the narrator's way has the suggestion of having ignored proper cares as chastised, for example, by Spenser.[19] That the wood clothes the narrator so that he becomes a prelate strengthens the association between his world and the false enclosed one of the nuns. This is again emphasised by the poem's presentation of the '*easie Philosopher*', exploiting language and imagery which display him as a decadent royalist. Blair Worden has noted how 'languishing' (which Marvell's 'forward youth' renounces in 'an Horatian Ode') was popularly associated with monarchical rule[20]. Anthony Low has proposed that this style of pastoralism became acquainted with a royalist elite and, certainly, the scene recalls a courtly indulgence with nature as a sycophantic courtier[21]:

> Then, languishing with ease, I toss
> On Pallets swoln of Velvet Moss;
> While the Wind, cooling through the Boughs,
> Flatters with Air my panting Brows.   (lines 593–6)

This is not to argue that *Upon Appleton House* tries to present its narrator consistently in royalist terms. Indeed, the previous celebration of the destruction of the nunnery as a religious act implied approval of a continuing parliamentarian Reformation. In contrast, Sir John Denham's more consistently royalist *Cooper's Hill* (published 1642) mourns the earlier destruction of the abbeys (lines 146–78), noting: 'May no such storm / Fall on our times, where ruin must reform' (lines 149–50).[22] Denham portrays Henry VIII's dissolution of the monasteries as resulting from personal greed couched in the language of reform, recognising that the interpretation of these events rests on the way those in power portray them (lines 161–4). The emphasis of Denham's poem is to seek a middle course between extremes. He rhetorically wonders why the Reformation cannot seek a mean: 'Could we not wake from that Lethargicke dreame, / But to be restlesse in a worse extreme' (lines 175–6). In opposition to this view, the narrator of *Upon Appleton House* is excited by the

earlier Fairfax's forceful involvement with the dissolution of religious
institutions: 'But waving these aside like flies, / Young Fairfax through
the wall does rise' (lines 257–8). His forceful action in occupying the
nunnery anticipates the glorious military conquests enacted by later Fairfaxes. Again, though, this contains a concealed criticism of Marvell's
employer. The family's past is a great one because founded on activity
not retirement. The poem may try to grant Fairfax's present inactivity
some credibility because it is based on 'conscience', a plant: 'Which most
our earthly gardens want' (line 356). Yet, the result of Fairfax's inactivity
and involvement with imaginary, not real, forts is that England's garden
is left without proper attention. (lines 345–52).

Sir John Denham's popular poem, *Cooper's Hill* (which reached a third
edition by 1650), provides an interesting context which helps reveal further indications of Fairfax's position in *Upon Appleton House* as being
more precarious than the poetic narrator's celebration of him is apparently
intended to reveal. Denham's poem seeks to celebrate the virtues of the
via media (both religious and political) as the right norms by which to
govern the state. At the conclusion of the 1642 version of *Cooper's Hill*
the state is portrayed being ideally governed as a river (the king) whose
flood is carefully contained in raised banks (the law) built by 'husbandmen'
(the subjects). If, however, these subjects:

> strive to force,
> His channell to a new, or narrow course,
> No longer then within his banks he dwels,
> First to a Torrent, then a Deluge swels;
> Stronger, and fiercer by restraint, he roares
> And knowes no bound, but makes his powers his shores. (lines 337–42)

In *Upon Appleton House* the act which most immediately perpetrates the
narrator's withdrawal to the wood is Denton's flood, with the result that:
'the river in itself is drowned' (line 471). Denton is, unlike the village
cattle or mowers, not an 'outside' force disrupting the estate, but another
of Fairfax's possessions. The narrator attempts to construe the flood as a
'pleasant act', but its effect, as with the mowers or cattle, is to cause an
alteration in the order of things and force a retreat to safety. Fairfax appears
incapable of controlling his possessions, let alone intruders. He is
presented as unable to husband the river properly, causing his authority
to be compromised: 'How salmons trespassing are found, / And pikes are
taken in the pound' (lines 479–80).

The whole concept of retreat in the poem becomes questionable, therefore, specifically at the moments where the narrator is apparently most
abundantly praising the ideal. This casts severe doubts about his ability
to interpret consistently and correctly. If the narrator misconstrues the

security offered by the wood, he may also misconstrue the nature of the forces which threaten its security and, perhaps, the supposed darkness outside. Marvell reveals the danger of embracing a poetic pastoral strategy which appears to offer an escape from dark forces. As the narrator retreats into an increasingly confined area within the Fairfax estate (leaving others to 'tell the paradox' the flooding creates, line 473), so he retreats into a poetic sanctuary. He adopts a mode which allows him to recast a threatening occurrence as another providential sign (the provision of the green ark), and to describe the wood as a place of liberty, not a confined fortress. The danger in this manoeuvre, as we have seen, is that the sanctuary provided by the poetic model has already been occupied by others within the poem (the nuns) and within other poems (the royalists), with whom the narrator would apparently wish to identify neither himself nor Fairfax. The narrator's poetic strategy is seen to be flawed, creating a sanctuary where artificial and illusionary qualities predominate.

Marvell's skilful exposure of poetic artifice as a means of undermining rather than strengthening the poem's apparent vision of Fairfax and the future can be made clearer by comparing *Upon Appleton House* with Ben Jonson's designs in 'To Penshurst', the country-house poem upon which Marvell's is founded and which he skilfully adapted. Like Marvell's poetic narrator, Jonson idealises a family and their property to depict an example of a materially and spiritually profitable place, a harmoniously balanced location in contrast to other 'proud, ambitious heaps' (line 101)[23]. In 'To Penshurst', as in *Upon Appleton House*, the reader is alerted to the location being, finally, a poetic place rather than a poetic description of a real one. Jonson's Penshurst is no more Kent, than Marvell's Nun Appleton is Yorkshire. Jonson's: 'For fire, or lights or livery: all is there / As if thou then wert mine, or I reigned here' (lines 73–4) pointedly suggests that the Penshurst of the poem is far more Jonson's fabrication than the possession of the Sidney family. Jonson, as the poem's author, does reign within his text, providing himself with a world where all his wants are satisfied – including a desire for authority. Jonson's Penshurst is a place where King James and Prince Henry discover their needs met as well; but royalty, just like the Sidneys, become dependent on Jonson to provide them with a world where peace, bounty, and satisfaction may be found.

'To Penshurst' is a version of the traditional ideal place provided by poetry, but is not here a mere magical place. Jonson has given it an actual location (not an ill-defined Arcadia) and the appearance of material existence, a sense of being real because the house does have a topography and a history. Jonson's skill rests in that he absorbs and masks the tensions between the 'real' house (the newly remodelled Penshurst was ancient in only a small part, not particularly abundant, or even the secure possession of the financially strained Sidneys) and his poetic creation[24]. The poem radiates Jonson's confidence in *his* possession, and the poetic organisation reflects this confidence: 'Thou has no lantern whereof tales are told, / Or stair or courts; but stand'st an ancient pile' (lines 4–5). Clearly, Jonson has told a tale (and a conventional one) by attributing an antiquity to the house which it did not truly possess. But, unlike in *Upon Appleton House*, a knowledge of the actual history of the house or family does not interfere with Jonson's conviction in his claim that his Penshurst is a place where King James and Prince Henry find all their needs met. The unity of the uninterrupted eulogy to the estate reveals that it is the poetic Penshurst, rather than the historical one, which actually provides king, prince, Sidneys and the reader with an illustration of the ideally organised life. Jonson's exposure of artifice in his manipulation of the actual estate, rather than disrupting his interpretive pattern, strengthens it. The more the reader becomes aware it is a mythical Penshurst Jonson celebrates, the more the poetic myth takes on an importance and 'location' of its own. The poem is where Jonson, its builder, 'truly dwels' (lines 99–102), and it is this, his possession, which is the better house. The celebration of Sir Philip Sidney's oak at the historic Penshurst as a type of poetic tree of Jesse (lines 10–16) is a good example of the way Jonson directs the actual estate to a higher fulfilment (and 'reality') in the Jonsonian myth: from Sidney's seed arises the greater poet, the greater and truer Arcadia.

In contrast, the narrator of *Upon Appleton House* lacks both the skill, and, even within the poem's world, the more stable circumstances of Penshurst to generate such a confidence in his poetic vision. Impositions such as the flood keep occurring, forcing him to adopt unconvincing strategies to explain these events, while trying to maintain a semblance of unity and coherence to his vision. Marvell not only subverts his narrator's projection by having him use imagery which compromises him, he also has the poem directly challenge the narrator's interpretive organisation. This is best illustrated through one of the poem's most unusual features, the imposition of an alternative explanation to events posed within the poem by 'bloody Thestylis'.

The narrator describes the mowers cutting the field as seemingly like Israelites: 'walking on foot through a green sea' (line 390). The imagery once more focuses on providential renewal: the mowers, like the Israelites, are a chosen people led to a promised land. When one of them unknowingly kills a rail he detests the action: 'Fearing the Flesh untimely Mow'd / To him a Fate as black forebode' (lines 399–400). Instead of continuing with the implications of this action, though, the poem is interrupted by Thestylis who ignores the dead rail as a destructive sign. She trusses it up and kills another announcing: 'He call'd us Israelites; / But now, to make his saying true, / Rails rain for Quails, for Manna Dew' (lines 406–8). Her procedure appears cynical, usurping the textual process which inscribes her as an Israelite and using the identification to justify her destructive act.

The narrator is forced to accommodate this rewriting of his design, exposing the tenuousness of his identification: 'Who seem like Israelites' (line 389)[25]. The mowers employ a supposed re-enactment of the gathering of providential manna as the excuse to slaughter the rails. 'The Mower now commands the Field' (line 418) – the narrator has no resources to contend with them as they enter into destruction. The consequences are unsettling. In one respect the simile of the mowers as Israelites is presented as incomplete and limited, but in other respects the simile continues to apply legitimately. The bounty of the innocent rails may be providentially provided as sustenance for a chosen people. Indeed, the mowers may claim the narrator's comparison has provided them with the authority to act in a manner which appears unexpected and apparently unintended by him.

The result is the 'careless victors' feasting and revelling (lines 425–32), which, like the narrator's subsequent 'careless' treading on strawberries, contains the elements of a vice-ridden *otium*, indulging in *luxuria* and lasciviousness[26]. It also recalls that the Israelites were frequently rebellious to God's commands with disastrous results. When Moses went up to the mountain to receive the Commandments, the Israelites constructed a golden calf and 'sat down to eat and to drink, and rose up to play' (Exodus 32:6). Moses returns to find them dancing and naked (33:19, 25). The result is bloodshed, like the mower's fear of 'a fate as black' as the rail's:

And he [Moses] said unto them. Thus saith the Lord God of Israel: Put every man his sword by his side and go in and out from gate to gate, throughout the camp, and slay every man his brother, and every man his companion, and every man his neighbour.   (33.27)

The result is three thousand dead (33:28).

The mowers also present another challenge to Fairfax, who, as owner of the estate, is celebrated for providing an order and proper organisation to it. In losing poetic control, the narrator allows mastery of the estate to be gained, at least momentarily, by those who pillage its resources, a pillaging they inscribe through usurpation of both a scriptural and pastoral model. The equation of natural order with a prevailing social order, a staple of country house poems (e.g. 'To Penshurst' lines 45–56), has been compromised[27].

Beyond the social and political usurpation by the mowers, the claim by Thestylis: 'to make his saying true' is a linguistic and literary usurpation. It appears an example of what Bakhtin characterises as 'novelisation', in which a plurality of voices cause a verbal and ideological decentring.[28] It is an instance of the way Marvell and his contemporaries could no longer control patterns perceived arising from literary or scriptural precedent. The mower, characterised both as Virgilian Thestylis – though ironically so since the original Thestylis (*Eclogue* II, lines 40–2) has nothing to do with being 'bloody' – and as an Israelite, does not contradict the textual process which inscribes her. Rather she changes the inscription from proposing a providential idyll to a scene more threatening in its implications. It is a process which can be discovered replicated in Marvell's world. The following, for instance, appears in the Church Warden Account Book from Lutterworth, Leicestershire, dated 10 April 1650:

Given Agnes Griffen was nailed to a branch or tree by hand and foot having 37 wounds in her head having part of her body cut being forced to eat her own flesh and drink her own blood by the rebels.[29]

The entry's reference to 'rebels' indicates that this act is being cited as an instance of parliamentarian cruelty, but the nature of the torture is not commented on. Agnes Griffen was clearly crucified and made to undergo a terrible Last Supper. Was this *parodia christiana* inflicted as a mockery on a woman who was felt to adhere to superstitious ceremonies for example? Or were her torturers merely applying patterns of torments whose familiarity caused them to ignore the ironic implications for themselves? The problem is complicated because the pattern is so strikingly uncanny. It is a bizarre manifestation of repetition, adhering to the scriptural injunction to 'do this in remembrance of me', but being strangely and disturbingly performed. This brief entry among accounts of routine church expenses provides no ready indication of what its position in this context is meant to signify. It is not clear what the writer's strategy was in this description, causing this sad event's relation to both contemporary history and to its 'literary' context in scripture to become problematic.

Renaissance poetry commonly attempts to impose a single coherent character on the world it sees itself reflecting. The establishment whose power dominated the culture is celebrated by inscribing heavenly and human virtues in its members and their actions. Opposition is characterised as ungodly and diabolic, savage and uncivilised, or in some other respect distinctly inferior and dangerous. Poets wrote events in order to join a coherent pattern established by previously approved structures, seeking to solve the problem of their age's representation (and their own position in it) by participation in a collective story.

The fragmentation caused by the Civil War created a context where the poet was no longer in a position to claim with any ease to be the voice of a coherent culture whose authority could be enforced by repressing and marginalising alternatives. The frameworks adopted to explain and to represent events were precisely those which varying groups adopted to

characterise alternatives, and which, as Agnes Griffen illustrates, could
be discovered used in uncanny ways throughout society. The fiction of
participation in a collective story collapses. The universal vision comes to
be recognised as a factional vision. Yet, the poet's resources and the poet's
role are still largely assumed to be virtually unchanged. Resources and
role invite an interpretation of events which offer a stable reality, a vision
of an achievable ideal.

The ideal Fairfax offered Marvell in 1650, however, must have been
an awkward one, particularly if we accept the genuineness of Marvell's
welcome of Cromwell's return from Ireland in 'An Horatian Ode'. Fairfax's retirement to Nun Appleton was an act which left him estranged
from the new Cromwellian order, and one implication of *Upon Appleton
House* is certainly that Fairfax is creating something new. The republican
culture to which Cromwell plays midwife is apparently being redesigned
by Fairfax's passive action. Fairfax, according to the poem, is still a player
on the national scene and the family will assume a leading role in directing
the future. As Michael Wilding has argued, the expectation that Fairfax
would again take an important role in national affairs, perhaps even help-
ing to effect a restoration of the monarchy was widely believed.[30] Marvell's poem, as I have indicated, reflects some uneasiness about Fairfax
acting according to royalist norms. But an even greater confusion was
present in the continuing instability about England's political and social
direction under the victorious parliamentarian forces, an anxiety to which
both Fairfax's action in retiring and Cromwell's action in pursuing the
invasion of Scotland gave new impetus. *Upon Appleton House* is more than
an example of a poet placed in the difficult position of needing to celebrate
an employer when he actually doubts the wisdom of his actions. It is an
example of poetry attempting to fulfil a role of historical interpretation
and foresight which its poet no longer feel confident with. The poet, no
more than any other player of the time, is a victim of uncertainty.

In lines from *Cooper's Hill* printed in 1642 but deleted from editions
after the Restoration, Denham betrays his uncertainty about analysing the
meaning of current events. His conclusion at first seems pointedly cynical,
aimed at discrediting parliament's early victories in the Civil War as the
result of *realpolitik* and not moral superiority. Yet the lines also seem to
propose the actual insecurity Denham felt about his authority in deciding
the meaning of events. Success may imply justness, not simply because
the victors impose an order in accordance with their laws, but because
victory may imply the moral and genuine superiority of the winning side.
Denham's lines seem close to the Marvell of 'An Horatian Ode' (especially
lines 33–40):

> For armed subjects can have no pretence
> Against their Princes, but their just defence,
> And whether then, or no, I leave to them
> To justifie, who else themselves condemne:
> Yet might the fact be just, if we may guesse
> The justnesse of an action from success.[31]

Cowley's 1656 preface portrayed the poet destroying fortifications built to defend a vision whose authenticity will be determined by the way the controversy will be decided. Marvell's *Upon Appleton House* attempts to build a defence for Fairfax, but one far from impregnable. We are becoming increasingly aware of how poetic styles, themes and theories were employed as strategies in the Civil War's larger social and political conflicts. However, it would be incorrect to try to present Marvell's position in this world as merely a skilful chess-player whose work is composed of a series of complicated manoeuvres within a political/poetic game. A sense that: 'Tis not what once it was, the World, / But a rude heap together hurl'd' (*Appleton House* lines 761–2) is shown to be a cause for serious anxiety. The illusion of poetic authority dissolves, but the reasons for this dissolution are themselves a proper subject for poetry. At the poem's end the narrator may be, like one of his salmon-fishers, hiding his head 'Tortoise-like' in his poem, wishing to retreat indoors from the encroaching, uncertain, 'dark Hemisphere' (lines 773–6). Marvell, though, remains outside, exposing this 'rational Amphibii' to his readers who discover, awkwardly, the poem does not prevent a dark hemisphere. As we see, *Upon Appleton House* deliberately and determinedly asserts the uncontrollable, unstable and unknowable quality of the world it seeks to encapsulate.

NOTES

1 Lines 63–70. *The Poems and Letters of Andrew Marvell*, ed. H.M. Margoliouth, 3rd edition (Oxford, 1973), I, p. 96. All references to Marvell's poetry are from this edition.
2 Leah S. Marcus, *The Politics of Mirth* (Chicago and London, 1986), p. 217.
3 Margaret Anne Doody, *The Daring Muse: Augustan Poetry Reconsidered* (Cambridge, 1985), pp. 46–7.
4 Louis Montrose, 'Renaissance Literary Studies and the Subject of History', *English Literary Renaissance* 16 (1986), 8.
5 Peter Schwenger, ' "To Make his Saying True": Deceit in *Appleton House*', *Studies in Philology* 77 (1980), 84.
6 Achsah Guibbory, *The Map of Time: Seventeenth-Century English Literature and Ideas of Pattern in History* (Urbana and Chicago, 1986); Katherine R. Firth, *The*

Apocalyptic Tradition in Reformation Britain 1530–1645 (Oxford, 1979); C.A. Patrides, *The Grand Design of God: The Literary Form of the Christian View of History* (London, 1972); for Marvell's involvement in this tradition: Margarita Stocker, *Apocalyptic Marvell: The Second Coming in Seventeenth-Century Poetry* (Brighton, 1986).

7 Kevin Sharpe and Steven N. Zwicker, *The Politics of Discourse: The Literature and History of Seventeenth-Century England* (Berkeley, 1987), pp. 5–7.

8 *Poems* ed. A.R. Waller (Cambridge, 1905), p. 455. The passage was not printed in Cowley's *Poems* in the 1668 collected edition.

9 *Divine Right and Democracy: An Anthology of Political Writing in Stuart England*, ed. David Wootton (Harmondsworth, 1986), p. 298.

10 *Ibid.*, p. 269.

11 Stocker, *Apocalyptic Marvell*, pp. 153–60.

12 See Frank J. Warnke, 'The Meadow Sequence in *Upon Appleton House*: Question of Tone and Meaning', in *Approaches to Marvell: the York Tercentenary Lectures*, ed. C.A. Patrides (London, 1978), pp. 234–50; James Turner, *The Politics of Landscape* (Oxford, 1979), pp. 33–84; Allan Gray, 'The Surface of Marvell's *Upon Appleton House*', *English Literary Renaissance*, 9 (1979), 169–82; Marcus, pp. 240–63.

13 Doody, *The Daring Muse*, pp. 30–56.

14 Schwenger, ' "To make his saying true" ', pp. 95–6; Marcus, *The Politics of Mirth*, p. 223.

15 Ovid, *Metamorphoses*, VI, lines 519–674.

16 Rosemary Woolf, *The English Lyric in the Middle Ages* (Oxford, 1968), pp. 232–3.

17 See Michael Wilding, *Dragons Teeth: Literature in the English Revolution* (Oxford, 1987), pp. 150–8.

18 *Winstanley: The Law of Freedom and Other Writings*, ed. Christopher Hill (Harmondsworth, 1973), pp. 191–2.

19 Brian Vickers, 'The Ambivalence of *Otium*', forthcoming in *Renaissance Studies*.

20 Blair Worden, 'Andrew Marvell, Oliver Cromwell, and the Horatian Ode', in Sharpe and Zwicker, *The Politics of Discourse*, p. 167.

21 Anthony Low, *The Georgic Revolution* (Princeton, 1985), esp. pp. 250–1.

22 For the 1642–50 version of 'Cooper's Hill': Brendan O'Hehir, *Expans'd Hieroglphicks: A Critical Edition of Sir John Denham's Cooper's Hill* (Berkeley and Los Angeles, 1969), pp. 120–1.

23 *Ben Jonson: Poems*, ed. Ian Donaldson (London, 1975), pp. 87–91.

24 See Don E. Wayne, *Penshurst: The Semiotics of Place and the Poetics of History* (London, 1986), pp. 86–105.

25 Harold Skulsky, '*Upon Appleton House*: Marvell's Comedy of Discourse', *English Literary History* 52 (1985), 601.

26 Discussion of the mowers in relation to the concepts of labour and *otium* has received much attention recently: *ibid.*, pp. 601–4; Gray, pp. 174–5; Low, p. 293; Annabel Patterson, 'Pastoral versus Georgic: The Politics of Virgilian Quotation', *Renaissance Genres: Essays on Theory, History, and Interpretation*, ed. Barbara Lewalski, Harvard English Studies 14 (Cambridge MA and London, 1986), pp. 260–2.

27 Turner, *The Politics of Landscape*, pp. 101–2.

28 M.M. Bakhtin, *The Dialogic Imagination: Four Essay*, ed. Michael Holquist,

trans. Caryl Emerson and Michael Holquist (Austin TX, 1981), esp. pp. 6–7, 12.

29 I am grateful to Dr Gordon Campbell for bringing this entry to my attention.
30 Wilding, *Dragons Teeth*, pp. 169–71.
31 O'Hehir, *Expans'd Hieroglphicks*, p. 131, lines 307–12.

10 'History digested': opera and colonialism in the 1650s

Why, truly, your great enemy is the Spaniard. He is. He is a natural enemy, he is naturally so. He is naturally so, throughout, as I said before . . . And truly when I say that he is naturally throughout an enemy, an enmity is put into him by God.
Oliver Cromwell, Speech at the opening of Parliament, 17 September 1656[1].

I

IN 1517, the Spanish missionary Bartolomé de las Casas, taking great pity on the Indians who were languishing in the hellish work-pits of the Antillean gold mines, suggested to Charles V, King of Spain, a scheme for importing blacks, so that they might languish in the hellish work-pits of the Antillean gold mines.[2]

Thus Borges describes the processes of colonialist displacement which invents non-European races for the intellectual consumption of the European. The noble savage and the barbarian, Ariel and Caliban, are equally products of a conceptualisation of an other, obviously invented to serve the value system of the representer, fabulator. Borges is drawing our attention to the logic of this process (in which Cromwell's speech participates), by which values and characteristics are attributed to 'natives' and other peoples only in order to inscribe them in the definitional codes of the naming nations.

The aim of this chapter is to explore the connotations of such displacements and constructions in four interregnum dramas and operas by William Davenant, performed under the restrictive conditions of production prevailing in the 1650s. The closure of the theatres in 1642 (and further strictures in 1647 and 1648) meant that to publish or perform drama became an obviously political act, though not necessarily a pro-monarchical gesture. Theatre could no longer be innocent of its ideological status either in terms of plots or in terms of the kind of representation displayed. All aspects of dramatic and theatrical texts were overtly politicised by the Civil Wars, the regicide and, in the 1650s, the continued ban of the theatre under the Protectorate. This is the context for my examination of *The First Days Entertainment at Rutland House*, *The Siege of Rhodes* (I and II), *The Cruelty of the Spaniards in Peru* and *The History of Sir Francis Drake*. This chapter explores the anxieties the texts manifest around the interconnected issues of their own status as drama and problems of rule and government, using Michel Pecheaux's simple insight that language ('words, expressions, propositions') is always incribed in ideological formations, and that words alter according to the position from which they are spoken.[3] I propose a reassessment of Davenant's work which contends with previous critical studies which have characterised it as either participating directly in an undivided and identifiable 'royalist' ideology, or solely in terms of the arrival of opera in England – a supposedly depoliticised and contextless event in dramatic and musical history.[4] I shall not be discussing the musical aspects of the opera, only the ideological implications of the drama presenting itself as such. The civil, ideological and epistemological crisis of the Civil War created a moment when the English 'nation' must be perceived as capable of many different kinds of definition (or none). The execution of the king, for example, made evident certain differences previously united under the mystifications of divinely sanctioned absolutism and helped to inaugurate that re-definition of the state played out during the later 1650s.

Patricia Coughlan's chapter, which follows, demonstrates the construction of Ireland as an 'other' to England. Here I am concerned with representations of colonial 'others' in discourses of colonialism in the drama written by Davenant and performed at Rutland House and at the Cockpit between 1656 and 1659. These plays constitute themselves in response to the particular ideological conflicts in politics and in the politics of theatrical representation. They appear to avoid all obviously dangerous political ground including the old genres, domestic topics and the representation of Christian kings. Analysis of their position must begin by pointing out that these are plays whose political involvement is inaugurated by their attempt both to avoid controversial forms and their inevitably doomed attempt to avoid reference to an unavoidably political present. Nevertheless, these plays can, at points, be linked fairly closely to Cromwell's foreign policies of the later 1650s.[5] The structure of the plays also provides evidence about the relationship between the legal and political and pragmatic status of performed drama under the Protectorate and it constitutes a response to the terms of the strictures against the theatre in the constructions of the new genre adopted. These new 'operas' also suggest the political implications of the instability of meaning, especially the meaning of the nation, at the moment of production. Additionally, with the exception of *The First Days Entertainment*, the plays' references to the internal politics of Protectorate England – the constant topic of many published dramatic pieces from the Interregnum – takes place through a discourse of the other.[6] Notably, two of the plays, *The Cruelty of the Spaniards in Peru* and *Francis Drake*, operate with reference to England's Elizabethan past. These references exist literally in terms of a glorification of Elizabethan foreign policy (similar to Cromwell's as suggested in the opening quotation) and in terms of a reworking of a Protestant politics, or analysis of the state (as in *The Siege of Rhodes*). Just as the formal aspects of the drama are distanced from pre-war public drama, so the representations of traditional 'others' distance the plays from obvious representation of domestic political conflict. Inevitably, these generic factors and the colonialist discourses interweaving in the plays actually form the mode of entry of these texts into political debate.

The plays Davenant wrote demonstrate anxiety about the position of drama. He himself, as a favourite dramatist of the Stuart court, was in some ways a surprising choice as an officially sanctioned Protectorate dramatist, although he was perhaps vulnerable because of his accidental presence in England. The political positions of dramatists appear to have been much more fluid than any notion of 'royalist' or 'cavalier' allegiance would suggest. Indeed, although Davenant was the only officially sanctioned theatrical figure during the Interregnum, he was not the only dramatist favoured by Henrietta Maria to have had work performed during the Protectorate 1650s – James Shirley's *Cupid and Death* was acted before the Portugese ambassador and he was author of the well-known, even notorious, *Triumph of Peace* (1634). Even John Tatham, who seems to have tried to approach the queen's circle with his first volume of poems and a dramatic pastoral *The Fancies Theater* (1640), made several movements between political positions in the 1650s and ended up writing for the reconstituted Lord Mayor's shows.[7]

Nevertheless, Davenant's performances were the only dramas sanctioned by the state (they were vetted by Thurloe, who might have had a closer involvement) and he may have been helped towards these productions by Bulstrode Whitelocke. These texts of the 1650s were operating in a legal and a discursive context formally, if not actually, determined by the moves against the theatre in 1642 and subsequently (including the harsh enforcement of these measures at the beginning of 1649). The fact that the rhetoric of these legal objections was to a degree moral provided the dramatists with their rhetorical and political positions.[8] It gave them the cue to reply with offers of a 'reformed' stage. Writers, including James Shirley, Richard Flecknoe and Davenant, used the new fashion for opera as a way of offering a reformed drama (in Flecknoe's case the drama was dedicated to Cromwell's daughter-in-law).[9] This was true of plays both for those who saw them and for those who put them on. Accordingly, Davenant's operas avoid the tragic formal structures which would imply a direct analysis of the issues of absolutism and other forms of government.[10] In terms of personnel, however, they were irrevocably linked to courts, kings and court entertainments.

II

Davenant's first intervention in the debate about the reformed stage was performed, unlike the others, on a quasi-public stage in his own house. *The First Days Entertainment at Rutland House* (staged on 23 May 1656) was the first piece of theatre permitted by the Protectorate government and it addresses directly the problem of the nature and value of theatrical representation, an issue also addressed by Edmund Gayton in his preface to the Lord Mayor's show of 1655.[11] The formal aspects of the play initiate the oblique generic relationship between these plays and pre-war genres, an obliquity which I interpret as a response to a perceived crisis in that which it is permissible to articulate. Like a masque, the piece was called after the occasion of its production, but unlike a masque it was called after that only; the title tells us nothing at all about any aspect of what is actually to be performed. Later we learn that the drama is to be 'by declamations and musick after the manner of the ancients'. Such a description clearly places the piece in the context of a reformed theatre: the play demands to be considered as a 'reformed' and 'moral' play. It also displays a radical uncertainty about what a theatrical representation might be, or might be permitted to be.

The drama itself continues the privileging of occasion over narrative found in the title, and the emphasis is on the morally beneficial effects of the stage upon spectators. Not only is it careful to say nothing to offend the government, but it consists largely of a debate between Aristophanes and Diogenes, on the topic of the pros and cons of 'Publique Entertainments by Morall Representations'. So it becomes drama about the possibility of staging drama and it seeks to answer allegations against the theatre on the moral ground set out by the 1642 and 1647 attacks on plays. However, outside the legal sphere, Davenant's opera was operating in the very different context of the Protectorate and had close links with government officers. The form of the piece reflects this in that it hardly resembles a play at all. Instead it is set up as a pair of public debates, which demonstrate literally that the stage could, indeed, teach by delighting.

The First Days Entertainment is a response to the specific ideological and political position in which the theatre found itself. It addresses the issues directly in both the adaptation of its shape from drama to discussion, and in the discussion itself which raises the question of the possibilities of a morally reformed theatre. While representing a revival of the theatre it also represents a visibly radical break with many pre-war conditions of the theatre, but in doing so it also shifts the modes of representation employed by public theatre perceptibly towards the kind found at the court of Charles I. This is evident in the way the title and its construction present it as an occasional piece, as well as in the abandonment of anything approaching narrative, and in the use of spectacle including perspective scenery. Henrietta Maria rarely visited the theatre and Charles I never went, in contrast to the Restoration custom. Arguably, in this piece we see the change between the pre-war and the Restoration stage actually taking place. It could be said that *The First Days Entertainment* was the occasion of the theatrical conventions which before the war had been primarily associated with the court moving on to a stage that was 'public' in the sense that it was open to the public. At any rate, *The First Day's Entertainment* sets the scene for theatre under the Protectorate as radically different from most things which preceded it. The other dramas by Davenant from this period do not emphasise their status as moral representations within arguments conducted as part of the play. It is possible that while this text does not contain elaborate analyses of theatrical representation derived from Aristotle (as do the theatrical treatises of Hedelin and Chapelian) the fact that debate about theatre was permitted in France is very likely to have influenced a dramatist who had been present at Henrietta Maria's court in France. Certainly, this drama is unique in Davenant's mid-century plays in the fact that it actually addresses the question of what a 'moral representation' might be. Nevertheless, the shape of the play, and its status as a particularly oblique kind of meta-theatre from beginning to end, is contiguous with the anxieties about the status and nature of drama in these other operas of the period. Davenant had held discussions with Thurloe before the plays began to be staged, and documents make evident the fact that the state had a close interest at least in the ideological nature of the plays.[12]

The drama which Davenant wrote and which was performed subsequent to the performance of *The First Days Entertainment* and the first part of the *Siege of Rhodes* was *The Cruelty of the Spaniards in Peru*, first performed at the Cockpit during 1658 and simultaneously printed by Henry Herringman.[13] In *The Cruelty of the Spaniards in Peru* the text evidently presents itself as a new kind of drama in its formal aspects and in its construction of Englishness through the representation of the 'natives' and the Spanish. This echoes both generically and in the literalisation of the colonialist metaphor Davenant's assertion in the 'Preface to *Gondibert*' that:

Such limits to the progresses of every thing (even of worthiness as well as defect) doth Imitation give: for whilst wee imitate others, wee can no more excell them, than he that sailes by others Mapps can make a new Discovery.[14]

It is a particularly novel piece of public drama in terms of the ideologies of the nation and of colonisation which it presents and in the relation between the play and the libretto which was simultaneously printed. It demonstrates even more obviously than *The First Days Entertainment* the drama's anxiety about its status and about the political position of opera as constituted both in the shape any performance might take and in terms of the actions represented.

The Cruelty of the Spaniards intermittently tells the story of the arrival of the English in Peru, where they rescue the natives from the evil Spanish. Thus it draws on mythologisations of the English as conquerors in South America established around Drake, Raleigh and others. At the same time the resolution of the play takes place in the future, in the form of a fantasy of the reconquest of South America by the English – and so the play unites past and future, ignoring anything which might pass between. It fuses mythologised past (the golden age of Elizabethan conquest) and the future (the age of reconquest) and so contextualises the present, or moment of production, in a historical continuum which has direct access to Elizabethan politics of nationhood and conquest, obliterating any Stuart history. The political implications of the displacement in Davenant's case are in many ways as obvious as the implications of the structure of both *The First Days Entertainment* and this play in terms of the status of theatrical representation.

The piece, like *The First Days Entertainment*, is not easily placed in generic terms. Music and song are used as a semi-choric comment on tableaux and mimed actions. The mimes also include a variety of tumbling, juggling and acrobatics. The piece does not offer any obvious narrative links between the various 'entries' which are presented as singular, though sequential, episodes. Thus the action provides tableaux which are commented upon in song and speech but which would not be easily understood as a narrative when performed. The connotations of each tableau and mime would not be wholly obscure to the audience, but connection between the scenes and narrative does not inhere wholly in the spectacle. However, in the central role accorded to the libretto, this drama acknowledges the multiplicity of meanings that any actual theatrical performance might generate. It also acknowledges the politicised nature of the interregnum audience. While the libretto is, clearly, there to help the audience follow what is going on, it also tells them what the play in front of them means. It seems of signal importance that Davenant took the trouble to send the text to Bulstrode Whitelocke before the play was produced.[15] This supports my argument that the text actually attempts to contain meaning. The problem of the theatre to the authorities in the 1650s is, in part, how to contain meaning, to deny and circumvent the radical instability of theatrical signs and the multiplicity of potentially subversive meanings generated by direction, acting and the ideological commitments of an audience. Davenant's drama is an isolated event permitted by a government which attempted to control theatre by a more complete suppression. It comes as no surprise, then, to find that the play's anxieties about the politicisation of meaning are 'internalised'. *The Cruelty of the Spaniards* makes a bid to foreclose on interpretation. The narrative, and thus much of the ideologically laden signification of the drama consists not in what actually happened on stage, but in a libretto sold at the door and giving a very detailed description of what is witnessed on stage. The libretto gives a 'definitive' interpretation of events on stage (i.e. scenes, songs and acrobatics) by fitting them into a narrative and ascribing meaning to that narrative.

The libretto supplies a hermeneutic code, which links the visual and aural codes into a narrative strongly suggesting an interpretation to the audience. The libretto inserts itself into the audience's interpretation by putting the meaning outside 'the play', outside whatever is actually taking place on stage. The publication of the libretto can also be seen as an attempt to fix the dynamics of actual theatrical production in one manifestation, that is in the printed, published text which can be presented as standing for the performance.

The natives of North and South America had been commonly represented as both vicious and noble savages.[16] If the savages here are noble then it is Arcadian and Edenic. And if it is Eden, then Spain is the serpent. Fulke Greville (for whom Davenant worked) described it in his *Life of Sidney* (published 1652) as the ultimate land of opportunity – for an overwhelmingly English way of life:

To Martiall men he [Sidney] opened wide the door of the sea and land, for fame and conquest. To the nobly ambitious the far stage of *America* to win honour in. To the Religious divines, besides a new Apostollical calling of the land of the heathen to the Christian faith, a large field of reducing poor Christians, mis-led by the Idolatry of Rome to their mother *Primitive* Church. To the ingeniously industrious variety of naturall richnesses, for new mysteries and manufactures to work upon. To the Merchant, with a simple people, a fertile and unexhausted earth. To the fortune-bound, liberty. To the curious, a fruitful womb of innovation. Generally the word Gold was an attractive Adamant, to make men venture that which they have, in hope to grow rich by that which they have not.[17]

As Roland Barthes puts it in *Mythologies*, the differential between the way of life there and the way of life in Europe was sufficient for the natives and their culture to become idealised, as they did to a degree for Las Casas on whose narrative the text and visual tableaux of *Cruelty of the Spaniards* are fairly closely based. This idealisation can be directly linked to material and national investments. Just as Greville, Davenant's mentor in his youth, associated the Americas with opportunity, wealth (gold) and the validation of masculinity, so Las Casas saw it as a paradise, an Eden spoilt by the exploitation of the noble natives. Davenant, like Greville, in turn both valorises the English and represents the natives as tractable, but also produces a scapegoat – Spanish nationalism, Catholicism and colonial ambition.

The Spanish are represented as truly vile, and their colonialism signals corruption through their indulgence in the rankest torture. In terms of the displacements effected in Davenant's interregnum work, here the Spanish are represented as venting tortures on the noble natives very similar to those which the natives themselves are sometimes represented as inflicting on Europeans. Vivid pictures of the cruelty of native South Americans to other natives are particularly found in such places as Purchas's *Pilgrims*. Here, for instance, the Mexicans are contrasted with the Peruvians, and the Spaniards are the 'civilising' influence,

They of *Peru* have surpassed the *Mexicans* in the slaughter and Sacrifice of their children . . . yet they of *Mexico* have exceeded them, yea all the Nations of the World, in the great number of men they have sacrificed and the horrible manner thereof . . . The *Spaniards* that saw these cruell Sacrifices, resolved with all their power to abolish so detestable and cursed butchering of men, and the rather, for that in one night they saw threescore or threescore and tenne *Spaniards* sacrificed.[18]

The play presents an almost exact replica of these circumstances, except that the torturers are the Spanish, the Peruvians the tortured. The libretto/narrative provides a particularly appetising description at Entry 5:

A dolefull pavin is plai'd to prepare the change of the Scene, which represents a dark prison at great distance; and farther to the view are discerned Racks, and other Engins of torment, with which the Spaniards are tormenting the natives and english Marriners, which may be suppos'd to be lately landed there to discover the Coast, two Spaniards are likewise discover'd, sitting in their cloaks and appearing more solemn in Ruffs, with Rapiers and Daggers by their sides; the one turning a Spit, whilst the other is basting an *Indian* Prince, which is rosted at an artificiall fire.[19]

Needless to say, the English triumph sees the Spanish grovelling and the natives gambolling in delight. They are no longer particularly similar to their virtuous English conquerors. The play sets up the co-ordinates of the colonial discourse which has three terms, the Christian conquerers, the pagan 'discovered' and the Spaniards characterised as a diabolic agency. Thus the status of the fantasised campaign is elevated to that of a crusade against not the Peruvians – whose country is a locus of desire, filled with possibility perceived as a country with a (European) future – but against the Spanish. The narrative presents a futuristic fantasy of a battle for primacy between a Protestant and a Catholic European nation acted out in a remote location. The colonial ambitions of England are justified and validated in their treatment of the Spaniards and, particularly as the narrative is set in the future, there is no need to address the dynastic question of in whom the rule over the noble Peruvians would be invested.

The play's analysis of colonial ambition reverses the positions of the civilised and the barbaric through this addition of a third term, a third nation, the Spanish. Ideologies of nationhood are not made explicit except in the broadest possible way: Roman Catholic Spaniards are defined against good Protestant English but no question is raised about whether the good Protestants are monarchic or republican Protestants. The disappearance of the present between past and future is one factor which enables the question of national authority to – conspicuously – disappear. Also, the discourses of colonial conquest engulf the pressing questions of nationhood.

A further dimension is given to *The Cruelty of the Spaniards* when we find that the narrative from which it was taken was inscribed very firmly in a specific ideological tradition. John Phillips who translated *The Teares of the Indians* (1656) dedicated it to Cromwell.[20] Phillips is voluble about the urgent need for the Peruvians to be protected by the English. He writes to Cromwell of 'the cry of Bloud ceasing at the noise of Your great transactions; while you arm for their revenge' (A3v). The 'revenge' for which Phillips argues is thus enacted in Davenant's narrative of a glorious future crusade. Analogues can be found for Davenant's use of sources with ideological profiles of high nationalism in the narrative material used in *The History of Sir Francis Drake*, Davenant's other interregnum play which dramatises a story from an Elizabethan expansionist past. Philip Nichols's *Drake Revived* (London, 1626) is the text on which *The History of Sir Francis Drake* is based. Nichols calls upon 'this Dull or Effeminate age, to follow in his Noble Steps for Gold and Silver', though here the context for the 'effeminacy' would appear to be the accession of Charles after James I. Davenant and Nichols replicate one another in their appeal to new regimes for an active foreign policy following broadly that of Elizabeth and it comes as no surprise to find *Sir Francis Drake Revived* reprinted in 1652. Moreover, the other Drake material, *The World Encompassed* (1636), offered itself 'especially for the stirring up of *heroick spirits*, to benefit their Countrie'.[21] Drake literature was periodically reprinted, and while it is of course possible that Davenant explicitly studied these books for his trip to Virginia, the narratives were also apparently woven into national consciousness and seem to have formed a part of the *mythos* of Elizabethan foreign policy. This policy Cromwell reiterated, for example in the 1656 inaugural speech to Parliament, where he combined it with a call to action: 'Truly our business is to speak Things; the dispensations of God that are upon us do demand it.' (Abbott, 4, p. 260). The colonialist representations of both *The Cruelty of the Spaniards* and *Francis Drake* echo Cromwell's foreign policy, call up memories of a heroic Protestant past and avoid issues of contemporary domestic import.

If the Americas provide a model of otherness against which a present Englishness can be established with reference to the past of the nation and its future, then the representation of the Turk in *The Siege of Rhodes* offers a more complex colonial representation. In the 'Preface to *Gondibert*' Davenant wrote of the Mohammedian 'vaine pride of Empire', and Walter Benjamin, writing on the German tragic drama aptly commented that for Europe, 'the history of the Orient [was] where absolute imperial power was to be encountered', yet in *The Siege of Rhodes* I and II, we find this mythologisation gradually subverted and unravelled.[22] It is also one which serves to illuminate Davenant's reinscription of Greville's political analysis and, to some extent, his dramatic poetics, into an almost Hobbesian analysis of the contemporary crisis in the right to rule. On the one hand the play provides a 'love and honour' drama in which issues of fidelity, honour and loyalty are raised. On the other hand it is a play which presents and partially undercuts historically determined notions of the Turk as Satanic and offers, at least potentially, a critique of militaristic and absolute government (while at the same time Cromwell drifted daily closer to being a *de facto* hereditary monarch). This complex representation of the Turk as both other and similar draws on diabolised mythologisations of the Turk alongside which trading relations had existed, but I would argue that this particular representation also utilises the implications of a particular event in the year in which the play was first produced.

The first part of *The Siege of Rhodes* followed a few months after *The First Days Entertainment*, in 1656, and was published in that year and again with *Francis Drake* in 1659. In 1661 both parts of *The Siege of Rhodes* were staged alternately at the Lisle's Tennis Court theatre, and in 1663 the revised version (and very different second part) were all published.[23] Substantial differences exist between the representation of politics in the first and second part. Here I shall examine briefly the representation of the Turk on the English stage in the 1656 version, and the issues of absolutism and the will of the people raised in the second part. The first part, sometimes described as the first English opera, is interestingly balanced between public and private theatre. The two parts of the play provide, firstly, a definition of European values in relation to an 'other' (the Turk). But later that scheme is questioned when the Turk, previously constituted as the other, comes to represent values similar to those of the Europeans.

The play describes the siege of Rhodes in 1522, when the English were involved in the garrisoning of the island. It presents the audience with two rival armies fighting over the town. The English ('lions') are represented in Rhodes, but the central conflict is between the Rhodian forces

and the Turks. The Turk is initially represented as a powerful force, with
his fleet moving towards Rhodes:

> ADMIRAL: Her shady wings to distant sight,
>   Spread like the curtains of the night
>   Each Squadron thicker and still darker grows,
>   The Fleet like many floating forrests shows.
>   1 *Siege of Rhodes* I.i. 11–14

Initially at the start the Turk is represented as an 'other' – dark, pleth-
oric, dangerous; an apparition to contrast with the European virtues of
Rhodes. However, as the play goes on this reassuringly different 'other'
shows evidence of increased affinity to the Rhodians. The initial presentation of the Turks draws on the historical status of the Turk as a threat
to European Christendom, to the kingdom of God itself. As C. A.
Patrides notes, the equation between the Sultan and Satan was a commonplace. The play activates those discourses with which (in the words of
Edward Said), the east 'has helped to define Europe . . . as its contrasting
image, idea, personality, experience'.[24] Just as in *The Cruelty of the Spaniards in Peru* a battle is joined, but here it is situated on the edge of Europe,
at the border with beyond. Instead of presenting two European powers
struggling for dominance in a landscape empty of values (or of questionable values), it presents a united Europe defending an outpost against an
enemy which was traditionally perceived as pressing on the frontiers of
the western world, threatening disruption, destruction and the end of
Christendom itself.

If the Ottoman empire historically provided an 'other' by which Europe
defined itself, then the genuineness of this 'otherness' was constantly
undermined by the close trading links between Turkey and Europe. *The
Siege of Rhodes* draws on the double standard by which the Ottoman
empire was seen as a recognisable 'other'. The play also presents an
uncanny similarity or replicatory re-presentation of the west to itself. Its
detailed hierarchies might be seen as in many ways analogous to European, or specifically English monarchies of types both *de facto* and *de jure*.
Furthermore, that which made the Turks available for this dual representation as 'other' and 'similar' was, in part, the fact that the Ottoman empire
suffered its worst defeat since Lepanto, when the Venetian fleet came close
to destroying the Ottoman fleet at the mouth of the Dardanelles on 26 June
1656 – months before *The Siege of Rhodes* was entered on the stationers'
register.[25] At the end of August 1656 Giavarina was finally granted an
audience with Cromwell and he reported the Protector's response to the
news of the Turkish defeat:

'he [Cromwell] added that now the strength of the Turks was so attenuated it would be advisable for all Christian powers to join forces.'[26]

The fact that Ottoman empire was at the time a declining threat to Europe allowed the Turk to be represented as both a grotesque of otherness and, at the same time, a humanisedly similar subject.

The Turk, in Davenant's play the 'external' subject, becomes in fact a mirror image of not merely European, but English questions about government. Earlier representations of the diabolic Turk are reinscribed in a context which is sensitive to the power of the notion of the religious unity of Islam. The discourse of colonialism is turned upon itself, and the issue of power and the struggles for power are presented as ubiquitous. Both the Sultan and the Rhodian leaders are represented as ultimately at the mercy of the will of the people. Both Solyman and the Grand Master of Rhodes confront the problem of negotiating a connection between absolute rule and the people's will. The powerlessness of the Turkish absolute monarch at the hands of his people is echoed in the rebellion of the Rhodians against the continuation of battle.

> SOLYMAN: Of spacious Empire, what can I enjoy?
> Gaining at last but what I first Destroy.
> Tis fatal (*Rhodes*) to thee,
> And troublesome to me
> That I was born to govern swarms
> Of Vassals boldly bred to arms:
> For whose accurs'd diversion, I must still
> Provide new Towns to Sack, new Foes to Kill
>
> . . .
>
> For I shall find my peace
> Destroy'd at home, unless
> I seek for them destructive Warr abroad
> 2 *Siege of Rhodes* II.ii. 52–64

The Sultan is presented both as an eastern despot, and as a ruler facing the inevitable problems of absolute rule. It is consonant with the representation of the Turks offered by Giovanni Botero:

The Turkes give their minds to nothing but warre, nor take care of anything else but the provision of armour and weapons: courses fitter to destroy and waste, than to preserve and inrich provinces.[27]

The uncontrollable force of the people is echoed in the Grand Master's acknowledgement of their will (2 *Siege* 1.263–71). Eventually, the people take control in Rhodes and Ianthe is elected as their ambassador to the Sultan: Villerius comments: 'Who can resist if they will have it so.' (2 *Siege of Rhodes* I.198–200). As Ann-Marie Hedbäck points out, this implies a quasi-Hobbesian analysis of power.[28] Neither the absolutist monarch nor the Rhodian militarised aristocracy are capable of overruling the desires of the people. The only difference between the Rhodians and the Turks is that the warlike disposition of the Turkish people forces the Sultan to acts of aggression whereas the Rhodian people demand peace; the question of who rules and how that rule is effected remains present. Villerius comments:

> Ianthe needs must go. Those who withstand
> The tide of Flood, which is the Peoples will,
> Fall back when they would onward row,
> We strength and way presume by lying still.
>
> (2 *Siege of Rhodes* I.i. 18–20)

The quotations show that by the end of the play the presentation of Rhodian and Turkish states as binary opposites has broken down. The Turks do not rebel, as the Rhodians do, but then their leader epitomises, rather than opposes, them. The representation of government as hanging on the will of the people strikingly echoes a line in Fulke Greville's *Mustapha*, when Rosten says:

> Towards *Solyman* they runne: and as the *Waters*
> That meet with baks of Snow, make Snow grow Water:
> So, even those Guards, that stood to interrupt them,
> Give easie passage, and passe on amongst them.[29]

Davenant also appears to draw on Greville's *Treaty of Warres* in *The Siege of Rhodes*.[30] Both the *Treaty* and *The Siege* initially appear to be ideologically committed to a defence of national war, and each text contains an inbuilt critique of its apparent assumptions. The *Treaty* slips and slides syntactically from one position to another until the whole issue of a just war is called into doubt. Ideas which each text implicitly question include the notion that a ruler's sanction justifies war, the assumption that colonial wars are justified and the assumption that a simplistic sort of obedience is the duty of the people to the ruler. It seems likely that Davenant was influenced here by both the literary output of his former employer and by the ideas in Greville's texts about government. However, the Protestantism of Greville is transformed in Davenant's text into an analysis which presents government as expedient and pragmatic, not an issue of right at all.

III

Walter Benjamin suggests that 'the theory of sovereignty which takes as its example the special case in which dictatorial powers are unfolded positively demands the completion of the sovereign as tyrant'. (*Origin of*

German Tragic Drama, p. 69). *The Siege of Rhodes* subverts this pattern found again and again in interregnum drama, whereby the sovereign is replaced by the tyrant, and avoids both generically and ideologically the tragic completion of the absolutist sovereign. Instead the drama untangles the interwoven issues of absolutism and tyranny, undoing the tragic pattern (and genre) simultaneously as it undoes the opposition between east and west. The rulers of Europe and Turkey are represented as equivalent, and powerless, at the moment at which the 'dictatorial powers' – absolutely absolute, tyrannical, powers – would otherwise come into being.

In this way *The Siege of Rhodes* seeks to dissolve the problematic pressure of civil politics. Elsewhere in these interregnum plays we find nationalistic and colonialist drama. These dramas mobilise mythologisations of old enemies – the Turks and the Spanish – to represent an 'other' against which to define present Englishness. Yet at the same time, in the case of *The Siege of Rhodes*, they undermine the validity of such enterprises. These plays seek to avoid exploration of problems of England's internal conflict and the uneasy position of the theatre itself in terms of that conflict. With the exception of *The First Day's Entertainment at Rutland House*, these plays seek to solve questions of rule and government by dramatising international crusades, in which the imperialist and colonialist English are seen not only to crush opposition, but are also the bearers of positive values of good government.

This way of reading Davenant's interregnum drama illuminates the situation of drama and theatre in the conflicts of the mid-seventeenth century. In Davenant's case an analysis of this interregnum drama in terms of suppression of pressing issues of national conflict and the substitution of colonial fantasies and histories, relying on the representations of 'others', provides a fruitful place to begin a re-reading of the drama of the interregnum period. This drama is implicated in positions and dialogues which cannot be represented as straightforwardly and consistently divided between royalist and republican interests. Davenant's interregnum drama can tell us stories about the representation of nationhood – but these stories are double edged. Generically, Davenant's interregnum drama challenges our continued assumptions about seventeenth-century drama and its relation to absolutism. Davenant's plays from this period represent a group of which it is significantly and unusually *not* true to say 'the sovereign . . . holds the course of history in his hands like a scepter' (Benjamin, p. 65). However, in so far as we can read these plays as marginally unravelling and de-coding the dominant myths of monarchical/absolute power, we must simultaneously read the concomitant displacement of the absolute power struggle into fantasies of colonial dominance.

NOTES

1 *Writings and Speeches of Oliver Cromwell,* ed. Wilbur Cortez Abbott, 4 vols. (Cambridge MA, 1947), IV, p. 261.
2 Jorge Luis Borges, 'The Dread Redeemer Lazarus Morell', *A Universal History of Infamy* (first published as *Historia universal de la infamia,* (Buenos Aires, 1954; Harmondsworth, 1973, 1975), p. 19.
3 Michel Pecheaux, *Language, Semantics, Ideology,* trans. Harbans Nagpal (1975; London, 1982), p. 111: 'words . . . change their meaning according to the positions from which they are used'.
4 See A.H. Nethercott, *Sir William Davenant* (1938; New York, 1967); Alfred Harbage, *Sir William Davenant, Poet Venturer 1606–1668* (Philadelphia, 1935), and *Cavalier Drama* (New York, 1936).
5 Eric Walter White, *A History of Opera* (London, 1983), p. 65.
6 Published plays dealing directly with the political crises of the 1640s and 1650s include Samuel Sheppard, *The Commitee-Man Curried* (1647), *Crafty Cromwell, or Oliver Ordering Our New State* (1648), *The Mistress Parliament* plays of 1648, John Tatham's *The Scots Figgaries* (1652) and *The Rump* (1659).
7 John Tatham provided shows from 1657 to 1663.
8 The Ordinance of 11 February 1647/8 speaks of plays in moral terms as 'condemned by ancient Heathens and much less to be tolerated among Professors of the Christian Religion'. Charles Firth, ed. *Acts and Ordinances of the Interregnum 1642–1660* (London, 1911) I, pp. 1070–1.
9 Richard Flecknoe, *Love's Dominion* (London, 1654). Flecknoe's dedication to the Lady Elizabeth Claypole runs, 'never a more Innocenter thing appeared in court . . . For the rest, I dare not interest you in its more publique Representation, not knowing how the palat of the time may relish such Things yet, which, till it was disgusted with them, was formerly numbered among its chiefest Dainties', A3r–A3v.
10 Franco Moretti in 'The Great Eclipse' writes of tragedy as the form which acknowledges the implications of absolutism. Moretti seeks to demonstrate that 'tragedy disentitled the absolute monarch to all ethical and rational legitimation. Having deconsecrated the king, tragedy made it possible to decapitate him.' *Signs Taken For Wonders* (London, 1983), p. 40. A similar reading of the relation between absolutism and the tragic genre can be found in Walter Benjamin's *Origin of German Tragic Drama* trans. John Osborne (London, 1977), pp. 69–72.
11 Edmund Gayton, *Charity Triumphant, or the Virgin-Shew,* acted 29 October 1655 (London, 1655), p. 3.
12 White, *History of Opera,* p. 65.
13 *The Cruelty of the Spaniards in Peru,* performed by July 1658.
14 *Gondibert,* ed. David F. Gladish (Oxford, 1971); 'The Author's Preface', p. 7.
15 Bulstrode Whitelocke, *Memorials of the English Affairs* 4 vols. (1732; Oxford, 1753), III, p. 462; IV, p. 273.
16 In Davenant's *Francis Drake* they are represented as both at different points in the plot. See also Peter Hulme's *Colonial Encounters: Europe and the Native Caribbean, 1492–1797* (London, 1986).
17 Fulke Greville, *Life of Sidney* (London, 1652), pp. 132–3.
18 Samuel Purchas, *Purchas His Pilgrims* (London, 1625), in five books, the third

204 SUSAN J. WISEMAN

part. Book V, p. 1037 line 25; p. 1039, line 50. Thanks to Ms. Claudia
Strasky.
19 *The Cruelty of the Spaniards in Peru* (London, 1658) p. 19.
20 Bartolome de las Casas, *The Teares of the Indians*, trans. John Phillips (London,
1656), A3v.
21 Philip Nichols, *Sir Francis Drake Revived* (London, 1621; reprinted 1626, 1652).
Quotation from titlepage of 1626 edition. *The World Encompassed*, (London,
1636).
22 'Preface,' *Gondibert*, p. 12; Walter Benjamin, *The Origin of German Tragic
Drama*, p. 68.
23 William Davenant, *The Siege of Rhodes,* ed. Ann-Marie Hedbäck (Uppsala,
1973). Hedbäck gives two editions – the 1656 edition and the 1663 additions
to the first part. The play exists in 4 quartos – 1656, 1659, 1663, 1670. 1SR
entered on Stationers Register, 27 August 1656.
24 C.A. Patrides, 'The Judgements of God' in *Premises and Motifs in Renaissance
Thought and Literature* (Princeton, 1982) pp. 137–51; Edward Said, *Orientalism*
(London, 1978), p. 1. See also Christine Woodhead, 'The Present Terrour of
the World? Contemporary Views of the Ottoman Empire c1600' in *History*,
72, 234 (Feb 1987).
25 Stanford Shaw, *History of the Ottoman Empire and modern Turkey* (Cambridge,
1976) I, p. 200.
26 Abbott, 4, p. 273.
27 Giovanni Botero, *The Traveller's Breviat* (London, 1601), pp. 41, 43. Incidentally, Joan Rees thinks that the *Breviat* may have influenced Fulke Greville's
Treatie of Warres which would seem to have in turn considerable bearing on
Davenant's *Siege of Rhodes*. See Fulke Greville, *The Writings of Fulke˙Greville*
(London, 1973). David Norbook, *Poetry and Politics in the Renaissance* (London
1984). 'Voluntary Servitude: Fulke Greville and the Arts of Power', pp. 157–74
provides a clear and convincing analysis of Greville's unease with the mystifications of kingship.
28 Ann-Marie Hedbäck, ed., *The Siege of Rhodes: A Critical Edition* (Uppsala,
1973), p. lxvii.
29 *Mustapha*, Actus Quintus, scena tertia 25–31 in *Poems and Dramas of Fulke
Greville*, ed. Geoffrey Bullough, 2 vols. (Edinburgh and London, 1939), II.
30 Fulke Greville, *Treaty of Warres*, G. Bullough, ed. *Poems and Dramas*, I.

11 'Cheap and common animals': the English anatomy of Ireland in the seventeenth century

IRISH HISTORY, while profoundly influenced at every turn by that of its neighbour, nevertheless does not answer very well to English periodisation. The dynamic is different. At the outset of the English Civil War Ireland contained plantations less than fifty years old, and while it had in the east and in the towns an ancient and sophisticated legal and political culture based on the English model, other areas of the country preserved in varying degrees of strength the still older native forms of political behaviour. Thus in the 1630s Strafford's Irish policies were an attempt to institute thorough centralising control over a society which was divided in quite other ways, and over issues quite different, from those which preoccupied contemporary England. Questions of church government and royal prerogative were heavily inflected in Ireland by ethnic power struggles, not merely by differences of religious or political principle or class tensions. But Irish divisions are not readily to be understood as simple ethnic polarities. Paradoxically a common religion uneasily united the 'Old English' elite – Catholics of Norman origin – with the native aristocracy in resistance to Strafford's autocratic tactics. Later, in the 1640s, the Irish wars were fought in patterns formed very much in that country, and with constant and bewildering shifts of allegiance, and are no more than 'inconvenienced' with English interventions on different scales until Cromwell's definitive 1649 expedition. And even then, the development of factions during the 1650s among apparently unified interest groups complicates the effects of the Cromwellian conquest. The 'new English' – the group of pre-1649, largely Elizabethan and Jacobean settlers – have by 1660, before the Restoration, come quietly into possession of the land and power so patently in the hands of the radical Cromwellians a decade before.

The study of English writings about Ireland in these two decades is complicated not only by these sharp differences from the familiar and prevailing English modes of understanding the period, but also by the brute facts of current historiography. While the interesting texts of the period in England have long been known, though not always studied sufficiently in relation to their context, there are as yet no synthetic accounts of the body of writings either in or about Ireland in the period. Historians have occasionally put to use particular texts (for example Petty's *History of the Down Survey*, published in 1852) as sources of factual information, and it is conventional to notice the influence of the 1641 massacre-descriptions on English public opinion. But there has not yet been any significant attempt to investigate the various writings of the period in themselves as symbolic representations (as distinct from seeing them as relatively inert and transparently readable pieces of evidence for the views or political positions of various factions). The unfamiliarity of the material which results from these considerations means that it must be approached very differently from well-known writings such as *Areopagitica*, Marvell's 'Horatian Ode', or even Lucy Hutchinson's work. I have therefore sometimes found it necessary in the case of the least known texts to offer a descriptive as well as an analytic account. Equally, the detail of contemporary Irish, as distinct from English, history needs to be recalled before the possible significations of a work totally imbricated in it can be at all usefully explored.

There is also, however, a sense in which the approach of this book appears in Ireland less surprising or new than it may do to those accustomed to English literary or historical perspectives. Irish experience has preserved quite unbroken the connection between history and literature, rhetoric and action, which has in England become problematic – though it was not so in the seventeenth century. To Irish consciousness the mutual interpenetration of texts and events is a given, not the perhaps slightly threatening and radical postulate it is in England. Because of its close and nervous relation to the ideology actually seen to govern political actions, colonial discourse shows with particular clarity a general dependence upon shared representations. These representations – for instance, of the roles of coloniser and colonised, and of socially desirable goals – cut across the generic boundaries between literary texts and other kinds of writing.

Seventeenth-century writings about Ireland did not, of course, construct their representations of the Irish *ab initio*. They worked by modifying and adjusting as seemed necessary those views about the Irish arrived at in earlier periods. There is not scope here to rehearse the long process of construction of these stereotypes, effected by the centuries-long interaction of prejudice and experience in the power relations of Irish and English.[1] The particular background against which the thought of mid-seventeenth-century writers was formed was that of the intensive phase of Elizabethan and Jacobean colonisation, which produced the classic expressions of early modern Anglo-Irish colonist ideology, among them the writings of Spenser and Sir John Davies. Spenser's *View of the Present State of Ireland* (written in 1596, though not published until 1633) is indeed the founding text of modern English discourse about Ireland, and was a specific influence in the civil war decades on Englishmen's approach to Ireland. It affords a particularly appropriate source for a summary account of those received representations which are the basis of seventeenth-century English thought and action in respect of Ireland.[2]

Spenser's images of the Irish, like those of his fellow-colonist writers, are based on the more general Renaissance typology of the wildness outside civil society, a set of representations which has been well described by Hayden White. As such they resemble those prevailing in other colonial situations in the period – for instance in Spanish interpretations of South American indigenes in the context of their rule over them – and can also be paralleled in English accounts of North American Indians. In spite of the major actual differences between these various places and peoples, their colonising interpreters came to them equipped with more or less the same model of civility versus barbarity formed in the tradition of European classical and Christian thought.[3]

Bearing in mind these pre-formed notions about the incivility of those without a native urban culture, in Spenser's attitude to Ireland and the Irish one may identify a negative and a positive moment, of which the negative is dominant. In the *View* it consists of an assumption that the Irish are a 'salvage' nation, who represent an irredeemable otherness and are impermeable to civility. They are sly, dissolute, fickle and imponderable. The only way to deal with them is by ruthless suppression and if necessary by eradication.[4] The territory of Ireland is presented as a hostile wilderness, alien to civilised understanding, in which these savage and implacable enemies fleetingly appear and disappear. It consists of 'great mountains and waste deserts full of grass', whose inhabitants are 'Scythian' in their propensity to wander with their cattle-herds from place to place and thus defy the imposition of civil order. There runs through the *View* a series of antitheses between these Irish, who 'swerve', 'straggle', 'miche in corners', 'wander loosely', are 'ydely roguing', and the English policy which is intended to repress such qualities, and which will have them 'shortly to be brought in by the ears', feel 'the bitternesse of the marshall lawe', and so forth.[5] The countryside too must be controlled, shut down, contained, by means of clearings, bridges and forts.

Very occasionally, however, in *The Faerie Queene* (especially I.vi and IV.iv) Spenser does invent some 'salvage' characters about whose development to fully human status he can express a sense of possibility, and who are basically benign in spite of living outside the bounds of normal society. The Irish landscape, too, is sometimes assimilated imaginatively to an ideal order, for instance in the Faunus and Diana episode of the Mutabilitie Cantos. This episode reconstructs the Munster countryside as an ideal territory, to which the beauty of perfect order is imputed by the genial personification of local mountains and streams (VII. vi. 46–55). This impeccably Ovidian fable has also strong echoes of Irenius' policy programme for Ireland in the *View*.

Finally, when in *Colin Clouts Come Home Againe* (1591), Spenser attempts to bring together both the moments of his vision of Ireland, the result is uneasily paradoxical and confusing, and strains the pastoral form. To Colin, Ireland is both a beautiful, fertile, fictionally native land, and a 'waste desart' full of human and inhuman horrors, 'the griesly famine and the raging sweard', 'wayling' and 'wretchednesse' (lines 91, 184, 312–19). In this uncertainty of perspective we may identify a characteristic which is of central importance in English writing about Ireland in the succeeding century. Ireland in the poem is being made to pose for Arcadia, but even in the transforming mode of pastoral poetry it cannot be made altogether to fit the role, any more than it will be readily accommodated to the new Utopian (rather than Arcadian) formulations of some seventeenth-century 'projectors'.

In spite of the rebarbatively negative tone of Spenser's version of Ireland in the *View*, it was nevertheless already being naturalised or refunctioned as distinctively Anglo-Irish discourse when it was first published in Sir James Ware's version, *The Historie of Ireland* (Dublin, 1633). Ware, a Protestant of English stock, embodied in his own repertoire of social roles the doubleness or multiplicity of perspectives often entailed upon those publicly active in colonial situations. He was, on the one hand, a trusted office-holder in Strafford's divisive and autocratic regime, and on the other an extremely important antiquarian, historian and collector of ancient Irish manuscripts, who maintained cordial communications with contemporary Gaelic poets and was responsible for the survival of precious early works.[6] His version of the *View* makes systematic and highly significant textual modifications to the original, all tending to a considerable softening of Spenser's harsh judgements about the native Irish and particularly the Old English. He further affects readers' reception of the *View* by reprinting along with it the rivers passage from *Faerie Queene* IV and the Mutabilitie Cantos, the two passages of Spenser's text which most idealise and offer a benign transformation of the Irish landscape. Ware also adds an eirenic preface which expresses (optimistically) his sense of an Irish unity now achieved.[7] A major shift of emphasis has occurred between Spenser's unbending condemnation of Irish actuality – delivered in the context of rebellion and confiscation – and Ware's foregrounding of the *View's* historical and antiquarian aspect, which can hardly have been in the 1590s the most salient part of the text.

An interesting contrast with Ware's refunctioning of Spenser is provided by James Shirley's play *St. Patrick for Ireland*, produced in Dublin on the eve of the Civil War, during the 1639–40 theatre season.[8] The piece presents Patrick's conversion of the pagan Irish as a civilising enterprise. The foreign arrival Patrick, who is 'of Brittaine, sir' (I.i.175), is made responsible for initiating Ireland's medieval glories of faith and learning in the teeth of the sullenly resistant, bloody and duplicitous Irish king and pagan priests, whose barbarism is strongly reminiscent of that attributed by Spenser in the *View* to the vengeful, blood-drinking, 'Scythian' Gaels. The play ends with an outward capitulation by the native king, but he is covertly determined to carry on a diehard opposition. This may well represent, in a manner gratifying to Strafford and his regime, the crass stubbornness of current Irish resistance to centralising English rule and the wisdom of treating cautiously any apparent native submission. Thus by a curious reversal of the legend's cultural significance *to the Irish*, the civilising influence Patrick represents comes to stand for that currently being exercised by the English. This would make the Irish (shown as stubbornly refusing enlightenment by Patrick) responsible for their own imputed barbarity, a condition already detailed in Spenser and other writings and vividly present to the English popular imagination since Elizabethan times.[9] In the context of the Caroline court, Shirley may appear to have had reservations about absolutist royal policies, but it would be as incautious to apply this as it would be many other English-based presumptions, without careful modification, to his stance in Ireland.[10] On a personal and professional level, certainly, the sour tone of Shirley's Dublin Prologues suggests an impatience with the Irish and their cultural limitations which lead to a refusal or an incapacity to support the drama adequately. Furthermore, there is no obvious evidence that his Catholicism had any moderating effect on his hostility to these – no doubt largely Old English and Catholic – audiences.[11] The most positive aspect of native Ireland in the play is perhaps the 'Bard', who, while primarily a comic figure, is nevertheless benign and ultimately willing to be converted and to follow Patrick. But on the whole, one can find little in Shirley's version of Ireland in this play which would reveal the development of any insight into the situation of the colonised in that country. Nor is there a capacity to apprehend the place from anything other than a strictly colonising viewpoint.

Understanding the possible political and wider cultural meanings of Shirley's text is a complex matter. Yet, though I wish to stress the absence of an enlightening vision of Irishness in Shirley, and set his work against Ware's in that respect, one must bear in mind that the two are products of the same cultural milieu, however different they are in character. This fact returns us to the observation I have made at the outset of a simultaneous continuity and tension within the surviving body of seventeenth-century Anglo-Irish texts.

After the Irish rising which began in October 1641, however, there appears a strain of English writings about the Irish which are of an alarming simplicity. The problem of what actually happened in 1641 is one of the most vexed questions in Irish historiography and political mythology, and I shall not attempt to examine it here.[12] But the *representations* of 1641 greatly influenced English thinking about Ireland for some time afterwards. The intention of the original Commissions of Enquiry was to record the quantity and value of money and property stolen from Protestants, but within a few weeks an equal or greater emphasis was being laid on the alleged atrocities committed.[13] Stories about the wholesale massacre of Protestants began to circulate in the early months of 1642, and the English Commons commissioned reports by Irish Protestant spokesmen such as Henry Jones, then Dean of Clogher, who had himself been a refugee from the rising. Jones's pamphlet *A Remonstrance*, published in March 1642, is relatively restrained compared to the subsequent lurid pamphlet literature on the subject, of which the classic example is Sir John Temple's prurient and repetitive *History of the Irish Rebellion* (1646). Jones's text nevertheless shows the qualities familiar from other contemporary atrocity stories, rehearsing many times a series of incidents which form a fixed repertoire of symbolically arresting and evocative horrors: stripping naked, dashing out of the brains of infants on stones, burial alive, mockery and trampling of the sacred book (in one case 'causing the bagpipes to play the while') and 'ripping up', especially of pregnant women.[14] These images passed into the popular propagandists' minds, and recur countless times in the news-sheets of the following decade or more, where they are used to whip up indignation against the 'bloody inhumane savages' in Ireland who were at war throughout the 1640s with parliament. The few protests against this dominant attitude – by some Levellers and by figures such as Henry Marten and Thomas Walwyn – have been detailed by historians of the radical opposition in England.[15] But for the duration of the wars and commonwealth the prevailing image in England was dominated by grotesque stereotypes: monsters of cruelty, living subhumanly in bogs and wielding 'skeines' (Irish *scian*, long knife), often by a scornful metonymy themselves labelled 'trowses' after Irish traditional warriors' dress. It is a picture not confined to the popular newsbooks; it is recognisable in several passages of Milton's writings, particularly (but not exclusively) in his *Observations Upon the Articles of Peace* (1648), the extraordinarily bitter and vituperative pamphlet written to attack the Irish royalist leader Ormond and the 'blockish' Belfast Presbyterians on the occasion of Ormond's truce with the Irish rebels.[16] Throughout the 1640s, any mention of the Irish seems to require an epithet such as 'bloody', 'cruel' or 'inhuman' to be communicatively effective. In the 1660s popular literature begins to find it possible again to include a more positive, though scarcely more nuanced, image of Ireland in its vocabulary. Brome's collection of *Rump Songs*, for example, contains several jolly national medleys each of which mobilised Irishmen along with the Scots and Welsh, and sometimes with the French and Dutch too, in a vague and wish-fulfilling proto-imperialist praise of Britain.[17]

There are few texts from the 1640s written in English from the perspective of the Catholics in Ireland.[18] One particularly interesting and specifically literary example is, however, Henry Burkhead's *Cola's Fury Or Lirenda's Miserie* (Kilkenny, 1646), whose subject is the Irish war, and which shares with the Protestant 1641 propaganda the quality of extreme emotional intensity. Burkhead, a Bristol merchant, was a Catholic, and his play is written from the royalist viewpoint. From 1642 to 1649 the Leinster town of Kilkenny was the headquarters of the Assembly of confederate Catholics, the coalition of native and Old English Catholics which had been formed to carry on the war in the name of the king against the English parliament. During the early 1640s this confederacy carried out a prolonged series of negotiations with the king's agents, trying to gain guarantees of religious liberty in return for promises to support Charles with their forces in the English Civil War. Burkhead's play may be dated between June 1645 and very early 1646.

Cola's Fury may be called a tragi-comedy, since it ends with the proclamation of a 'cessation' of fighting, and near the end of the piece fair portents are presented to the good characters. But its form seems barely able to contain its subject-matter, and is visibly strained by the burden. The play tries to account for the current Irish war in two ways at once, ways which are largely incompatible. At the start of the play the war is presented as a comprehensible political conflict about power, possession of territory and religious differences. But it later becomes apparent that the Angoleans' commander, Sir Carola Cola, is in the grip of a dementia, the 'fury' of the title, which is represented as rationally inexplicable and which causes him to multiply senseless cruelties against the Lirendeans.[19] In the character of Cola, Burkhead seems to suggest a transcendent intervention in human political affairs. Near the end the spirit of Revenge begins to haunt him, promising his imminent destruction, and when he is soon after shot dead, the hand that eliminates him is understood by the reader to be providentially guided.[20] By resorting to the formal resources of masque – dance, superhuman apparitions, an enchanted sleep – Burkhead conjures a magical resolution of the play's conflict in place of the political one he could not, within the given framework of actual history, find a way to envisage.[21]

One might read this recourse to a wished-for transcendence as the relinquishing of the Catholics' politically hopeless position to fate, the equivalent of an inarticulate cry as if at the dismemberment of a body politic. The parallel with Spenser's idealising escapè tactic in the Mutabilitie Cantos is striking. Though from politically opposite perspectives, the intractable matter of political actuality is, so to speak, converted into metaphysical energy so that it can fuel the desire for an order stably established. The difference between Spenser's and Burkhead's gestures is a reversal of direction: in Burkhead the Irish are the victims rather than the exemplars of inexplicable irrationality, subject to, not the originating subjects of, insanely destructive behaviour. Providential sanction is invoked by Spenser for the work of Lord Deputy Grey and English authority, and equally by Burkhead for the allied Catholic and Irish resistance to that authority, as embodied in 1645 by the London Parliament.

After Cromwell's Irish expedition in 1649, however, invocations of transcendence cease to consist in turning to a metaphysical elsewhere. Nothing is plainer than the strong sense of Providential mission felt by many of the godly ''49 men', but there is a very particular relation of pragmatism to piety in the applied Protestantism of Ireland's governors during the 1650s. Divine approval is something to be actively achieved in the here and now, by the vigorous exercise both of force majeure and intellectual acumen. Thus new post-Baconian endeavours to increase the sum of knowledge, such as the Boate brothers' *Irelands Natural History* (London, 1652), went forward with two intriguingly mixed motives: the conviction of a Providential appointment to eradicate the bloodthirsty and oppressive powers of Catholicism, and an impulse further to colonise and exploit more efficiently the natural resources being described and enumerated. The *History* was to be a new full and empirically based description of Ireland, which was enthusiastically promoted by Samuel Hartlib, in whose Puritan and post-Baconian projects the Boates, scientists of Dutch origin, were partakers.[22] One might imagine extravagantly emotional outbursts to be almost programmatically excluded from the actual text of a Baconian scientific work such as the *History*; but in practice this is not so. Its promise of scientific detachment is misleading. Written in the later 1640s, it shares with *Cola's Fury* and the 1641 texts a high degree of emotional intensity. The circumstances of its composition help to explain this charged atmosphere, while not abolishing the implicit contradiction between it and the Baconian programme of objectivity. The Boates were close to a group of 'new English' settlers in Ireland – chiefly to the former ruthless chief justice and acquisitive planter Sir William Parsons (probably the character called Pitho in *Cola's Fury*) who had been 'driven thence' by 'the bloody combustions' of 1641.[23] So even though the *History* was intended to confine itself to the noteworthy *natural* characteristics of Ireland – harbours, climate, the potential of the woods and mines – and not to discuss the people till a later section, nevertheless it repeatedly breaks out in expressions of violent revulsion against the native Irish, 'a nation extremely barbarous in all the parts of their life', who have resisted all the 'great pains taken by the English, ever since the Conquest, for to civilize them, and to improve the Countrie'.[24] The spectres of 1641, no doubt raised by the Parsons, the Boates' informants, are often in evidence. The depredations of 'that horrible Rebellion of the bloody Irish' upon the fair improved lands of English and Ulster Scots are repeatedly described. Further, having poured scorn on the alleged inaccuracies of fact in earlier historians of Ireland such as Giraldus Cambrensis and Camden, the Boates themselves employ representations of the Irish at least as stereotyped, and (ironically, considering their commitment to a Baconian instauration) perhaps actually deriving from such earlier accounts. Thus they say that Ireland's mineral seams have been under-exploited, because the Irish – 'one of the most barbarous Nations of the whole Earth' – have been 'so far from seeking out' any such enterprise, that only the 'New-English' have begun this task. Here the Baconian enthusiasm for discovering the resources of the earth and putting them to use has coalesced with a traditional element of the Irish stereotype – ineradicable laziness.[25] And in 1641 this pathological sloth was compounded with wanton destruction, as in the story of the wrecking of a silver mine in County Tipperary:

not content to lay wast the Mine, and to demolish all the works thereunto belonging, [they] did accompany this their barbarousness with bloody cruelty against the poor workmen . . . the which some of them being English and the rest Dutch (because the Irish having no skill at all in any of those things, had never been imployed in this Mine otherwise than to digg it, and to doe other labours) were all put to the sword by them, except a very few, who by flight escaped their hands.[26]

One is prompted, against the Boates' evident intentions, to wonder whether the very lack of a stake in the mine was not more potent than the imputed barbarous ignorance in bringing about its destruction. Thus even in a discourse which avowedly concentrates on the material features of the country, the Boates' fevered prejudices about human nature in Ireland are quite manifest. They apply even more absolutely than Spenser an essentialist model of ineradicable Irish wickedness, and (perhaps unsurprisingly, given their political allegiances) they place all faith for the country's future in a complete transfer of control to the new English.

But the Boates are minor figures by comparison with the main bringer of the new empiricist approach to Ireland, William Petty. Petty, born in 1623, was a self-made man and a polymath: Marx called him the founder of political economy, and he was a distinguished mathematician, inventor, anatomist, surveyor and cartographer, and a pioneer of statistics. In his youth Petty had lived in Holland and France, where he knew Descartes and the Mersenne circle, and assisted Hobbes during the writing of his *Opticks*. They studied anatomy jointly, and Petty was subsequently professor of anatomy at Oxford. He came to Ireland in 1652, when he was appointed Physician to the army there, but by December 1654 he had been appointed to carry out the 'Down Survey'.[27] This was to ascertain, in the wake of the recently completed Cromwellian conquest, the exact boundaries of those lands which were to be forfeited by all those deemed not of 'constant good affection' to the parliamentary forces during the 1640s.[28] Petty himself became an Irish landowner, acquiring vast territories in South Kerry in payment for his work on the Survey, and retained them at the Restoration, setting up an iron-works and a pilchard fishery on them.

Petty's writings about Ireland are of great interest from our present perspective because they differ so markedly from most earlier colonist writing, showing a steady pragmatism, a determined lack of interest in controversy or recrimination, and a peculiar, vivid practicality of style. They include his documented *History of the Down Survey* (*c.* 1659), several pamphlets on Ireland's economy and administration, and many brief notes and speculations, composed up to the last years of his life, in the 1670s.[29] Petty's first published work – the *Advice to Hartlib* (London, 1648), a Baconian essay on a reformed educational system – predates his association with Ireland. But it clearly limns the outlines of his lifelong intellectual project, which he set out to bring to bear upon Ireland. These are the impulse towards quantification, or some other exact fixing, of the matter to be dealt with, and the accompanying concept of the division of labour in executing a project, and a determination to privilege things over words and the objects of the material world over rhetoric. There is a resulting emphasis on empirical acquaintance with the object of study, which one must examine, as he says, *per autopsiam* – as in a modern anatomy, not merely in theory or relying on a textbook, but for oneself, materially and in practice.[30]

As we have seen, in the 1641 narratives endlessly recurring 'ripping up', tearing and dismembering are represented as the characteristic action of the Irish upon the bodies of the English settlers; the Cromwellian reconquest and the ensuing transplantation plans (which depend on the Down Survey) are specifically conceived as turning back upon the Irish all that violent cutting up. For an anatomy to be performed, the body in question must first be dead, and therefore totally available to the wielder of the knife: to the anatomist, such as Petty had been, it is as new material upon which to practise. If one considers Petty's surveying work on Ireland as an anatomy, the precedent killing has been carried out by the Cromwellian military campaigns, and when Petty came, just over a decade later, to write his major discussion of Ireland, he called it a *Political Anatomy*.

In his Preface, Petty explicitly says he is using the 'judicious Parallel' made by Bacon between the body natural and the body politic. He continues:

Furthermore, as Students in Medicine, practice their inquiries upon cheap and common Animals . . . I have chosen Ireland as such a Political Animal, who is scarce 20 years old; where the Intrigue of State is not very complicate, and with which I have been conversant from an Embrion . . . 'Tis true, that curious Dissections cannot be made without variety of proper Instruments; whereas I have had only a commin Knife and a Clout.   (Hull, I, p. 129)

This was written in 1672; the '20 years' run from the Act of Settlement in 1652, which as we have seen was also the year of Petty's arrival in Ireland to be physician to the army. The passage reveals his sense of the difference of the Cromwellian intervention from all previous ones. Politically and intellectually, the work of the 1650s is continuous, in his mind, with that to be done in subsequent decades, but it constitutes a break with Irish history before 1649.[31] Petty would not have been alone in expressing such an opinion in the 1650s, when the sense of a fresh start, and the use of such images as a clean slate or a white paper was common among the Cromwellians in Ireland, full of the 'moral energy' which had driven the bloody reconquest.[32] Henry Cromwell's chaplain, Thomas Harrison, expressed a common feeling when he called Ireland 'clay upon the wheele, ready to receive what forme authority shall please to give it'.[33]

But despite the initial similarity, Petty's sense of a break with the past has a different quality from that of these godly witnesses in two main ways, one a positive quality, the other an absence. First, the emphasis on newness is part of the utopian character of his thinking: 'Ireland is as a white paper', he wrote (Hull, I, p. 9). Looked at positively, from Petty's viewpoint rather than that of those dispossessed, the Down Survey, too, has an utopian character in the completeness of its working upon the forfeited lands of Ireland; it is named from the fact that unlike previous surveys it not only lists the territories but puts them *down* on new-made maps. The existing civil bounds and Catholic proprietorships are rendered null and by that means the country as previously named becomes a nowhere, literally an utopia. The second differentiating feature of Petty's expression of newness in Ireland is its striking secularity: it is the result of a fresh political, rather than divine, dispensation and the attendant promise of rationalising reforms. For all his early participation in and patronage by the Hartlib group, for whom, as we have seen, millenarian religious feeling was closely linked with Baconian projections for Ireland's future and with colonist personal ambition, Petty very rarely manifests on his own account any specifically religious aspirations, as distinct from scientific, intellectual and political ones. His contact as a young man with Hobbes, who was the reverse of an enthusiast in the religious sense, no doubt influenced the formation of his disenchanted attitude; in his later manuscript writings he emerges as a Lockean sceptic and a latitudinarian, perhaps even a deist, for whom religion is primarily a matter of social custom.[34] In this connection, his attitude to 1641 is highly unusual. The *History of the Down Survey* contains none of the customary execrations of those events, and compared to the attitudes of Milton, Cromwell, or the Boates, Petty appears in general extraordinarily dispassionate. In later writings, he distinguishes himself explicitly from such anger as theirs, and perhaps Cola's, in Burkhead's play:

Some furious spirits have wished, that the Irish would rebel again, that they might be put to the Sword. But I declare, that motion to be not only impious and inhumane, but withal frivolous and pernicious even to them who have rashly wish'd for those occasions. (Hull, I, p. 155)

He nowhere engages in ritual expressions of abhorrence at the massacres, raising the topic only in order to suggest a division by at least four of the numbers alleged to have been killed (Hull, I, p. 150). About the whole period of the wars, he suspends judgement: 'But as for the Bloodshed in the Contest, God best knows who did occasion it'. He makes no exalted claims about the rights or moral mission of the English in Ireland, as his choice of metaphor shows:

But upon the playing of this Game or Match upon so great Odds, the English won and have (among, and besides other Pretences) a Gamester's Right at least to their Estates. (Hull, I, p. 154)

Given the self-righteousness of other colonists' rhetoric and the feverishness of the usual 1641 references it is difficult not to find such distance a relief and be tempted to accept empirical method at its own valuation, as a wholly progressive invention. Petty's mathematisation of the world, and specifically of Ireland, is part of a process of rationalisation. His cool, detached style is a respite from the often fulminating succession of English discourses on Ireland, and sometimes he pinpoints the underlying cause of a problem with insight, economy and wit.

Quantification is Petty's dominant tactic in his dealings with the multifarious particulars of social life; he constantly uses it to resist merely interested argument and looks for 'some Rule in Nature whereby to value and proportionate the Lands of Ireland' (Hull, I, p. 180). All his texts tend towards tabulation and listing, in accordance with his assertion that 'Arithmetick and Geometry' are 'the best grounded parts of Speculative knowledge' (*Advice*, p. 7). As the following typical passage from the *Pol-*

itical Anatomy shows, statistical description becomes a dominant method
of procedure in his writings:

Now in Ireland a Milch-Cow . . . breeds upon two Acres of Pasture, and with as
much Hay as will grow upon Half an Acre of Meadow, will yield 3 Gallons of
Milk for 90 days . . . and one Gallon at a Medium for 90 more . . . Wherefore it
follows, that such a Cow upon such Feeding, gives above one Tun and a half.

(Hull, I, pp. 172–3)

In his own thought we can see a kind of division of labour operating. He
sees himself as engaged in a new kind of planning and description, which
is meant to escape entanglement in the Irish melee of competing interests
and factions. He declares that 'I profess no Politicks', and 'I never intended
to complicate Religion with the Matters of this Essay', which may be
interpreted merely as pragmatic attempts to assure his current position,
but are also characteristic expressions of a coherent intellectual programme (Hull, I, p. 129; II, p. 578). The problem is to be simplified so
that it may be discussed. He tries to remove from his consideration all the
vexed questions of Irish history – land ownership, religion, ethnic origin,
power, usurpation – thinking of the resultant passions as 'a mere Caprice
and Perverseness', things not rationally explicable and therefore imponderable. Sometimes he has an air of cutting the Gordian knot, as when he
classifies the present inhabitants of Ireland not in the usual categories of
native Irish, Old English, and pre- or post-1649 arrivals, or 'much less' as
'Protestants and Papists, and such who speak English, and such who
despise it', but as soldiers, landowners, tenants, labourers, etc. Thus he
substitutes economic and therefore in his eyes rational differences for the
irrational, factional ones actually functioning to make for Irish 'intrigue'
and 'complication' (Hull, II, pp. 562, 576).

For Petty, divisive political passions are bound up with the defects of
language. He sets the project of 'a Political Arithmetick and a Geometricall
Justice' against the errors of the world, which cannot be mended by 'Wit',
'Rhetoric', or 'Interest'. Here 'Wit' and 'Rhetoric' – the stuff of words –
are linked with 'Interest' as equally incapable of remedying the defective
facts of actuality (Hull, I, p. 240). In the *Advice*, he says learning to read
should come only after an intimate acquaintance with material objects and
tools, which is the means of acquiring a more rational and purposive form
of knowledge than that normally imparted: 'it would be more profitable . . . to spend ten or twelve years in the study of Things . . . then in
a rabble of words' (p. 8). This Baconian idea of a struggle in the mind
between things and their names finds a particularly interesting application
in Petty's thought about Ireland. In his work on the Down Survey he
projects an effective eradication from the material terrain of Ireland of the
'meer Words and Chymaerical Notions' which have given it its outlandish

and incomprehensible names and articulated it in the minds of its native inhabitants. He complains about the traditional methods of naming lands in Ireland:

For as a Territory bounded by Bogs, is greater or lesser as the Bog is more dry and passible, or otherwise: so the Country of a Grandee or Tierne [Irish: *tiarna*, lord] in Ireland, became greater or lesser as his Forces waxed or weaned . . . The limits of their Land-agreements were no lines Geometrically drawn; but if the Rain fell one way, then the Land whereon it fell, did belong to A., if the other way, to B, & c.   (Hull, I, p. 206)

Such procedures he sees as irrational, subject to wholly imponderable shifts in power, fluid and impermanent as bogs and rain. The adequacy of these arrangements for the earlier Irish cattle-herding society practising seasonal nomadism and organized according to clan or sept simply does not enter into Petty's frame of thinking. Such indeterminacy to his mind must entail confusion and probably knavery. For Englishmen in Ireland, of course, the relation between words and things, names and the people or places they attach to, had always a peculiarly problematic status, because the names themselves were alien and offended by their incomprehensibility. The 1665 Act of Explanation contained a royal order that the 'barbarous and uncouth names of places' be changed for new, English ones. Like most of his countrymen Petty experienced this difficulty; probably much more than most, because of his work in the survey. He calls the old names 'uncouth, intelligible' (Hull, I, p. 208). But having said that 'the various spellings of Names not understood' must be 'prevented' and 'set out by Authority to determine the same for the time to come', he nevertheless remarks that:

It would not be amiss if the significant part of the Irish Names were interpreted, where they are not, or cannot be abolished.   (Hull, I, pp. 207–8)

It is Petty's distinction that he can see that the Irish names *have* a 'significant part'; here one might say that the names have as it were become things, potential objects of study, part of knowledge and not of that confusion which in his eyes is its antithesis. When, in his late work *A Treatise of Ireland*, Petty proposes a total union of the two nations, and a 'transmutation' of the Irish into English, he argues from the dispensability of mere names:

Now if the two Nations be brought into one, the Name of the lesser Nation must needs be abolished, whilst the Thing and Substance is exalted.
                                                                                    (Hull, II, pp. 577–8)

What matters is not the name, but what he calls the 'Thing and Substance' – the material conditions of the people's lives: 'The Cabineers of Ireland . . . will be removed out of their wretched Beastlike habitations; unfit for making Merchantable Butter and Cheese' (Hull, II, p. 578). Not only will the names be altered, in Petty's proposal, but the things also, and for the better. The act of renaming is a response to a rational intention of improvement, not a destructive impulse.

It is by this eminently Baconian move of concentrating on material facts that Petty tacitly dismantles the stereotype of the Irish which had served most earlier English writers. He makes no apparent assumption of a *natural* inferiority in them; instead of their nature, he considers their circumstances. In his eyes their manners are environmentally produced – by a 'want of Imployment and Encouragement to Work' – rather than by any natural or moral deficiency (Hull, I, pp. 201, 202). It follows that they are alterable. Where Spenser and the Boates call the people 'barbarous' or 'uncivil', Petty says that '6 of 8 of all the Irish live in a brutish nasty Condition, as in Cabins, with neither Chimney, Door, Stairs nor Window'. The Hobbesian phrase is applied not to an inevitable, innate quality of the Irish poor, but to the state of their houses, which offends primarily because it runs counter to 'the advancement of Trade', for which Ireland is 'by Nature fit' (Hull, I, p. 156; and see pp. 170, 215, 217). This is a striking departure from the traditional colonist assumption of an innate and stubborn difference in the Irish, which drove Spenser and subsequent writers to think them sub-human, 'salvage'.

But the overall impression left by Petty's writings on Ireland is not an entirely positive one. The unfortunate prejudices he seeks to excise were rooted in Irish history before 1649, the only beginning Petty was prepared to acknowledge; and this refusal to attend to the 'Chymerical notions' of the past is gravely damaging to his projects. The Cromwellians' impression of newness – whether formed by the conviction of a divine mission to avenge the 1641 outrages, or produced by a prospect of progress in Ireland towards a more rationally organised society – was a misleading one, as subsequent Irish history showed; in the historian T.C. Barnard's words:

Ireland was not *tabula rasa*. There were old institutions; there was a native population, both Protestant and Catholic, whose support was necessary to any regime's permanence.[35]

Even the Survey itself, for all its comprehensiveness, could not simply impose a completely 'new geography' (Hull, I, p. 6). This was not just because there had been some earlier surveys of parts of the country, but because in surveying civil, as well as natural, boundaries, Petty was obliged to accept earlier, Irish, cultural and social interpretation of the material landscape. There had to be someone to point out to the measurers in the field where the 'meres' or boundaries of the lands lay. Petty several times makes it clear that these 'meresemen' were usually or always 'Irish Papists'. However clean a sweep the Cromwellian military activities had made, creating a civil administration totally *ab initio* was not possible. The forms in which Ireland had been moulded on previous potters' wheels, the history already inscribed in the social landscape, were far from utterly broken or erased.

Petty enumerates and quantifies to the point of political and ideological myopia. His resort in his works to 'Arithmetical and Geometrick' methods allowed him not just to achieve detachment, and a new precision of description, but, more problematically, to put a *cordon sanitaire* round whole areas of experience and edit them out of his discourse. Spenser's work on Ireland, dismayingly harsh and oppressive as it is, nevertheless is of a piece. He brings to bear on the problem the full vocabulary of Renaissance humanist forms, with their intimations of completeness: pastoral, allegory, political dialogue. However questionable one may find his political position, one cannot justly claim that he tries to suppress its practical implications in any part of his work. This very wholeness leads to the internal tensions and contradictions in his work which I have described. But Petty's discourse *is* partial. In the Survey, for instance, he can concentrate on his scientific and administrative project because, by a division of labour on the larger scale, the military basis for it has already been established. As his Victorian editor C.H. Hull says, it

is not that he literally experimented upon Ireland himself, but that he examined by the best available means, the effects of such experiments as had been made there.   (I, p. lxvi)

And in his later writings, by an application to Ireland's condition of the principles of exact and mathematical description, he sometimes achieves a clarification at the cost of missing the main point. The falseness of Petty's claim to completeness was discerned by Jonathan Swift when he chose Petty's style as his parodic model in *A Modest Proposal*. But in a longer perspective, that of the slow transformation of a specifically conquering and colonial ideology into an Irish national identity which during the succeeding century would come to define Ireland as an entity whose interests are not necessarily identical with England's, one might argue that Petty ought to join Swift as a founding figure: Petty's writings, for all their limitations, mark significant progress in the transforming endeavour to dismantle the inherited stereotypes, as do Ware's, while Spenser's afford the classic example of that which is to be transformed.

Such a formulation as this implies that this collection of texts can be divided more or less clearly into those which reinforce and seek to perpetuate the inherited, stereotypically negative, representations of the Irish, and those which, however partially and cautiously, seek to nuance, interrogate, escape, resist or at best discard them. This is one way to consider them. But it may be preferable to say that all the writings I have been examining are contributions to the continuing English discourse about Ireland in the seventeenth century, and are best considered together as a body of writings whose true anatomy can be discovered only by a careful attention to its internal relationships and mutual influences. The fundamental assumptions of the colonist position are held in common by all the writers I have discussed, except possibly by Burkhead. English rule and nationality are taken as preferable to Irish; it is assumed that the Irish would be better off by becoming English, where possible; and the rights of England to exercise authority and power in Ireland are not questioned. But once, within that general framework, one looks more closely, one finds major divergences in attitude, varying interpretations of the specific implications of the general position. Even in the brief period of the English Civil Wars themselves, a tension is apparent between the implied secularity and empiricism of the new science, which is to lead, in Petty's project, to different, more rational and distanced forms of colonial domination, and a quasi-apocalyptic vision of Irish evil destroyed by English righteousness.

NOTES

I wish to acknowledge the generous assistance and encouragement I received in the conception and execution of this project from the following: Tom Dunne, Anne Fogarty, Maire Herbert, Trevor Joyce, Clare O'Halloran, and Dorinda Outram.

The research for this chapter was done with the assistance of a grant from the Faculty of Arts, University College, Cork.

1 See Joseph Leerssen, *Mere Irish and Fior-Ghael* (Utrecht, 1986). See also R.O. Bartley, *Teague, Shenkin and Sawney* (Cork, 1954), for specifically literary instances of sixteenth-century English stereotypes of Irishness.
2 Spenser's Irish writings 'touching the reduction of the Irish to civility' are approvingly mentioned in a letter of Cromwell's (*Commonwealth Book*, A/28, PRO, quoted in Pauline Henley, *Spenser in Ireland* (Cork, 1928), pp. 206–7); see also Vincent Gookin's 1655 pamphlets against transplantation.
3 See Hayden White, 'The Forms of Wildness: Archaeology of an Idea', in *Tropics of Discourse* (Baltimore, 1978), pp. 150–82, Anthony Pagden, *The Fall of Natural Man* (Cambridge, 1982), Margaret Hodgen, *Early Anthropology* (London, 1964), and James Muldoon, 'The Indian as Irishman', *Essex Institute Historical Collections* 3, 4 (1975), 267–89. For a fuller discussion of Spenser's representations of Ireland, see Patricia Coughlan, ' "Some secret scourge which shall by her come unto England": Ireland and Incivility in Spenser', in

Patricia Coughlan, ed., *Spenser and Ireland: An Interdisciplinary Perspective* (Cork, 1989).

4 See Nicholas Canny, 'The Ideology of Colonization in England and America', *William and Mary Quarterly* 30 (1973), 573–98, and 'Edmund Spenser and the Development of an Anglo-Irish Identity', *Yearbook of English Studies* 13 (1983).

5 See for example, *View* pp. 219–20. References are to the Variorum Edition, ed. E. Greenlaw *et al.* (Baltimore, 1949).

6 See T.W. Moody *et al.*, eds., *A New History of Ireland*, III (Oxford, 1976), pp. lvii, lx, 567–8.

7 His textual alterations are listed in the Spenser Variorum Vol. X, 519–23.

8 *St. Patrick for Ireland*, ed. J.P. Turner (New York, 1969). See A.H. Stevenson, 'Shirley's Years in Ireland', *Review of English Studies* 20 (1944), 19–28, and 'James Shirley and the Actors at the First Irish Theatre', *Modern Philology*, 37 (1942), 147–60; on Shirley's sources, see Turner, 'Introduction'.

9 See Bartley, *Teague, Shenkin and Sawney*, pp. 7–47; Leerssen, *Mere Irish and Fior-Ghael*, pp. 33–66, 85–99.

10 See Stephen Orgel, *Illusions of Power* (Berkeley and London, 1975), pp. 77–83, and Martin Butler, *Theatre and Crisis 1632–1642* (Cambridge, 1984), p. 236.

11 The Prologues are reprinted in his *Poems* (London, 1646); see pp. 38–49.

12 See Aidan Clarke, 'The 1641 Depositions', in Peter Fox, ed., *Treasures of the Library* (Dublin, 1986), pp. 111–20; Walter Love, 'Civil War in Ireland: Appearances Through Three Centuries of Historical Writing', *Emory University Quarterly* 22 (1966), 57–72; M. Perceval-Maxwell, 'The Ulster Rising of 1641 and the Depositions', *Irish Historical Studies* 83 (1979), 145–67.

13 Clarke, 'The 1641 Depositions', 112, 120.

14 Jones, *A Remonstrance* (London, 1642), pp. 8, 9, 48, 58–9, 61, 63, 68. On contemporary lists of atrocities attributed to Cavaliers in parliamentary propaganda, which employ a similar vocabulary or repertoire, see T. Corns *et al.*, 'Archetypal Mystification: Polemic and Reality in English Political Literature, 1640–1750', *Eighteenth-Century Life* 7 (1982), 3.

15 See Christopher Hill, '17th-Century English Radicals and Ireland', in P.J. Corish, ed., *Radicals, Rebels and Establishments* (Belfast, 1985), pp. 33–47; Norah Carlin, 'Ireland and Natural Man in 1649', in Francis Barker *et al.*, eds., *Europe and Its Others*, II (Colchester, 1985), pp. 91–111; and Chris Durston, '"Let Ireland be Quiet": Opposition in England to the Conquest of Ireland', *History Workshop Journal* 21 (1986), 105–12.

16 See *Church-Government*, III, p. 228; *Eikonoklastes*, V, p. 77, *History of Britain*, X, pp. 49 and 174 (references are to the Columbia edition).

17 *Rump Songs* (London, 1662), I, pp. 254, 258; II, pp. 112, 171ff.

18 Exceptions are the political pamphlets and arguments written by Old English Catholics, of which the lawyer Patrick Darcy's speech to the Irish Parliament in June 1641 (Waterford, 1643) is a fine example; so is the work of Nicholas French, Bishop of Ferns, composed in the 1660s. For the many works in Latin by Irish Catholic clerical controversialists, see Benignus Millett, 'Irish Literature in Latin, 1550–1700', in Moody *et al.*, *New History of Ireland*, pp. 561–86.

19 Cola may be intended for Charles Coote, whose military ferocity was notorious; see T.P. Coonan, *The Irish Catholic Confederacy and the Puritan Revolution* (Dublin, 1954), pp. 125–7. See Patricia Coughlan ('Enter Revenge': Henry Bunklend and *Coln's Fury*', *Theatre Research International* 15 (1989), 1–4.

20 IV 46–7. Revenge is accompanied by 'three spirits in sheets'.

21 Greeted with very little enthusiasm by the Lirendean generals, the concluding cessation is for a year and a day, like the Ormond truce of 1643 which it clearly represents; on the disputes about its acceptability which divided the Confederates, see P.J. Corish, 'The Rising of 1641 and the Catholic Confederacy, 1641–5', in Moody et al., New History of Ireland, pp. 289–316.

22 See Charles Webster, The Great Instauration: Science, Medicine, and Reform (1626–1660) (London, 1975), pp. 428–35; K. T. Hoppen, The Common Scientist in the Seventeenth Century (London, 1970), pp. 11–15, 21.

23 Kearney, Strafford in Ireland, p. 174; and see Carl S. Bottigheimer, English Money and Irish Land (Oxford, 1971), p. 177.

24 Arnold Boate, 'To the Reader', sig. A7; Natural Historie, p. 185.

25 See Leerssen, pp. 48, 55–6; Gerald of Wales, History and Topography of Ireland, ed. J.J. O'Meara (Dublin, 1982), p. 103.

26 Natural Historie, p. 144. This incident is described, in a rather lower key, in Thomas Morley's otherwise sensationalist Remonstrance . . . Of the Barbarous Cruelties . . . by the Irish Rebels (London, 1644).

27 There are two biographies, Lord Edmond Fitzmaurice, Life of Sir William Petty (London, 1895), and E. Strauss, Sir William Petty (London, 1954).

28 See T.C. Barnard, 'Planters and Policies in Cromwellian Ireland', Past and Present 61 (1973), 33–69, and Carl S. Bottigheimer, 'The Restoration Land Settlement in Ireland: A Structural View', Irish Historical Studies 18 (1972), 1–21.

29 The History of the Down Survey remained in manuscript till it was published by T.A. Larcom (Dublin, 1851; reprinted in facsimile, New York, 1967); most of his other writings are in Economic Writings of Sir William Petty, ed. T.H. Hull, 2 vols. (London, 1898; referred to below as 'Hull'), or in The Petty Papers, ed. Marquis of Lansdowne (London, 1927).

30 See Advice, p. 21; History of the Down Survey, p. xvi.

31 See T.C. Barnard, Cromwellian Ireland (Oxford, 1975), p. 246.

32 See Carl S. Bottigheimer, English Money and Irish Land, p. 27.

33 Cromwell himself said that Ireland after 1649 was 'as a clean paper'; Colonel John Jones, a Parliamentary Commissioner from 1650 to 1654, believed that the English were providentially in Ireland 'to frame or form a commonwealth out of a corrupt rude mass', and the chief justice of Munster, John Cook, likened Ireland to 'a white paper'. All quoted in Barnard, Cromwellian Ireland, pp. 14, 268.

34 See Petty Papers, ed. Marquis of Lansdowne (London, 1928), I, pp. 117–18; in his will, dating from about 1685, he expresses 'my love and honour to almighty God, by such signs and tokens, as are understood to be such by the people with whom I live' (Tracts (Dublin, 1749), p. xii). And in the Political Anatomy he notes that the religion of the Irish poor is 'rather a Custom than a Dogma amongst them' (Hull, I, p. 200).

35 Barnard, Cromwellian Ireland, pp. 14–15. The eventual passing of a great deal of the land allocated to the soldiers, and even to the Adventurers, into New English hands, is pointed out by both Barnard and Bottigheimer.

PART V

Aftermaths

12 'The Colonel's Shadow': Lucy Hutchinson, women's writing and the Civil War

ON 11 SEPTEMBER 1664 John Hutchinson died a prisoner in Sandown Castle on the coast of Kent. It was an inconspicuous and ignominious end to a life dedicated to the service of what we have learned to call the English Revolution. He had served as parliamentarian governor of the Castle and Town of Nottingham during the Civil War[1] and had been elected to the Long Parliament in 1646 (p. 164). He was subsequently a member of the commonwealth's Council of State (p. 191), Sheriff of Nottingham during Richard Cromwell's brief Protectorate (pp. 212–13) and Nottingham's representative in the Convention of 1660 (pp. 226–7). More particularly, he had been one of the commissioners at the trial of Charles I and a signatory to the death warrant (pp. 189–90). In 1660 he was not one of those excepted from the Act of Oblivion, and so, 'pardoned, released, acquitted, indemnified and discharged' from 'all manner of treasons, misprisions of treasons, murthers, felonies, offences, crimes, contempts and misdemeanours', he was legally entitled to expect that no act previously committed should 'hereafter rise in judgment' against him to the 'prejudice' of his life, liberty, estate or reputation.[2] On 11 October 1663, however, he was arrested on suspicion of complicity in the Derwentdale Plot[3] and committed to the Tower (pp. 243–9, 272). Examination by Secretary Bennet (afterwards first Earl of Arlington) failed to uncover incriminating evidence, and John Hutchinson was never charged, let alone brought to trial; but his was a liberty too prejudicial to the reputation of the restored authorities to be tolerated. While the monarchical and episcopal regime was tightening its hold on power and pursuing, through persecution, propaganda and censorship, the complete annihilation of the cause to which John Hutchinson had committed his life, he himself remained in confinement until the dilapidated and damp conditions of Sandown, 'a lamentable old ruin'd place . . . not weather-free' (p. 262), brought him to his inglorious death in 1664.[4]

To 'moderate her woe' and to 'console' herself in her bereavement (p. 1), Lucy Hutchinson undertook during the later 1660s to write her *Memoirs of the Life of Colonel Hutchinson*.[5] At the time of the book's composition, however, she endured more than the private anguish of her loss:

the collapse of the Good Old Cause posed for her, as for all the defeated Puritans and their nonconformist successors, a daunting case of conscience. The 'revolution' of 1660 (in the seventeenth-century sense of that word) tempted her, and them, to betray their Puritan allegiance, to doubt God's providential dealings with his elect nation, and to despair. The Restoration so effectively, so painlessly, and so quickly frustrated the whole range of Puritan aspiration that its beneficiaries could not but see it as a divine mercy: 'Never was there so miraculous a change as this, nor so great things done in so short a time', wrote the 72-year-old Bishop of Winchester, Brian Duppa, 'But *a Domino Factum est istud*; no humane wisdom can claim a share in it'. And so it seemed, for the Restoration occurred 'in a trice', as Richard Baxter wrote, when it was thought 'next impossible' and the royalists, in Abraham Cowley's view, had not 'the least glympse of Hope' of it.[6] Cowley was in no doubt that this, not the Civil War nor the constitutional experiments of the Interregnum, marked God's intervention in history:

> Where are the men who bragged that God did bless,
>   And with the marks of good success
> Sign his allowance of their wickedness?
> Vain men, who thought the divine power to find
> In the fierce thunder and the violent wind.
>   God came not till the storm was past,
> In the still voice of peace he came at last.
> The cruel business of destruction
> May by the claws of the great fiend be done.
> Here, here we see th' Almighty's hand indeed,
> Both by the beauty of the work we see't and by the speed.[7]

The bewilderment and disillusion which might be caused by this inexplicable disappointment of all for which the Puritans had worked and fought is at the heart of Milton's *Samson Agonistes*:

> God of our fathers, what is man!
> That thou towards him with hand so various,
> Or might I say contrarious,
> Temper'st thy providence through his short course.

The apparent perversity of God's dealings with his chosen ones wrings this exclamation from the Chorus as it views the degradation and humiliation of that 'glorious champion' Samson. In Samson's plight Milton describes that of John Hutchinson and many a nonconformist during the next twenty-five years: a 'prisoner chained', scarcely able to 'draw / The air imprisoned also, close and damp, / Unwholesome draught'. He and the Parliamentarians had, like Samson, been 'solemnly elected' by God 'To some great work, thy glory, / And people's safety, which in part they effect', but to what end? It was the royalists' interpretation of history's providential design which the Restoration appeared to confirm. What could be said in response to the Chorus's disillusioned conclusion: 'Just or unjust, alike seem miserable, / For oft alike both come to evil end'?[8]

To answer that question is Lucy Hutchinson's larger purpose. Her work takes its place beside *Samson Agonistes*, Baxter's *Reliquiae*,[9] and the body of nonconformist writing, as an attempt to perceive and accept God's purpose in and after the Restoration.[10] In the *Memoirs* the royalist view is gloatingly put by Bennet, who, vindictively confident God is on his side, comments on 'the sad condition' of John Hutchinson, his family and estate; ' "you may here take notice how the justice of God pursues those murtherers, that, though the King pardon'd both his life and estate, by the hand of the devine justice they were now like to come to ruine for that crime".' (p. 254). It is this notion of divine justice, this identification of God's providence with illegal royalist machinations, this characterisation of the Puritans as criminals and murderers, that the *Memoirs* would refute. Lucy Hutchinson sets out not only to 'preserve the memory' (p. 1) which the royalists would consign to oblivion, but also to 'honor' the 'wealthy stock of [John Hutchinson's] glory' (p. 2), to vindicate his part in the Civil War and Interregnum, and to affirm that, despite political defeat and public obloquy, he retained his allegiance to the cause no less resolutely than the Milton who defiantly asserted 'I sing . . . unchanged'.[11] Psalm 43.1, 'Judge me, O God, and plead my cause against an ungodly nation', which John Hutchinson cited in his own 'narrative of his imprisonment' (p. 260), would serve equally well as Lucy Hutchinson's epigraph.[12] The *Memoirs* are apologetic and celebratory, a record of triumph and victory despite the vicissitudes of the fallen world, an acclamation of the glory of the inglorious.

To this end, John Hutchinson holds centre stage. He comes before us as every inch the hero, and, more particularly, a Renaissance hero. He was, as we might expect, exemplary, honourable, virtuous and valorous, and as 'well-proportion'd' in his body as in his temperament (p. 3). We might not expect his physical attractiveness, with 'thick sett' hair 'softer than the finest silke' (p. 3), 'a great ornament to him', which prompts some sharp reflections on the sobriquet 'Roundhead', 'very ill suited to Mr. Hutchinson' (p. 63). He had an 'amiable countenance, which carried in it something of magnanimity and majesty mixt with sweetenesse' (p. 3). He was 'apt for bodily exercise', 'could dance admirably well', had 'skill in fencing', 'a greate love to musicke', 'shott excellently in bowes and guns' and 'had greate judgment in paintings, gravings, sculpture, and all excellent arts, wherein he was much delighted' (p. 4). In London in

1653 his 'only recreation . . . was in seeking out all the rare Artists he could heare of, and in considering their workes . . . insomuch that he became a greate Virtuoso and Patrone of ingenuity'. He purchased some of the paintings which had been in Charles I's collection, including a Titian (pp. 207, 320 n.1 to p. 207). He was an ideal manager of his estate, with 'a greate delight in improovements, in planting groves and walkes and fruite-trees, in opening springs and making fishponds' (p. 4; cf. p. 239). He was generous and thoughtful to his retainers (p. 208), 'lov'd hospitallity', though he 'hated riot' (p. 12), and, with a 'liberall heart', kept 'a house open to all worthy persons' (p. 216). With all his attainments, he was yet judicious, 'never disdain'd the meanest' nor envied 'superiors' (p. 11), was 'exactly just' in all his dealings (p. 9), prudent (p. 7), temperate in his appetites (p. 13), a man so composed as to have escaped vulnerability to fortune: 'When the most noble delights were taken from him, he could bend his mind to recreate it selfe as well in any or in no diversion as in the richest curiousities' (p. 12; cf. p. 264).

Except, perhaps, that we hear it from the wife of a regicide, there is nothing surprising about Lucy Hutchinson's depiction of the masculine gender role. John Hutchinson is the complete gentleman. Gentlemanliness is the touchstone throughout her characterisation: his skill in fencing was 'such as became a gentleman' (p. 4); he was 'a farre greater schollar than is absolutely requisite for a gentleman' (p. 8). Lucy Hutchinson has stolen the royalists' clothes: John Hutchinson excels in precisely those accomplishments upon which royalists prided themselves, which, indeed, they supposed distinguished their civility from the vulgarity of all rebels and schismatics. The Colonel is *not* common. This depiction thus serves her apologetic purpose well, but it is not upon John Hutchinson's gentlemanliness that Lucy Hutchison rests her case, nor does he share anything with the kind of libertine gamester who carouses his way through cavalier lyrics. When he left to attend the Long Parliament John Hutchinson went 'to serve his country as faithfully in the capacity of a Senator as he had before in that of a souldier' (p. 166). He was a patriot, but a patriot, 'Senator' suggests, in the tradition of Roman republicanism, as opposed to the ambition and dictatorial power of Cromwell, which perverted the 'happie, rich' and prosperous commonwealth established by parliament (p. 205), as to the dissolute absolutism of the Stuarts. Cromwell's 'little courtiers' and the Oriental despotism of the Major-Generals, 'like Bashaws' (p. 212), were 'disdain'd in his owne noble heart' (p. 212) as surely as the 'caterpillars' of the Stuart court (p. 45). John Hutchinson gave unqualified allegiance to, and waited passively upon, no man: rather, on every occasion, he waited for 'a cleare call from the Lord' (p. 65).

It is the fidelity of this Christian witness which vindicates him. 'By Christianitie', Lucy Hutchinson explains 'I intend that universall habitt of grace which is wrought in a soule by the regenerating spiritt of God, whereby the whole creature is resign'd up into the devine will and love' (p. 5).[13] John Hutchinson was regenerate and obedient, a Moses in his commitment. If, like Moses, he was 'but allow'd a Pisgah's sight of Canaan' (p. 35; cf. Deut: 34.1–5), that no more calls in doubt his vocation or the justness of his cause than it does that of the man who, 'by faith', chose 'rather to suffer affliction with the people of God, than to enjoy the pleasures of sin for a season' (Heb. 11:25). After 1660, 'the integrity of his heart in all he had done made him as chearfully ready to suffer as to triumph in a good cause' (p. 229). In defeat 'he attain'd confirmation in many principles he had before, and dayly greater enlightnings concerning the free grace and love of God in Jesus Christ' (p. 234). Prison was for him, as for John Bunyan, the 'school of Christ', a place of spiritual education and liberation.[14] As his worldly fortunes fail, so 'the advancement of his Cause by the patient suffering of the Martyrs' (p. 242) becomes the theme of the last part of the *Memoirs*. At Sandown, he 'endur'd . . . all so chearfully that he was never more pleasant and contented in his whole life' (p. 264). Her account of the Colonel's suffering is the badge of the saint, for those 'whom the Lord loveth he chasteneth' (Heb. 12:6). Lucy Hutchinson herself wrote that 'the more patient our sufferance is, the more glorious our crowne will be; the more painefull our labour, the sweeter our rest; the more wee humble ourselves under the mighty hand of God, the more eminently will he in his due time exalt us'.[15] John Hutchinson's death itself is remarkable for its 'Christian courage, and constancy of mind' (p. 272), betraying none of the terrors of the damned: in meeting it, he was, no less than Milton's Samson, 'victorious over the Lord's and his enemies' (p. 277; cf. pp. 12–13). 'Victory' is the final word of the *Memoirs* on a life which, to the world, appeared a dismal failure.

Colonel Hutchinson is, then, the unchallenged protagonist of the *Memoirs*. It is his spiritual progress which is traced, his character and behaviour which are vindicated. Lucy Hutchinson herself, 'the faithfull depository of all his secrets' (p. 7), plays a very slight part in his history. The concerns of the *Memoirs* are overwhelmingly those of masculine discourse: war, politics and patriarchal religion. And with these, women have very little to do. John Hutchinson's dealings with his bride-to-be, though they 'would make a true history of a more handsome management of love than the best romances describe', are 'not worthy mention among the *greater* transactions of his life' (p. 32, my italics). To those 'greater transactions' the life of Lucy Hutchinson is marginal; they require of her submission, obedience and passivity. The Colonel was a loving husband, but 'not uxorious', nor 'remitted that just rule which it was her honor to obey, but manag'd the reines of government with such prudence and affection that she who would not delight in such an honourable and advantageable subjection must have wanted a reasonable soule' (p. 10). This identification of willing submission to masculine authority as the mark of a rational woman characterises Lucy Hutchinson's references to her relationship with her husband: she was 'a compliant subject to his . . . wise government' (p. 33), no more the ungovernably brash Puritan hussy of royalist caricature than is John Hutchinson the oafish artisan. On the contrary, only through obedience is her woman's identity to be realised. Lucy Hutchinson has no existence save through her husband; it is his reflection which confers on her substantiality and individuality: 'he was the author of that vertue he doted on, while she only reflected his owne glories upon him: all that she was, was him, while he was here, and all that she is now at best is but his pale shade' (p. 10). Though she is the writer, he is the author of her, not she the creator of him, a paradox to which we shall return. The image recurs in more developed form some pages later:

he soone made her more equall to him than he found her, for she was a very faithfull mirror, reflecting truly, though but dimmely, his own glories upon him, so long as he was present; but she, that was nothing before his inspection gave her a faire figure, when he was remoov'd was only fill'd with a darke mist, and never could againe take in any delightfull object, nor returne any shining representation. The greatest excellence she had was the power of apprehending and the vertue of loving his. Soe, as his shaddow, she waited on him every where, till he was taken into that region of light which admitts of none, and then she vanisht into nothing.   (pp. 32–3)

This is a moving testimony to her love, but it is a testimony which can express itself only through metaphors of self-negation and self-dissolution. The less intrusive Lucy Hutchinson is, the less corporeal she becomes, the more entirely she loves for the more completely she depends upon John Hutchinson. Lucy Hutchinson may be made 'more equall' by the Colonel, but she cannot be made equal. This rhetorical strategy allows no role reversal. Indeed, its premise is that the Colonel should not be uxorious, that he should not depend upon her as does she upon him, that the relationship should comprise only one person, and one reflected image. My face may appear in thine eye, but not thine in mine.

In short, Lucy Hutchinson's conception of the feminine gender role was entirely traditional.[16] Mary Astell would ere long see in celibacy and female companionship a way to women's liberation,[17] but Lucy Hutchinson can envisage no alternative to matrimony – witness her caustic remark on Edward the Confessor who was 'sainted for his ungodlie chastitie' (p. 280). She articulates none of that deep dependence on women friends, nor that longing for retirement from the destructive clamours of 'tyrant man', to be found in Katherine Philips on Anne Finch, Countess of Win-

chelsea; nor does she ever chafe at the bonds of marriage.[18] On the contrary, she is in no doubt that women belong in patriarchal societies and
households because their fallibility, incompetence and vulnerability
require the guidance and correction of masculine governors:

as our sex, through ignorance and weaknesse of iudgement (which in the most
knowing weomen is inferior to the masculine understanding of men), are apt to
entertaine fancies, and [be] pertinacious in them, soe wee ought to watch ourselves, in such a day as this, and to embrace nothing rashly; but as our owne
imbecillity is made knowne to us, to take heed of presumption in ourselves, and
to leane by faith upon the strength of the Lord.[19]

Accordingly, women are throughout the *Memoirs* expected to be the dutiful and submissive wives which Richard Allestree's *The Ladies Calling*
(1673), like many another conduct book and guide to godliness, said they
should be.[20] Praise and blame are meted out according to their performance in this role. John Hutchinson's mother, Margaret, a woman of 'generous vertue', was especially remarkable for being 'a most observant and
affectionate wife, a great lover of her father's [Sir John Biron's] house . . .
a wise and bountifull mistresse in her famely', who, though brought up
at court, 'managed all her famely affaires better than any of the homespun
huswifes that had been brought up to nothing elce' (p. 18). Her courtly
education, that is to say, had not spoiled her but better fitted her for the
performance of domestic duties. Similarly, Lucy Hutchinson's daughter-
in-law, Jane Ratcliffe, is commended for being 'naturaliz'd into [her husband's] house and interests, as if she had no other regard in the world',
even though she came from a royalist family, and for 'loving home, without melancholly or sullenesse, observant of her father and mother [in-
law], not with regrett but delight, and the most submissive affectionate
wife that ever was' (pp. 239–40). *Submissive* to patriarchalism and
exogamy: that is her defining excellence as a woman. The reprimands
handed out in seventeenth-century sermons, guides and handbooks to
bold and assertive women find a sympathetic echo in Lucy Hutchinson's
text.[21] For aspiring wives, it has only scorn: Cromwell, for all his faults,
may yet have been 'gallant and great', but his 'wife and children . . .
setting up for principality . . . suited no better with any of them than
scarlett on the Ape' (pp. 208, 209). The independence of 'Wicked or vaine
weomen' and their profligate ways are condemned, if not as misogynist-
ically, certainly as categorically as androcentrism could desire (pp. 26–7).
  Despite her republican repudiation of monarchy, patriarchy thus
remains for Lucy Hutchinson the natural order of things. Indeed, though
a vindication of a rebellion, the *Memoirs* is also, and equally, a vindication
of patriarchy. Catastrophe waits on those who would evade or invert its
allocation of responsibility. Of this, there are two striking examples. Lucy

Hutchinson strongly disapproved of Thomas Lord Fairfax's decision to resign his commission in 1650 rather than lead the campaign against Charles II and the Scots, since it paved the way for Cromwell's ambition. In her account of the episode, she makes no mention of the conscientious scruples which weighed with Fairfax: that the invasion was a breach of the union and peace between the two kingdoms sworn in *The Solemn League and Covenant*. Rather, she attributes his regrettable decision to the malign influence of a woman: Fairfax, 'perswaded by his wife and her Presbiterian Chaplains', was 'as unmoveable by his friends as pertinacious in obeying his wife' (p. 195). Thus, a woman exercising an authority to which she was not entitled was responsible for handing over the young commonwealth to Cromwell's tyranny.

Still more remarkable than this collusion between woman's misrule and Presbyterian self-interest is Charles I's culpability for causing the Civil War. It lay less in his inclinations towards absolutism than in his capitulation to a woman; not in the tyrannical imposition of patriarchy but in its subversion. He was 'a most uxorious husband', 'enslav'd' to 'a papist, a French lady of a haughty spiritt', Henrietta Maria (pp. 46, 49), and

never is . . . any place happie where the hands that are made only for distaffes affect the management of Sceptres. If any one object the fresh example of Queen Elizabeth, let them remember that the felicity of her reigne was the effect of her submission to her masculine and wise Councellors; but wherever male princes are so effeminate to suffer woemen of forreigne birth and different religions to entermeddle with the affairs of State, it is always found to produce sad desolations. (p. 48)[22]

Furthermore, when Lucy Hutchinson remarks of the wife of the Mayor of Nottingham, a man who 'had no more but a Burger's discretion', that she was possessed 'of more understanding than women of her rank usually have' (p. 70), she betrays as small expectation of the lower classes as of the female sex. The woman who was so sensitive to the gentility of John Hutchinson and proud that her children were educated 'befitting their father's house' (p. 207), reminds us that the first Duke of Buckingham, for all his greatness, was only a 'fourth sonne' (p. 46), and she speaks with asperity of Archbishop Laud's 'meaness' (p. 48). Dr Huntingdon Plumtre, one of John Hutchinson's critics at Nottingham, lacked not only 'courage' but, equally damningly, 'quallity' (p. 71). Captain Gervase Lomax might have been 'a very honest man', but, still, he 'could not be reckon'd among the gentry, though he were call'd by the name of Mr' (p. 73). For all her political and religious Independency, her Baptist and sectarian sympathies, Lucy Hutchinson had none of Cromwell's straightforward preference for 'plain russet-coated' captains over 'gentlemen'.[23] She was scornful of the indecorousness of lower-class enthusiasts (p. 63), found John Lilburne 'turbulent spirited' (p. 191) and was frustrated that the constant recourse of the 'religiousest and best' in the garrison at Nottingham to the promptings of their individual consciences made them so 'pragmaticall' as to be ungovernable (p. 106). She did not at all care that John Hutchinson should become too familiar with them. He should preserve a 'distance' from his soldiers as from his wife, that he might secure the obedience of both (p. 156).

This history of opposition to patriarchal tyranny in the state is thus not radical but conservative in its unequivocal insistence on the need for obedience to proper superiors, and, especially, on the propriety of women's subordination to men. And yet, in these very terms, Lucy Hutchinson's whole text is a gross impropriety. Its mere existence contradicts its own avowals. The text denies Lucy Hutchinson any being apart from John Hutchinson even as, without him, it confers on her an enduring identity; it characterises her as his shadow when his surviving image is hers; it presents him as her author when he is her literary creation. Every page thus constitutes an implicitly ironic and assertive gloss on the text's explicitly deferential submissiveness. Lucy Hutchinson's enterprise is at odds with itself, and at odds with the woman's role it endorses. Hands that should not grasp at sceptres had no more business grasping pens:

> I am obnoxious to each carping tongue
> Who says my hand a needle better fits,
> A poet's pen all scorn I should this wrong,
> For such despite they cast on female wits . . .
> Men have precedency and still excel,
> It is but vain unjustly to wage war;
> Men can do best, and women know it well.
> Preeminence in all and each is yours. [24]

That is the New England Puritan Anne Bradstreet in the apologetic 'Prologue' to her *The Tenth Muse* (1650). Half a century later Anne Finch went beyond Anne Bradstreet in her direct recognition that her sex necessitated an apologetic preface to her poetry since, for a woman to write, constituted a threat to androcentric order: it was to encroach on men's prerogative:

> Alas! a woman that attempts the pen,
> Such an intruder on the rights of men,
> Such a presumptuous creature is esteemed,
> The fault can by no virtue be redeemed. [25]

It is horror at the monstrosity of such a perversion of the natural order of things which inspires the virulence and sordidness of Pope's attack on Eliza Heywood. [26] 'Let thy words be few' (Eccles. 5:2) was a text applied with particular homiletic fervour to women in whom 'excessive talkativeness' was typically taken (as by Allestree, for example) to be endemic, and a sad evidence of the sex's propensity to immodest boldness. 'A laxative running tongue', wrote Richard Baxter, citing Proverbs 10:19, is 'the most common miscarriage of your Sex'. To 'be well thought of and honoured by men, you can scarcely take a surer way, than to let your words be few and weighty'.[27]

If, then, 'the great indecency of Loquacity' is 'universally an insolent unbecoming thing' but (as is usual when blame is being allocated) 'most peculiarly so in a Woman', for a woman to be not only loquacious but loquacious in print was 'a scandal to the modesty of her sex' in its unashamed self-assertiveness. This scandal Dryden saw exemplified in Aphra Behn,[28] and many contemporaries in Margaret Cavendish, Duchess of Newcastle; or, if not a scandal and a monstrosity, then a kind of madness: 'Sure', wrote Dorothy Osborne, 'the poore woman is a little distracted, she could never bee soe rediculous else as to venture at writeing book's'.[29] As Jane Spencer has pointed out, the situation was nicely summed up in 1702 by a critic who objected that 'the Language won't bear such a thing as a She-Author' since ''tis false Grammar, there's no Feminine for the *Latin* word [*auctor*], 'tis entirely of the Masculine Gender'.[30]

For Lucy Hutchinson to write at all was thus to emerge from the shadow of John Hutchinson by laying implicit claim to the prerogatives of the masculine gender. It was an insubordinate, immodest and unfeminine act, if not an entirely surprising one from the woman in whose poetry John Hutchinson himself detected 'rationality . . . beyond the customary reach of a she witt' (p. 29), and who confessed 'for my needle, I absolutely hated it' (p. 288). It is true that she did not publish,[31] but this neither mitigates her effrontery nor argues a submissive reticence. Her book was confined to manuscript because she *could* not, rather than *would* not, reach a wider public. Though its prefatory address is to her children and the 'particular' readership envisaged the Colonel's 'owne posterity', Lucy Hutchinson's *Memoirs* also preserve the memory of John Hutchinson 'to instruct the erring children' not of her body but 'of this generation'. Her 'monument' is erected 'for the benefitt of all' (pp. 1–2). Circumstances prohibited printed address to this larger audience: no licence for such an historiographical apologetic could have been expected. When, however, circumstances changed, and Julius Hutchinson was able to publish the *Memoirs*, he was but realising the author's intention. In any case, composition and possession of the manuscript in itself legally constituted publication and, in this instance, was certainly to be guilty of seditious libel, and probably of treason, in that the *Memoirs* contemplate the death of a king, defend the abolition of monarchy and advocate republicanism.[32]

So far was she from being deferential that Lucy Hutchinson not only rebelliously wrote but wrote approvingly of rebelliousness.

She was well aware of the resultant anomaly, 'Could my sex . . . derive honour from writing', she wrote in 1675, she would have wished for something worthier of the first Earl of Anglesey's patronage than her translation of Lucretius; but the possibility does not arise: a woman's 'more becoming virtue is silence'.[33] Yet 300–odd pages hardly constitute silence, nor are the words of the *Memoirs* few. Lucy Hutchinson consequently sought in various ways to subdue her literary rebelliousness to conformity with the ideal of feminine reticence which her own text recognises as a woman's only proper demeanour. She endeavoured, in fact, to write herself out of the book even as she wrote it, marginalising her own role in its matter and repeatedly disclaiming any credit for its manner. Hers is a 'naked undrest narrative' (p. 1), a 'rude draught' (p. 2) drawn by her 'unskillful hand' (p. 3; cf. pp. 12, 14), which, she fears, will 'injure' rather than 'honor' John Hutchinson's memory with its 'imperfect image of him' (pp. 1–2). Hers is 'only a female pen' and therefore no more able to do justice to the Colonel than was Aphra Behn's to honour Oroonoko.[34]

This proper acknowledgement of the impossibility of feminine achievement in this venture is tactful, but Lucy Hutchinson takes a far more significant step to reduce her artistic presence. The earlier part of the *Memoirs* is 'transcrib'd out of a more particular collection' (p. 157), that is, a journalistic notebook, still extant, kept more or less contemporaneously with events up to February 1645 (p. xxii). The Puritan habit of diary-keeping is well known and well documented, and there is nothing remarkable in either a woman keeping such a journal or in its being written up subsequently.[35] What is remarkable is that this journal was written up not as autobiography but as biography, and furthermore, as third person biography. Throughout, Lucy Hutchinson figures as 'the Colonel's wife', 'the Governor's wife', 'his wife'. Her son is 'his sonne' (p. 239); Sir Allen Apsley stays not with her but at 'the Governor's house' and he comes not because he is her brother but because 'the Governor's wife' is his 'sister' (p. 170). Such pronouns and circumlocutions deny Lucy Hutchinson an author's authority over her book and reduce her to a minor character within it, and a minor figure defined by her relationship to a man. In the text of the *Memoirs*, the words of the Governor's wife *are* few. Furthermore, though they may be reported, she does not speak in the first person. Lucy Hutchinson has, in fact, attained that silence which is woman's more becoming virtue.

This is a narrative strategy which frees the *Memoirs* not only from dependence upon a woman but also from subjectivism.[36] Clarendon would similarly invest his *History* with authority and objectivity. In this respect, the title *Memoirs*, which the first editor supplied (p. xxii), is misleading. *Memoirs* are written by one who remembers, who was involved in, and has a personal relationship with, what is remembered. Lucy Hutchinson's own title far more accurately reflects the impersonality of her method: *The Life of John Hutchinson.* Within the narrative she is, as she should be, the devoted, loving and obedient wife of John Hutchinson. 'His wife' could have no business writing, and she does not. She neither recollects her memories nor recalls the intimacies of a relationship. A disembodied historian records the public activities which comprised the *Life* of John Hutchinson.

To this narrator is granted a liberty denied to the Colonel's wife: she can address the reader in the first person. She most commonly intrudes to explain some point about the management or direction of the narrative. The situation in 1642, for example, is rehearsed 'so farre as is necessarie to be remember'd for the story I most particularly intend' (p. 60). It is 'I' who digresses from 'the story which I would carry on' (p. 69), who returns 'to his story where I left it' (p. 199), and who confesses 'I have bene a little tedious in these descriptions' (p. 72). This controlling 'I' has made a generic choice – she does not write romance (p. 114) – and deploys her material as best suits the Colonel's biography (p. 173), though on occasions she 'cannot here omitt one story, though not altogether so much of the Colonell's concerns' (p. 242). This is 'his', the Colonel's, story, but 'I' trace it (p. 53).

The Colonel's wife, then, could not write his *Life*, but 'I' can. This separate 'I' is not, however, merely writer and historian: she is an independent intelligence, capable of adopting a point of view on both the Colonel and his wife, a satirist and polemicist of acerbic acuity, and a person wholly committed to a particular interpretation of the events narrated. On occasions, these opinions assume masculine authority by being fused with those of the Colonel. At the free school at Nottingham the young John Hutchinson was disgusted by the 'nice superstitions and pharisaicall holiness, straining at gnatts and swallowing camels' (p. 24) of Episcopalians. The narrative voice is sharp in its epithets and Biblical allusion (Matt. 23:24), but apparently articulates John Hutchinson's rather than its own sentiments. When the narrator speaks of John Hutchinson's 'happie progress in discovery of the false, carnall and Antichristian Doctrines of Rome' (p. 35), an explicit evaluation is made of his religious development, but it is merely the appreciative one the feminine owes to the masculine. Similarly, the narrator is entirely in accord with her subject's growing abhorrence, as he attended chapel worship at Peterhouse, Cambridge, of 'their stretching superstition to idolatrie' (p. 25). However, when she adds that, at this stage in his development (in the early 1630s), 'he consider'd not the emptinesse and carnallitie, to say no more, of that publick service which was then in use' (p. 25), she is no longer merely recording and approving John Hutchinson's views. On the contrary, she is commenting on what he had then not noticed. The decision 'to say no more' can be made only by one who could say more. This parenthetical reticence betrays the narrator's autonomous identity. 'I' have not only the capacity to choose what to write but hold opinions on which, had 'I' so chosen, 'I' might have enlarged.

And very often she does enlarge on them, saying a good deal more with no appeal to John Hutchinson as her authority. 'I can truly relate' the state of the kingdom at the outbreak of Civil War from 'what I was then able to take notice of' (p. 37). This first person narrator does not, like the Colonel's wife or Milton's Eve, acquire her knowledge second-hand from her husband, but first-hand. 'I know upon certeine knowledge' (p. 191) that those who declined to serve at Charles I's trial or to sign the death-warrant 'retreated not for conscience, but for feare and worldly prudence' because 'I' 'lived' through that time (p. 190). The Colonel's wife may have no memories, but 'I' have (p. 63). And what 'I' make of this experience is forcefully personal: 'I am sure' (p. 51).

This certitude invests the many pages of the narrator's survey of England on the eve of war with a partisan belligerency. It reverberates through her attack on the transference to kings of the adulation previously accorded popes (p. 3); on the machinations of the 'wicked' Queen of Scots, guilty of 'murthers and adulteries' (p. 39); on the political 'dissembling' which prompted Elizabeth 'to destroy' the Earl of Essex who alone had 'a courage to have kept out' James I (p. 41); on the luxury of James's court, 'a nursery of lust' (p. 42); and on monarchical aspirations to absolutism, so contrary to the true constitution enjoyed by the free-born English (p. 40). Thomas May's *History of the Long Parliament* (1647) she finds of 'more indulgence to the King's guilt than can justly be allow'd' (p. 53). She herself has no intention of indulging malignants, nor even those who eschewed partisanship. Unlike Richard Baxter, 'I cannot reckon' moderate Protestants 'as a vertuous Medium' between Papists and Puritans, since they are either nominal Christians or secret Romanists (p. 38). The zealous commitment she admired is found only among Puritans, who draw from her a rhetorically sustained and cumulatively patterned defence (pp. 43–4). The 'greatest of the Governor's defects' was 'through the candidnesse and sincerity of his owne nature, he was more unsuspitious of others, and more credulous of false pretenders, than suited with so great a prudence as he testified in all things else' (pp. 133–4). Credulity is not a defect shared by the narrator. Her portraits prickle with indignation at the disloyal, scheming and selfish wiles of those who so inadequately served John Hutchinson at Nottingham – the 'fowle adulterer', of 'noe pietie or holinesse' and 'not understanding enough to judge the equity' of Parliament's cause, Sir John Gell (pp. 67–8); the physician

Huntingdon Plumtre, a man of 'great pride' (pp. 70–1); James Chadwick, with his 'insinuating witt and tongue' (pp. 71–2); Charles White, 'of meane birth and low fortunes' who had 'the most factious, ambitious, vaineglorious, envious, and mallitious nature that is imaginable . . . the greatest dissembler, flatterer, traitor and hipocrite that ever was' (p. 69). Her contempt for what she portrays as their conspirational activities is vital in its animus (e.g., pp. 132, 137, 138, 140, 141, 145), as is her belittling of Major-General John Lambert's suppression of Sir George Booth's royalist uprising (a 'very cheape victory', achieved 'through the cowardice of the enemy'), (p. 216). Equally acerbic is her rejection of the Restoration settlement. For this, she holds the Protectorate's betrayal of the Good Old Cause responsible (p. 209), an opinion she delivers in her own voice before we hear it from John Hutchinson (p. 211). In 1660 the 'sunne of liberty then sett, and . . . gave place to the fowlest mists that every overspread a miserable people' (p. 224). 'The mercies of the wicked' is her scathing application of Proverbs 12:10 to the Act of Oblivion (p. 232). 'I reject' astrological speculation as 'vaine and foolish' (p. 276): and 'I' can reject as 'barbarous' (p. 275) the turn of political affairs no less vehemently or absolutely.

There are, then, two Lucy Hutchinsons in the *Memoirs*: the obedient wife, her husband's shadow, who has no voice, and the creatively independent, defiant and opinionated narrator who speaks for the former.[37] Consistently to maintain the distinction between the two halves of this split self would require considerable adroitness in role-playing, and, not surprisingly, there are occasional venial slips: 'Our horse' who fled before a Cavalier attack on Nottingham in 1644 (p. 114) inadvertently engages the narrator as a participant rather than a commentator, and though 'Mrs Hutchinson' was up late when forced entry to the Hutchinson home was attempted in the winter of 1661/2, 'wee since heard' Sir Edward Golding was responsible (p. 241). More revealingly, not even the narrator can keep Lucy Hutchinson entirely in her feminine and wifely place. Early in the *Memoirs* there is evident narratorial satisfaction in the refusal of the youthful Lucy Hutchinson to conform to the feminine stereotype. The reader is introduced to a *femme savante*, careless in her dress (p. 31), 'giving herself wholly up to studie and writing' (p. 32), 'loath to displease' her parents 'but more herselfe in marrying such as she could find no inclination to' (p. 31).[38] The narrator as well as Lucy Hutchinson triumphs over the 'mallitious practises' of those women who, 'with wittie spight', sought to engage John Hutchinson's affections by representing 'all her faults to him, which chiefly terminated in the negligence of her dresse and habitt and all womanish ornaments' (p. 32).

This independence of mind survived marriage, and could exert considerable influence on John Hutchinson himself. When, in 1646, the Colonel broke up a 'private meeting' to placate Presbyterian opinion, it was Lucy Hutchinson who read the meeting's notes on paedobaptism and, 'hap'ning to be with child', 'communicated' to her husband her resultant doubts concerning 'the misapplication of that Ordinance . . . and . . . that greate mistake of the nationall Churches'. Though the point was raised with a due feminine desire for masculine instruction, its consequence was that the Colonel came to reject paedobaptism and the Hutchinsons were 'revil'd . . . and call'd fanaticks and anabaptists' (p. 169). Sometimes, she was less deferential, plainly telling her husband 'she could not bear' the Scots Presbyterian engaged as their chaplain, with the result the man was dismissed (p. 178).

Her interventions could be of more consequence. 'Peek'd' at reflections on John Hutchinson's unworthiness in apparently deserting her when Prince Rupert's troops prevented his return home in 1642, she presented the Colonel's brother as her husband. This scheme to safeguard his honour misfired (pp. 65–6), but in 1660 she was far more decisive, and no less deceptive. Finding, after the King's return, the Colonel 'ambitious of being a publick sacrifice' she 'drove him out of her owne lodgings, into the custody of a friend, in order to his further retreat if occasion should be' and would 'by no meanes heare of his surrendering himself'. Having secured his safety by persuading him 'to a strong engagement that he would not dispose of himselfe without her' (p. 229), she then wrote and forged his signature to a petition of submission and repentance to the Speaker of the House of Commons (pp. 290–2), with the result that they voted 'for his absolute discharge' (p. 230).[39] There is no doubt who took charge in this emergency, but the event was not entirely happy. In resolving to disobey the Colonel's injunction 'to keepe quiet' (p. 229) she 'thought she had never deserv'd so well of him as in the endeavours and labours she exercis'd to bring him off' but discovered she 'never displeas'd him more in her life' (p. 234). Denied his martyrdom, John Hutchinson found himself suspected by both royalists and republicans as a turncoat (p. 234). The later pages of the *Memoirs* are tense with the determination of the Colonel to pursue what his wife resists as a suicidal course, impatience striving with patience:

Once when his wife was lamenting his condition, having sayd many things to comfort her, he told her he could not have bene without this affliction, for if he had flourisht while all the people of God were corrected, he should have fear'd he had not bene accounted among his children if he had not shared their lott; then would with thankfulnesse repeate the kind and gentle dealings of the Lord at all times toward him; and erect a firme and mighty hope upone it, and wonderfully encourage her to beare it patiently. (pp. 265–6)

As in this example, the narrator continues to insist gender roles are being properly fulfilled: it is the wife who repines, he who 'erects' a firm and mighty hope. This repining wife was nevertheless well able to engage men as equals. She was sufficiently determined to resist attempts to inveigle from her evidence incriminating the regicides, claiming, with palpable untruth, that she knew 'nothing of State managements' (p. 237). In 1663, when her husband was imprisoned in the Tower, she was a suitor to the Privy Council, and was 'sent' by the Colonel to Secretary Bennet (p. 253), as, many years before, he had sent her to Ireton to be relieved from serving on the Council of State (p. 191) and had, in 1659, 'caus'd his wife to write a letter' to Major-General Charles Fleetwood after a scuffle with soldiers in their home (p. 221). John Hutchinson had good reason thus to rely on her self-possession, sharp-mindedness and forceful persuasiveness. As in 1659 she had with fine composure dealt with the soldiers' commander, 'smiling' as she plainly told him 'all the whole country would shortly be weary of their yoake' (p. 221), so in 1663 she was more than a match for Bennet. She reminded him her husband was 'compriz'd in the Act of Oblivion', was disingenuously unable 'absolutely [to] say' the petition to the Speaker was in her handwriting 'though it had some resemblance', and was alive to the irony of so 'wise' a statesman suspecting the romance nomenclature of young girls' correspondence – Amalthra, Araminta, Clarimond, Thyrsis and so on – to be the secret code of seditious plotters (pp. 253–4, 326 n.1 to p. 254).

   Clearly, to survive in the aftermath of 1660, and to ensure her husband's survival, Lucy Hutchinson had to be not only decisive but devious and even reckless. Such behaviour had been demanded of her and of many other women ever since 1642. The Civil War, separating wives from husbands, challenged them to forgo the passivity and submissiveness supposed to be naturally womanly and to assume instead an 'unnatural' masculine courage and resolution in meeting its threats and in enduring the disruption and hostilities which it visited on every part of the kingdom. Their response to this challenge so plainly contradicted the received notion of the feminine[40] as to encourage a questioning of, and a disregard for, traditional androcentric assumptions. Women not only acted in unaccustomed roles; they began to express themselves in unaccustomed ways, discovering the audacity to engage in political and religious controversy, to dispute constitutional and ecclesiastical settlements, and to petition parliament.[41] The war thus tended, if only partially and temporarily, to the liberation of women, much to the horror of conservative contemporaries who inveighed against the 'modern' phenomenon of the 'manwoman'.[42]

   One evidence of this enlargement of woman's place is the greater readiness of both parliamentarian and royalist women to grasp masculine pens. From her statistical analysis of seventeenth-century printed books by women, Patricia Crawford concludes that: 'The impact of the Civil Wars and Interregnum upon women's publications was remarkable.' From under ten in every five-year period before 1640 the number of new titles by women in 1641–5 rose dramatically to over forty, and to sixty-nine in 1646–50, to continue at nearly that level until 1660.[43] Since Keith Thomas's pioneering article[44] we have realised that the more radical of these texts said some very remarkable things, suggesting that the religious and political egalitarianism of the enthusiastic sects is to be associated with a move towards sexual equality. Such a tendency might have made possible for some women confident self-expression and the assumption of the rights of authorship, but their number was, like their social standing, insignificant. Lucy Hutchinson represents the predicament of the far greater number, whose radical creativity, inspired by the unprecedented turmoil of Civil War, was constrained by the conservatism engendered by education and social mores. Here is neither the persona nor the voice of the single-minded radical. Rather, she is a kind of mirror-image of Mary Astell: where Mary Astell's prophetic feminist thought was married to a staunchly conservative Tory politics and episcopalian religion, Lucy Hutchinson's radical religion and politics could tolerate only wifely domesticity in women.[45]

The consequence is an inescapable tension within her text. Although she openly and willingly embraced her woman's role, it was a role incompatible with the literary creativity released by the experience of war, defeat and bereavement. Since a wife should, as John Hutchinson instructed his, 'keepe quiet', she could not at one and the same time be obedient and articulate. It was when, with the Colonel's death, the wife 'vanisht into nothing', that the writer came into being. Even then, Lucy Hutchinson could not associate the two roles. Consequently, the independent 'I' who alone could 'speak the truth of all' (p. 172) had perforce to speak for the wife and widow. However, if the distinction between Lucy Hutchinson and the narrative 'I' was an expedient which allowed the wife to speak while disguising her disobedience in so doing, it was also an expedient which implicitly conceded the inability of the wifely role to answer to the complete individuality of Lucy Hutchinson. For who is this 'I' but Lucy Hutchinson, and who is Lucy Hutchinson but the Colonel's wife? Yet how can two be one?

To write the *Memoirs* was, then, to be compelled into a narrative deviousness akin to the political deviousness necessitated by the Restoration, a role-playing such as the unpredictable contingencies of Civil War had often demanded of women. And as that role-playing had made possible kinds of achievement and self-realisation unattainable through conformity to the feminine gender role, so the disguise of the narrative persona of the *Memoirs* liberated Lucy Hutchinson. Consequently the text is problematic, self-reflexive and self-defeating. Through her *alter ego* the silent wife delivers more vigorous and striking utterances than ever we hear from the Colonel; for all her disavowals and self-effacement, she is his author, he her creation; though she marginalises her own participation, she remains much the most forceful and decisive character in the action. She, not he, animates a text devoted to him.[46] Yet this she can do only by dissevering herself into silent wife and vocal narrator. The duplicity which one strand in feminist criticism sees as the inevitably strategy of women writing in androcentric cultures has here become an actual doubleness,[47] a doubleness we may feel reflects the literal situation of the Colonel's wife and of seventeenth-century women. Wifely silence and womanly loquacity were incompatible. Bifurcation was the condition of articulation. For Lucy Hutchinson, univocity was impossible.

NOTES

I am deeply grateful to my colleague Angela Smith for her comments on an earlier draft of this essay.

1 Lucy Hutchinson, *Memoirs of the Life of Colonel Hutchinson*, ed. James Sutherland (1806; London, 1973), pp. 83, 106. Parenthetical references in the text are to the pages of this edition.
2 Andrew Browning, ed., *English Historical Documents 1660–1714* (London, 1966), pp. 164–5.
3 On this episode, see Henry Gee, 'The Derwentdale Plot, 1663', *Transactions of the Royal Historical Society*, 3rd ser., 11 (1917), 125–42, and Richard L. Greaves, *Deliver Us from Evil: The Radical Underground in Britain, 1660–1663* (New York, 1986), pp. 165 ff., which discusses Hutchinson's involvement.
4 Lucy Hutchinson suspected a 'ling'ring poyson' had been administered to him by Sir John Robinson, Lieutenant of the Tower (*Memoirs*, pp. 261–76).
5 The *Memoirs* were completed by the summer of 1671 (*Memoirs*, p. 325, n.3 to p. 244). Lucy Hutchinson consequently had that 'sense of connection' with her subject which Natalie Davis considers to have been necessary to prompt women to attempt historiography, and which led them 'to write about the world [they] knew' (Natalie Zemon Davis, 'Gender and Genre: Women as Historical Writers, 1400–1820', in Patricia H. Labalme, ed., *Beyond Their Sex: Learned Women of the European Past* (New York and London, 1980), pp. 155, 156–7); this essay mentions, but does not discuss, the *Memoirs* (p. 165).
6 Sir Giles Isham, ed., *Correspondence of Bishop Brian Duppa and Sir Justinian Isham*, Northants Record Soc. Publ. 17 (1956), p. 180; Richard Baxter, *Reliquiae Baxterianae* (1696), I, p. 100, § 145; Abraham Cowley, *The Essays and Other Prose Writings*, ed. Alfred B. Gough (Oxford, 1915), p. 46.
7 Abraham Cowley, 'Upon his Majesty's Restoration and Return', lines 134–44, in G.A.E. Parfitt, ed., *Silver Poets of the Seventeenth Century* (London, 1974), p. 228.
8 John Milton, *Samson Agonistes*, lines 7–9, 633–45, 667–704, in *The Poems of*

John Milton, ed. Alastair Fowler and John Carey, 2nd corrected impression (London, 1980), pp. 347, 367–70.

9 N.H. Keeble, 'The Autobiographer as Apologist: *Reliquiae Baxterianae* (1696)' in Thomas N. Corns, ed., *The Literature of Controversy: Polemical Strategy from Milton to Junius* (London, 1987), pp. 105–19, discusses the *Reliquiae* in this respect.

10 On this thrust in nonconformist writing, see N.H. Keeble, *The Literary Culture of Nonconformity in later seventeenth-century England* (Leicester, 1987), esp. pp. 83–5, 187–97; the previous paragraph draws on pp. 17–18, 188–9 of this study.

11 John Milton, *Paradise Lost*, VII.24, in *Poems*, p. 776.

12 John Hutchinson, *A Narrative of the Imprisonment and Usage of Col. John Hutchinson . . . now close Prisoner in the Tower of London* (1664), in *The Harleian Miscellany or, a Collection of . . . Tracts . . . found in the late Earl of Oxford's Library*, 8 vols. (1744–6), III, pp. 31–6.

13 Lucy Hutchinson explains more fully her thinking on regeneration, faith and grace in [Julius Hutchinson, ed.], *On the Principles of the Christian Religion* (London, 1817), esp. pp. 51–80.

14 John Bunyan, *Prison Meditations* (1663), line 102, in *The Miscellaneous Works of John Bunyan*, gen. ed. Roger Sharrock, 12 vols. in progress (Oxford, 1976–), VI, p. 45.

15 Lucy Hutchinson, *Principles of the Christian Religion*, p. 131. On this as a characteristic theme in nonconformist writing, see Keeble, *Literary Culture*, pp. 189–91, 198–204.

16 For descriptions and discussions of this role see particularly Ruth Kelso, *Doctrine for the Lady of the Renaissance* (Urbana IL, 1956), esp. pp. 5–37, 78–135: and also Juliet Dusinberre, *Shakespeare and the Nature of Women* (London, 1975), pp. 77–136, 196–231.

17 Ruth Perry, *The Celebrated Mary Astell: An Early English Feminist* (Chicago and London, 1986), pp. 105–6, 112–13, 120–4, 129, 136–42.

18 For examples of women who did, see Patricia Crawford, 'Women's Published Writings 1600–1700', in Mary Prior, ed., *Women in English Society* (London, 1985) pp. 116–17.

19 Lucy Hutchinson, *Principles of the Christian Religion*, pp. 5–6.

20 [Richard Allestree], *The Ladies Calling* (1673), part II, p. 33. Cf. e.g., Richard Baxter, *A Christian Directory* (1673), p. 531, §§1–6; John Bunyan, *Christian Behaviour* (1663), in *The Works*, ed. George Offor, 3 vols. (London, Glasgow and Edinburgh, 1860–2), II, 560–1. See also the discussion of William Gouge's *Of Domesticall Duties* (1622) and Richard Braithwaite's *The English Gentlewoman* (1631) in Hilda Smith, *Reason's Disciples*: Seventeenth century feminists (Urbana, Ill. 1982) pp. 51–2.

21 E.g., Thomas Bentley, *The Monument of Matrones* (1582), iii.35 (quoted by Crawford in Prior, ed., *Women in English Society*, p. 216); [Allestree], *Ladies Calling*, part I, pp. 29–47 ('Of Meekness'); Baxter, *Christian Directory*, pp. 531–2, §§7–8.

22 This passage is mentioned in Antonia Fraser, *The Weaker Vessel: Woman's Lot in Seventeenth Century England* (London, 1984), p. 136.

23 W.C. Abbott, ed., *The Writings and Speeches of Oliver Cromwell*, 4 vols. (Cambridge MA, 1937–47), I, p. 256.

24 Jeannine Hensley, ed., *The Works of Anne Bradstreet* (Cambridge MA, 1967), p. 16.

25 Anne Finch, Countess of Winchelsea, *Poems*, ed. J.M. Munnay (London, 1928), p. 24.
26 Alexander Pope, *The Dunciad Variorum* (1729), II.149–58, III.141–5, in *The Poems*, ed. John Butt (London, 1965), pp. 384–5, 408.
27 [Allestree], *Ladies Calling*, part I, pp. 7–8; Baxter, *Christian Directory*, p. 532, §10. Cf. Smith, *Reason's Disciples*, p. 53.
28 W. Scott, ed., *The Works of John Dryden*, rev. G. Saintsbury, 18 vols. (Edinburgh, 1893), XVIII, p. 166.
29 G.C. Moore Smith, ed., *The Letters of Dorothy Osborne to William Temple* (Oxford, 1928), p. 37.
30 *A Comparison Between the Two Stages* (1702), pp. 26–7, quoted in Jane Spencer, *The Rise of the Woman Novelist* (Oxford, 1986), p. 6.
31 Fraser, *Weaker Vessel*, p. 135 is mistaken in saying Lucy Hutchinson 'sprang into print in order to write a justificatory memoir of the husband she adored'. The *Memoirs* were first published in 1806.
32 See Keeble, *Literary Culture of Nonconformity*, pp. 98–101.
33 Charles Firth, ed., *Memoirs*, 2 vols. (London, 1885), II, p. 400.
34 Aphra Behn, *Oroonoko and Other Stories*, ed. Maureen Duffy (London, 1986), p. 64; for other examples of women pleading 'the ideology which made them inferior as an apology for their inadequacies', see Patricia Crawford in Prior, ed., *Women and English Society*, p. 219.
35 See Owen Watkins, *The Puritan Experience* (London, 1972).
36 Noting that Lucy Hutchinson wrote in the third person (but not that she also used the first), Dale Spender, *Mothers of the Novel* (London, 1986), p. 32, makes this point (cf. B[ridget] G. MacCarthy, *Women Writers: Their Contribution to the English Novel 1621–1744* (Cork, 1944), p. 104).
37 Cf. Sandra Findley and Elaine Hobby, 'Seventeenth Century Women's Autobiography', in Francis Barker *et al.*, eds., *1642: Literature and Power in the Seventeenth Century* (Colchester, Essex, 1981), p. 26.
38 Lucy Hutchinson's *Of Theologie* (in *Principles of the Christian Religion*, p. 139 ff.) shows extensive classical, patristic and historical reading. Roger Thompson, *Women in Stuart England and America*, (London, 1974) p. 200, cites her as an example of one of the 'relatively few' who managed to distinguish themselves 'by bucking the system' of poor education available for middle- and upper-class women. But compare Dorothy Gardiner, *English Girlhood at School* (London, 1929), p. 254.
39 MacCarthy, *Women Writers*, p. 103, calls attention, as does Firth, ed., *Memoirs*, I, p. xxi, to a second, later, petition to the House of Lords (II, pp. 395–8) which 'seems to prove that Col. Hutchinson's share in this matter was not confined to the passive and silent acceptance of his wife's expedient'. That Lucy Hutchinson does not mention this petition may be thought to reduce her husband's culpability by taking the responsibility for his recantation solely upon herself; but, equally, it does cast him in a (feminine) 'passive and silent' role, and herself in a (masculine) assertive one.
40 See Fraser, *Weaker Vessel*, pp. 163–221, for examples.
41 Patricia Crawford, 'Women's Published Writings 1600–1700', in Prior, ed., *Women in English Society*, pp. 213–14, 223–4; Patricia Higgins, 'The Reactions of Women, with special reference to women petitioners', in Brian Manning, ed., *Politics, Religion and the English Civil War* (London, 1973), pp. 179–222.
42 Fraser, *Weaker Vessel*, pp. 222–30.
43 Patricia Crawford in Prior, ed., *Women in English Society*, pp. 212–13, 265.

The 1646–60 level was only afterwards equalled in 1686–90 and 1696–1700 (p. 265). The number of political and prophetic works in the earlier period was not again achieved in that century (p. 269).

44 Keith Thomas, 'Women and the Civil War Sects', *Past and Present*, 13 (1958), 42–62 (esp. p. 47).

45 On Mary Astell's religious and political conservatism see Perry, *Celebrated Mary Astell*, pp. 163–6, 169–231; Bridget Hill, ed., *The First English Feminist Mary Astell*, (London, 1986), pp. 39–49; and Joan Kinnaird, 'Mary Astell and the Conservative Contribution to English Feminism', *Journal of British Studies*, 19 (1979), 53–75 (reprinted in revised form in Dale Spender, ed., *Feminist Theorists* (London, 1983), pp. 28–39).

46 This point is made in Fraser, *Weaker Vessel*, p. 135.

47 This view is summarised in Toril Moi, *Sexual/Textual Politics* (London, 1985), pp. 58–60, with particular reference to the thesis of Sandra M. Gilbert and Susan Gubar, *The Madwoman in the Attic* (New Haven, 1979).

13 Exporting Enthusiasm: John Perrot and the Quaker epic

THE CULTURE of radical religion was the new, flourishing and excitingly varied feature of English society in the twenty years after 1640. However small a proportion of the population the early nonconformists were, they had a large voice in the press, the pulpit and at times in government. The image of the 'sects' as socially disruptive and psychologically destructive 'enthusiasts' was a fear which remained long after 1660, a reminder of how dangerous a threat they were seen to present to the social and religious order. Unless we pay attention to how the radicals wrote as well as to what the radicals said and did, this hostile image – as much a hindrance to sympathisers as a blindfold to enemies – will remain.[1] In consequence, our knowledge of their culture – their construction in language of the self, the divine, and their notions of social practice – will remain impoverished, lost in the pejorative stereotypes generated by hostile contemporaries. The following essay seeks in part to remedy this situation by taking one case of an extreme religious radical and exploring the role of his literary production in the context of his activities, considering both in the light of the aesthetic consequences of the Civil War and Interregnum.

I

In the dayes of *Luther,* GOD moved in the *Darkness* upon the *face* of the *deeps* thereof; but they which made *him* their *Rest* are *confounded,* and their *head* is *broken* as Clay. He appeared *brighter* by *Behman* and *Brown;* but they which built their *Travels* as *Towers,* the LORD *confounded* with many *Languages,* even running up to the height, *Baptists, Seekers,* and *Ranters,* some made *bounds* for the pure, and others in their *lusts* revolted.[2]

Thus John Perrot, Quaker, in his testimony of 1661, *Battering Rams against Rome.* The quotation makes reference to two authors whose writings prefigure, in different ways, the nature of early Quaker belief. Perrot regards the Lutheran Reformation as a new creation, so he imitates the language of Genesis 1:2. Like the Creation, the Reformation is but a beginning, and there is more truth to be revealed. Robert Browne was the Elizabethan theorist of separation, of the gathering of the church apart from the impure and worldly.[3] Jacob Boehme, the German mystic popular in England from the mid-1640s on, saw the emanating abyss of the Godhead in nature and in man: the world was the perpetual 'out-speaking' of divine nature.[4]

Putting Robert Browne and Boehme together, despite Perrot's castigation, helps us to understand the two principles which the Quakers manifested and which locate them as products of the ferment of radical religion in the English Revolution: separation (though in a very different sense from Browne's) and reliance upon the 'inner light' speaking perfection – the presence of Christ, within all men, if only they would come to see it.

There is a further possibility. References to Robert Browne during the 1640s and 1650s by religious radicals are fairly rare. It may be that Perrot is referring to Sir Thomas Browne, and comparing *Religio Medici* and *Pseudodoxia Epidemica* with Boehme, as related accounts of the presence of God in nature. If Perrot is referring to Browne the natural philosopher, the interest in natural objects in Perrot's poetry is more understandable.[5] Moreover, there are strong grounds, as we shall see, for connecting Perrot the Quaker with the Hartlib circle of scientific reformers, who were usually not quite such extreme enthusiasts as was Perrot, but whose aims found a sympathetic hearing among the supporters of the Commonwealth.[6] Perrot's enthusiasm is an expression of mid-seventeenth-century nature mysticism, as much a part of the intellectual revolution as of the Puritan one.

The Civil War was fought in part over religious difference. Through the experience of religious toleration, and through the tendency of extreme Puritanism towards fragmentation and an increasingly subjective witness to divine assurance, the Quakers emerged in the early 1650s as an extreme version of radical religion. In these early years, the Quakers were not the unified movement, firmly under George Fox's control, which they were to become in the Restoration.[7] They were a disparate body, though their general acclaim of the inner light led to their persecution by the interregnum government because it was seen as a denial of the historical Christ who died at Jerusalem.[8] Their presence in the New Model Army, their apparently fierce, even violent language, and their habit of speaking to the world in sometimes extravagant bodily gestures or symbolic actions, caused people to fear them. The spectre of Münster was raised in hostile minds. The Quakers, it has been contended, helped to scare the nation into a Restoration in 1660.[9]

The 'light within' was more important for Quakers than the literal word of the Scriptures. Speech, as a record of the light within, could become privileged over the Bible. Moreover, for the Quakers, there was a continuity between body, world and speech or text, in a way that was not possible even for other radical religious groups, be they Baptists, Fifth Monarchists, Ranters, Muggletonians or one of the individual prophets active in these years. All speech, writing or gesture, all material objects, human and natural, were signs, or figurative sacraments, in which the presence of the inner light could be detected. For most early Quakers, human language was entirely natural (unlike the view of other radicals) but it should ideally represent traces of the 'seed' and 'light', the forces by which the perfected ones knew each other.[10] Quaker prophetic writings were devoid even of the sense of personality present in so much 'mechanick preaching' as they simply let their Old Testament (though often also Johannine) prophetic language speak directly:

thou thinkest those people have none to take their parts, and indeed they have not in the Earth, but I the Lord have undertaken their cause; and weeping, and howling, and [g]nashing of teeth, shall be the portion of all their Enemies for I will overturn, overturn overturn all powers and people, till he comes to Reigne whose right it is to Reigne, I will contend with all flesh, till they acknowledge my righteous Judgements.[11]

If the divisions between writer and text disappeared, or rather, if the textual presence of prophecy could obliterate an assumed unprophetic identity in the person outside the text (the author), the actions and experiences of the individual could become just as much a 'text' as the writing or 'testimony' itself. The two became interchangeable. This is not an observation made in the light of post-structuralist, Foucauldian or Greenblattian critical ideas, but a reality of Quaker theology. The body, internally and externally, became a sign of the sacred, and records of the experience of the person were published as the sufferings of that individual witness to the light. Conversely, aspects which in other theologies would be confined to the discursive, found an outlet in the 'speech' of action and gesture.

'Justifying the ways of God to men' for a Quaker meant going out into the world to testify in speech, gesture and writing in the hope of convincing others of the truth of the inner light. Writing meant writing pamphlets in which testimonies of truth were contained, but these testimonies could also be saved up, with accounts of journeys, sufferings and convincements, and published later, as the history of the 'seed' (those with the inner light) unfolded.

II

What was the relationship between these forms of testimony and Puritan culture at large? And how are they to be located within the field of early modern literary activity? Despite the misgivings which Independents and Baptists had concerning the Quaker denial of predestination doctrine, and their almost total denial of a visible church, there are continuities between the lesser and the greater extremes of Puritanism.[12] The most important of these was an acknowledgment of the Holy Spirit as evidence of an experiential encounter with the divine. This itself produced a discursive homogeneity, the differences within which reveal the problems which the collision of subject with key text (the Bible) created. N.H. Keeble has demonstrated the existence of a nonconformist literary culture, one shared by *Paradise Lost* and *The Pilgrim's Progress*.[13] Not only did Puritans, radical or otherwise, share theologies which can be detected in very different genres and forms, but also those theologies could transform inherited genres. This is one of the effects of nonconformist culture. The reaction of action with discourse, and of genre with theology, and the comparisons possible between different pieces of writing, help us to comprehend the dissemination and reception of radical religious activity.

A Sea of the Seed's Sufferings, Through which Runs A River of Rich Rejoycing, a series of poems of some 1448 lines, was written by John Perrot while he was in captivity in Rome in 1658 and 1659, and published on his return to England in 1661. Perrot was an Irish Quaker, previously a Baptist, and 'convinced' by the prominent early Quaker Edward Burrough in 1655.[14] After some time proselytising in Ireland, and then in England, he set sail in May or June 1657 with some other Quakers for the eastern Mediterranean. Their aim was to take their message to the Sultan of Turkey, and to proceed to Jerusalem. In fact, the group split up on several occasions, and the adventures which befell Perrot formed the basis for a particular 'testimony' which resulted in the only serious challenge to George Fox's authority in the Quaker movement in the 1660s.

Six Quakers set out on this mission: John Luffe, John Buckley, Mary Fisher, Mary Pierce, Beatrice Beckley and Perrot himself. They were ashore in Livorno on 6 August and had reached Zante (off the western coast of the Peleponnese) by 6 September, spreading their message as they went. The party divided at Zante, Perrot and Buckley travelling overland across the Peleponnese, via Corinth and Athens to Negroponte (now Evvoia), from whence they were able, after some difficulties, to meet the others who had sailed to Smyrna (now Izmir). The English Consul at Smyrna, perhaps desiring to protect the reputation of English merchants as much as to look after the Friends, advised Perrot and his companions to leave Turkey, telling them that their quest would be fruitless. They embarked for Zante again, and it is here that the group fragmented, leading to Perrot's particular tribulations.

Perrot and Luffe took sail for Venice. After a treacherous and unpleasant voyage, they entered the Gulf of Venice on 25 February, 1658, and were quarantined in the Lazzaretto, the leper colony confined to a small island near what is now called the Lido. After forty days, Perrot and Luffe were able to enter Venice itself, met the Doge and members of the Jewish community, and left Venice for Rome on 7 May, again with the eventual hope of seeing Jerusalem.

A month later, on 6 June, Perrot and Luffe reached Rome and established lodgings in the Piazza Farnese, near to the English College. Displaying a remarkable if by now unsurprising innocence, Perrot approached the English confessor in St Peter's Basilica, and asked how he might open communications with the Pope, Alexander VII, and so convert him. The confessor, a Jesuit, Thomas Courtney, passed him on to another Jesuit, John Crey, an Irishman and Chaplain to the Pope. Apparently, Perrot told Crey his intentions and the chaplain acted as Protestants feared Jesuits did. On 8 June, Perrot and Luffe were arrested at their lodgings, and taken to 'one of the New Prisons' where Perrot was interrogated by the City Governor and promised a public trial. Instead of the trial, however, Perrot was transferred a week later to the Inquisition prison where he was held for some eighteen weeks. Upon further examination, he was accounted mad and taken to the 'Pazzarella' or 'Prison of Madmen'. Perrot and Luffe both seem to have been held in solitary confinement, and by the end of 1658, Luffe was dead. It was given out that Luffe had died from starvation while fasting, but there is other evidence, none of it conclusive, to suggest that Luffe had been secretly hanged.[15] Perrot spent the next three years in the Pazzarella in squalid conditions, a lot of the time chained by the neck or by the ankle, and sometimes tortured, until he was released after the intercession of some other Quakers (namely, Jane Stokes and Charles Bayley) in Rome.

During this period of imprisonment and torture, Perrot produced a mass of writings in which he found a unique language for his sufferings by exploiting the potential for the allegorising of Scripture and the interiorising of verbal symbols which is so central to Quaker theology. Perrot developed this form of expression much earlier in his travels, so that the poetry written in Rome was the culmination of a series of largely prose writings which he delivered to particular groups during his journey, notably the Jews at Livorno, the Greeks at Negroponte and the Turks at Smyrna. Though his poetry's rhetoric of suffering is distinctive, it occurs also in these other pamphlets, and his own discovery of inner revelation was intimately linked to that which others were supposed to find. These writings all found their way back to England, most of them after Perrot's release, and they were published, partly in support of Perrot's claim against Fox and the other prominent Quakers that hats should be kept on in the Meeting during prayer. 'Hat heresy' is an even more extreme form of gestural anti-ritualism than that pursued by most Quakers. In his writings may be seen interpretative and experimential stances which formed that heresy. It will become clear that Perrot's particular witness, and his sufferings in Rome, lead to an attempt to refashion the signifying power of poetic language and of allegory, at that point in time when the status of literary allegory itself was questioned.[16] The modern reader is faced not only with the curious prospect of a new kind of poetry as an expression of something as bizarre and apparently trivial as 'hat heresy', but also with an answer to what one of the radical theologies produced in the English Revolution did to the poetic resources of the English language. This answer itself sheds new light on the relationship between social change and literary activity in the period, especially with regard to the works of well-known figures like John Milton.

III

In *Paradise Lost*, in order to express the emergence of fallen man eventually under the Covenant of Grace, Milton needed two heroes, Satan and Adam, in order to express the sense of rebellion and loss, and the arrival of conscience, when 'inward silence broke' (IX. 895) in Adam. The Quaker scheme works in the opposite direction, not from innocence to (ultimately) *felix culpa*, but from reprobation to grace and perfection. Milton splits Virgil's Aeneas into two presences in his poem, and some would argue that the narrator becomes another form of hero. Perrot, in his voyages, becomes the Quaker hero: the record of the sufferings is an epic record of the founding not of a nation but of inner peace. Clearly, *Paradise Lost* is an epic by virtue of its consciously formulated generic structure, and not purely the 'poetry of the spirit', as *A Sea* is meant to be. Also, *A Sea* in no sense matches the achievement of *Paradise Lost*. Nonetheless, Milton's own notion of inspired presence does compare with Perrot's poetic, the narrator in *Paradise Lost* threatening to allegorise himself in the characters of Satan and Adam, a position which is only forestalled by the Homeric and Virgilian language which dominates the poem.

In Perrot's writing, however, especially *A Sea of the Seed's Sufferings*, self is split into several allegorical presences, most notably the worm and the seed. These are threatened by a series of hostile elements, until the true nature and location of God is discovered. During the course of the poem, Perrot is able to express his own sense of gradual regeneration, his sense of the enormity of God in the natural world, and, in an unusual way, his experience of torture at the hands of the officials in the Pazzarella. If *Paradise Lost* is concerned with the definition of self according to Milton's theology through the relationship among prophetic narrator, Satan and Adam, *A Sea of the Seed's Sufferings* is an equivalent theodicy generated through a Quaker version of the signifying function of language and appropriate to the missionary experience of the Quakers.[17]

The poem is not an epic in the strict and classical sense of the word. Rather, it is a series of contemplations and songs, in a variety of poetic forms, which form the representation of the 'inner light' epic of Perrot's life. It is allegorical in two senses. First, it is an allegory in that it has natural objects or names which 'figure forth' abstract qualities. Secondly, it embodies the Quaker principle of interpreting scripture language as an allegory of a process of regeneration which takes place within the individual. This means that the poem lies somewhere between a late Spenserian idea of allegory, and something new which is a result of radical Puritan theology. In this sense, it may be compared with *Paradise Lost* again, where a radical Puritan theology is also used to transform an inherited form, the classical epic. Where Milton 'likens spiritual to corporeal' things when necessary, while generally claiming to speak a literal and substantial divine truth, Perrot uses his allegory in the first sense to place the spiritual *within* the corporeal. This is the literary correlative of the 'inner light' theology, one which Milton approached, but was not able finally to reach.[18]

There are two dominant discursive models for *A Sea*, and their choice would be unsurprising were Perrot's treatment not so extravagant. The Book of Job and Psalm 22 provide the obvious starting point, though the story of Jonah is detectable in the background. For Perrot, Job provides the main vocabulary for suffering and the model for the intense questioning of the divine which follows. Like Job, Psalm 22 was popular, especially with members of the gathered churches in their confessions of experience.[19] The text shares with Job the reference to man as worm, and the awareness of return to the womb as an archetypal experience for the sense of return to origins in the power of the Lord. But Perrot does not simply imitate. The entire poem is a series of debates between different voices, each voice being a different part of the allegory, so that the Biblical models are given differing functions. The allegory begins immediately as the reader's awareness of the first person shifts between worm and seed:

> I am a worm poor and low, which in the Earth doth creep,
> Hid as the tender Plant with Snow, in time of winter deep,
> So saith the Seed, grievous Oppressions long have bin
> My weighty burthens: ages spreading clouds of sin
> Have wrapt me up, and roul'd me under trouble
> I stand the same, they perish'd as a bubble.   (p. 3)

It is apparent that while the seed does create another identity in the worm, there is no distance between these two identities and that of Perrot's. Two pages later, at the beginning of the next section, Perrot's own voice is back with us: 'Hearing the Seed's *sore cryes*, my heart did think, / How bitter is the *Cup* given thee to drink' (p. 5).

Also noticeable is a hint regarding Perrot's diction and its sources. 'Bubble' does not occur in the Authorised Version. Rather, the word seems to come from seventeenth-century sacred poetry: Herbert uses 'bubble' twice (in 'Nature' and 'Vanitie II'), and there are other instances in Quarles and Thomas Washbourne.[20] Perrot was a man with reading, though he did not attend university. He was familiar with a wide range of techniques in contemporary verse, as the sixteen different sections of *A Sea* reveal. What is of interest is his development of these locutions. In fact, the *topos*, '*homo bulla*', here is the same as the elaboration on the Greek epigram published by Thomas Farnaby in 1629 and ascribed to Sir Francis Bacon:

> The world's a bubble, and the life of man
>   less than a span;
> In his conception wretched, from the womb
>   so to the tomb.[21]

The impressions which strike the reader most are those to do with the body: the actions of the body, especially physical symptoms of a harrowing emotional state – tears, bleedings, sighs, groanings, pangs – become situated in the larger allegory. Much of this vocabulary was developed by soteriologists (especially Puritan ones) as an affective means of encouraging self-understanding, and of enhancing the relationship between conscience and body with the divine.[22] In Perrot this usage is subtly changed, both dramatically animated in the urgent voice of the seed/worm, and mythologised as the fragmented physical anguish of self is set within the wider sea of the poem's universe. Moving bowels, which were associated with pity or tender feelings, become the most striking way of communicating the pressure on the conscience in response to suffering. It is both a literal and a figurative disembowelling:

> Thou Drop, Thy Channel's more than many Brooks,
> On Thy Grief's Streams my mourning spirit looks;
> Yea, for thy sake my Bowels are a River,
> Pour'd on the ground's, my Reins, my Heart and Liver   (p. 7)

The sight of God causes the self to tremble (to 'quake'), and more remarkably, the sources of physical life to imitate the way in which the natural world reveals divine presence:

I girt my *Loyns* with strong *Steel-bands* of *fear*
Dread *fill'd my house*, whilst *Jah's face* did *appear*,
My *Vitals* all became a *Silver Stream*,
In *substance*, melted not, as in a *Dream*,
Nor under *bonds* of *Magick's* gloomy hour;
But in true feeling of *Coelestial Power*.   (p. 9)

The poem tells of a journey, as the seed/worm swims precariously in a
sea full of frightening, predatory creatures, or 'Flocks of *devouring Birds*'
(p. 6), until the light within is reached. The natural part of man makes
him as brutish and oppressive as beasts. Moreover, through this course,
the reader is able to learn the significance of the allegorical language,
specifically its reference through natural imagery and naming to internal
illumination. Here, Perrot reveals a familiarity with contemplative occult-
ism, an interest not uncommon amongst the radicals and certainly an
influence upon their theology of perfection. The doctrine of correspondence, that in this case the life of the soul may be referred to in the same
terms as the outer world, illuminates Perrot's poem further: 'Then follows
Faith and Hope, which gives alone, / Th'Internal Knowledge of the vertuous stone' (p. 32).[23] Biblical imagery and natural observation combine
to express the beneficence of the Creator:

Through what his *Love* unnatural *compounds*
Of *Roots*, *Stones*, *Oare*, and *Dirt* of divers grounds.
It's but *one* simple *Virtue* doth *unfold*,
Which touching *Mettals* makes all *pure Gold*.   (p. 13)

Flesh becomes the '*Adamant*', the hard loadstone or diamond, which the
sweating blood of the worm fails to move or melt. In consequence, the
blood rises around the worm threatening to drown him. Sea and blood
begin to take on an equivalent status.

During the journey to Rome, there was plenty of time to experience
the hardship of voyage at sea. Perhaps the large amount of sea reference
expresses the experience of Perrot and Luffe at sea. The first vision of the
Seed appears to be made by a person standing in '*shallow waters*', observing
marine life. Then the speaker moves into deeper water, under which he
swims, watching the persecution of the Seed, until returning to land to
watch the persecutions of more beasts (p. 5). Was such an ordered pro-
gression partly bred by the observation of sea-life? Shallow water would
have surrounded Perrot when quarantined in the Lagoon of Venice. He
must have crossed the treacherous strait between the Greek mainland and
Negroponte, where violent currents flow in both directions. In his non-
poetic account of the voyage between Zante and Venice, Perrot describes
how he and Luffe were victimised by the Italian captain and his English,
Dutch and German crew. The captain threatened to cast Perrot adrift in

a barrel, while some of the sailors '*gritted their teeth upon me, and could even have found in their hearts to have bitten off my flesh from my bones*'. As a punishment, God visited what appears to have been an electric storm upon the ship, in which the mast was hit by lightening and split, and fireballs rained down, killing two passengers, an Armenian merchant and a Turkish servant. After this, Perrot and Luffe lost no opportunity to distribute some of their writings in Italian in the hope of gaining new convincements. This account from *Battering Rams against Rome* (1661) is one type of testimony. But in *A Sea*, the allegory transposes sailors and other persecutors into preying fish:

> Like as the least, I saw thee made the bait,
> The little Dolphin's spaun, in ev'ry hour
> Pursu'd by fishes, which would thee devour.
> And whilst I waited, the Deeps did me cover,
> Wherein I saw, where thou swim'st swift to hover,
> The Whale, the Shark, the Porpos, and the Hake
> In scools do chase thee fierce, a prey to make. (p. 5)

In Rome, the threats of physical punishment were realised. In the Pazzarella, the chains made Perrot temporarily lame, while he was periodically beaten and bruised with a bull's penis, sometimes beaten by madmen, and at others tempted with the pleasures of women and wine if he relented. Presumably he was being beaten into sanity. In *Battering Rams*, Perrot says that he 'cannot express well by *Pen*' his suffering, but in *A Sea*, the experience of violent torture is sedimented in the poem's vocabulary: '*Oh! Pressures, Pressures, Bleedings, Sorrows, Cryes!*' (p. 7). There is worse still:

> *Hunger, thirst, Nakedness*, and *Cold*, yea, *pangs of pain* I eat,
> To which *Oppression* doth me *hold*, *Tears* are my *drink & meat*;
> *Sighs* in the deeps do gird *me*, as a *swadling-band*;
> The Night's *black womb* of *wrath's* my *bondage* in the Land. (p. 3)

Such language is attached to the minor figures in the poem who represent different aspects of the seed: the '*Orphant*', '*wanting Bread . . . Most grievous Cryes*, the *Ecchoes* as a *Dart* / And *piercing Lance*, wounds me unto the *heart*' (pp. 23–24), while '*Like as a Lamb* I *bleat*, I *bleed*' (p. 24).

None of this harrowing poetry need be related to the voyage in such a literal way. The shark, the whale and the hake are decidedly non-Mediterranean sea creatures, so that the journey of the persecuted in Italy is over-laid by a realm of reference which goes back to Britain and Atlantic waters, or to native literary resources. The concern with sperm and with the appearance of these fish has one root in Browne's *Pseudodoxia*.[24] Through the peculiarity of the internalised Quaker allegory, the reader apprehends a simultaneity of extreme literalism, equating inner and outer experiences in a very rigid way, and an openness of reference which takes the reader into a universe of semi-abstract symbols where divinity, the 'inner light', is mediated.

The counterpart to the language of physical oppression seems to be one in which knowledge of the natural world is a means of appreciating the power of God. The divine is greater than the immediate authorities of imprisonment and so such contemplation reminds the prisoner that he is ultimately in safe hands. Also, Perrot's much-repeated exercise of asking who has the ultimate knowledge of a great variety of natural processes functions to take the prisoner's mind away from the immediate squalor in an almost mnemonic exercise which helps to pass the time: 'Can he the *nature* of the *Lilly's Seed*, / Change into an *offensive* hurtful *Weed*?' (p. 15). It is indeed prison poetry, where sin is as much a dungeon to the self as is actual confinement (p. 31). Significantly, God answers back in questions too, completing a reciprocal exercise. Perrot refers to Shiloh (Genesis 49:10) as a name for the Messiah, present in nature, vertuous and emanating, the power which transforms nature and man:

> Whilst *Shiloh*, which in *flames* reposes,
> Of *burning Coals* makes *sprout* forth *Damask Roses*
> . . .
>
> Whose *Light's* thick *Darkness*, spread by *Shiloh's* Candle:
> To whom *all souls* must come by *Transformation*.   (p. 15)

Perrot's natural world is a theatre for salvation, and the sequence of events here resembles in much condensed form that exploration of the underworld in *Paradise Lost* I and II. In another vision ('Through *cloven Mountains* things I clearly did / *Behold*', p. 7), Perrot sees in '*Earth's womb*' a treasure of precious metals and jewels, the names of some of which are not even known to man, mixed up with 'corrupted *dross* and *Reprobate*', including a 'smother'd *substance*, in whose bowels seal'd / Is all *fulness* of *Virtue* and *Perfection*' (p. 7). Before these lines, there is a description of the '*fiery-flying Serpent*' (p. 6) whose flight dominates and intimidates while the seed remains buried and choked by weeds in the ground above the mountains. As in *Paradise Lost*, space is being used to suggest the experience of fallenness. In the epic, Satan's character and his journey suggest the pain and the vastness of loss, while the objects below the ground in Hell are a demonic counterpart to the virtuous buildings and earth in Heaven. Corrupt only according to their users, it is the mountains which are thrown first by the angelic army against the rebels (VI.639ff.). This neutrality of nature is determined by Raphael's stricture that he is talking about spiritual matters in corporeal terms, finding a heroic, dramatic and mythic form for the ethereal war. In Perrot, the serpent is not without, but, by virtue of the allegory, within, flying around in the sea of life, while nature or matter is coterminous with the body and its state of salvation or perfection. Just to compound the intermixture of mediums, mountains exist for Perrot on land and under the sea. Here Perrot's poem appears to be transforming the language of the popular translation by Josuah Sylvester of du Bartas's *Semaines*, published as the *Divine Weeks and Works* (1592–1608). Animal similes are used in du Bartas as extended similes for human action, especially persecution. Du Bartas's serpents are often false illusions, but they still terrify as predators:

> as a *Sturgeon* or a Pike, dooth skoure
> The Creeks and Pills in Rivers wheare they lye,
> Of smaller Fishes and their feeble frie.[25]

The difference effected by Perrot is in his internalising allegory, but the interrogative form is found in du Bartas as well as in Perrot, as is the sense of wonder at natural processes. In du Bartas, it is God who becomes the captain of fish at sea, leading them by natural law to their seeding grounds.[26] In *Paradise Lost*, the serpent of Job 41 is Leviathan, to whom the Norwegian pilot anchors his fishing boat (I. 200–8). Milton's 'captain' is reduced to emphasise the enormity of Satan. Perrot returns to du Bartas's model, but has God as the presence both within and without the narrator. In Perrot's natural world, flying fishes have been given wings by God so that they may change medium, and escape hungry sharks by entering the air and leaving the sea. Just so, earth must be left for ascent with the Sun and the '*Day-star*' (p. 31). The day-star (2 Pet. 1:19) is Christ, who becomes identified as the light within when the poem begins to draw to a close. Unlike Milton's version of nature, Perrot's is one within which redemption is already inscribed by God. In Milton, only unfallen nature is so revivifying (according to the most basic interpretation), and even then it is the 'link of nature' which draws Adam into the Fall with Eve.

IV

On his return to England, Perrot rapidly gained notoriety within the Quaker movement for his 'hat heresy', which Fox and the other prominent Quakers saw as vain and lacking in humility. The writings produced in prison in Italy were published as part of Perrot's campaign for his belief. Outside they brought ridicule upon him, one pamphlet actually imitating letters from the Pope to Perrot in Perrot's own style.[27]

Some Quakers accused Perrot of effeminacy because he addressed Quaker women by referring to himself in the feminine.[28] In the light of the seed, womb and blood imagery in *A Sea*, it might be conjectured that

Perrot was attempting to cross or merge genders, perhaps as a means of expressing the universal significance of his suffering. The regenerate narrator seems to assume the identity of Christ as the Bridegroom in the Song of Solomon:

> Let me *descend* from *Sion's* glorious *Mountain*,
> To shew a *Seed* the *Vale* wherein's the *Mountain*;
> For surely I could freely lay down *Life*,
> With *Blood*, to buy a *stranger* for my *Wife*.   (p. 31)

It is a curious mixture of marital and progenerative phrases from the Bible which is used to construct Perrot's language of inner regeneration. The frequent references to the sweating or dripping of blood suggest menstruation. Perrot seems to mean these instances as symbolic imitations of atonement, though equally, if taken in an Old Testament sense, they could be seen as representations of spiritual impurity. In Perrot's account of the apocalypse, a single drop of blood becomes an immense sea, upon which a diamond spark cuts an earth of brass, which becomes the firm land connecting all the islands in the sea, a sure passage upon which the saved shall march (pp. 20–1). In the matter of the use of blood, was he engaging with a sub-code within Quaker women's writing and prophecy? The use of metaphor as a means of enhancing Quaker community by early Quaker women has been identified by Barbara Ritter Dailey.[29] Some Quaker women spilt the blood of animals on Church altars as a gestural protest against the celebration of communion, which they saw as idolatrous. This question seems even more pressing in the light of the journey with his female companions: Mary Fisher, it should be remembered, achieved her goal, though she did not publish any pamphlets. Perrot was markedly unsuccessful in his goal, though he wrote and published reams. The near-androgynous representation of the self was certainly a means of signalling perfection among some of the more extreme and occult enthusiasts during the early 1650s, but by 1660, it was regarded as frivolous by a movement seeking respectability in the eyes of a new hostile government.

Perrot was also accused by William Penn of affectedly wearing a beard.[30] This was probably an imitation on Perrot's part of Rabbinic appearance, something not uncommon among the radical religious prophets, and another instance of signs of prophecy and perfection residing in style. The seed is like Perrot's Jew, 'alienated' (p. 4). It also indicates the very important connections in the 1650s and 1660s between Quakers and Jews, both parties showing an interest in each other because of their shared millennial concerns. Perrot took advice from the Jews in Livorno, and Charles Bayley spoke to them in Rome, both times on matters to do with persecution. The Jews were a preferable alternative in Venice to the decadent, finely-dressed and masked Venetians, whose dress offended Perrot. The mysticism and scepticism of some Jewish philosophers, known to some Quakers, might also have its relevance to *A Sea*.[31]

In Dublin, Perrot had known the scientific reformer and Surveyor General in Ireland, Benjamin Worsley. Perrot had tried to raise funds from Worsley and perhaps also from Hartlib for his mission. The evidence for the latter is suggested by a manuscript letter in the Hartlib Papers, perhaps in Perrot's hand, which is his account of God's visitation upon him with the instruction to go to Turkey.[32] Worsley let Hartlib have some correspondence from Perrot, which might suggest that Worsley himself had some sympathy with the Quakers in 1657. On 10 September 1657, Perrot wrote to Worsley from Zante, affirming the community of the Seed: 'thou mayst Read wthin, my love & affection to the seed wch is my soules desire may live, & that it may rather be borne in a manger, then strangled in the most glorious chambers of the wombe'.[33] The sexual language returns, this time as an indication of the preferability of Christ-like birth, against stillbirth through strangling on the umbilical cord (see Jer. 20:17–18). The womb here is the zone of persecution, the deep. The knowledge in nature which Perrot seeks is truly divine and not natural, ever to be left in the womb, that is, on earth, which is the realm of mere human 'invention':

> Some in their time have *swollen* like the *Seas*,
> And chose them *paths*, even what their hearts *did please*.
> *Invention* up did spring, and they were *bound*,
> In *Chains* of *blackness*.   (pp. 40–41)

If Perrot was a Baconian or a Hartlibian speculator, he certainly had a very different conception of the possibilities and ends of human knowledge to Hartlib and to Worsley.

V

There are some harrowing accounts of meetings between Perrot, Fox and other Quakers, where the former would protest in tears that he did nothing which was contrary to the work of Fox, Burrough, Howgill and Farnworth. Of the early Quaker leaders, only Isaac Penington, who had an interest in occult philosophy, and who had entertained very extreme positions in the early 1650s, was prepared to see some good in Perrot.[34] The others were unrelenting. Some said he had taken on the ministerial role too soon; most were agreed that his poetry was an offence to plainness.[35] As early as 1662, Perrot became a voluntary exile in Barbados. Like Nayler, whom he did not support, Perrot had been excluded for the sake of the new and (given the times) necessary discipline and quietism of the Quakers.

In Barbados and Jamaica, Perrot settled and worked as a court clerk. Though still a Quaker, he was paid to extract those oaths which the Quakers refused to give. He was also famous for sporting a splendid velvet coat, another contradiction of his profession. On a limited scale, the publication continued, and Perrot became associated with Robert Rich, the sometime follower of Nayler, and guardian of the radical spiritualist tradition.[36] After Perrot's death, Rich published Perrot's letters to Fox and others: a final testimony in a foreign land.[37]

As for the poetry, *A Sea* is not founded upon decorum, as *Paradise Lost* was, but it is a significant and unusual example of radical religious writing. Prophetic decorum is replaced by prophetic performance: suffering. The English Revolution resulted in a transformation of subjectivity, and the Quaker sense of self was an extreme and enduring manifestation of that change. If we are to understand Perrot's poem properly in this context (quite apart from any question of whether the poem is 'good' or 'bad'), we must understand it as a product of Quaker theology. Milton's theology and that of the Quakers had similar roots in Puritanism, but the differences between the two positions account in part for fundamentally different attitudes towards language. This is why Perrot's allegory is so peculiar. Moreover, *A Sea* must be understood as a part of Perrot's other ways of bearing witness to the inner light, so that it is part of a wider passage of statement, behaviour and experience in this life. The poem ends by finding the true centre of self, universe and Godhead, without forgetting what had been suffered:

> The DAY of *God's* at hand, the LIGHT's his *Word*;
> GOD comes with *Fire, Plague, Famine* and with Sword,
> To plead with *all flesh*, living in *Corruption*,
> Upon their *heads* to bring *swift* fierce Destruction.
> . . .
> GOD's Pow'r with *His*, is like a *Fort of Steel*,
> My *Brethren* in the *Life* you may me *feel*;
> For I am with you all under your *Deep*,
> Where all the Fishes *swim*, and *Worms* creep.   (p. 46)

It is something new in the radical religious tradition, though definitely a part of that tradition, in which discourse and action were intimately connected. It is also something new in the history of poetry, looking forward to the introspective poetry of the eighteenth century. Yet it was in Rome, the heart of Protestantism's and Puritanism's greatest professed enemy, that this radical religious subjectivity was found.

NOTES

1 J.C. Davis, *Fear, Myth and History: The Ranters and the Historians* (Cambridge, 1986) is a good example of a study which demonstrates conclusively the non-existence of most of the claims made by hostile commentators of this particular sect. What Davies does not proceed to examine is what the individuals who were called Ranters considered themselves to be.

2 John Perrot, *Battering Rams against Rome* (London, 1661), pp. 11–12.

3 Robert Browne, *A Treatise of reformation without tarying for anie* (Middelburg, 1582).

4 Serge Hutin, *Les disciples anglais de Jacob Boehme* (Paris, 1960), pp. 49–77; Nigel Smith, *Perfection Proclaimed: Language and Literature in English Radical Religion, 1640–1660* (Oxford, 1989), pp. 185–225.

5 References to Sir Thomas Browne in radical circles are as rare as those to Robert Browne, but there is at least one reference in a controversy involving radicals: Nigel Smith, 'Sir Thomas Browne and the Levellers', *Notes and Queries*, n.s. 30 (1983), 421–2. Perrot's interest in natural philosophy would link him with other early Quaker naturalists, such as Thomas Lawson, and other radical religious and Behmenist observers of the natural world, such as Richard Franck and Thomas Tryon.

6 Perrot's correspondence with Benjamin Worsley, University of Sheffield, MS Hartlib 26/28.

7 William C. Braithwaite, *The Beginnings of Quakerism*, 2nd ed., rev. Henry J. Cadbury (Cambridge, 1955); Hugh Barbour, *The Quakers in Puritan England* (New Haven, 1964); Richard T. Vann, *The Social Development of English Quakerism* (Cambridge MA, 1969).

8 Blair Worden, 'Toleration and the Cromwellian Protectorate', *Studies in Church History*, 21 (1984), 199–233.

9 Barry Reay, *The Quakers and the English Revolution* (London, 1985). On gesture, see Richard Bauman, *Let your words be few: Symbolism of speaking and silence among seventeenth-century Quakers* (Cambridge, 1983), pp. 84–119.

10 For contradictions in Quaker attitudes towards language, see Smith, *Perfection Proclaimed*, pp. 276, 279, 287, 291–9.

11 Solomon Eccles writing from Newgate Goal, 24 June 1662, in Richard Greenway, *An Alarm from the Holy Mountain* (1662), p. 8. Jackson I. Cope, 'Seventeenth-Century Quaker Style', *PMLA* 71 (1956), 725–54 for the Johannine element in Quaker language. The texts in the passage are Isa. 38:14; Matt. 8:12; Ezek. 21:27.

12 First demonstrated in G.F. Nuttall, *The Holy Spirit in Puritan Faith and Experience* (Oxford, 1946).

13 N.H. Keeble, *The Literary Culture of Nonconformity in Later Seventeenth Century England* (Leicester, 1987), pp. 68–92; Georgia B. Christopher, *Milton and the Science of the Saints* (Princeton, 1982), pp. 59–174.

14 I am indebted to Kenneth L. Carroll, *John Perrot: Early Quaker Schismatic* (London, 1971). I have taken additional information from Friends House, MSS Swarthmore, 4, 5, 6; MSS Port. 17; MS Crosse (1 vol. only); Perrot, *Battering Rams against Rome*; Perrot *A Narrative of some of the Sufferings of J.P. in the City of Rome* (London, 1661).

15 Charles Bayley, *A Seasonable Warning and Word* (London, 1663), p. 6; Braithwaite, *The Beginnings of Quakerism*, pp. 424–5.

16　Stephen Fallon, 'Milton's Sin and Death: The Ontology of Allegory in *Paradise Lost*' *English Literary Renaissance* 17 (1987), 329–50, p. 332.

17　For missions, and attitudes towards them, see Braithwaite, *The Beginnings of Quakerism*, pp. 401–33.

18　On the similarities between Miltonic and Quaker theology, see William Riley Parker, *Milton. A Biography*, 2 vols. (Oxford, 1968). I, p. 497.

19　Smith, *Perfection Proclaimed*, p. 44.

20　Francis Quarles, *A Feast for Wormes* (1620), p. 10; Thomas Washbourne, *Divine Poems* (1654), p. 66.

21　Reprinted in 'Appendix Five: A Poetical Essay' in Francis Bacon, *The Essays*, ed. John Pitcher (Harmondsworth, 1985), pp. 286–7.

22　David Leverenz. *The Language of Puritan Feeling: An Explanation in Literary, Psychological and Social History* (New Brunswick NJ, 1980) explores the Puritan roots of this type of language. Nonetheless, such language is also central to Counter-Reformation devotional writing, which is known to have influenced English Protestants.

23　*Battering Rams against Rome*, Sig. A4v.

24　Sir Thomas Browne, *Pseudodoxia Epidemica*, ed. Robin Robbins, 2 vols. (Oxford, 1981), I, pp. 273, 370–1.

25　*The Divine Weeks and Works of Guillaume Saluste Sieur du Bartas*, trans. Josuah Sylvester, edited with introduction and commentary by Susan Snyder, 2 vols. (Oxford, 1979), II, p. 556.

26　*Ibid.*, I, p. 236.

27　Anon., *Perrot against the Pope* (London, 1662).

28　Perrot, *A Wren and the Burning Bush* (1660), p. 10.

29　Barbara Ritter Dailey, 'The Husbands of Margaret Fell', *The Seventeenth Century* 2 (1987), 55–71.

30　William Penn, *Judas and the Jews* (1673), pp. 16–17.

31　David S. Katz, *Philo-Semitism and the Readmission of the Jews to England, 1603–55* (Oxford, 1982), p. 238.

32　Sheffield University Library, MS Hartlib, 26/28/4.

33　*Ibid.*, 26/28/1.

34　MS Crosse, pp. 6–7.

35　Thomas Ellwood, *The History of the Life of Thomas Ellwood*, ed. C.G. Crump (London, 1900), pp. 150–1.

36　Robert Rich, *Love without Dissimulation* (1666), pp. 6ff.

37　Robert Rich, *Hidden Things Brought to Light* (1680).

Index

Printed in Great Britain
by Amazon.co.uk, Ltd.,
Marston Gate.